EQUILIBRIUM VERSUS UNDERSTANDING

The theories we use shape the way we look at the world and influence our explanations of people's behaviour.

Equilibrium versus Understanding argues that neoclassical theory is incapable of explaining or understanding people's conduct. As a result it is unsuitable for explaining decisions and choices. The author asserts that a different sort of economic theory is required if economists are to understand and get to grips with social problems. As an alternative, he proposes a hermeneutic theory.

The book is divided into two parts. The first contrasts the positivist methodology of neoclassical equilibrium theory with that of an interpretative approach to social theory. The author rejects the 'third-person perspective' of the former in favour of a subjectivist theory incorporating a 'first-person perspective'. He goes on to discuss what a hermeneutic theory entails; why it is a suitable framework for explaining people's conduct; how it differs from orthodox economics; and how it enlarges the scope of economics.

The second part of the book uses the problem of industrial location to illustrate how both third- and first-person perspectives explain business decisions. The analysis shows how the explanations provided by traditional location theories mislead us and also provides insight into the nature of investment decisions. Throughout the book, the discussion of methodologies affords a novel critique of equilibrium theory and insight into the nature of business decisions and uncertainty, the issue of prediction, and the use of mathematics in economics.

Mark Addleson is Associate Professor in the Program on Social and Organisational Learning, George Mason University, Virginia. He has previously taught at the University of the Witwatersrand's Business School, South Africa and he has also held a directorship in a firm of economics consultants. His publications include contributions on the methodology of Austrian economics and on industrial decentralisation policy.

i

ROUTLEDGE FRONTIERS OF POLITICAL ECONOMY

EQUILIBRIUM VERSUS UNDERSTANDING

Towards the restoration of economics as social theory

Mark Addleson

London and New York

First published 1995
by Routledge
11 New Fetter Lane, London EC4P 4EE

Simultaneously published in the USA and Canada
by Routledge
29 West 35th Street, New York, NY 10001

Typeset in Garamond by
Ponting–Green Publishing Services, Chesham, Bucks
Printed and bound in Great Britain by
Biddles Ltd, Guildford and King's Lynn

British Library Cataloguing in Publication Data
A catalogue record for this book is available from the
British Library

Library of Congress Cataloguing in Publication Data
Equilibrium versus understanding: towards the rehumanization
of economics within social theory / Mark Addleson.
p. cm.
Includes bibliographical references and index.
ISBN 0–415–12814–5
1. Equilibrium (Economics)
2. Decision-making. 3. Uncertainty.
4. Economics–Methodology.
HB145.E678   1991
339.55–dc20   95–11822
CIP

ISBN 0–415–12814–5

Once men have been made to realise the crippling mutilations imposed by an objectivist framework – once the veil of ambiguities covering up these mutilations has been definitely dissolved – many fresh minds will turn to the task of reinterpreting the world.

Michael Polanyi (1973), *Personal Knowledge:*
Towards a Post-Critical Philosophy, 381.

The objective and the subjective. The former to be embraced, the latter to be suppressed and eliminated. It is strange that Science, that vast work of original thought, should be so contemptuous of its origins.

G.L.S. Shackle (1972), *Epistemics and Economics:*
A Critique of Economic Doctrines, 354.

CONTENTS

CONTENTS

LIST OF FIGURES

ACKNOWLEDGEMENTS

I owe an enormous intellectual debt to Ludwig Lachmann. He was a friend and mentor for many years and I missed his wise counsel when working on this book. As the epitome of a gracious scholar he always listened and read with interest. His enthusiasm for his subject was rare, but irresistible, and I hope he would have found the main ideas congenial.

This work started life as a Ph.D. dissertation submitted in the Faculty of Management, University of the Witwatersrand, Johannesburg. It is generally considered unwise to use a Ph.D. dissertation as a vehicle for exploring intellectually controversial, even heretical, themes. Having done so I was fortunate to have been aided and abetted by two very capable supervisors at Wits – Mark Orkin, a sociologist-philosopher, and Karl Mittermaier, an economist-philosopher. Such a coincidence of wants is rare, and without their support the ideas would not have seen the light of day. The Business School at Wits provided a particularly congenial atmosphere for pursuing an eclectic piece of research. Of my many colleagues there, who contributed by their help as well as their tolerance, I would like to single out Nick Binedell, Ian Clark, Di Kruger, and Keith Yeomans.

In deciding to rewrite the Ph.D. as a book, I was heartened by the warm reception that Don Lavoie, of George Mason University, Virginia, gave to the original ideas. I have been delighted to find someone who not only shares the view that hermeneutics holds great promise for social theory but also has been instrumental in building a university department around people with similar interests.

My main debt is to my long-suffering family. Although it is customary to include them in one's acknowledgements, there would certainly have been neither a Ph.D. nor a book without my wife, Jen, who not only continues to enrich my understanding of hermeneutics and modernism but also, through her companionship and wonderful sense of humour, has contributed immeasurably to the writing process, helping me to keep matters in perspective and generally making the effort worthwhile. I am also very grateful for Robbie's help. He was particularly understanding about having a neglectful father and I want to thank him for his patience. This book is dedicated to my mother and to the fond memory of my father.

Part 1

INTRODUCTION

AN OVERVIEW OF THE MAIN IDEAS

Economics is about how people organise and manage the production of goods and services, as well as the resources that are used in the process of production. The subject matter of economics covers an enormous range of issues, problems, and questions, including questions about how production is organised; why particular activities are undertaken and whether they should be; the nature and functions of the institutions that are associated with organising and carrying out production activities – from banks and manufacturers to shipping and training; and the efficacy of the production processes – what criteria should be used to evaluate them, what purposes they serve, and so on. It is the task of economic theory to elucidate these problems and issues which all have to do with people's activities and, at the root of their activities, their decisions and plans.

Although it did not matter much at the time, from my earliest encounter with neoclassical economics I remember feeling uneasy about this portrayal of decision-making and choice. The 'theory of consumer choice', unfortunately, was the undergraduate's introduction both to economics and to a neoclassical model. Explaining the purpose of this model, our lecturer spoke about selecting an optimal shopping basket. In spite of the penchant that undergraduates are supposed to have for swallowing whole whatever they are told, the analogy of compiling an optimal basket when faced with an income constraint, while detailing a huge range of possible things on which one might spend money, seemed a long way from the experience of going shopping or from buying the things that family members want. I imagine that students still feel this way about the models, and in teaching economics to graduate management students (who are a critical bunch at the best of times) I used to try to make these models more palatable, arguing – using Hayek's terminology – that one could think of them as attempting to bring out the logic of what is involved in making effective (optimising) decisions, i.e. as a 'pure logic of choice'.

I now think that this sort of rationalisation is specious. Part of the purpose

3

of this book is to substantiate the assertion that neoclassical models of 'decision-making' and 'choice' will always be unpalatable, because they have nothing to contribute to our understanding of how people make decisions about managing resources. Orthodox or 'mainstream' economics is unable to explain choice and conduct because its methodology demands that the scholar look at problems in a way that makes it impossible to understand choice. What a person does and the choices that she makes – whether it is a spouse, a new car, or a career that she is choosing – depends on how she *understands* her social circumstances. This consideration is formally recognised in social theory in the tradition of *Verstehen*, or subjective understanding. A theory that purports to explain people's conduct – what they do and why they do it, including the choices and decisions they make – which is certainly a central task of social science, must be based on a satisfactory explanation of how they themselves understand. Yet the 'perspective' of an agent that is embedded in neoclassical theory, as a determinate equilibrium theory, has no bearing on how an individual does 'see' things; nor could a person conceivably understand in the way that the rational agent is supposed to 'know' about the world.

Now the sentiment expressed above, that neoclassical theory is unrealistic, is shared by many people who are exposed to mainstream economic theory, even some of its most ardent supporters. It is a view that is often articulated and is both an expression of dissatisfaction with the theory as well as an indication of a wish to try to set matters right. The criticism that the theory is unrealistic generally takes one of two forms. Either the story the theory tells is somehow inappropriate, in that it fails to reflect what we know about how things work, or the explanation provided by the theory is incomplete, in that there are certain important things which evidently have a bearing on what happens, but the theory leaves these out; they are not part of the story. The theory of consumer choice exemplifies the first sort of criticism by suggesting that the rational consumer can – or ought to – rank a whole range of often completely disparate 'alternatives', while the second is contained both in Frank Hahn's (1982) regret that general equilibrium theory typically does not allow for agents to learn and in Oscar Morgenstern's (1972) observation that the neoclassical concept of competition makes no reference to dissembling or to other motives associated with competitive conduct.

Such problems are often presented as mere deficiencies of orthodox theory, which can be remedied with sufficient effort and ingenuity. I begin this book, however, with an explanation of why these are not just gaps in a theory which can be plugged in order to make it more satisfactory. On these and other matters neoclassical theory will always be 'wrong'. My object is to show why it is not possible to make the theory more realistic, in terms of explaining and understanding people's conduct; why orthodox economic theory is incapable of taking account of things that properly belong in a theory of human conduct and decision-making; and why, as a consequence, it is incapable of serving the purposes which social scientists require of their theories – the ability to enlighten them on how the social world 'works'.

A second equally important task is to show that a different sort of economic theory is required if economists are to address issues which even top-ranking neoclassicists concede they should do. The alternative that I propose is a hermeneutic theory and I will explain what a theory of interpretative understanding entails, why it is a suitable framework for explaining people's conduct, how it differs from orthodox economics, how its use enlarges the scope of economics, and what decision-making means in the context of a hermeneutical framework.

My main thesis is that both the epistemology and ontology – what knowledge is, how it is acquired, and what it is about – of the neoclassical scheme have nothing to do with how people understand. Human conduct, however, is a result of understanding, and explanations of human conduct require an understanding of how people understand. Thus neoclassical economics and any theory with similar foundations (which includes any equilibrium theory or any theory that postulates that 'rational' individuals engage in some form of optimising behaviour) is unsuitable for explaining people's conduct. A hermeneutic theory, of the sort that I have in mind, has different epistemological and ontological foundations which make it appropriate to the task of explaining conduct.

The approach that I use to accomplish both the task of establishing the limitations of mainstream theory and that of identifying an alternative conceptual framework, will be unfamiliar to many readers and this introduction is intended as an overview of the methodological issues that underpin my main thesis, which are the fulcrum of the analysis.

In contra-distinction to the widely held view that there is a single correct scientific method, my standpoint, associated with what has come to be labelled the 'hermeneutic turn' in the methodology of science, is that scholars can and do formulate and apply fundamentally different conceptual frameworks in order to explore social and other problems. This book is concerned with two such frameworks or theories: on the one hand neoclassical economics, which derives from one particular set of beliefs about how to 'do science', a Cartesian conception of science; on the other hand, a hermeneutic theory based on the tradition of interpretative understanding, or *Verstehen*, which holds that when scientists set about doing science they cannot and do not practise a Cartesian methodology. Rather, from a hermeneutical standpoint, science is a human endeavour and, like all human endeavour, involves understanding. Understanding is not the same as 'observation' as positivist science uses that term.

A Cartesian-inspired framework and a hermeneutic one are in no way compatible or interchangeable when it comes to applying them to problems of society or of nature. Each is constructed upon its own foundations, is intended to serve specific purposes, and is capable of serving only the purposes for which it is 'designed' or which its foundations enable it to fulfil. Science, in the Cartesian mould (i.e. a positivist-empiricist or 'modernist' notion of science), has the task of establishing relationships amongst observable phenomena, which according to the modernist credo is the way that scientific knowledge is produced. For hermeneutics, knowledge comes with understanding. Understanding is interpretation and science, like other (social) human activities, has the task of contributing to understanding. Only in rare instances, and not when we are dealing with other people and their family or business decisions, for example, does understanding require or involve establishing empirical relationships.

The statement that different conceptual frameworks serve different purposes can be clarified by looking upon a theory as a language for exploring phenomena. The concepts and terminology of a theory actually shape the way the theorist looks at the world and they influence what he is able to say about it. A conceptual framework like neoclassical general equilibrium theory encourages – actually forces – the scholar to think of everything, including human conduct and choice, in terms of tendencies towards equilibrium. In this regard he needs to conceive of the things he is interested in as part of a complete system. A hermeneutic theory, on the other hand, looks to the nature of understanding, highlighting people's motives, interests, and their relationships with other people, as aspects of how they understand and how we as theorists understand them and explain their activities.

The implication here is that the language of orthodox economics and that of a hermeneutical approach are capable of illuminating different sets of problems because each provides a different way of looking at and of describing the world. Each amounts to a different perspective on what constitutes the scheme of things and although each is capable of yielding different insights, each also constrains the theorist, forcing him to look at things in the way dictated by the elements of the theory. So while a hermeneutic theory has its constraints, I will argue that it is nevertheless a profoundly appropriate framework for exploring problems that have to do with people's decisions and their conduct. This is so because hermeneutics is about understanding, and that is precisely what the social scientist concerned with explaining conduct needs to do because people's activities, decisions, and choices, reflect their understanding.

Showing why neoclassical theory is unsuitable while hermeneutics is appropriate for exploring human conduct involves an explanation, first, of the differing views of the scheme of things that each provides, i.e. what is within and what lies beyond the theorist's 'field of vision'. The question in each case is how does the theorist 'see' or understand the scheme of things. Most of the first chapter is taken up with answering this question. I contrast the '*third-person perspective*' – which is the way mainstream theory and any equilibrium theory requires the theorist to conceive the scheme of things – with a '*first-person perspective*' of interpretative understanding. The former, by focusing on a system and the interrelationships within it, puts all matters that are pertinent to understanding the social nature of conduct – such as people's motives and their social relationships and obligations – beyond the theorist's intellectual grasp, while the first-person perspective of a hermeneutic theory, the nature of which is explained in Chapters 4 and 5, makes these central to explanations of conduct and thus facilitates the task of showing how they bear upon what people do.

The source of the limitations of neoclassical economics is the modernist conception of what science is and of how scientific knowledge is produced or acquired. At the root of this conception, which shaped the evolution of orthodox theory, is the idea that the world is something that has a real existence 'out there', somewhere beyond the theorist. His function, once he has purified himself of any preconceptions or prejudices regarding how the world works, is to learn about what is happening out there by observing and hypothesising about relationships between things that he observes. Thus the ubiquitous modernist notion of science is founded upon particular epistemological and ontological presuppositions. It prescribes both what knowledge consists of and how it is acquired. Knowledge is all true facts about the things that make up the world and is produced by attempting to falsify hypotheses about relationships between things that are observed out there. The ontology of the modernist conception of science defines the world (including knowledge) as a set of objects (constants and variables) that exist independently of people and what they do or think, and these objects together comprise an entity. The world that exists out there, parts of which the scientist observes, is a self-contained complete system and an important task of theory to represent the system and, by establishing the nature of the interrelationships within it, to show how it works.

My position is that the notion of determinateness and its manifestation in the economist's preoccupation with the concept of equilibrium is a product of modernism and its associated, but particular and peculiar, epistemology and ontology. It is these that enable, indeed require, the scholar to think of any phenomena, including social problems, in terms of a complete scheme, or system, which can have an outcome. At the same time the epistemology and ontology of mainstream theory are also what prevent the theorist from exploring and explaining conduct and choice. To the hermeneuticist, in order to do the latter, a language or conceptual framework is needed which is capable of expressing how people actually understand when they make decisions. The theorist needs to be able to reflect on how and why people do things: how they plan, what motivates them, what are the consequences of their fears or doubts, and how their decisions are affected by their financial and moral obligations towards others. These are the sorts of things that 'determine' what people do and, in order to be able to make them part of the explanation of conduct, what is needed is a theory that is not just about things that exist in the world, but one that recognises that human beings construct or constitute their understanding in conscious thought and that they do so in the light of their relationships with other people.

A language of human action, one that enables the scholar to explore understanding, has different epistemological and ontological foundations from those of a determinate equilibrium scheme. Understanding is not about establishing or enumerating formal causal relationships between things that pertain to a world which is conceived as a whole, external to the individual, and which the individual experiences in a passive way. Rather, understanding is a process in which the individual 'interacts' with her world, constituting that world as her conscious thoughts, defining it in terms of her interests. Understanding is intimately tied to the individual's being-in-time. It pertains to her experience at a moment in time. Moreover, because her understanding is a product of her past and present social circumstances, it is essentially *prejudiced* by her 'milieu' and her relationships with others. So her understanding and thus her decisions are shaped by the people she happens to be with – whether these are friends, teachers, or colleagues – and what she happens to be doing – whether she is on the beach on holiday or is giving a paper at conference. Understanding is not formal knowledge of an external world that exists independently of what people are doing. In understanding, the individual is part of *her* world and she makes her decisions in terms of *how* she understands and *what* she understands, which are both related to her being-in-time and are also shaped by her social 'history'.

The first-person perspective of a hermeneutic theory is an explication of how the individual understands, as a basis for explaining her decisions and her conduct. In general, except when thinking about a game, the plot of a novel, a work of art, an intellectual puzzle such as a crossword, or other things such as the solar system that are understood and can be represented as a complete entity, understanding does not encompass the idea of a system. Events or circumstances, as the individual understands, are not interacting parts of some pre-existing, external structure, but are constituted anew in time. The orientation of conscious thought is towards an open future which will be constituted and reconstituted in the context of the individual's yet-to-be formed interests in future moments. Her interests will shape her future. From this it will be apparent that the notion of equilibrium and optimisation is irrelevant to the first-person perspective. Experience is not, and cannot be, complete. The things in which she is interested, such as what particular people have done or will be doing and how this may affect her, are not thought of as parts of a system nor seen as elements of some whole entity. In representing plans and decisions in this way, as neoclassical theory does, we transcend understanding itself, which is precisely the problem of the third-person perspective of a determinate, equilibrium scheme. Not surprisingly, we fail to comprehend and to explain human conduct. The 'explanation' that orthodox theory provides, that runs in terms of individuals' attempts to optimise and supposedly indicates how they would do so, is utterly misleading.

A condition of completeness, which is necessary to maintain the illusion of a state of affairs where the individual would be able to optimise, is that she has nothing to learn or that any 'knowledge' that she will acquire must be conceived as a function of, or as predetermined by, what she already knows. While a notion of equilibrium which incorporates the decisions or plans of different people demands that the theorist treat each of these plans or decisions as utterly comprehensive in scope – covering all possible 'choices' – and, in combination, as forming an exhaustive set. All these conditions would mean that the individuals who are represented in this scheme have ceased to experience, to learn, or to understand. They must already know everything there is to know. I submit that a conceptual framework based on this epistemology cannot possibly help us to explore and to explain human conduct.

Equilibrium theory has served economists through some two centuries of economic thought. Is there really a need to abandon equilibrium now in order to explain conduct? Why can't the considerations raised here – people's motives, their hopes or expectations, and their relationships with others, for example – simply be brought into mainstream economics? First, I point out in Chapter 3 that this is exactly what some neoclassical theorists of high standing have been trying to do in recent years. Indeed economists have been attempting to do so for a long time. The problem is that a motive like 'the desire to work close to home' or to 'be with people who understand me', the expectation that 'things will improve next year' or that 'this product will give us an edge over the competition', and a relationship based on, say, collegiality or friendship, cannot really be accommodated by the third-person perspective of a determinate scheme. They are the sorts of considerations that are relevant to explaining what people do, but they belong to a different language, with an epistemology and ontology that is compatible with the notion of understanding.

Building his theory around the idea of an economy or market as an equilibrium system, the neoclassicist is interested in functional interrelationships and in establishing stability conditions. These are the sorts of considerations that will form part of a description of the scheme of things from a third-person perspective. They are essential elements of the theory, which define the language of orthodox economics. Take them away and you are no longer dealing with neoclassical economics. Also, whatever the theorist wishes to explain he has to do in terms of tendencies towards equilibrium or towards some optimum (which may or may not be attained) and in terms of interrelationships between parts of a system (which may or may not 'fit together' so that the system converges to an equilibrium). Once again, the nature of the explanation is not arbitrary. It is consistent with the language of neoclassical theory, but this way of 'seeing' the world is entirely unsuitable for providing insight into human conduct which is not about optimising or about making one's decisions harmonious with the decisions of other people. These involve a different epistemology and ontology.

The individual, as I have explained, does not understand a system. She does not and cannot possess the sort of knowledge that would enable her to optimise. Her expectations are judgements about what will or may happen. They are conjectures and not probability statements about states of a pre-existing world. They involve neither quantification nor do they presume a complete *set* of outcomes, as implied in the assignment of statistical probabilities. Other people, too, conjecture and constitute their 'worlds' in terms of their interests. Their decisions are not things-in-the-world, like pieces of a puzzle, against which she can measure the 'fit' or compatibility of her own plans. We need a different sort of language to explain conduct. Every attempt that is made to bring concepts like choices, decisions, plans, knowledge, expectations, uncertainty, or motives, into mainstream theory results in the meaning of these concepts being lost. In order to make them part of the 'story' of neoclassical economics, they have to be compatible with that language and with its underlying epistemology and ontology. If the phenomena do not fit the language of equilibrium and optimisation, they either have to be discarded ('we do not yet have a theory which can deal with such considerations') or they have to be redefined – their meaning has to be changed – so that they fit the requirements of the language.

I explain in Chapter 3 that this is exactly what has happened when orthodox economists have tried to tackle an issue like uncertainty. Uncertainty becomes part of the (in principle complete) system about which there is *not yet* complete knowledge; it is a *thing* which, with sufficient planning and by rational calculation, can be minimised in each time period and, since people do not like it, they try to minimise the amount of it in their decisions. Expectations are also conceived as things and treated as variables which, like the pieces in a kaleidoscope, are transformed in each period. The values of expectations are *determined* by other variables and, like their decisions, different people's expectations may be compatible or incompatible. In a determinate equilibrium scheme, motives are translated into tangible, measurable 'objectives', like maximising or minimising, which are conceived not as a person's hopes or fears, but as parts of a world that exists out there. The objective is attained (in the sense of being acquired, like a prize at a funfair sideshow) when the individual 'chooses' the right combination of things from amongst the complete set known to exist out there.

Whether the meaning of the phenomena is changed by bringing them into the theory or whether certain notions are simply discarded as not having a place in the theory, the result is unsatisfactory and accounts for neoclassical economics being viewed as 'unrealistic' in both senses of the term that I identified above. Yet, because it is the language that is at fault, these deficiencies cannot be overcome. The upshot is, as the title of this book suggests, that economists have to make a fundamental choice between understanding and explaining human conduct on the one hand, or building equilibrium theories on the other. If economists wish to explain conduct and choice, and I believe that as social theorists concerned with how resources are managed this is one of their tasks, they are left with what for many will be the unpalatable prospect of having to abandon equilibrium theory.

What is to replace neoclassical economics? What is economic theory like without equilibrium? Because of the complete dominance of modernism and of neoclassical economics, scholars have not had much occasion to ponder these questions and to consider whether or not there can be an economics without equilibrium. Competing approaches to economics like neo-Ricardianism and post-Keynesianism also rely heavily on notions of equilibrium and, if the nature of my arguments is accepted, this rules them unsuitable for the task at hand. Austrian economics may be a possibility, and in some respects it is an attempt to provide the sort of theory we are looking for but, as I argue in Chapter 6 conventional Austrian subjectivism is not an effective alternative to mainstream theory, for it has been developed around concepts of equilibrium and it shares the epistemology and ontology of neoclassical economics.

The hermeneutic approach to which I have referred is not in any sense a well-developed framework and an important task of mine is to clarify the foundations of interpretative understanding. This I do in Chapters 4 and 5, taking the reader on a brief excursion through the evolution of the tradition of subjective understanding in social theory from Max Weber, through the phenomenology of Alfred Schütz, to the modern hermeneutics of Hans-Georg Gadamer. The latter provides important insights into the subjective and intersubjective nature of understanding. By clarifying the meaning of the hermeneutic circle of understanding, Gadamer helps us both to appreciate the importance of the double hermeneutic that is at the root of all social theory and all thought about human society, and to establish the foundations of a first-person perspective. With additional contributions from Schütz and others, my aim is to clarify the meaning of subjectivism associated with a first-person perspective, which I regard as the appropriate epistemology-ontology for a framework that aims to provide an understanding of human conduct. At the end of the first half of the book, and after examining the subjectivism of Austrian economists, I consider some of the implications for economics of pursuing a theory based on interpretative understanding.

As to the nature of an economics without equilibrium, I tackle this issue in the second half of the book, using the theory of industrial location as a convenient vehicle for contrasting a third-person perspective on 'decision-making' as optimisation, with a first-person perspective on how managers make investment decisions. In the light of what has been said above, perhaps it will not come as a surprise to find that viewing plans and decisions in the context of interpretative understanding completely undermines the conclusions drawn from orthodox theory about what a location decision is and what motivates such decisions.

In addition to investigating the two languages of economic theory, along the way the book offers a cook's tour of many matters that are relevant to the current methodological debate in economics. Understanding the epistemologies and ontologies of the third-person and first-person perspectives and how they differ proves to be useful in treating a number of issues that are of concern to economists. The distinction throws light on the long-standing debate about the use of mathematics. As a language of economic theory, I argue that mathematics goes hand in hand with the third-person perspective. It is entirely appropriate in this context where it supports the epistemology and ontology, but it is inappropriate as a language for explaining human conduct. The concept of uncertainty, the use of statistical probability theory to express uncertainty, and the distinction between risk and uncertainty, is another set of topics which is clarified by understanding the difference between the third- and first-person perspectives, as is the whole question of prediction in social theory. Being able to contrast the two languages even reveals why the notion of a social welfare function is a completely inappropriate basis for conceptualising the formulation of economic or social policy.

The views in this book are controversial. I doubt that at the end of the book I will have been able to persuade a reader, who may be patient enough to pursue the arguments to the bitter end but who is strongly committed to neoclassical economics and also wants a useful theory of human conduct, of the folly of his or her ways. Convinced as I am that neoclassical economics has run its course and also that the economics profession has not gained a great deal from it, I hope to have accomplished two things. First to have shown both how and why a hermeneutic approach, as an economics without equilibrium, represents a radically different alternative to neoclassical economics, and then to have provided a glimpse of the fact that such an approach has much to offer in its own right. From the limited exposure to a hermeneutic framework that this book provides, interpretative understanding is not just desirable as an alternative to neoclassical economics. Certainly it is that, and hermeneutics offers a way of escaping from the rut in which economics finds itself. More than this, it is a means of exploring important and genuinely interesting social problems which remain hidden to equilibrium theory. In this regard, I believe, it enables economists to address matters in which, as social theorists, we should be interested, which help us to understand the market economy, and which both broaden and greatly enrich the subject matter of economics.

1

TWO LANGUAGES OF ECONOMIC THEORY

The language of economic theory, like any language provides a framework for thought: but at the same time it constrains thought to remain within that framework. It focuses our attention; determines the way we conceive of things; and even determines what *sort* of things can be said. . . . A language, or conceptual framework is, therefore, at one and the same time both an opportunity and a threat. Its positive side is that (one hopes) it facilitates thought within the language or framework. But its negative side arises from the fact that thought must be within the framework.

(Coddington 1972: 14–15)

THEORY AS LANGUAGE

In the epigraph to this chapter, Alan Coddington uses the apposite metaphor of theory as a language in order to explain why it is important to examine the nature of one's theory and to determine whether the theory is appropriate. On the face of it, neoclassical theory appears to be a very useful and versatile language. It is the pre-eminent language of economists and is applied to a host of practical problems from education to the location of industry. In spite of its widespread acceptance, however, over the past two decades and more, orthodox economic theory has been the subject of sustained critique in what is generally known as the 'crisis in economic theory' (see Bell and Kristol 1980 for an early assessment).

A common complaint, even from people well versed in neoclassical economics, is that the theory is 'unrealistic' or 'highly abstract', although when pressed on the matter they may find it difficult to pinpoint the source of their dissatisfaction. It is also sometimes said that economists have two types of theory, a formal one and one that they use to explain practical problems. The implication being that the formal language is not suitable for dealing with practical matters, and yet it remains the *lingua franca* of economists and is used almost exclusively and universally for teaching economics. One object of this book is to identify the source of the problems with neoclassical economics, explaining how and why the use of the theory is so narrowly circumscribed that it is unsuitable for investigating the problems with which economists are and should be concerned. I will argue that developing an appropriate language for economics means turning our backs on orthodox theory.

In the late nineteenth century, several writers contributed to reshaping the subject matter of economics. Leon Walras, Carl Menger, and William Stanley Jevons laid the foundations of modern economics and in so doing brought problems of decision-making and choice to the forefront of the economist's attention. Notwithstanding its present position, I contend that the language of neoclassical theory, formulated around the economist's preoccupation with the notion of equilibrium, is unsuitable for explaining individuals' choices. The villains of the piece are the epistemology and the ontology of a determinate equilibrium scheme. These are congruent with the methodology of logical positivism and its successor logical empiricism which shaped neoclassical equilibrium theory, but the problem is that they constrain the language of theory in such a way that it cannot serve to explain how and why people make choices. I argue in this chapter that different languages or conceptual frameworks are used in formulating and exploring problems of choice and problems of equilibrium. Different languages are necessary for each task, but are characterised by incompatible epistemologies and ontologies. Neoclassical theory fails as an appropriate language of economic theory because it unsuccessfully attempts to combine the two sets of problems – those of equilibrium and choice – and to deal with them in a single conceptual framework. In order to explain how people decide and choose, we must be able to understand how they themselves understand and to do this we have to separate human conduct from problems of equilibrium, for the language of equilibrium theories forbids understanding.

The idea that a theory may be suitable for explaining some things but not others is supported by Hicks (1976a: 208), who emphasises an important corollary of Coddington's argument that each theory directs one's attention to particular things. Hicks says that a limitation of every theory is that the view it provides is circumscribed.

> Our theories, regarded as tools of analysis, are blinkers. . . . As we use them, we avert our eyes from things that may be relevant. . . . It is entirely proper that we should do this. . . . But it is obvious that a theory must be well chosen; otherwise it will illumine the wrong things.

Questions which are not often asked, but which I want to tackle, are how do the theories of economists circumscribe or blinker their field of view, and why do they do so? An examination of the epistemological and ontological foundations of different theories assists in answering these questions and this is what I propose to do. What the examination reveals, perhaps more starkly than has hitherto been apparent, is that because a particular theory cannot serve all purposes, economists themselves have to make fundamental choices. My standpoint is that one of the choices that they face is between obtaining insight into the nature of decisions or dealing with problems of equilibrium.

I hold that once economists are working with a particular theory, they have to confine themselves to those problems and phenomena that the language of theory enables them to investigate. In orthodox theory these phenomena include the existence and stability of equilibrium and the conditions of equilibrium itself. As long as the theorist's main concern is problems of the existence, uniqueness, and stability of equilibrium, neoclassical theory, with its particular epistemology and ontology, has its purpose. It is quite beyond the capabilities of a determinate scheme, however, to investigate other sorts of issues, such as how a decision-maker understands or interprets inter-personal relationships and other people's motives, and how these bear upon her decisions. If economists wish to investigate social problems associated with how and why people make decisions and to understand the con-sequences of those decisions – issues that are conventionally regarded as the proper domain of economists – neoclassical theory will not do. A theory with different epistemological and ontological foundations is required.

It is vital, therefore, to resolve the thorny questions of what economics is about and what economists are trying to do. Answers to these questions are sought in Chapters 2 and 3. Because they determine whether neoclassical theory is a suitable language for economists to pursue their objectives, the answers also influence the fate of orthodox theory.

In considering different languages of theory and their suitability for different tasks, the approach of this book is bound up with a broader philosophical conversation that is taking place in which the precepts of science have come to be questioned and criticised. The idea that there are different theories characterised by different epistemologies and ontologies, and that each constitutes a language capable of illuminating different prob-lems, would not have struck much of a chord until quite recently; it is a consequence of developments in the philosophy of science that have trans-formed our conception of what science is and what it can do. The approach and the problematic of neoclassical economics has been forged out of a positivist-empiricist methodology and a Cartesian conception of scientific endeavour and of what theorising is about. This methodology is also referred to as 'modernism'. The idea that, like any methodology, positivism-empiricism defines a relationship between the theorist and his subject matter that embraces a particular epistemology and an ontology was not widely recognised until fairly recently. Today there is acceptance of the notion that by applying any methodology the theorist comes to 'see' things, or to understand, in a particular way; he has a particular 'world view'. I will argue that the world view associated with modernism, and applied to the formula-

15

tion of equilibrium theories, frustrates attempts to explain people's decisions and to understand human conduct.

THE HERMENEUTICAL VIEW OF SCIENCE

The recognition that the methodology, epistemology, and type of problems that a theory can investigate are interrelated is consistent with the view that interpretation is at the root of all human endeavour and that the language of a theory shapes that interpretation. Today there is wider, though still restricted, acceptance of this conception of science as a hermeneutical endeavour. The term 'hermeneutics', originally associated with textual exegesis, refers to a philosophy that treats knowledge as understanding, and understanding as interpretation.

In the work of modern hermeneuticists, like Hans-Georg Gadamer, interpretation is creative or constitutive; 'reality' is what the individual – as consciousness-in-time – makes it. From the standpoint of hermeneutics, the problems of science, like all problems, are subjective. They are constituted by the scientist and reflect his interests, prejudices, and passions.[1] The subject matter of science does not exist as 'brute facts' as logical positivists would have it. Instead individuals endow problems and issues with meaning, in the same way that the literary text is 'brought to life' by the interpretation of the reader when she interacts with it. Without the reader's involvement there would be only printed marks on a page. The characters, their landscape and interactions are constituted by the prejudiced reader, who brings her own interests, emotions, and cultural heritage to bear on her reading or interpretation. Different people constitute the text in different ways. So it is with the identification and exploration of scientific problems. All sciences, including the natural ones, are interpretive. People bring their interests, biases, ideologies – all influenced by their associations with other people – and the language of their theory to bear on their scholarly activities, with the corollary that scientific discourse is neither neutral nor all-encompassing in its scope as positivists would like to believe.

The hermeneutical notion of science as social discourse and inquiry finds support among certain philosophers today and is part of a post-empiricist philosophy of science (see Bernstein 1983; Rorty 1980). With hindsight, this interpretation of science has been evolving for some time, as Ebeling (1986: 46) indicates with a concise explication of the meaning of the hermeneutical turn:

> for the last hundred years the hermeneutical aspect to all human understanding has slowly become apparent. . . . Once 'the facts' are seen as theory laden, i.e. bound by context . . . the interpretive element in both evidence and argumentation becomes an essential quality in all understanding. *All* sciences become . . . *human* sciences, for it is minds

and not matter that serve as the tentative arbitrators concerning the world and its working.

Bernstein (1976) refers to the 'image of science', meaning the view of whether a common, unified method of science should be applied, or whether dual methods are warranted for the social and natural sciences. The image of science has been thrown into confusion by the hermeneutical turn. When applied to the philosophy of science it not only challenges the positivist's conception of, and search for, a single conceptual framework that will serve to answer all scientific questions, but also redefines the basis on which divisions between the social and natural science are drawn.

For more than a century some scholars have repudiated the methodology of positivism-empiricism and advocated separate methods for the social and natural sciences. The case for methodological dualism is usually associated with Max Weber's *Verstehende Soziologie*. Peter Winch (1958) revived that case on the grounds that explanation in the social sciences must take cognisance of individuals' ability to understand social action and their need to apply this subjective understanding in order to interpret the motives and meanings in activities of others. In this older and more conventional view of the differences between the natural and social sciences, both are devoted to elucidating the nature of the world as it exists out there, but the things to which they refer in the world are different. The conventional view makes the scientist or theorist an 'observer' as far as both the subject matter of the natural sciences and the activities of people are concerned, but people's activities have meaning in them because (as a human being) the 'observer' understands that the activities of people are directed at attaining ends. There is, however, no meaning in or 'behind' the phenomena of the natural sciences. Thus in the older view of the method of *Verstehen*, the social and natural sciences warrant different methodologies because while the two sets of sciences share the same ontology, in each case the scientists have different types of knowledge about the phenomena that exist out there in the world.

The modern hermeneutical view of science has altered this assessment and also the nature of the debate concerning the relationships between the natural and social sciences. That debate is no longer confined to the issue of dual methodologies *versus* a single, all-embracing methodology for all sciences. The social sciences are not different because they are based on, or take account of, interpretation. On a hermeneutical reading all science is interpretative. The more fundamental question now is whether to treat science as epistemology or as hermeneutical discourse. Rorty (1980) regards these two conceptions of science as dichotomous. Hermeneutics frustrates the idea of an all-embracing epistemology which can lay bare the inner-workings of the universe; i.e. a comprehensive, objective language in terms of which all phenomena can be explained at all times.[2]

On a hermeneutical reading, scientific problems do not exist in the world but are constituted by the scientist using the language of his science as the basis of interpretation. Each and every language of interpretative understanding is limited in its sphere of application. The philosophy of science has to discover what languages people use to understand why and how they use them, to establish how useful a particular language is in the context of a particular set of scientific problems, and what sort of theory is needed to elucidate the particular problems that interest the scientist.

An implication of the hermeneutical turn is that the social sciences require a conceptual framework which is appropriate for their purposes, one that accommodates various 'levels' of interpretation and understanding that are associated with any attempt to explain people's conduct. By different levels of understanding I mean that from a hermeneutical standpoint all understanding is interpretation. Science is cognition, *ergo* science is a hermeneutical endeavour. But the subject matter of social science is people and their activities, decisions, and choices. These activities involve individuals in understanding. Thus *social science embraces a double hermeneutic*. The social scientist (as an understander) has to explain how individuals – as objects of study – understand, since their activities are related to their understanding.

The notion of a double hermeneutic of social science is attributable to Giddens (1977: 12) and is discussed by Bleicher (1982), though its potentially far-reaching implications remain largely unexplored. The double hermeneutic means that the methodologist has two levels of understanding or interpretation to think about. One level pertains to the theorist's understanding – the nature of the world that he identifies and describes in his theory. This level of the double hermeneutic is common to all enquiry. Then there is a level that is peculiar to social science. The focus here is on the individuals whose social conduct is the object of analysis. What does the theorist permit them to know? What sort of world do they 'see'? How do they understand their circumstances?

Questions such as these highlight the paramount position in methodological debates of the relationship between the theorist and his subject matter and this relationship is the central component of my methodological analysis. The distinction that I draw in the next section between the world view of neoclassical equilibrium theory and that of a subjectivist scheme hinges on their different characterisations of this relationship. Subsequent chapters expand upon the portrayal of the relationship in mainstream theory and also on how modern hermeneutics interprets the relationship.

The epistemological problems associated with the relationship between the theorist and his subject matter are not completely alien to economists. The theme of Hayek's justly celebrated article, 'Economics and Knowledge' [1937] (1948c) is the epistemological assumptions underlying the idea that individuals base their equilibrating conduct on market-price 'signals'. In the opening paragraphs of his book on methodology, Boland (1982a: 2) also highlights the need to investigate epistemological matters.

Any decision-maker must have some knowledge from which to determine, and by which to assess the options available. What do we presume about the individual decision-maker's knowledge? Or better still, what do we presume about the individual decision-maker's methodology that allows for rational choices? If ... economics is supposed to explain, or even to describe, the process of making decisions, surely the methods utilized by the decision-maker must play a central role in the *process* and thereby in the outcome of the process.

The question of what the decision-maker knows or understands – how he interprets the world – is one that suggests itself from a hermeneutical reading of the nature of decision-making. Yet, like Hayek, Boland refers to only one level of the double hermeneutic – what individuals know and how they come to acquire and to use that knowledge.[3] Equally important on a hermeneutical reading of the nature of science is what the theorist knows and how he acquires his knowledge. This issue has not been ignored and is itself a long-standing source of controversy within the scientific community. Essentially an epistemological problem, it is at the root of the debate about objectivity, or the *Wertfreiheit*, of science. That the matter also includes an ontological dimension is apparent in asking what are the 'facts' of any science? Are there objective facts? Where do these facts and the world itself exist? Are they in some sense separate from and independent of the theorist? What is it that the theorist observes or knows?

Recognition and acceptance of the double hermeneutic of social science give rise to a host of questions to which the methodologist must attend; questions that concern not only the nature of understanding at each level, but also whether understanding is the same at both levels of the double hermeneutic. Does the theorist understand in the same way as the individuals whose conduct he is studying, and what are the implications for the formulation of social theory if his understanding is either the same or different? It is worthwhile listing some of the issues that arise on regarding social theory as a hermeneutical activity.

What does the theorist know about the way in which people, who are the object of analysis, construct or constitute their world? How is this knowledge acquired? Is the theorist's knowledge of his world, of which he has experience, somehow different from his knowledge of the world of the individuals who populate the scheme? Does the theorist acquire knowledge of his world in a way that is different to the way in which he acquires knowledge of those individuals' world?

Questions of an ontological nature include the following. Where does the theorist's world – the one to which his experiences refer – exist? Is it something out there? Or is it of his own making, one that he 'creates' through his activities? And what of the world of the individuals whom he is studying, where does this exist for the theorist? Is it a part of his world, or something separate?

19

On the other level of the double hermeneutic, what does the individual know of the world and how does she acquire this knowledge? What 'theory' of knowledge does the individual apply in dealing with the world? Is the knowledge of all individuals the same? Or, if in some sense they create or '*constitute*' their worlds, how do they do so?

Ontological questions about the 'world' of the individual include: where does that world exist? Is it a pre-given world out there which exists 'around' the individual, or which she confronts (an objectivist view), or, is it a world of her own making (a subjectivist or relativist view)?

Gadamer is quoted by Bleicher (1982: 34) as saying that the instrumental languages of positivist-empiricist science 'have no community of speech or life as their basis but are introduced and employed merely as means and tools of communication. It is for this reason that they have to presuppose actually practised understanding' and this is why neoclassical theory either takes the answers to these questions for granted or assumes that they have been resolved, but does not debate them. Because the language of neoclassical theory knows nothing of interpretation or understanding, which arises in a social context and is intersubjective, all these questions about understanding are beyond the theorist's field of vision or comprehension. The positivistically inspired language of the neoclassical theorist does not enable him to say anything about these matters. They are hidden from him and so are their implications for people's conduct. I call the epistemology and ontology of mainstream economic theory, which defines the relationship between the theorist and his subject matter, a 'third-person perspective'. Central to the third-person perspective is the idea that the world is simply 'given' for the theorist. Without him having to interpret it or understand it, it just exists out there as a complete, comprehensive scheme. The 'agents' who inhabit that world do not understand either. A theory formulated from a third-person perspective does not require them to do so; knowledge is just something, a part of the world, which the agent possesses or acquires.

Positivism-empiricism is the foundation of the third-person perspective. Neoclassical theory is constructed on the premise that the scientist's task is to undertake an objective investigation of a world of tangible things that can all be observed and that exist out there somewhere beyond and separate from the scientist. The purpose of theory is to classify and predict and the canons of this methodology give rise to a language of theory where interpretation and understanding, which is subjective rather than objective, is expressly precluded.

Juxtaposed with positivism-empiricism, with its conception of science and its allied epistemology and ontology, is hermeneutics. Throughout the book I use the term 'interpretative understanding' to denote the concept of *Verstehen* that I associate with modern hermeneutics. 'Interpretation' and 'understanding' are both terms that apply to the individual as being-in-time, which is the focal point of hermeneutically based theory. Interpretation and understanding refer to a conscious, sentient, social being, making sense of her circumstances. A positivist methodology tries to paint the scientist-observer as someone who casts a detached, dispassionate eye on something that is happening over there and is removed in place and time from the observer's existence, experience, and interests. Hermeneutics regards science as understanding, and understanding is not a matter of observation as positivism misleadingly portrays it. In understanding we make the thing or the ideas relevant to our own interests, bringing the issues into the context of our interests of that moment. All knowledge is gained in, or through, understanding. Indeed *knowledge* is understanding, which is part and parcel of making our way in life. Understanding does not yield a set of universal truths nor is our understanding permanent and immutable; the way we understand and what we understand changes. In order to understand we do not test our comprehension against benchmarks of truth as if the truth somehow resides outside, or beyond, ordinary comprehension. Truth is what people understand and we 'test' our understanding in the social context of the hermeneutical circle, in discourse with others and in the light of our own experience. Doubt – wondering whether we have 'seen the point', or questioning ourselves about whether things are going to change unexpectedly – is an inevitable and fundamental part of understanding (see Warnke 1987: 32–3; Bernstein 1983: 36–7), which also involves recognising and dealing with the novel and unanticipated.

Natanson (1962: 196) points out that understanding is self-validating. It is also self-referential in that what a person understands is what interests her, although she shares her ideas with others who are part of her social world, and they too influence her understanding. Understanding is personal. It concerns the individual's assessment of things in relation to her interests of the moment and is always prejudiced, for it is shaped by social convention, by one's beliefs, and by the nature of one's relationships with other people, whether they are people in authority, subordinates, friends, or elders.

From a hermeneutical standpoint, decisions reflect individuals' comprehension, and explanations of decision-making and choice must be based on an understanding of how individuals understand. I use the term 'subjectivist' to characterise those theories that are formulated to elucidate human conduct and to address problems of decision-making and which treat understanding as paramount in such explanations. Subjectivist and positivist theories are incongruent both in terms of the objectives they endorse and their epistemologies and ontologies. Contrasting it with the third-person perspective of neoclassical economics, I refer to the epistemology and ontology of a subjectivist theory as a 'first-person perspective'.

21

THE FIRST- AND THIRD-PERSON PERSPECTIVES

The remainder of this chapter is concerned with explicating the first-person and third-person perspectives, beginning with the latter. The object is really to be able to understand how the two conceptual frameworks that incorporate these perspectives differ in terms of the way they portray the relationship between the theorist and his world. How does the theorist see things and, ultimately, what does he allow the subjects of his theory to see and how do they understand their worlds? An understanding of the differences between the two frameworks is crucial to revealing why neoclassical theory cannot serve to explain conduct. By contrasting the epistemologies and ontologies of the two languages of theory, I will also be able to identify features of a subjectivist theory framed from a first-person perspective.

There is a widely held belief that orthodox economic theory explains phenomena such as prices, profits, and competition from the point of view of a 'detached, external observer' (see, for example, Coddington 1972: 12–13). The theorist's world view is supposedly that of an observer, sometimes referred to as an 'omniscient observer', taking cognisance of how people behave, and constructing a theory from his observations. I want to emphasise that this is not the viewpoint of an observer, in the ordinary sense of someone who watches from the sidelines, someone not involved in the activities himself but who studies the activities of others going on over there, with all his training and expertise. If this is what we ordinarily understand by an observer, then the 'detached observer' which is the third-person perspective of neo-classical theory is something entirely different and has no bearing on the way in which a person observes or understands. In terms of both what is known and how it is known, the third-person observer's knowledge is fundamentally different to the knowledge of an individual who is both observing and understanding. By exploring the implications of the third-person perspective, we discover that the 'omniscience' of the detached external observer defines a special epistemology and ontology which makes this an unnatural viewpoint in terms of what an ordinary person observes and of how she understands. An investigation into the epistemology and the associated ontology of someone contemplating a world that comprises an equilibrium scheme helps to explain why this is so.

In defining the notion of general equilibrium, Arrow (1968: 376) states it has 'two basic, though incompletely separable, aspects'. These are 'the simple notion of determinateness' and 'the more specific notion that each relation represents a balance of forces'. Determinateness means that 'the relations that describe the economic system must form a system sufficiently *complete* to determine the values of its variables' (emphasis added). What does completeness mean if applied to an economy or market? What would a 'complete world' be like? Can we define the circumstances of someone who was able to experience completeness by trying to understand how the world of an

22

equilibrium scheme would appear to someone who 'experienced' it? If you saw the world as the 'observer' of neoclassical theory is supposed to do, what would it mean to say that relations that describe it form a complete system? How would you understand that world? What would you know? Such an approach is useful in exposing both the epistemological premises of an equilibrium theory and the ontological implications of such a scheme. It helps to reveal the meaning of the third-person perspective.

The third-person perspective, of someone 'viewing' the world as an equilibrium scheme, denotes a comprehensive world view associated with the grasp of a scheme of things that is truly, comprehensively complete. The most important feature of this epistemology is that it is literally a *world* view, embracing at one instant everything that there is to know which has a bearing on the equilibrium or optimisation problem at hand. All conceptions of determinate systems and optimisation problems involve a third-person perspective, whether the system is an economy, a market, or even the optimising 'decisions' of individuals and firms. The epistemology of the third-person perspective is identified by the postulate that 'the system' will produce certain results, or have an outcome, and that the workings of the system can be determined in order to define the outcome. A theory that postulates that economic activities could, or do, terminate in equilibrium states asserts that individuals' interactions are determinate and conceives the world in this way.

The notion of equilibrium demands, and the third-person perspective characterises, a world that is absolutely bounded and complete, to the extent that nothing is unknowable. What is 'given' signifies the full extent of the world. Even if some of what really exists out there is hidden from view in this 'time period', it is nevertheless known that it does, or will, exist out there to be uncovered, or 'learned', in some later time period (see Hahn 1973a). This is what determinism and the third-person perspective imply: there is knowledge of exactly what, and how much, it is possible to know. Even if knowledge has to be acquired in the 'future', a part of the scheme – one of the givens – is how knowledge in one period is transformed into other knowledge in subsequent periods. Everything that is needed in order to explain how the system works is within one's grasp; and it is possible to conceive of the entire scheme of things as being simultaneously and instantaneously present.

From an ontological point of view, the scheme that constitutes the particular optimisation or equilibrium problem is conceived as consisting entirely of things or objects.[4] Thus, from a third-person perspective, all the elements of the world, such as 'resources', 'tastes', and 'technology', have a real, material existence and every single bit can be identified, defined, enumerated, measured, and compared with every other bit. 'Knowledge' is also something in the world and has the same qualities as all the other things. It consists of 'items' or 'pieces' like a child's blocks that can be 'acquired' or 'grasped'. Every piece of knowledge refers to, and has a counterpart in, a concrete piece of the real world. The things that make up the world have an existence 'out there'. They are beyond and independent of, or separate from, every individual in the sense that the existence and properties of things in the world make no reference to and have no bearing on the circumstances, perceptions, or interests of any person. Yet it is the awareness of his or her circumstances by every person that denotes understanding and is indicative of one's spatio-temporal being, or one's being in the *durée*. Thus, the scheme of things as 'seen' from a third-person perspective is not the 'my world' of the participant who has an interest in, or is part of, events and who is involved in social relationships. An inventory of things in the world makes no reference to experience, insight, or understanding. In this regard one could say that the things that make up the world, including knowledge, do not have meaning to anyone, in that they do not have to be interpreted or understood but merely exist out there.

A third-person perspective, in purporting to represent a scheme of things that is complete, is an artificial thought scheme. It depicts a world that transcends (or passes beyond) ordinary comprehension or understanding. This is not the world that any individual 'sees'. The third-person perspective cannot be reconciled with anyone's point of view. Ordinarily when we speak of 'understanding' or 'a point of view' we refer to someone's (the knower's) interests and her particular view of things, which is a first-person perspective. The third-person perspective is an attempt to eliminate countless personal points of view in favour of a single, all-encompassing description of a world out there. The phrase 'third-person perspective' contains an inherent contradiction because a perspective is always some*one's* point of view – a first-person perspective. I use the phrase deliberately, in order to convey the paradox of the epistemology and ontology of positivist theories; that they suppose the absence of any personally constituted point of view. All knowledge, and the world itself, exists out there, without a knower, or an understander.[5] In attempting to articulate a problematic notion, Van Peursen (1977: 188) has the following to say about 'perspective', as an essential aspect of human cognition.

> Human life, its acts, its thoughts unfold in perspectives. To come 'out of perspective' is incompatible with being human. . . .
>
> Perspective expresses the idea that a thing or scene is not looked at from all sides at once. Things show a certain part of themselves, depending on the side from which we approach them. Ideas are likewise grasped in perspectives.

Just as a complete scheme of things abolishes the individual's understanding and perspective, so it eliminates the notion of time experienced as duration; Bergson's notion of the *durée* – the inner stream of duration in which we are immersed, when other moments follow this, the present moment (see Schütz 1972: 45). The stream of experience is about discovering

24

and continuously becoming aware; the 'world' unfolds as we constitute it in the *durée*. Van Peursen comments that eliminating time 'amounts to extract-ing the world from its horizon. That would make the world unreal; it would no longer be a world for man, or a world related to human consciousness' (Van Peursen 1977: 194). Yet, the third-person perspective is just such a view outside of time. Perception and understanding is time-bound, related to the individual's existence in the *durée*. The lived-in *durée* of being and inten-tionality is continuous understanding; i.e. becoming aware, finding out, learning. This 'acquisition of knowledge', or understanding, in the *durée* is such that I (as being-in-time) did not, and could not know or understand this before my comprehension-of-the-moment. Comprehension is my being-in-time, related to my interests, and I never conceive of my world as complete. In order to do so, I would have had to stop thinking.

Spanos (quoted in Leitch 1988: 199), attributes the abolition of the *durée* to a 'dominant "ontotheological tradition"', which I associate with the scientific method that emerged from positivism and empiricism, that 'trans-formed . . . the temporality of being-in-the-world into an overall insidious "world picture"'. Conveying the essence of the third-person perspective, Spanos states that the transformation

> allows *Dasein* [human being] to *see* existence from the beginning, i.e., all at once. In so doing it dis-tances him, i.e., it disengages his Care, makes him an objective, or disinterested or careless, *observer* of the ultimately familiar or autonomous picture in which temporality – its threat and its possibilities – has been annulled.

This analysis should help to clarify how the scheme of things has to be conceived by an equilibrium theorist, or one who sees human conduct as solving optimisation problems. Now what of the knowledge possessed by an agent who inhabits an equilibrium scheme? How is this represented by the theorist who, conceiving the world from a third-person perspective, holds that conduct is determinate and that individuals aim to optimise?

It is difficult to see how, or why, the theorist and the agents whose activities he is studying should be subject to different epistemologies, i.e. why '*homo oeconomicus*', the 'rational' agent of economic theory, should have a world view that differs from the third-person perspective of the theorist. A conventional approach to this matter is that of Talcott Parsons, who argues that the actors of social theory should be represented in exactly the same way as the theorist.[6] This argument means that while there is consistency across both parts of the double hermeneutic, the actor is conceived as capable of knowing an entire system.

> Since science is the rational achievement par excellence, the mode of approach here outlined is in terms of the analogy between the scientific investigator and the actor in ordinary practical activities. The starting

point is that of conceiving the actor as coming to know the facts of the situation in which he acts and thus the conditions necessary and means available for the realization of his ends.... [T]here is, where the standard is applicable at all, little difficulty in conceiving the actor as thus analogous to the scientist whose knowledge is the principal determinant of his action so far as his actual course conforms to the expectations of an observer who has, as Pareto says, 'a more extended knowledge of the circumstances'.

These views are quoted by Schütz (1943: 130–1) who attacks the methodology that Parsons advocates in the quotation, arguing that the standpoint of the scientific observer, as reflected in Parsons's archetypal scientist, is not the way in which individuals 'see' the world. It is equally inappropriate to portray actors and the theorist as if they had, or conceivably could have, a third-person perspective. Because the theorist knows or understands in the same way as an ordinary individual – i.e. his is a first-person perspective – the theorist's understanding is fundamentally different from the way in which the knowledge of the positivist scientist is conceived. The theorist, as an observer, understander, and interpreter of people's conduct does not have the knowledge of people and the world that is attributed to the positivist scientist, so the theorist cannot possibly provide an adequate explanation of their conduct from this level and it is entirely inappropriate to regard individuals as coming to know the world in the same way as the positivist scientist. As Schütz explains the problem, the 'level' of the research in which an archetypal positivist scientist is engaged is associated with a different meaning of the term 'rationality' to that of the individual making decisions in the 'life-world'. He says (Schütz 1943: 134, emphasis added) that,

[i]n our daily life it is only very rarely that we act in a rational way if we understand this term in the meaning envisaged in Professor Parsons' previously quoted statement. We do not even interpret the social world surrounding us in a rational way, except under special circumstances which compel us *to leave our basic attitude of just living our lives*.

The distinction between the epistemologies of the third-person and first-person perspectives helps to clarify the meaning of Schütz's criticism. It can be restated along the lines that the epistemology of the scientific observer as well as that of the rational optimiser is not congruent with the way in which an individual (or the theorist) ordinarily understands. Schütz is saying that it is absurd to imagine an individual having a grasp of a complete scheme of things out there as is attributed to the rational, optimising agent of economic theory. This is where the shortcomings of neoclassical economics are to be found.

A positivist methodology presupposes a third-person perspective by upholding the idea of a single, all-encompassing language that is capable of explaining all phenomena. Behind this idea is the conception of an entire world or universe, portrayed as a single system and consisting of things, all parts of which could be explored and explained using a single, all-embracing language of theory. Misinformed by the methodology of positivism, which suffers from the significant limitation that it precludes enquiry into the nature of knowledge, the individual's epistemology is inappropriately and mistakenly conceived as the third-person perspective and people who cannot have a third-person perspective are treated as attempting to optimise when, in terms of *what* they know about the world as well as *how* they know, they cannot even conceive of doing so. The agent in social theory comes to be regarded, and modelled, as a rational optimiser and some type of optimising behaviour[7] is always associated with the rationality postulate that underpins the determinateness both of individual conduct and of individuals' interaction, as expressed in the notions of market or general equilibrium. Where does this confusion originate? In the epistemology and ontology of the third-person perspective; a conception of the scheme of things that is compatible with the assumption that individuals try to optimise, but is at odds with the knowing, observing, or understanding that we do as human beings.

What knowledge would an individual have to have in order to believe that she could optimise? How would a person intent on optimising have to 'see' the world? These questions have been tackled by Schütz (1943: 136) who describes 'the knowledge that a man living naïvely has about the world' and contrasts this with the knowledge that would be required for the postulate of rational optimising action (ibid.: 142).

Admitting he can hardly begin to cover all aspects of the knowledge that a person would need in order to optimise, Schütz suggests that it would include knowledge of the 'place of the end to be realised' as well as its 'interrelations with other ends'. Concerning the means to attain her ends, the individual would have to know 'the different chains of means which technically or even ontologically are suitable' and she would have to know whether and how the means interfered with other ends. Schütz also recognises that the problem merely of identifying what 'items' of knowledge are implied in the maximisation postulate multiplies once the social context of action is taken into account (ibid.: 142–3). The implication of his list is that just in order to optimise, every actor would have to know everything there is to know about the world. Each would have to be able to conceive of the world, or the problems with which each is dealing, as complete in every respect and, in terms of being able to evaluate and to compare all the options, the world would have to conform to those ontological conditions that I have ascribed to the third-person perspective.

This means that what the optimiser confronts 'now' is all there is and all there ever will be. Everything is accessible to her and nothing can even be imagined or anticipated beyond what is already known; nothing is still-to-be-revealed; nothing is uncertain, so she is never in doubt. All the implications of whatever she might 'choose' to do, including the ways in which every other individual will respond to what any one else does, must be known or must be calculable. Her knowledge has to be comprehensive so that even if some knowledge about the world is currently unavailable she must know precisely what is 'unknown', meaning that there is a means available to her now of generating the 'knowledge' for 'future' time periods.

To know of everything in the world means that the world already exists entirely beyond (outside of) the individual and is not something that is part of her existence, something that she creates with her thoughts and activities. The optimiser must be able to determine how far she is from attaining her goal with each 'choice', or 'course of action', that she could possibly make. She must be in a position to compare the consequences of all 'choices' in order to determine which are best for her. Everything that pertains to her actions must be regarded as having a concrete existence in the world out there. So 'tastes', 'resources', 'technology', and even 'knowledge', have properties which enable them to be compared in respect of the contributions each makes to the agent's 'goals'. The goals are not personal or subjective, they are not associated with impressions, feelings, judgements, or thoughts, but reside in things out there – in maximising utility or in minimising costs, for example. It is the thing itself out there, the bundle of goods, or the investment opportunity, that contains the 'goal' of utility or profit maximisation and when the right one is selected, the individual 'attains her goal'. The ontology of knowledge is the same. Knowledge can be 'acquired' and 'change'; it is something physical that exists in the world as a thing.[8]

An individual who had not yet tried out and exhausted all the opportunities for action, and did not know all the consequences of pursuing all the opportunities, would not be able to optimise. She would have to conjecture about what might be the right thing to do, but having done it she could not be sure that it was optimal. The idea of optimising implies stasis, meaning inactivity or stagnation. All opportunities can be, and have been, discovered, which is why the notion of a stationary state plays such a prominent role in equilibrium theory. More precisely, the idea that the world of the optimiser is complete means that it is timeless, without a future, since the future means the yet-to-be-understood. The full extent of the world is not known or 'tested'. There are courses of action that are as yet unconceived, and will only be apparent in time to come. Uncertainty, surmise, and conjecture, which go hand in hand with thinking about the future, have to be extraneous notions in the complete world of the optimiser.

If the third-person perspective is 'wrong', in that the methodology of positivism and empiricism has distorted our picture of what and how the individual knows, by transforming understanding, or being-in-time, into a complete world view, the logical question to ask is: what is the 'correct' way of representing the social world of the individual? To the hermeneuticist the question is inappropriate if it implies the need for an objective and definitive description of the individual's world. Understood in this way, the question stems from a misplaced Cartesian desire to know and to show the world as it really is. The relevant question is: how does the individual understand? How does she constitute her 'world'? The object of a subjectivist theory, one that espouses a first-person perspective, is to explore how the individual understands.

From the time Max Weber brought the notion of *Verstehen* – interpretative, or subjective, understanding – to social theory, the subjectivist approach which he developed has undergone a process of continuous evolution. Different stages in the evolutionary process, which are examined in later chapters, all recognise that understanding what is happening involves interpretation, or attaching meaning to events, though initially subjectivism associated *Verstehen* only with understanding the activities of other individuals. Contrasted with the third-person perspective of the agent confronting a world that consists of things out there, the more recent subjectivist positions of phenomenology and modern hermeneutics depict understanding as ubiquitous (because consciousness is interpretative understanding) and creative (the individual contributes to her world rather than passively experiencing it). The individual's 'world' is literally her thoughts, but these thoughts always concern other people who share her social world, so understanding is always intersubjective. As opposed to the friendless and solitary agent of orthodox theory, the first-person perspective takes cognisance of each individual's associations with, and involvement in, the activities of other people and how these influence understanding and action. The 'life-world', as the individual knows it, is a social world.

Understanding is time-bound, related always to the present moment and to the individual's interests – reflected in her thoughts or perspective – at a given moment. Time, here, means the *durée* of conscious thought, not the mathematician's notion of extension that is associated with orthodox theory. The latter sustains and preserves the illusion of a complete world because events in one period are mechanically transformed into those of another period by some predetermined formula. In the *durée*, understanding is like a continuous dialogue or conversation in which, with experience, fresh insights are gained and one's standpoint changes. The individual constitutes her 'world' anew, in terms of her interests in the *durée*. She is caught up in a hermeneutic circle of discovery, of finding out, forming new opinions, and reshaping her beliefs. Her interests and perspective continually change, and perhaps she modifies her views.

In general, economists do not appreciate that the *durée* frustrates attempts to construct a complete scheme: that being-in-time and equilibrium belong to different conceptions of the scheme of things. Two notable exceptions are G.L.S. Shackle and L.M. Lachmann. This is surely the meaning of Shackle's epithet (1972a: 151; also Preface and 105) that 'time is alien to reason'. 'Reason' is synonymous with 'rational action', meaning the ability to optimise. In order to optimise one has to have complete knowledge and only someone who has no sense of time, who has stopped experiencing and understanding, could have complete knowledge. In a similar vein Lachmann (1977b: 36) states that '[t]ime and knowledge belong together. As soon as we permit time to elapse, we must permit knowledge to change.'

What a person knows depends on her understanding (literally, what she knows is her understanding), and this is always prejudiced in the sense that understanding is a reflection of one's interest of the moment, shaped by relationships with other people and one's 'history'. The idea that the individual is only conscious of the moment is what is meant by her perspective. Understanding is a perspective. Her attention is focused on certain things and her perspective is one that she constitutes or creates in terms of her interest. Interpretation and insight is always a personal perspective, and in the hermeneutic circle the individual does not accumulate knowledge, nor is knowledge grounded in facts 'out there'. Both these conceptions of knowledge are a characteristic of the ontology of the third-person perspective. Experience is not about revealing more of a world that exists out there, it is just about understanding – making acquaintances, forming business and other relationships, finding out what people are doing and what has happened, and discovering whether things have gone according to plan; in the light of which we draw inferences, form judgements, and develop new interests.

Understanding is not just a personal perspective on some*thing*, or on a series of experiences that unfold in the *durée*. Understanding is creative or constructive in that one's understanding is constituted in a social context. The constitutive nature of understanding is explained by Bernstein (1983: 123), who summarises Gadamer's interpretation of the concept of play and of the individual observer's involvement with works of art: issues which Gadamer himself explores at length. By close analogy, Bernstein offers a view of the individual's 'relationship' with the social world, for the argument applies not only to the interpretation of works of art or of texts, but also more generally to understanding – events and relationships with other people.

> A work of art is not to be thought of as a self-contained and self-enclosed object (something *an sich*) that stands over against a spectator, who, as a subject, must purify himself or herself in order to achieve aesthetic consciousness of the work of art. There is a dynamic interaction or transaction between the work of art and the spectator who 'shares' in it.
>
> Even this way of speaking can obscure the fact that a work of art is essentially incomplete, in the sense that it requires an interpreter. And the interpreter is not someone who is detached from the work of art but is someone upon whom the work of art makes a claim. The spectator, then, is present to the work of art in the sense that he or she participates in it.

30

Gadamer's characterisation of the spectator as interpreter repudiates the conception of the detached observer. His argument means that the epistemology of the 'actor' and the 'observer' are one and the same. Positivism is prefaced upon the myth of an objective, potentially omniscient observer. There is no such creature, or if there is he is not a conscious human being whose understanding we can understand. Observation is part of understanding and of being-in-time. Both the actor and the observer are understanders and interpreters and each 'sees' things from his own standpoint. The world of the observer is, in some measure, his own world, of his own making, reflecting his interests in the *durée*. The distinction between actor and observer pertains only to the level of the double hermeneutic. The actor's perspective refers to how the individual 'sees' her world. The observer's understanding involves an interpretation of the interpretations or understanding of other people. The social scientist, whose object is to explain conduct, is always an observer, engaging the double hermeneutic, understanding the understanding of others. Understanding is discovery, not claiming to pile fact upon fact until the whole scheme is revealed (which is the Cartesian idea of knowledge as objective and impersonal).

Sometimes we speak of the individual's perspective, as if that were somehow given without understanding or interpretation. But the theorist is as much interpreter as the individuals whose activities we wish to explain. While claiming consistency across both elements of the double hermeneutic, these arguments reverse the conventional approach to the epistemologies of the actor and observer as reflected in Talcott Parsons's position, quoted earlier in the chapter. Interpretative understanding is always there, both on the part of the theorist or observer and on the part of the actor. The first-person perspective, though concerned with the individual's understanding, is about how, as theorists who are understanders, *we* understand and depict or explain that understanding. One thing is clear; we do not understand people's activities as attempts to optimise. The theorist who represents them in this way, or who constructs a theory around the possibility that individuals could optimise, has lost sight of his understanding and has also lost the ability to bring to bear on his scientific pursuits the insight that he has into human conduct, gained from his own understanding and 'observation' of people. Instead he has to construct a scheme without reference to what he, or anyone else, actually knows.

Critics of both the form of hermeneutical subjectivism described here and its implications, will no doubt find it subversive of scientific methodology and perhaps even nihilistic, because it implies that there is nothing certain in the world, nothing on which to ground an objective analysis of what things are really like. This criticism is a valid assessment of the position of hermeneutical subjectivism, but the response to it is that the criticism is based on a Cartesian ontology which holds that the world, comprised only of things, exists ready-made in an analysable form out there, and that knowledge consists of the sum of all true facts about the things in the world. Knowledge then is acquired by observing the world using a framework or language that is neutral and objective. The hermeneutical turn, embodied in the first-person perspective, is radically sceptical of these claims. From the standpoint of hermeneutical subjectivism, both the knowledge of the theorist and his task are conceived in a fundamentally different way.

Hermeneutics starts by questioning the foundation of knowledge or understanding and, according to Natanson, this is something a positivist methodology precludes. The recognition that social action is founded upon intentional experience which Natanson credits to phenomenological methodologies, however, permits 'questions about the nature and status of intentional experience ... [to] be raised and resolved within the same framework' (Natanson 1962: 158). He argues (ibid.: 159) that

> [a]t the conceptual level ... the method of natural science and the method of social science [phenomenology] are radically different; the former is rooted in a theoretical system that may never take itself as the object of its inquiry without transcending its own categories; the latter, in its phenomenological character, necessarily becomes self-inspecting yet remains within the conceptual system involved. . . . Furthermore, whereas the phenomenological approach begins by raising the question of its own philosophical status, the naturalistic standpoint cancels out the possibility of self-inspection by its own claim that natural science provides the essential method for stating and evaluating philosophical claims.

In enquiring into the foundations of knowledge – understanding – I conclude that the underpinnings of a determinate scheme are utterly misleading in their portrayal of what people know and how they know. The epistemology and ontology of the neoclassical agent – a third-person perspective – bears no relationship to understanding. In explaining the limitations of neoclassical theory, or its unsuitability as a language for dealing with human conduct, this point is central. The epistemologies and ontologies of the third-person perspective and the first-person perspective are *incommensurable*. Rorty (1980: 316) defines 'commensurable' as 'able to be brought under a set of rules which will tell us how rational agreement can be reached on what would settle the issue on every point where statements seem to conflict'. Theories embody either a third-person or a first-person perspective, but they cannot be brought under a set of rules in order to compare them in terms of, say, their respective abilities to meet some criterion, such as explaining economic phenomena. Each theory has a different task, each operates according to different methodological rules. The one is concerned with interpretative understanding: what it is, how people understand and constitute their worlds, and with interpreting their conduct. The other is about identifying, defining, classifying, and describing the relationships

32

among things that are conceived to be out there, to exist in the world without understanding, without a knower. It is uncertain, at best, whether it is possible to construct a set of meta-rules which would make the theories commensurable, and without this there is no means of translating the concepts which are part of a theoretical framework based on the epistemology and ontology of a third-person perspective into concepts which belong to a first-person perspective. The concepts simply belong to two different world views, or two different 'languages'.

Theories constructed from first-person and third-person perspectives appear as disparate and non-overlapping thought-schemes. Shackle (1972a: 246) comes as close as anyone to identifying the ontological incongruities between the two perspectives when he argues that neoclassical theory (the third-person perspective) depicts a world consisting only of things, and argues that economics should acknowledge that actions are 'based on' thoughts, implicitly recognising the hermeneutical basis of action. The contrast between a first-person and third-person perspective makes the epistemological and ontological roots of the two types of scheme explicit. A theory with a third-person perspective cannot accommodate those notions (including plans, decisions, and choices) which are associated with, and acquire their intersubjective meaning in, social interaction in the hermeneutic circle of social discourse. A third-person perspective is not about understanding or about constituting problems in conscious thought; it is about a system of things that exist out there. But plans and decisions are understanding and conduct reflects understanding. This is why neoclassical theory, the language of the third-person perspective, is unsuited to explaining people's conduct, their plans, and decisions. It is also the reason why we have to choose between understanding and explaining conduct or constructing determinate, equilibrium theories.

2

NEOCLASSICAL METHODOLOGY

The notion that there is a permanent neutral framework whose 'structure' philosophy can display is the notion that the objects to be confronted by the mind, or the rules which constrain inquiry, are common to all discourse, or at least to every discourse on a given topic. Thus epistemology proceeds on the assumption that all contributions to a given discourse are commensurable. Hermeneutics is largely a struggle against this assumption.

(Rorty 1980: 315–16)

THE ISSUES

I have identified two types of theory distinguished by their radically different epistemological and ontological foundations. My contention is that the theories are dichotomous in that each serves a different purpose, and that a determinate equilibrium theory, which necessarily involves a third-person perspective, is unsuited to the task of explaining human conduct and people's choices.

This assertion raises the important question of what it is that neoclassical economists wish to do with their theory. Writers who are dissatisfied with orthodox economics usually criticise it for being 'unrealistic', but Coddington (1975b: 540–1) makes it clear that realism does not constitute adequate grounds for either accepting or rejecting a theory. All theories are unrealistic and none purports accurately to represent reality. How then can we decide whether or not our theories are 'good' or 'bad'? In providing an answer, Coddington explains why it is important to understand what purposes theory is meant to serve.

Before one can effectively set about appraising a theory, it is necessary to be clear about what relationship theories have to their subject matter: what they are theories about or what they are theories of. . . . [T]his relationship is not, and cannot be, a straight-forward matter of 'correspondence' between theory and subject matter. . . .

34

[A]ll theories are 'unrealistic'. But the question can still be asked, whether the conceptual framework is adequate to sustain the intellectual tasks that we set ourselves. Accordingly we cannot provide a context-free appraisal of a theory, but only an appraisal in the light of what we are trying to do, what question we are trying to answer.

Because each of the two categories of theory has a different methodology and serves a different purpose, my classification of theories according to their epistemologies is particularly appropriate for answering the question regarding the suitability of a conceptual framework to its purpose. Natanson (1962: 196) identifies and highlights the different tasks of theories which originate in different methodological traditions. His comparison refers to the received notion of science on the one hand, which traces its origins to Francis Bacon and Descartes, and to the tradition of phenomenology and hermeneutics on the other hand. The former, he argues, judges theory by what it does,

> what it produces, what its applications are. . . . [A]ccording to its fruits the theory is judged valid, weak, or impotent. The acid test . . . is performance, and performance is itself judged in accordance with the canons of standard scientific method. . . . Knowledge is validated by its capacity to transform the world . . .

According to the Cartesian view of science, the purpose of theory is to provide knowledge of what exists out there beyond the theorist, and in order to do this a theory has to codify, classify, categorise, and predict that world. This methodology is demanding in divorcing the theorist from the world (his subject matter).

Another view of the task of theory, associated with the hermeneutical reading of science, has a different lineage and according to Natanson (ibid.) originates with Plato and comes down through the work of St Thomas Aquinas. The fundamental idea is that knowledge is understanding

> and that understanding is self-validating. The task of theory is comprehension; and not comprehension for the sake of something else, but comprehension for the sake of comprehension. The criteria for a good theory are its internal coherence, its capacity to illuminate the structure of reality, its power to transform not the world but the theorist, to make him a wise man.

Comprehension is synonymous with understanding and I have argued that understanding means that the individual approaches matters, and attaches significance or constitutes the relevance of something, in terms of her own interests. Understanding means that the person 'shares in' the situation and creates the understanding. The scientist adopting a Cartesian approach does not subscribe to the notion of understanding; nor do his epistemology and ontology permit him to understand. The phenomena that he is supposed to investigate, and the way he is supposed to go about doing so, do not belong to 'his' world (one which he understands), but to 'a' world, an alien thing, the mechanics of which are only revealed by successive attempts to refute hypotheses about how it works.

The methodology of neoclassical economics endorses a Cartesian view of scientific practice. I will approach in stages the question of whether the theory is appropriate for its purposes. Initially in this chapter I examine the premises of a positivist-empiricist methodology. This methodology does not appear to be entirely suitable for enquiring into the sorts of issues that the forerunners of modern neoclassical theory were contemplating. So why did economists settle on it? In order to answer this question, it is necessary to examine the interests of early neoclassicists. The next step, which takes us to Chapter 3, is to establish what the current generation of theorists are doing in terms of the sorts of questions that they are trying to answer. My contention is that a group of neoclassical theorists, that includes some of the most prominent figures in neoclassical economics today, are asking questions which a positivist methodology cannot answer. Theirs are not the equilibrium theorist's traditional concerns about the existence and stability of equilibrium but are rather associated with the hermeneutical view of science. What the theorists seek is an understanding of the nature of choice. They are the sorts of questions which a theory of decision-making must endeavour to resolve. The fact that on the theorists' own admission they arise in the course of their efforts to 'extend the scope' of the traditional theory and conventional methodology, suggests to me that these theorists have encountered the limits of their method when their object is to obtain insight into the nature of decision-making.

MODERNISM

The dominant methodological tradition of science is the one that McCloskey (1983: 484) refers to as 'modernism' in order to 'emphasise its pervasiveness in modern thinking well beyond scholarship'. Modernism is an 'amalgam of logical positivism, behaviourism, operationalism, and the hypothetico-deductive model of science'. Its intellectual origins are mixed and the lineage of some strands in this heritage of modern science stretch back at least to the Middle Ages when, according to Benton (1977: 19),

[t]he new movement in philosophy was intimately connected with innovations in scientific knowledge and constituted a challenge to the intellectual authority of tradition, divine revelation and faith, at least in those spheres being opened up to scientific knowledge. And this challenge was not, of course, a purely intellectual one. It had social and political implications of the most profound kind.

36

Modernism is particularly associated with the philosophy of Descartes which made its way into the social sciences through the tradition of empiricism. It did so via scholars such as John Locke and, supplemented by the Kantian conception of an ultimate objective basis for grounding knowledge, came to social science through Auguste Comte and positive philosophy (see Benton 1977; Losee 1972). Perhaps the purest expression of this empiricist philosophy of science is to be found in the writings of members of the Vienna Circle, such as Carnap and Schlick in the 1920s and 1930s, which are identified with logical positivism (see Caldwell 1982: ch. 2).[1] The Cartesian legacy is vested in the methodology of modernism as a belief in a meta-framework, in terms of which all thought is subject to the same criteria for evaluating the correctness of knowledge. The Cartesian 'dream or hope', according to Bernstein (1983: 71) was that

> with sufficient ingenuity we could discover, and state clearly and distinctly, what is the quintessence of scientific method and that we could specify once and for all what is the meta-framework or the permanent criteria for evaluating, justifying, or criticizing scientific hypotheses and theories.

He adds that

> [t]he spirit of Cartesianism is evidenced not only by rationalists but by all those who subscribe to strong transcendental arguments that presumably show us what is required for scientific knowledge, as well as by empiricists who have sought for a touchstone of what is to count as genuine empirical knowledge.

Rorty's (1980) reference to modernism as an 'epistemology'[2] underscores the point that, informed by the modernist paradigm, a central theme of epistemology has been the search for criteria by which to distinguish scientific knowledge from non-scientific knowledge. In Rorty's view (see especially 1980: 317–18), this search reflected a narrow and rigid conception of the nature of intellectual endeavour and also narrowly circumscribes the problematic of philosophy, the role of which is to serve as referee in respect of claims to knowledge. The quotation at the start of this chapter emphasises that both the perception of philosophy's role in resolving disputes about knowledge and the ability to distinguish between scientific and non-scientific knowledge are prefaced upon the existence of a single framework, common to all discourse, in terms of which different claims can be compared.

For a long time the Cartesian model of scientific endeavour held sway and, although this account of science glosses over complex problems with which successive generations of philosophers grappled, there was substantial consensus about the task of science. From a Cartesian standpoint the purpose of science, to borrow Rorty's felicitous expression, is to provide a mirror on nature. The metaphor identifies the subject matter of science as something that exists 'out there', separate from, and independent of, the individual. Discovering nature, out there, involves observation, and observation must be neutral and objective. The object of science was to discover empirical relationships, and philosophical issues revolved around the problems of *how* to construct the neutral, objective 'language', or conceptual scheme, for expressing the relationships.

To justify its claim as such, knowledge must be a true representation of what happens out there. The problem is that observation, being partial and subjective, cannot be counted upon to yield a true representation, and even language and terminology gets in the way of describing the world as it really is. How can one tell whether a proposition actually conveys knowledge? Only by subjecting it to an empirical test and confirming its status as knowledge if it passes the test. Science, then, consists of observing the world out there, formulating hypotheses about it, and then testing these hypotheses against further observations made about the world to ensure that the hypotheses convey real knowledge.

With regard to this testing, when the methodology of logical positivism was reaching its height, Karl Popper made a compelling case against inductivism which formed the basis of positivism. Arguing that evidence accumulated through observation is never sufficient to prove the validity of a theory and that the scientist's task is rather to attempt to falsify hypotheses, Popper defined another form of empiricism, 'logical empiricism', and sounded the death-knell of the Cartesian–Lockean–Kantian view of method. Science, he argued, progresses by first conjecturing about new relationships and then attempting to refute these. In explaining his philosophical position, Popper (1963: ch. 1) makes it clear that science is a social activity, that observation 'presupposes interests, points of view' (ibid.: 46) and that it proceeds by conjecture, verbal argument, and trial and error. Because Popper rejected the idea of value-free observation, Bleicher (1982: 35) describes his position as being 'between scientism and the new [hermeneutically-oriented] philosophy of science'.[3]

What is a theory within the modernist methodology? How is it developed? What purpose does it serve? As explained by Benton (1977: 64–5) and Caldwell (1982: 25–6), a theory is essentially a hypothetico-deductive system involving a hierarchical structure. It is a system for generating theoretical generalisations about the world, propositions about observable phenomena – hypotheses – which can be tested. This is the one view of the purpose of theory identified earlier in the chapter. Theory is judged according to its results, its applications, and its performance in yielding knowledge about what happens 'out there'.

In this conception of theory, a higher level of (synthetic) statements consists of axioms or postulates of a deductive system. The mathematical variables at this level often refer to unobservable properties of entities or processes which are termed 'theoretical' concepts, as distinct from 'observational' concepts at the lowest level of statements, which identify properties that can be observed or measured directly. From the higher-level statements, propositions can be deduced which identify quantitative relationships between variables. The lower-level statements, which are deducible from the former, describe observable phenomena and are the propositions which may be tested by observation.

In order to make the system empirically meaningful, there must be a means of linking the theoretical concepts at the higher level (which often refer to unobservable entities) to the lower-level observational concepts which express empirical generalisations. This is achieved through linking statements, designated 'correspondence rules' or 'bridge laws', which express functional relations between the two classes of variables. The acceptance of non-observable theoretical entities as part of scientific discourse means that not all statements or assertions within a theoretical system can be directly tested. Instead, theoretical statements acquire their validity, as claims to knowledge, indirectly, when the theory as a whole is confirmed by testing the deduced consequences against the data. This concept of theory covers both of the meanings that are generally ascribed to the term in the modernist tradition, and are identified by Hollis and Nell (1975: 8). 'Theory' is either the set of hypotheses in the hypothetico-deductive system, or the means of transforming the hypotheses into testable predictions about data. Often, however, the meaning is left implicit and this is a source of possible confusion.

According to the canons of empiricism, scientific explanation involves bringing a phenomenon or a law under a higher-level law. This is known as the 'covering law', or deductive-nomological (D-N) conception of explanation. The D-N model, which dates from the 1940s, is explained by Caldwell (1982: 28–9). (See also Losee 1972: 158–61).

> [A]ny legitimate scientific explanation must be expressible in the form of a deductive argument in which the explanandum, or sentence describing the event to be explained, is a valid, logical consequence of a group of sentences called the explanans. The deductive nature of explanation is stressed; if the initial conditions along with the general law(s) obtain, the phenomenon described by the explanandum *must* occur.

This notion of explanation enables the scientist to establish where something (that exists in the world) belongs in the world out there. It fulfils the role of classifying phenomena. The thing is 'explained' because it is recognisable as part of class of other phenomena: it has similar properties or behaves in a similar way. In addition, judging science by what it produces makes prediction a focal point of scientific endeavour. If something has been properly explained, meaning that its relationship to other phenomena or events has been adequately established, it should be possible to predict its occurrence or behaviour by its relationship with these other phenomena. The D-N model establishes the logical, structural symmetry of explanation (in the particular sense in which the term is used) and prediction. The only difference between the two is a temporal one. If the phenomenon described by the explanandum has already occurred, the theory 'explains', if it is still to occur, the theory 'predicts'.

Besides taking cognisance of the resonant voices that have been raised against this notion of explanation, it is worthwhile noting that for instrumentalists – represented in economics by Milton Friedman (see Boland 1979; 1982a: ch. 9; Caldwell 1982: ch. 8), whose methodology is widely imitated – even the connotation of classification in explanation is irrelevant. What matters is simply the practical, predictive success of a theory. As the means of producing predictions, a theory is a 'black box', in that the content is immaterial as long as it produces the right results. Benton (1977: 69–70) states that instrumentalism rejects 'the "underlying" or "generative" mechanism conception of cause, as against the positivist conception of causality as "constant conjunction" or "necessary and sufficient condition"'. Although the hypothetico-deductive model of theory treats theoretical statements (about unobservable entities) as valid if the theoretical system as a whole is confirmed by testing it, Benton (1977: 67) argues that the instrumentalist conception of scientific theories is the only one strictly available for verificationists of the logical positivist Mach–Carnap school variety.

The main principles of modernism are captured by McCloskey (1983: 484–5) in eleven statements (numbered 1 to 11). There are appreciable overlaps between these and a list of ten tenets of the positivist-empiricist tradition identified by Hollis and Nell (1975: 10) (numbered i to x). Differences between the two sets of statements merely reflect the different interests of the authors and the central elements of the modernist paradigm are clearly visible. The task of science is prediction and control (1 and $viii$). Claims to knowledge are based solely on observation (2 and i). In order to observe, it is necessary to devise objective, reproducible experiments (3 and vii). Things cannot be known a priori (7 and iv).[4] There is a need – implicit in the notion of modernism as an epistemology – to draw a strong line between the positive and the normative, so judgements of value have no place in science (8 and ix). In addition, McCloskey's list highlights issues which constitute important modernist 'beliefs' (his term). Precept 10 states that scientists, 'for instance economic scientists, have nothing to say as scientists about values, whether of morality or art'. Precepts 6 and 11 – 'Kelvin's Dictum' and 'Hume's Fork' – both identify the elevation of mathematics and statistics to a position of pre-eminence within the modernist scientific tradition. Tenet *x* of Hollis and Nell adds the rider, which is central to the debate on the methodology of the social sciences, that 'sciences are distinguished by their subject matter and not by their methodology'. The world out there is a single entity. Different groups of scientists, from physicists to psychologists, are interested in (observing) different bits of it. This conception of science that neoclassical theory adopted is prefaced upon the existence of an all-encompassing meta-framework as the basis of scientific investigation and it rules out the possibility of a dichotomy between natural and social science.

My suggestion that a modernist methodology is inappropriate for pursuing the task of explaining individual conduct means that I must address various questions which are specifically about the methodology of economists. The first concerns the way in which neoclassicists came to espouse modernism, after which we will deal with what is perhaps the more pertinent matter of whether economists actually practise the methodology that they espouse.

By implying that the early neoclassical economists had a choice of methodologies and deliberately selected a positivist-empiricist one, the question of why early neoclassical theorists came to adopt a positivist methodology may be unfair in that the only logical path for them to take would have been to accept the dominant positivist methodology of science. Nevertheless, at the time that the seeds of modern economics orthodoxy were being sown, there were other methodologies on offer and it does not seem inevitable that the sorts of problems that interested these writers should have been squeezed into a positivist mould. For example, the tradition of *Verstehen* was beginning to emerge in opposition to Comtian philosophy and Max Weber was proclaiming the desirability of methodological plurality, with different methods for the natural and social sciences. These ideas, as we will see, did make some impression on the Austrian School of economics and Tarascio (1968: 4) says that '[d]uring the nineteenth-century development of economics, there was a kind of intellectual interregnum during which the procedures used by economists were vague, shifting, and tentative'. He adds that 'economists, as well as sociologists, felt the need to "rationalise" their aims and procedures'. Why did they do so around positivism and with what implications?

MODERNISM AND A THEORY OF 'CHOICE'

The 'marginal' or 'subjectivist' revolution that heralded the arrival of neoclassical economics marked a fundamental shift in the interest of economists compared with their classical predecessors.[5] Both the contributions of the protagonists of the marginal revolution as well as the character of the revolution itself continue to be analysed and assessed (see, for example, the papers in Black *et al.* 1973) but, as Blaug (1973: 10) has noted, the term 'marginal' (as well as 'subjectivist') is apt to be misconstrued.

The term used by Hicks (1976a: 212–14) and by Schumpeter and Mises before him, 'catallactics', has the advantage of conveying something about the interests of the protagonists in that revolution and also of highlighting the shift of emphasis that occurred at the time. Hicks juxtaposes catallactics – involving exchange, markets, value, and the formation of prices – with the concept 'plutology' – the study of the 'flow of wealth' (of nations) – which is the interest of classical political economy. As the forefathers of the revolution, W.S. Jevons [1871] (1957), Carl Menger [1871] (1950), and Leon Walras [1874–77] (1954), independently all formulated contributions that revolve around the main catallactic themes of markets and prices and individuals and their 'choices' or 'decisions'. With their contributions, decisions or choices became central elements of economic theory.

Today it is accepted that there are important methodological differences among their writings and there is considerable debate about what methodologies they espoused as well as the significance of their methodological differences, especially between the contributions of Walras and Menger.[6] It is the work of Menger, founder of the Austrian School, whom Jaffé (1976) describes as 'the odd man out' methodologically, which provides the clue that a theory of choice need not be based on a strict positivist methodology and, indeed, that positivism may be the wrong approach when the object is to explain choice.[7]

In Menger's *Grundsätze*, individuals' valuations of things in a process of exchange are central to explaining market prices. Menger (1950: 120–1) says of value that unlike the classical concept of value as 'cost of production', it is not something 'inherent in goods, no property of them, nor an independent thing existing by itself [but rather] . . . a *judgement* economizing men make about the importance of goods at their disposal' (emphasis added). The idea that individuals' valuations are 'behind' market prices suggests that in the formulation of catallactic theory prominence ought to be given to considerations about a person's motives and how her judgement enters the picture. It also suggests that if economists contemplated the epistemological and ontological foundations of catallactics, they would reflect on the implications that the introduction of values, motives, and judgements had for their methodology. As Max Weber made clear, it is difficult to reconcile a theory of decision-making and action, which recognises the notion of purpose, with the positivist conception of a world consisting of things that exists out there. Purposes are not things that we observe in the world.

The fact that these considerations are all but irrelevant to mainstream theory can be ascribed to Walras's (1954) legacy. He gave neoclassical economics the general equilibrium scheme and it was the notion of general equilibrium, rather than decisions or valuations themselves, that captured the imagination. That the conceptual scheme of Walras left the deepest imprint on the new economic theory[8] is evident in Schumpeter's (1967: 918) elevation of Walras's contribution above those of his catallactist contemporaries. Schumpeter's assessment is widely supported by economists.

> So soon as we realize that it is the general-equilibrium system which is the really important thing, we discover that, in itself the principle of marginal utility is not so important after all. . . . [M]arginal utility was the ladder by which Walras climbed to the level of his general-equilibrium system. . . . [Jevons and the Austrians] . . . too, found the ladder. Defective technique only prevented them from climbing to the top of it. . . . [T]hey saw in marginal utility the essence of their innovation instead of seeing in it a heuristically useful methodological device. . .

This quotation is revealing in a number of ways. It underscores the economist's enchantment with equilibrium and, in Schumpeter's disparagement of the Austrians' technique, it identifies methodological differences between them and Jevons, on the one hand, and Walras, on the other. The Austrians are blamed for focusing too much attention on individuals' valuations and for the failure to realise that the 'correct' approach to economic theory lay in leaving such matters behind in order to reach the concept of general equilibrium. In other words, in the final analysis, marginal utility, and with it valuations, is not really what interest economists: rather, equilibrium is the thing. I have argued that an equilibrium scheme must describe a world that is complete, so with equilibrium comes the epistemology of the third-person perspective.

The epistemology of equilibrium draws the theorist away from understanding. Neither the optimising agents who inhabit the scheme nor the theorist have any need for understanding. Interpreting a person's motive or purpose is utterly irrelevant in a complete scheme because choices merely exist in the world, they are there as things, unrelated to what anyone thinks, understands, or believes. Choices are there as parts or pieces that are necessary for determining an equilibrium but there is no sense in which choices can be explained within such a scheme. All that can be 'explained' is whether and how the pieces fit together in equilibrium. The equilibrium scheme is fully congruent with the positivist conception of a world of physical objects that exists out there.

If it is deemed desirable or necessary to come to terms with choices, to understand the reasons why a particular decision was taken, to consider what influenced someone to do something, or to speculate about what a person might do, neoclassical theory is of no value and Walras has to shoulder the blame for some of this. So the question arises, what was he trying to do? If, as we accept, he was interested in the catallactic themes of markets and prices and people's interaction in markets, what purpose did he intend his scheme to serve? The answer is by no means certain. One view is that of Jaffé (1980), the translator of the *Eléments* and acknowledged expert on Walras, who argues it was not Walras's aim in this work to describe or represent the workings of any actual economy. Walras was not really concerned with what happens in markets and why it happens. He would not have been interested in explaining individuals' decisions. Basing his argument on textual interpretation, Jaffé (1980: 530), suggests that 'the *Eléments*, instead of aiming to delineate a theory of the working of any real capitalist system, was designed to portray how an imaginary system *might* work in conformity with principles of 'justice' rooted in traditional natural law philosophy'. Another view is expressed by Morishima, a modern interpreter of Walras. Quoting from Walras, he contends that the author was applying accepted scientific principles in order to 'obtain a scientific description of the real world' (Morishima 1980: 551, 552).

Whatever the reasons for working with an equilibrium scheme, ironically for a theory that ostensibly revolves around or at least is founded upon them, choices have all but disappeared from neoclassical economics. It is largely Pareto's (1971) conceptualisation of the problem of choice that is responsible for this state of affairs. Pareto succeeded Walras in the Chair at the University of Lausanne and it was he who brought a Comtian, positivist conception of scientific rigour to economics. Tarascio (1968: 30–8) argues convincingly for the influence of Comte's methodological approach on Pareto, despite the latter's accusation that Comte's principles were 'pseudo-experimental' and that he had regressed from the 'experimental' (positive) phase of intellectual evolution to the lowest, 'theological' (supernatural) phase (see also Caldwell 1982: 135, n. 1). Later, via the work of Hicks and Allen (1934) and others, Pareto has had a major impact on the formulation of modern 'axiomatic' neoclassical theory.

Pareto's object, supposedly (see Pareto 1971: 109–18), is to represent 'rational choice'. In his formulation, however, and indeed a necessary requirement for a scheme that equates rationality with optimising, the individual 'chooser' is endowed with a complete world view. All the decisions she could possibly make are simultaneously present to her mind. Choice is identified with the existence of a comprehensive set of things in the world, modelled in a set of indifference curves. The individual who comes equipped with a set of 'decisions' to cover every eventuality has no interests of the moment and hence no perspective in the *durée*; she never has to make up her mind. Questions such as for whom is she making the choices, what is the occasion, what is she aiming to do now (other than to maximise satisfaction), are all supremely irrelevant when the world as a whole is laid bare in one instant. Choice is divorced from the flux of time and thus from experience and understanding. This is the third-person perspective *par excellence*.

Although he overlooks the epistemological transformation that accompanies the shift from choice as understanding to choice as things-in-the-world,

Shackle's (1972a: 96, 245–6, 365) elegant articulation of why he demurs at calling the Paretian conception of decision-making 'choice', is worth quoting at length as it bears upon these arguments and illuminates implications of the third-person perspective.

> Economic choice does not consist in comparing the items in a list, known to be complete, of given fully specified rival and certainly attainable results. It consists in first creating, by conjecture and reasoned imagination on the basis of mere suggestions ... the things on which hope can be fixed. These things, at the time when they are available for choice, are thoughts and even figments.
>
> Rational choice, choice which can *demonstrate* its own attainment of maximum objectively possible advantage, must be fully informed choice. But there can be no full information except about what is past,[9] or else what is exempt from the world of time altogether. ... Rational choice, it seems, must be confined to timeless matters.
>
> To be free to take some course, rather than to obey some necessity, is to be confronted with a number of rival courses of action. ... The same must be true of other men. ... But the sequel to the course he takes will be shaped in part by the particular respective courses that they take. To be free to choose one's action implies that its sequel cannot be known.

In the Paretian scheme the individual as understander, or sentient being, whose understanding is intimately linked to her being-in-time and her relationships with other people, has disappeared. Indeed, Pareto himself accepted that once individuals have left a record of their preference orderings or 'tastes', they are no longer needed in the scheme (Pareto 1971: 120). According to Hahn (1973a: 33), who is evidently troubled by the matter, the absence of a role for the individual still persists in the more modern Arrow–Debreu general equilibrium theory: '[t]he theory does best', he suggests, 'when the individual is of no importance', when individuals cannot influence what happens in the scheme. Others have noted that once the preference function is established there is no need to explain how choices are made (see Rothbard 1956; Lachmann 1977c: 9–11). Whims or passing fancies, ambition, a desire to please – factors that influence decisions and identify our social existence by reflecting our feelings towards other people – are not part of the language of 'choice' but have been replaced by 'tastes' and have become things that exist in the world.

It is surely absurd to claim that this is a way of representing, or furthering the understanding of, choice and decision-making. Hicks (1976b: 317) makes a similar point, though less bluntly, arguing that

> there are many purposes ... for which that assumption [of a fully formed scale of preferences] can be justified. But it is itself a very odd

45

assumption; to take it, as many economists do, as being justifiable for all purposes, must, I now believe, be wrong.

The question is, just how 'odd' must an assumption be before it is of no value whatsoever?[10]

The idea of a fully formed scale of preferences, which underpins Paretian welfare economics, provides an admirable illustration of the complete world of the third-person perspective. It shows just how alien this epistemology is to our understanding and how unsuitable the language of neoclassical economics is as a foundation for policy. I take issue with Cowen (1991) in arguing that the main conceptual problem with Paretian welfare theory does not lie in comparing individuals' levels of welfare or in the difficulties of aggregation. The difficulty is with the notion of a 'level of welfare' itself which is prefaced upon a positivist epistemology and is meaningful only in this context. In order to establish a welfare optimum all possible levels or states of welfare must be known or be discoverable; the world has be conceived as truly complete. Both these notions pertain to an epistemology that makes them incomprehensible to a policy-maker.

The concept of a welfare maximum, involving a complete set of choices, relies on the positivist image of the theorist confronting a world that exists out there and consists entirely of material things. In contrast to this image, how can a policy-maker possibly respond to an injunction to do something only if no one is going to be worse off as a result of his actions? He can conjecture about whether people may be worse off in the future or he can surmise whether some might already be worse off. Even if people's 'levels of welfare' could be measured, he would still need to interpret what a 'higher level of welfare' meant and speculate about whether or not a relative increase in one person's welfare made someone else worse off. His is not and cannot be a complete world, where everyone is 'fully known' to him (whatever that may mean). So the question to be asked is whose welfare is of interest to him. These are the people whom he might consider and it may be important to understand how he identifies them, why he does so, and what he knows or thinks about them. Is he motivated by self-interest or has someone told him to do something to improve the lot of a particular group? Then the question would be: how does he understand the concept of welfare? What does he deem to be important and why? Does his view correspond with that of the people concerned? Does he have any means of finding out what they think and is he interested in doing so? Suppose he wished to find out whether anyone in this group would be adversely affected by what he plans to do. Even the people themselves would only be able to tell him whether they *thought* they would be better off. They might say this, but later have reason to change their minds.

The notion of a complete set of choices in a complete world is problematic from an epistemological standpoint but it is also pernicious in obscuring the value-judgements and the moral issues that are necessarily associated with decisions and have a bearing on policy matters. The policy-maker is prejudiced by his relationships with particular people as well as by his social upbringing. He cannot view the world neutrally for he constitutes it in terms of his own understanding. He has to exercise his judgement and his actions must be discriminatory simply because he does things for one reason but not for another. He has to use his discretion when it comes to deciding whether to do something; moreover how he uses it turns upon his perception of the situation, sometimes prefaced upon moral and ethical judgements. Without first recognising the ramifications of the idea that a policy-maker 'understands', and without an understanding of how and what he understands, we fail utterly to recognise the biases, prejudices, and interests that are at the root of all decisions.

Hence a belief that Paretian welfare theory – which eliminates understanding – is in some sense useful for examining or guiding policies and decisions, involves the assertion that one can meaningfully investigate people's activities and even predict what they will do without considering issues such as their acceptance of authority, or their loyalty, their attitudes to corruption, power, self-interest, their regard for tradition, and even their sense of survival. Comparing the conceptual frameworks that economists use with the understanding that we have of the way in which things work (or fail to work), it is small wonder that economics has so little to offer with regard, say, to the mismanagement of resources in third-world countries. My point is not that economists' frameworks are unrealistic, but that they are wholly unsuitable.

So far I have said nothing about the partial equilibrium approach of Alfred Marshall (1966) which was developed alongside the Walras–Paretian general equilibrium scheme and constitutes the other main antecedent of modern neoclassical theory.[11] Does the Marshallian approach make up for the deficiencies of general equilibrium, in terms of being able to analyse the decisions made by people in business or government or 'households'? Does a partial equilibrium framework provide a basis for understanding these decisions and their consequences?

Certainly Marshall is as much concerned with catallactic problems as are the other forerunners of neoclassical economics, and the differences between his approach to economics and those of Walras and Pareto are marked. Apart from the obvious methodological difference associated with his use of a partial equilibrium framework, modern interpreters highlight Marshall's period analysis and the importance of time in his work (see Boland 1982b; Clower 1975; Gram and Walsh 1983: 520–2; Loasby 1978; Shackle 1972a: ch. 28). In the following quotation, Gram and Walsh (1983: 520–1) indicate that Marshall was interested in analysing the choices of firms, but forcing Marshallian analysis into a (timeless) general equilibrium mould loses the essence of what Marshall was trying to achieve.

The interpretation of Marshall as a *partial* equilibrium theorist suggests that a consistent version of his short-period analysis would entail all the properties of a timeless Walrasian *general* equilibrium of supply and demand. But this is to misinterpret Marshall. His analysis is partial in the more interesting sense that firms are managed by entrepreneurs operating in a short slice of *historical* time[12] – they make decisions under conditions of uncertainty (as distinct from calculable risk). To subject the Marshallian model to a rigorous formulation within a coherent system of general equilibrium would suppress precisely what Marshall wanted short-period analysis for: the study of the choices of a particular entrepreneur ... which may turn out to be wrong, but which nevertheless result in the firm being in equilibrium (given the expectations guiding its conduct) for a short period of time.

A partial equilibrium scheme, which focuses on a particular market or industry rather than on interrelationships in the economy as a whole, is particularly suited to Marshall's purposes, for in both the *Principles* (1966) and *Trade and Industry* (1919), the author keeps an eye firmly on business practices in late Victorian England. Things are changing around the firm all the time and, without the impediment of having to analyse their effects on all markets at once, it is possible to examine their impact on firms and 'the industry' in a methodical manner. Description and formal analysis can be combined in a way that is precluded by the complexity of the formal structure, interrelationships, and stability conditions, of general equilibrium analysis. Loasby (1978) lists various ways in which modern axiomatic neoclassical theory departs from the spirit of Marshallian economics and explains why it is important to distinguish between Marshall's ideas and the modern orthodox scheme, while Leijonhufvud (1976: 107, n. 66) and Moss (1980) emphasise the differences between the Marshallian and 'conventional' neoclassical theory of the firm.

Marshall's approach does not bring us closer than the general equilibrium strand of neoclassical theory to being able to explore the nature of individuals' decisions. Although it is a rich contribution and it avoids many of the pitfalls of modern orthodox theory, his equilibrium framework is still prefaced upon a third-person perspective and this epistemology is an encumbrance when the object is to understand the decisions of individuals or firms. The existence of time in Marshall's analysis does not reveal an appreciation of the *durée* – the being-in-time of consciousness – and the framework does not permit us to explore the individual's understanding in the *durée*. Instead his is a 'view' by someone with a complete picture of the market in each period, for whom the uncertainty of individuals, like all other things, is a given. Market conditions change from period to period but no one understands or interprets the changes. Things are just different because the longer period allows more changes to occur.

In a partial equilibrium model as much as in its general equilibrium counterpart, the third-person perspective means that relationships between firms or individuals are formalised and expressed as if they were physical structures or things that exist in the economy. Thus, entities like 'the market' or 'the industry' are givens, meaning that they appear as concrete and distinct things that are there in the world, with an existence and function that is unambiguous and can be taken for granted. For this reason a partial equilibrium framework is an unsuitable basis for explaining the nature and scope of competition though orthodox economics uses the partial equilibrium framework for this purpose.

Competition is about rivalry and in order to discuss the extent and effect of competitive conduct it is necessary to have a basis for understanding who the rivals are and how and to what extent they regard each other as rivals. There is no reason to believe that different individuals will have the same conception of the market, so that they constitute 'their' markets in different ways and their ideas in this regard are likely to change as well in the course of time. An individual's perception of who constitutes a rival probably depends on her firm's size and its geographic position. Her judgement may be influenced by the consideration that she once worked for the same company as her rival. The 'field of competition' will not necessarily comprise all businesses in the same industry. The sorts of questions which the manager may ask herself are: is her market secure for the time being or is her company likely to lose customers and sales; and if so, why and to whom? Unless it can accommodate different, changing points of view about the reasons why people first prefer one manufacturer's product but later buy from another, or different interpretations on the part of managers about what makes each of their offers attractive to potential buyers, the theory does not provide a suitable platform for constructing a theory of competitive rivalry or for formulating policies on competition.

Looking back over its history, the diversity of contributions lumped together under the heading 'neoclassical economics' is striking. Rather than a precisely delimited school of thought with a well-defined list of professing members, orthodox economics is a paradigm, a set of theories with a shared metaphysic and similar assumptions. In the course of more than a century, positions on the scope and subject matter of economics as well as methodological conventions have changed and some of the principal players have changed their minds and repudiated earlier views (compare Hicks 1976b: 137–8 and Hicks 1980 with Hicks 1937). A positivist-empiricist methodology, or modernism, is none the less clearly manifest in the widely used conceptual scheme which Loasby (1978) refers to as 'axiomatic economics'. Its substance as described by Hausman (1984b: 345), who identifies eight 'lawlike statements', has at its heart the central role ascribed to equilibrium outcomes (either market or general) which are based on individuals' and firms' 'decisions' or 'choices'. At the base of this scheme is a form of methodological individualism which Boland (1982a: 33–9) terms 'psycho-logistic' individualism and which is associated with a particular conception of rationality that involves maximising utility or profits (see Hausman (1984b: 344) for a succinct statement of the conditions associated with this notion of maximising). Equilibrium and rational optimising conduct signify that individual choice or behaviour is determinate. These elements all combine to provide the foundations for the epistemology of the third-person perspective.

As an assessment of what motivated the evolution of modernism, McCloskey's (1983: 486) irreverent view is worth noting. 'Modernism', he says, 'is influential in economics not because its premises have been examined carefully and found good. It is a revealed, not a reasoned, religion.' McCloskey's assertion applies to economics. The insight of Kuhn (1962) is that induction into a paradigm is like training for the priesthood. The 'official rhetoric' of neoclassical economics, to borrow McCloskey's phrase, is modernism. By implication, 'doing economics' is about formulating and rejecting hypotheses that do not pass muster against a rigorous testing procedure. The object is to develop a body of knowledge that mirrors the economic laws, which exist in the world out there, in order to predict. The knowledge gained will serve to master that world and perhaps to transform it.

But how seriously do orthodox economists take their modernism? My reason for posing this rather cynical question is the conviction that 'doing science' – any sort of science, let alone economics – involves more than working with a neutral, 'observation language', 'correspondence rules', discovering 'covering laws', and making predictions. In the course of the last thirty years, inspired by the seminal contributions of Kuhn (1962), Lakatos (1970; 1976), and Feyerabend (1978), the question of what it is that scientists actually do has been subjected to detailed examination.[13] A view that is attracting increasing support is that, even if some of what scientists do fits our description of positivist-empiricist science, scientific practice is much more about trying to find out what is happening, which means interpreting and discovering through discourse and interaction, than about generalising about what exists out there. Significantly, in order to have reached this point in the critique of the nature of scientific endeavour, philosophers of science themselves have had to step outside the conventional positivist-empiricist framework of observing, hypothesising, and testing. Instead, they have relied on interpretation and on an understanding of what scholars and scientists are doing.

In the next chapter I begin by examining the practices of economists who are divided into two groups – 'applied' and 'theoretical' – for the purpose of describing the methods that they employ and the problems that they pursue. My object is to draw together the views of various writers who argue that even though economists have adopted the epistemology and ontology of a positivist world view, they are not good modernists in their scientific practices. After this, it should hardly come as a surprise to find a group of neoclassical economists who are quasi-hermeneuticists. Unable to satisfy their intellectual curiosity by applying a modernist methodology, they are actually posing hermeneutical questions which a rigorous modernist would shun. Much of the chapter is devoted to supporting this interpretation of the interests of some of the leading neoclassical theorists.

3

THE PRACTICES OF
NEOCLASSICISTS

Every scientific method has its metaphysics. Logical positivists used to report the death of metaphysics, but, as Mark Twain remarked on reading his own obituary in the newspaper one morning, the reports were exaggerated. . . . That itself is no fault (although positivists would presumably think it one).

(Hollis and Nell 1975: 21)

MODERNISM IN NEOCLASSICAL ECONOMICS

The 'methodology' chapters of introductory textbooks offer a superficial impression that the heart of positivism beats as vigorously as ever in neoclassical economics, but this impression is belied by a closer examination of what mainstream economists actually do.

For the purpose of examining their methodologies, it is useful to adopt the classification proposed by Coddington (1975b: 544) and to divide the practitioners into two categories: those 'using theories as an instrument of applied investigation; and [those] . . . developing, refining, and extending them as a theoretical exercise or contribution to analysis.' I will refer to these two groups as 'applied' and 'theoretical' economists respectively although the categories are not rigid, and the contributions of some – Friedman and Samuelson come to mind – put them firmly in both groups. My main interest is in the second group, which could also be divided into theoretical economists whose interest lies in 'pure theory' – conceptualising economic problems and relationships – and those who aim to apply the concepts and to establish empirical relationships. The former includes the individuals most closely associated with the development of general equilibrium (GE) theory and, after an initial overview of the scientific practices of neoclassical economists, this chapter identifies the hermeneutical questions posed by a group of general equilibrium theorists and examines the methodological implications of these questions.

There are various assessments of the methodologies of applied neoclassical economists (see, *inter alia*, Boland 1982a; Caldwell 1982;

Katouzian 1980; O'Sullivan 1987), and the characteristics of 'typical', modern contributions in this category are identified by Boland (1982a: 116–19). All these writers agree that it is essential to distinguish between what economists say that they do (the methodologies they espouse) and what they actually do. McCloskey (1983: 485) highlights the contradictions. As far as the claims are concerned, having noted that 'few in philosophy believe as many as half of ... [the] propositions' that he identifies as the main tenets of modernism, he suggests that 'a large majority of economists believes them all'. McCloskey adds that economists do not try very hard to pursue positivist goals. In his view this is fortunate because the modernist paradigm is unacceptable and economists could not anyway hope to pursue these goals in a rigorous fashion (ibid.: 486–93). Instead, they have a 'workaday rhetoric', which is an important element in their arguments, explanations, and 'proofs', and which diverges from the official rhetoric of positivism. Coddington (1975b: 545) argues in a similar vein. Discussing economists' attitudes towards the 'scientific' criterion of falsifiability, he states bluntly that '[a]s far as what economists actually do with theories is concerned, "falsity" is simply an irrelevant category'.[1]

Caldwell is somewhat kinder. He offers various reasons as to why applied economists' reputations as scientists should not be determined by the consistency with which they uphold the tenets of modernism, especially that of testing or attempting to falsify a theory. His arguments include the consideration that the subject matter of economics, as a social science, does not provide the conditions for evaluating unambiguously the outcomes of tests (Caldwell 1982: 238–42). In discussing whether it is important that economists are scrupulous in rejecting a theory when it fails to pass a test, Caldwell notes that empiricists 'recognize that empirical criteria are often insufficient for unambiguous choice among competing theories. Their solution is to supplement the empirical criteria with other criteria' (ibid.: 231). If economists do not practise what they preach, is there anything to be had from advocating an empiricist or modernist research agenda? Caldwell adopts an ambiguous position on this question. 'The invocation to try to put falsificationism into practice in economics need not be dropped, though it seems that there is little chance for its successful application' (ibid.: 242).

If neoclassical theorists neither accept nor reject theories on the basis of what they find, what is the purpose of subjecting them to empirical testing? As an answer to this question, Boland's (1982a: 128) iconoclastic ideas are well worth considering.

[I]f the usual published positive neoclassical articles ... are actually considered contributions to 'scientific knowledge', then it can only be the case that the hidden objective of such positive economics is a long-term *verification* of neoclassical economics. Specifically, each paper which offers a confirmation of the applicability of neoclassical economics to 'real world' problems must be viewed as one more positive contribution towards an ultimate inductive proof of the truth of neoclassical theory. Our reason for concluding this is merely that logically all that can be accomplished by the typical application of neoclassical theory to 'real world' phenomena is a proof that it is *possible* to fit at least one neoclassical model to the available data.

This interpretation is a serious indictment of claims that economists try to sustain a rigorous methodology in order to meet the requirements of positive science. If Boland is correct, the espousal of positivism is a sham. The methodology has become an end in itself, pursued mainly because each generation of mainstream economists requires that new entrants into the profession are proficient in the application of a positivist-empiricist methodology.

Criticisms of the theoretical contributions of neoclassical economists are also wide-ranging and often devastating. Katouzian vigorously attacks mainstream theory from a number of different directions and, as a conclusion to his critique, examines the subject matter of a sample of contemporary theoretical writings in journals (Katouzian 1980: 184–204). His audit is spiced with a good deal of understated humour, probably to emphasise his exasperation at what he finds (see 'analysis of the evidence', ibid.: 204–6). He says that '[t]here is a rising trend among economic theorists to propose ideas which are *not* empirically test*able*. It looks as if, in practice, Positive Economics is virtually non-existent.' Also, Katouzian notes the 'precedence of form over content, of technique over problem, of mathematics over economics' (ibid.: 204). Finally he contends that '[m]any – and, especially most of the more mathematical – theories are abstractions with little or no conceivable counterparts in the world of reality' and the subject matter is 'analytical puzzles as opposed to substantial problems' (ibid.: 205). Later in the book I echo this view, arguing that all the examples of 'decision-making' used to illustrate how people optimise, since they have to be congruent with the epistemology of the third-person perspective, are conundrums and puzzles rather than the practical problems with which businesses and individuals have to deal.

One point of difference between Katouzian's position and mine concerns the use of mathematics in economics. He offers a lucid assessment of this much debated topic and is particularly scathing about the elevation of mathematics to an almost mystical status (Katouzian 1980: 164–72). Nevertheless, rather than arguing that mathematics is an inappropriate language for exploring economic problems, his is a plea for greater methodological tolerance. Thus he says that

the irrational, uncritical and authoritarian elevation of mathematical economics is prone to ... very serious dangers. ... Economic science can afford mathematical economics in a 'peaceful coexistence' or even 'détente' with other approaches. What it cannot afford is the professional hegemony of mathematical economics especially if this is effected by a combination of chauvinism and professional power-politics.

My standpoint is that the language of mathematics has its place when the problems involve structural and other formal relationships rather than understanding, for then the scheme satisfies the epistemological and ontological requirements of the third-person perspective. The language of mathematics exemplifies the ontology of the third-person perspective. It is associated with a world that exists beyond and separately from the theorist; one that consists entirely of physical objects, each of which has a distinct identity and can be represented by symbols and a set of equations. A constant refers to a specific thing – it has a real counterpart in the world out there – while variables refer to distinct and identifiable things that change in a predetermined way and take on new values, as they are physically transformed over time.

Mathematics is thus inappropriate in a hermeneutical theory that aims to provide answers to questions about how individuals judge, what they believe, and how they know or understand. In order to explain people's conduct, the social scientist needs to have answers to questions such as these, so a hermeneutic theory, embracing a first-person perspective, is indispensable. From a first-person perspective the world does not exist but is constituted with the individual's understanding. Its becoming is associated with the individual's existence in the *durée*. Because the ontology of understanding is not that of things that exist in the world, an attempt to express understanding and conduct mathematically requires the integration of two incommensurable ontologies. As this cannot be accomplished, the consequence is that understanding is transformed into a different ontology of things-in-the-world, into a language that makes it impossible to understand understanding. The consequences of this transformation are well known through neoclassical theory, where for example expectations, like tastes, are things that adapt and change under the specific influence of other variables. Although he does not identify the issues as ontological, Shackle (1972a: 26) evidently has in mind considerations such as these when he states that '[m]athematics can explore the meaning of what is already implicitly stated, of what is already *given*. A mathematical model ... has no place for ... *novelty*.' What is 'given' pertains to the third-person perspective, while 'novelty' concerns the continuous coming-to-be of consciousness or understanding in the *durée*.

These views of the methodologies of neoclassicists acknowledge both that neoclassical theory is not good positivism and that whatever methodology is being practised produces unsatisfactory theory. How then should neoclassicists deal with the situation? Should they be more conscientious about their modernism or, as some of these critics imply, should they be taking other methodological directions? In general the response from inside the neoclassical establishment to the 'crisis in economic theory' has been a muted one, and this can be ascribed to the way that modernism itself hinders intellectual debate. Both its hegemonic claim to provide the only valid criteria for assessing the 'truth' of a theory and the narrow set of criteria that it lays down for doing so are to blame. The preceding arguments suggest that at best it is unclear whether tests of economic theory reveal anything about the truth, or quality, of a theory, so it is difficult to imagine a dyed-in-the-wool positivist being prepared to abandon his theory in the light of what tests reveal. Either people judge theories and are willing to give them up in the light of other considerations, which is McCloskey's (1983) view or, when an entire profession is built around a particular approach, the theory is likely to go on being used whatever results it produces. The practitioners are secure in the belief that, like nearly everyone else, they are on the right track and do not feel obliged to listen too attentively to criticisms of their methodology.

A small but highly influential group of general equilibrium theorists, including Kenneth Arrow, Franklin Fisher, and Frank Hahn, have listened to and tried to address some of the criticisms. Not surprisingly they claim that modernism is essentially sound, but that orthodox theory needs to be developed in order to circumvent certain limitations (see, for example, Hahn 1982: 15). In their preliminary attempts to remedy the shortcomings of orthodoxy they provide a ruling on the direction that neoclassical theory should take and, unwittingly, it is an unorthodox one. The issues with which they are concerned are hermeneutical ones and should not even be raised by people who are committed to modernism. This reinforces the view that obeisance to positivism is no more than lip-service and also signifies that economists, concerned with human conduct, must have, and will eventually come round to, a framework that enables them to understand conduct. Positivism cannot serve this purpose so it has to be abandoned. In explaining what these theorists are doing, I will begin by outlining why I regard their contributions as hermeneutical and why their approach represents a rejection of positivism.

The Cartesian view of science as epistemology disregards the theorist's position or predicament entirely. It contains no reference to the theorist's knowledge (understanding) but only to knowledge as such. Epistemological science (Rorty 1980) is concerned with what is actually happening out there. It presupposes that there is consensus both about what knowledge is and about how it is acquired. Science merely enjoins the theorist to apply a particular framework in order to classify what is happening out there and thereby acquire, or 'find', knowledge. This is the approach of positive science. In contrast, the hermeneutical view of science – the view that science is understanding – regards questions about the theorist's knowledge as central to assessing scientific progress, to examining methodology, and also to understanding what constitutes the 'state of the art' in science itself. Any evaluation of scholarly activity involves an understanding of what theorists – who form part of a community – feel or believe about the things that constitute their scientific interests. How sure are they about discoveries? How do they deal with the doubts that they have?

Understanding is about gaining insight and making things meaningful by putting them into a context in which the people concerned can make sense of them. These notions are alien to modernism. Understanding is self-reflexive and always refers back to the understander in the *durée*, constituting problems in terms of her interests. Understanding is subjective, though as social beings scholars constantly communicate their views, ideas, findings, and beliefs. The theorist's voyage of discovery is fundamentally one of self-enlightenment, struggling with problems that interest him and on the way realising – or understanding – what he does not yet understand. Understanding, whether in science or in daily life, is about resolving the meaning of phenomena or events; not by establishing once and for all how they fit into the cosmos through their relationships to everything else, but in terms of how they bear upon one's present circumstances. Understanding does not remove doubt, but identifies the sources. The object of understanding is not to discover what is out there but to make headway in one's social life with other scholars, or with friends and family, or perhaps business associates. Scholarship, in my view, involves the same notion of understanding. 'Scientific progress' means the evolution of understanding in a scientific community, when a group of scholars accepts a new, or different, way of understanding things.[2]

The group of orthodox economists to which I have referred are asking questions which admit that they do not have firm convictions about what the world is like and are engaged in a process of interpreting problems. Instead of consensus about the nature of the world and about how to investigate and to describe it, these neoclassical theorists are trying to understand. They are seeking enlightenment, and not – at least not immediately – the ability to predict.

It is doubtful whether many economists are aware that the turn to interpretative understanding has happened. Fewer still are likely to admit that the methodology of modernism is being made obsolete by the types of questions that are now being posed. The questions about how to represent and to model conduct are those of the methodological sceptic and are self-reflexive in questioning the comprehension or understanding of the theorist. How do individuals learn? What does uncertainty mean, and how can it best be incorporated into economic models? How can these things best be explained? These quintessentially hermeneutical problems are not 'legitimate' ones for the modernist to pose, though it must be admitted that such questions are not entirely new. Throughout the history of neoclassical economics, writers have identified that the theory does not provide an accurate picture of the nature of human conduct and decision-making. In retrospect, one can see what they were getting at. The problems first of comprehending and then of modelling human conduct are reflected in earlier attempts, such as that of the Swedish School, to take account of expectations (see Kregel 1977). They are also at the heart of what Shackle (1965: 44) identifies as the contrast between Keynes's spirit and the method of the *General Theory*. The hermeneutical problem of how the theorist should interpret and explain human conduct is behind the analogy used by Keynes in a letter to Harrod (quoted in Lachmann 1986: 160) to convey the fact that, as a 'moral' science, economists need to take account of 'the apple's motives ... and whether the ground wanted the apple to fall, and on mistaken calculations on the part of the apple'.

Only quite recently have neoclassical economists shown an interest in the significance of these questions and it is important also not to give the impression either that this hermeneutical turn is the result of a deliberate choice of method or that it is widespread within neoclassical economics. Most neoclassicists are modernists and they espouse methods that conform to this genus, though they do not necessarily practise them. It is only a small group who have posed questions that take them well beyond the parameters of a modernist framework. I will call them 'reformists' and what makes their contribution particularly significant is that they are in the top ranks of orthodoxy. Even so, we will see that these economists are uneasy with the issues that they are investigating and readily retreat into their accustomed theory by defining or rephrasing the problems, so that these are amenable to analysis within the conventions of the third-person perspective of a determinate equilibrium scheme.

HOW THE HERMENEUTICAL PROBLEMS ARISE

The skirmishes with hermeneutical problems began in the 1970s when a number of articles with similar themes appeared, coinciding with a deepening awareness – reflected in wider discussion – of the crisis in economics. The purpose of those articles in most cases is to suggest how new types of equilibrium theories can be constructed which eliminate problematic devices and unrealistic assumptions of Walrasian and Arrow–Debreu formulations of GE. The devices that come under close scrutiny, which the reformists wish to avoid in reformulating GE, are employed to ensure that agents' independent 'decisions' are co-ordinated. These devices date back to Walras's notion of '*tâtonnement*' and Edgeworth's (1881) procedure of 'recontracting' and the hermeneutical questions often emerge in the context of posing the question how is equilibrium attained without *tâtonnement* or recontracting, when agents have 'limited knowledge' and when they have to 'learn' about opportunities to trade.

An investigation into the role that these devices play in equilibrium theories helps to explain why the effort to circumvent them inevitably brings the theorist face to face with hermeneutical issues and also their indispensability in an equilibrium theory. The devices solve an epistemological puzzle and without a solution it is not possible even to conceive of equilibrium. I have stressed that equilibrium requires, and pertains to, a scheme of things that is comprehensively complete. Because they serve to bestow 'completeness' on the scheme of things, devices like recontracting make it possible to associate an equilibrium solution with problems of 'choice'. Equilibrium is a creature of a third-person perspective but cognition and decisions do not involve a third-person perspective. Because individuals' decisions are supposed to underlie economic equilibrium, an equilibrium scheme requires devices that serve to create a closed system and to foster the illusion that decisions could be made with regard to a scheme of things that is complete. These devices are absolutely fundamental to equilibrium theory in that they sustain the third-person perspective. It can be appreciated that without constructs that fulfil the same purpose, equilibrium based on choice is literally inconceivable, so it is futile to try to do without such devices unless the theorist is willing to abandon all notions of equilibrium associated with people's decisions.[3]

The necessity of these devices and their epistemological role in equilibrium theories can be illustrated by considering problems associated with the temporality of decisions, to which Shackle draws attention. Contractual market activities are the 'real world' counterparts of solving a set of simultaneous equations in order to determine an equilibrium solution. The people making verbal or written contracts take cognisance of the activities of other people, aware that what others do may have a bearing on their own decisions. Despite the fact the market participants are always uncertain about what the future holds – they do not know, cannot know, and sometimes do not even care about what other people will do in future – an equilibrium scheme must 'care' about these things: it cannot allow people not to know, but must assert completeness. The epistemological role of devices like recontracting is to transform a first-person perspective (not knowing and sometimes not caring what other people will do) into a third-person perspective (knowing everything) and so support the illusion of a complete world. That they are able do this depends on invalidating being-in-time – the individual's existence in the *durée*.

Shackle explains that because the outcomes of a person's 'choices' depend on what other individuals do (and even on how they respond to him), equilibrium, which involves the consistency of 'plans' in the aggregate, requires that choices are 'pre-reconciled' (Shackle 1972a: 53–4, 252–4, 264–6). In order to pre-reconcile choice, it is necessary to resolve a paradox: how can individuals choose their own best courses of action while, at the same time, knowing what other individuals are going to do? The paradox is resolved because equilibrium market prices convey all the information that agents need. They contain information about all individuals' 'choices', and every person, taking his orientation from the equilibrium market prices, can adjust his 'actions' to the 'actions' of others.[4] But pre-reconciliation involves a sleight-of-hand, and Coddington (1975a: 154 n. 2) identifies the nature of the deception.

> [T]he result that . . . market prices are perfect knowledge surrogates is something of a swindle or, at best a piece of conceptual conjuring. This is so because all the epistemic problems have to be solved in *reaching* equilibrium. . . . The reason that market prices 'reflect' everything that traders need to know about the market is because – somehow – they have been rigged to do so.

How is the market rigged? Numerous different devices are used to solve the epistemic problems, but the role of each is essentially the same: to eliminate all vestiges of experience in the *durée* and the idea that individuals can conjecture, but do not necessarily know. For many years, until the late 1950s, GE formulations invariably depended upon '*tâtonnement*' processes to ensure stability. A condition of no trading out of equilibrium was imposed, and for the most part the models were confined to situations of 'pure exchange', rather than including production.[5] If, in 'dynamic' formulations of GE, consumption and production are permitted, which affect the excess demands for goods in subsequent 'periods', what generally happens is that the 'time' in which adjustments of prices to equilibrium occur is separated from the time of consumption and production (see Fisher 1976: 7). Economists who have wanted to construct determinate schemes have also found the notion of a stationary state particularly useful because it removes all the problems of indeterminateness associated with time. Marshall, who attaches importance to the 'period of production', refers to the notion as the 'famous fiction' (Marshall 1966: 304–6). Another assumption which negates being-in-time is a complete set of futures markets (see Arrow 1978). Edgeworth's (1881: 15–56) process of recontracting, Walras's 'fictive tickets' (a term coined by Leijonhufvud 1968) or '*bons*',[6] and even Pareto's indifference curves – because they prescribe the full extent of all 'preferences' and 'choices' – contribute to solving the problem of defining a complete world. Finally, the notion of perfect competition is purely and simply a device for pre-reconciling choices and for paving the way for the existence of equilibrium.

Perfect competition is a set of conditions that enables 'firms', independently, to adjust their output to demand, without having to know what other firms are doing. By stipulating conditions necessary to define a perfectly elastic demand curve for each firm, the notion of perfect competition gets around the paradox of how firms can take the market price as given while determining the price through their combined activities. It has nothing to say about competition – rivalry – among businesses. A theory of rivalry has to be based on interpretative understanding because rivalry is not some thing that exists in the world.

We will soon see that the theorists bent on reforming neoclassical theory have discovered that when these devices are replaced by 'more realistic assumptions' about human behaviour (that people will not wait until equilibrium is attained), and about how the institutions of the market economy work (there is no auctioneer), problems of decision-making in time as *durée* begin to be felt and uncertainty on the part of the agents enters the picture. The scheme no longer appears to be complete and the existence of equilibrium is in doubt. It is in this context that the hermeneutical considerations emerge and, moreover, existence can only be ensured in many cases by making strange assumptions about human conduct, no less 'unrealistic' than the devices described above.

THE HERMENEUTICAL TURN

Frank Hahn is not only in the top rank of GE theorists but also is sensitive to the criticisms of orthodoxy and, in responding to these, he has devoted considerable effort to illustrating what GE theory has achieved and to what it can still hope to achieve (see Hahn 1970, 1973a, 1973b, 1978, 1980, 1982). The hermeneutical nature of the problems with which he is grappling is most conspicuous in his work and, paradoxically, it emerges in the context of his defence of GE theory.

Expressing disquiet at the achievements of GE, Hahn (1980: 123) observes that GE continued down the road on which Adam Smith 'started us off', but he holds that the Arrow–Debreu version is 'near the end of that road'.[7]

> Now that we have got there we find it less enlightening than we had expected. The reason is partly ... that the road we pursued was excessively straight and narrow and made – we now feel – with too little allowance for the wild and varied terrain it had to traverse. We have certainly arrived at an orderly destination, but it looks increasingly likely that we cannot rest there.

The sentiments expressed in the quotation might be paraphrased as follows: 'Our conceptual framework was too narrow (or, perhaps, even wrong) and it prevented us from investigating the complex issues that we now deem to be important.' What is it that is required of an improved theory? Hahn's answer is that it should 'deal with a larger range of questions than it now does' (Hahn 1980: 130). When he identifies how the range should be extended, Hahn reveals that the problems of direct concern are not the traditional ones of existence and stability although, for the GE theorist, ultimately the problems must be placed within the context of existence or stability.

At issue are questions about how 'agents' matter, not only in terms of the typical GE concern with numbers – of, say, adding more markets and increasing the opportunities for exchange – but also in respect of how their conduct ('behaviour') should be understood in order better to model that behaviour. What is this conduct that now (in the context of the limitations of Arrow–Debreu GE) forces itself upon the theorist's attention? What does it mean to say that the individual learns? How does the theorist understand the notion of learning and how should this be represented? (Hahn 1973a: 18–21). Agents hold 'theories'; what causes them to change their theories? (ibid.: 25). Hahn's candid response to the latter question discloses his dilemma in the face of hermeneutical issues: 'not at all clear of what the precise formulation should be. . . . I content myself with the ill-specified hypothesis that an agent abandons his theory when it is sufficiently and systematically falsified.' The theorist's solution is to retreat to the safety of the assumption that agents are logical empiricists.

It is entirely plausible, especially if one brushes aside the formal language in which his arguments are couched, to suggest that Hahn is grappling with hermeneutical problems. His discussion, which involves the formation of expectations, motives, beliefs, and learning, certainly seems to imply that as the theorist gropes towards a better theory he has to take account of things that we understand – in the sense of *Verstehen* – in the conduct of others (Hahn 1980: 132–3). Even if this interpretation is too radical, his arguments certainly place him well outside the framework of the modernist paradigm. Agents may have to deal with things that they cannot observe (ibid.: 132). In entering into new areas, areas with which they should be concerned as theorists who wish to provide a more enlightening theory (Hahn says the old theory was 'unenlightening'), 'we certainly have no axiomatic foundations . . . and scarcely have we a psychologically plausible account' (ibid.: 132). These considerations justify the impression that neoclassical economics has moved beyond the realm of an epistemology and into that of a hermeneutical discipline in Rorty's sense. The type of explanation being sought is not that of rendering a phenomenon familiar by showing that it is one more instance of a covering law. Theorists concerned with these 'new' problems seek enlightenment, insight, or understanding, which comes not from testing hypotheses against actual events or from applying a particular predetermined framework, but from discourse.

In order to extend the usefulness of GE, Hahn (1978: 65) proposes to introduce 'conjectures' into an equilibrium scheme in which 'the auctioneer is replaced by the agents who change the prices at which they are willing to trade'. '[T]he designated equilibrium states depend on the conjectures with which we have endowed the agents – e.g. on their beliefs of the relation there might be between their ration and the announced price' (ibid.: 66). It appears to Hahn, and to us, that conjecture opens a Pandora's Box. Unless arbitrary constraints are placed on what a person can conjecture and how conjectures are 'formed', inventing a system for conjecturing – as has been done, say, with a distributed lag mechanism in attempts to model expectations – anything is possible. There is no necessary relationship between prices that are announced and the conjectures that people hold. Hahn's basic concern is the question of how to make conjectures 'less arbitrary', for only by doing so will it be possible once again to return to the comfort (for the GE theorist) of the complete world of the third-person perspective. Faced with the discomfort of having to deal with questions of how individuals may interpret and conjecture, the answer is to fashion the notion of conjecture to fit the language of an equilibrium scheme. Conjectures come to be conceived as mathematical variables; things with values that are determined by some mechanism.

To the extent that it raises issues of a hermeneutical nature, Hahn's contribution is not unique and his arguments are echoed in the writings of other neoclassicists. The examples selected to illustrate this have been chosen not only because they exemplify the same type of thinking, but also because the authors are neoclassicists of high standing.

As a further example of a neoclassical writer confronting hermeneutical issues, Fisher (1976; 1979)[8] is sensible to the fact that the old rules do not apply in the sphere of the issues he is contemplating. The enigma that Fisher encounters is that of dealing with 'consciousness of disequilibrium'. To his credit, he does not simply resort to ready-made equilibrium models and thereby immediately discard the problem that has surfaced. Instead he points to limitations of these models and the fact that they do not permit certain matters to be raised, such as a 'consciousness of disequilibrium' (Fisher 1976: 22–3).

> Could we do this adequately [step outside the model and allow consciousness of disequilibrium], it would be a great advance. However, we have no adequate theory of disequilibrium behaviour and all these [neoclassical GE] models impose equilibrium-derived behaviour on a disequilibrium process. This is obviously unsatisfactory wherever it appears.

Fisher's notion of 'disequilibrium consciousness' refers to a situation where individuals do not know what is going to happen and have to conjecture. The problem with a theory that permits people to think about what might happen and to act, or not to act, accordingly is that, just as Hahn finds when he introduces conjectures, the scheme loses completeness and the notion of equilibrium may simply vanish. Thus Fisher notes that stability literature requires the 'present action postulate', the purpose of which is to ensure completeness because any excess demands – which is what 'drives' prices – must be expressed as actual demands and cannot be reserved for the future as potential demands, otherwise 'the system will bog down' (Fisher 1979: 6). In the absence of futures markets, which are included to ensure that the scheme of things is complete, 'the fact that I expect to require toothpaste ten years hence is made to propel me into the spot market for toothpaste even if I am having some liquidity problems'. In an equilibrium scheme, agents cannot have the latitude to do as they choose! Their behaviour has to be governed by very clear-cut, but – from the point of view of human conduct – arbitrary rules. Fisher's toothpaste example is particularly interesting for another reason. It illustrates how the third-person perspective grips the imagination of the equilibrium theorist. In spite of the conceptual problems associated with 'disequilibrium consciousness', there is no difficulty in imagining that the individual has a complete dated set of preferences for toothpaste.[9]

As a final example of a neoclassical theorist confronting hermeneutical issues, Arrow's (1974) presidential address to the American Economic Association is an interesting case for two reasons. One can see that he has on his mind the same sorts of problems that concern both Hahn and Fisher. At the same time his approach to the problem of uncertainty is a marvellous insight into the language of equilibrium theory and how it influences and distorts the way in which we think about things. In this regard it even surpasses the toothpaste example. Arrow holds that 'the uncertainties about economics are rooted in our need for a better understanding of the economics of uncertainty; our lack of economic knowledge is, in good part, our difficulty in modelling the ignorance of the economic agent.' (Arrow 1974: 1). This is a formalistic way of referring to what Shackle (see 1983) terms 'unknowledge'; the fact that much of what we do necessarily involves conjecture. Arrow is concerned with the individual who confronts a world with a less than complete set of futures markets, who 'cannot know the future' and 'faces a world of uncertainty' (Arrow 1974: 6).

Both in this article and a subsequent one (Arrow 1978), the essence of the issues can be discerned, and even though Arrow speaks about 'our intuitive understanding, our *Verstehen* ... of the market as an institution' (Arrow 1974: 4) he fails to apply the same notion to the interpretation of human conduct. By doing so, he would have provided a quite legitimate means of investigating what uncertainty means for the individual. 'If expectations are ... important, the mode of their formation becomes critical' (Arrow 1978: 158). The issues are not, as Arrow somewhat grudgingly concedes, the traditional problems of equilibrium theory. In his words, this is not the world of the 'pure neoclassical model' (ibid.: 7) but one where buyers and sellers are not 'willing to make commitments which completely define their future actions' (ibid.: 8). In terms of the need for a determinate theory to be complete, the lack of such commitments is a fatal flaw for equilibrium theory.

How does Arrow propose to deal with uncertainty? When he speaks of 'modelling ignorance' (1974), he does not proceed to explain what people do when they are uncertain, when they do not know. His starting point is the third-person notion that agents could, in principle, know everything. Knowledge is a thing that the agent has, which corresponds to what the world out there is like. Ignorance means that this knowledge is incomplete. Some part of the agent's measurable, quantifiable stock of knowledge is missing and does not mirror, fully, the world out there. Since equilibrium is dependent upon being able to treat the scheme of things as complete, if individuals do not have complete knowledge (if they are 'ignorant'), then quite logically, in order to make the scheme complete, the theorist must include in his formulation what people do *not* know. In this context 'complete knowledge', a defining characteristic of the third-person perspective, means being able to specify or to define (as knowledge) the knowledge that people do not have. The world consists of the 'knowledge' plus the 'ignorance' of each agent. Ignorance is the difference between the world in its entirety and what each individual agent 'knows' of the world out there.

All the examples referred to illustrate the consequences of attempting to deal with uncertainty within the epistemology of an equilibrium scheme. The resulting notion of uncertainty or ignorance is nonsensical. The much more reasonable attitude of O'Driscoll and Rizzo (1985: 3–4) to the issue of ignorance is directly relevant to this position and should be contrasted with it.

> Ignorance is not something that, at least at some level, can be avoided or overcome. It is not a state of imperfect knowledge that some process asymptotically eliminates. As long as we remain in a world of real time, unexpected change is inevitable and ignorance is ineradicable. . . . Ignorance should not be transformed into a variant of knowledge.

AN ASSESSMENT OF THE HERMENEUTICAL TURN

The 'internal' criticisms by would-be reformers of neoclassical theory that I have cited recognise the failure of neoclassical theory to deal with phenomena or issues that are relevant in explaining people's behaviour. The theorists are exploring traditional concerns of the existence and stability of equilibria by using a 'more realistic theory' of behaviour. Their suggestions are supposed to extend or 'broaden' the scope of the existing theory as they eliminate some of its weaknesses. What happens if the notion of the auctioneer is abandoned and sellers fix prices while buyers search for the optimal price? Will the system converge to a competitive equilibrium (see Fisher 1976: 23–5)? Will the equilibrium still be stable if agents may choose whether or not to exercise their demands in the future?

At first blush the answers appear to turn on how to dispense with staple elements of GE in the form of devices like auctioneers, recontracting, or futures markets. But discussion of these devices, and the problem of removing them, is quickly seen to be a veneer which masks the issues identified here. Once the surface layer is peeled away, the problems are those of how to deal with uncertainty, with time as *durée* (as the context of decision-making) rather than time as extension, with expectations, and with learning. In the literature, the problems are identified as price adjustment problems or as problems of local or global stability. They are actually about what individuals know and how they know, as seen from the perspective of the theorist who has to model the behaviour of those individuals. How should the theorist 'see' the world out there? What aspects of individual behaviour should be included in an equilibrium theory which conveys, more satisfactorily than hitherto, what goes on in an economy?

Reformists have begun to explore questions that lie beyond their customary purview and issues that, from a positivist-empiricist point of view, belong to metaphysics rather than to science. So the question of whether the modernist paradigm is appropriate to their interests is hardly at issue any longer. These problems all reflect the theorist's uncertainty about how to proceed in the face of the 'inadequate state of our present knowledge'. Such problems can properly be called hermeneutical ones, concerned with interpreting individual behaviour and finding out how to represent that behaviour. The reformists stumbled upon these issues unwittingly in the process of trying to escape from the 'straight and narrow road' which, as Hahn says, led to such disappointing results. Yet, realising that detours are fraught with potential dangers, they are ill at ease in the company of such issues. They are prone to point out that the implications of pursuing a particular idea are too complex, or that the present state of knowledge is too unsatisfactory, to move out of a well-circumscribed area. So when new ideas are mooted (e.g. Hahn 1978; Fisher 1979) the issues are cast in such a way as to force them back into the GE mould, presenting the problems from a third-person perspective. Fisher's reflections (1979: 3) serve to illustrate this point.

> Even allowing agents to alter their expectations in sensible ways does not permit them to take into account the fact that their expectations may be wrong. Simply put, agents in the present model always behave as if they lived in a world of certainty. . . .
>
> I do not see the way towards a satisfactory solution here. Microeconomic theory is primarily an equilibrium subject. We know very little about the individual behaviour in disequilibrium. Further, a full-dress treatment of behaviour under uncertainty in a disequilibrium situation strikes me as too complex for incorporation into this sort of model at least in the present state of our knowledge.

Compare this with Hahn's view of a few years earlier (Hahn 1973a: 20–1). Defining the equilibrium action of an agent as the action which 'an outside observer, say the econometrician, could describe . . . by structurally stable equations', Hahn adds that

> [w]hen the agent is learning however, then there is a change in regime so that one would require a 'higher level' theory of the learning process. Such a theory is not available at present. . . . In our present state of knowledge . . . it is . . . not behaviour which we can hope to describe.

Having identified an area where the orthodox theory is less than satis-factory, the reformists quickly recognise that any thorough-going attempt to deal with the problem means leaving the safe-haven of determinism. The desire to understand human conduct is then sacrificed in the name of 'scientific rigour'. But pursuing this path is not a solution. All it does is to produce a more complex, but not necessarily a more satisfactory, theory. The theory is still 'stuck' in the epistemology of the third-person perspective which is the reason why neoclassical economics is 'unenlightening', and the economist has little option but to abandon this. One may interpret the reformists' concerns as a tacit admission that there is no single conceptual framework and methodology that can be applied to all the questions that the theorist may pose and which 'in our present state of knowledge' is entirely independent of the researcher's social and cultural milieu. This is a conception of science as a hermeneutical endeavour (see Warnke 1987: ch. 5).

Although hermeneutics is beginning to get a hearing amongst economists (see Lavoie 1991a) in general, as these examples show, they are reluctant to seek solutions beyond their customary habitat. Yet if the issues raised here are indicative of the limitations of Arrow–Debreu GE theory, they reveal that neoclassicists are flirting with hermeneutical problems – the individual's consciousness of his world, how he learns about the world, what learning and uncertainty mean for his (equilibrium) behaviour, and how expectations affect his equilibrium behaviour – because for people concerned about human conduct (who are even temporarily unencumbered by a modernist frame-work) they are logical questions to ask. The distinction between first-person and third-person perspective helps to reveal why the reformists' problems cannot be dealt with in an equilibrium framework, for they are associated with a different way of looking at the world. The reformers are in a bind. To get out of it, it is necessary to go the whole hermeneutical way, taking cognisance of the *durée* and the subjectivism of understanding. My object over the next few chapters is to explore the nature and implications of a subjectivist scheme based on interpretative understanding. One consequence of adopting subjectivism is clear: we turn our back on equilibrium by sacrificing completeness and abandoning determinism.

4

ON SUBJECTIVISM

The primary goal of the social sciences is to obtain organised knowledge of social reality. By the term 'social reality' I wish to be understood the sum total of objects and occurrences within the social cultural world as experienced by the common-sense thinking of men living their daily lives among their fellow men, connected with them in manifold relations of interaction. It is the world of cultural objects and social institutions into which we are all born ... and with which we have to come to terms.

(Schütz 1977: 228–9)

THE TERM 'SUBJECTIVISM'

Taken at face value, Schütz's statement in the epigraph to this chapter, that the purpose of the social sciences is to obtain 'organised knowledge of social reality', is likely to find acceptance with social scientists. The disagreements among them concern the rest of this passage and revolve around the key questions of what 'social reality' is, what is meant by 'organised knowledge', and how this knowledge is acquired. Adopting a theme of post-Wittgensteinian analytical philosophy, echoed in the views of Coddington about the language of theory as examined in Chapter 1, I have argued that the social reality which a theory can explain depends on the methodology it employs. The methodology, and its associated epistemology and ontology, is influenced by our conception of 'organised knowledge' which, in turn, influences what we can do with our theories.

Like Schütz, who speaks of the individual's 'experience', I have argued that there is a need to include the individual's understanding of her social world in the 'organised knowledge' that economists seek, for without this, we as theorists do not have a basis for explaining what people do, or why and how they do it. Because he is as much an understander as his subjects, the social scientist engages a double hermeneutic. I have also inferred from the contributions of particular neoclassical writers, who refer to 'conjecture' and 'disequilibrium consciousness', that they too recognise the need to describe how the individual understands; only the methodology of neoclassical theory thwarts this essentially hermeneutical task. It is the scholars committed to the methodological tradition of *Verstehen* – i.e. subjective, or interpretative, understanding – who have sought to provide a language to clarify how individuals experience the 'social world' and, in the belief that this tradition provides an appropriate foundation for social theory, I want to examine the foundations of a subjectivist methodology.

Although I regard the term 'subjectivist' as suitably descriptive of the methodology of social science associated with the tradition of *Verstehen*, there are different approaches to interpretative understanding and different conceptions of subjectivism. My main interest is in the subjectivism of modern hermeneutics, which leads to the idea of a double hermeneutic associated with social problems and which describes the epistemology and ontology of the 'first-person perspective'. In endorsing the first-person perspective as the basis of social theory, I must discuss the nature and implications of a theory incorporating a first-person perspective. In order to do so, however, it is necessary to proceed in stages. The first stage involves examining the use of the term subjectivism and explaining its suitability when applied to a theory of interpretative understanding. This, and the clarification of various implications of subjectivism, forms the substance of the chapter. In Chapter 5 I deal with the evolution of the tradition of *Verstehen*, showing how modern hermeneutics has evolved out of earlier forms of subjectivism, in order to describe the first-person perspective. Chapters 6 and 7 survey Austrian economics with the object of comparing Austrian subjectivism – the best-known subjectivist theory in economics – with the subjectivism of a first-person perspective.

Subjectivism, associated with the clarification of understanding, has its origins in textual interpretation and, more recently, in the methodological problems associated with social science. As I use the term, the philosophical movement representing subjectivism includes the considerable contribution of Max Weber on *Verstehen* and the phenomenological writings of Edmund Husserl and Alfred Schütz, as well as modern hermeneutics associated with Hans-Georg Gadamer and others. No doubt some readers will oppose my use of the term 'subjectivist' when it is applied to some of these philosophical movements. Others may simply find the term unacceptable in any context, arguing that there is no conventional 'subjectivist tradition'. It is appropriate for me, then, to examine and to defend the use of the term.

In the first place the term subjectivism is used in contrast to objectivism, a philosophical tradition of which there is a conventional definition. The epistemology and ontology of the third-person perspective, associated with positive science, characterises an objectivist position. Objectivism treats all reality as external to the mind and knowledge as based on the observation of objects and events. According to Bernstein (1983: 9), in its conventional or 'dominant' form, objectivism is

> the claim that there is a world of objective reality that exists independently of us and that has a determinate nature or essence that we can know. In modern times objectivism has been closely linked with an acceptance of a basic metaphysical or epistemological distinction between the subject and the object. What is 'out there' (objective) is presumed to be independent of us (subjects), and knowledge is achieved when a subject correctly mirrors or represents objective reality.

The ontology of objectivism specifies a world that exists, self-contained, out there at a distance from the observer. Its existence is separate from the observer and the world is known only by observation. To the objectivist, the theorist's role is to observe and to 'describe' the world as it really exists.

There is, however, much less agreement over what subjectivism means (see Gewirth 1954 on different ways in which the term 'subjectivism' can be used), and there is no generally recognised subjectivist philosophy. The term is not widely used by philosophers or others which explains why, when it is used in economics, it tends to be used very loosely,[1] and is consequently subject to misinterpretation. In short, considerable confusion surrounds its use. In economics, subjectivism is generally, though not exclusively, associated with Austrian economics and that, too, is confusing.[2]

Natanson (1962: 157) warns against applying the term 'subjective' to the sort of methodological approach that I advocate. His objection is that the term is often misunderstood and 'is equated . . . with personal or private or merely introspective, intuitive attitudes'. The problems in using the term are twofold. Most alternatives are not sufficiently general to embrace a tradition and are already associated with a particular type of subjectivism or with a phase in the development of a subjectivist paradigm. Natanson prefers 'phenomenological' to subjectivist, but admits to the possible confusion that its use may engender. 'Hermeneutic' might serve as an alternative, but in exploring the implications of the double hermeneutic, or a first-person perspective, my approach owes much to the phenomenological ideas of Alfred Schütz, which are not normally associated with hermeneutics. Also, the connotations that are often applied to subjectivism are neither necessarily applicable (e.g. equating subjectivism and solipsism) nor ones that I would want to see applied.

The reason for using the term is not only that it is difficult to find a readily acceptable substitute but also because, properly understood, it is an appropriate label for an approach which, in Natanson's words, describes '[methodological] positions that stress the primacy of consciousness and subjective meaning in the interpretation of social action' (ibid.: 157). Modern hermeneutics emphasises that the individual's understanding is relative, in the sense of being bound up with her social and temporal existence, so there is no need to reject the term in order to avoid the connotation of relativism. But because there is still room for confusion as a result of preconceptions that readers might have about the term, it is important to explain further the meaning of subjectivism.[3]

THE MEANING OF SUBJECTIVISM

Subjectivism in social science is traditionally identified with questions about how people 'observe' the conduct of other people and how an observer's knowledge of others should be conceptualised. The position that I adopt and associate with modern hermeneutics, is that subjectivism is more fundamental than this and addresses all understanding or knowledge in asking how people know.

Subjectivism was initially concerned with what could be termed a 'single hermeneutic': the problem of interpretation occasioned by the 'observation' of human activities, or the results of such activities, where, it was argued, the purpose or intention 'behind' the activities could be understood by the scientist who was a neutral observer. The earlier advocates of *Verstehen* held that the observer distinguishes between the observation of things and the observation of people and their activities and, when dealing with the latter, purposes have to be recognised and considered in explanations of conduct. Purposes, though not directly observable, are automatically recognised 'in' phenomena such as houses, the business of financial institutions, works of art, money, literature, the country's constitution, shopping in the super-market, and scientific research.

In studying people's activities, the observer recognises that, to them, a house is not just an object made of various construction materials, but something which serves a purpose. The term 'house' in the phrase, 'I prefer my house to the new one down the road', has a meaning to the individual concerned, and recognition of that meaning is interpretative understanding (*Verstehen*). A house is a 'home' with connotations of belonging to a family and relationships among family members, it confers status on the owner, and provides the family with a sense of security. The meaning that a house has to people cannot be observed. When explaining conduct, for example why a person has sold her house and bought another one of the same size, the observer is able to ascribe meaning to things because he too is an individual with purposes and plans who is able to understand (*Verstehen*) the meaning that things have for others. Meaning is 'subjective' both because the con-notations are intuitive rather than observed, and also because things have a different meaning to different people.

The rationale for calling this 'subjectivism' is explained by Weber (1964). Setting out his framework for sociological analysis, he states (ibid.: 88) that action includes 'all human behaviour when and in so far as the acting individual attaches a subjective meaning to it'. In defining 'meaning', Weber (1964: 89) argues that

> [i]n no case does it refer to an objectively 'correct' meaning or one which is true in some metaphysical sense. It is this which distinguishes the empirical sciences of action, such as sociology and history, from the dogmatic disciplines in that area, such as jurisprudence ... and aesthetics, which seek to ascertain the 'true' and 'valid' meanings associated with the objects of their investigation.

More modern interpretations of understanding, adopting Edmund Husserl's ideas, recognise that meaning is not just something that the individual attaches to things out there; the individual is actively involved in the construal of meaning, not as observer or as eyewitness to what is happening over there, and not as a passive recipient of information, but as creator of meaning. Interpretation and the constitution of phenomena are one and the same. Individuals do not interpret what exists out there. What exists is how they understand or 'see' events. In Bernstein's words (1983: 126), 'meaning is not self-contained – simply "there" to be discovered; meaning comes to realisation only in and through the "happening" of understanding'. In the modern hermeneutical form of subjectivism, attributed to Hans-Georg Gadamer, meaning is the result of a coming together, like a 'fusion' of the text and of the reader's ideas about it (see Warnke 1987: 81–2, 107–8). Meaning is also not fixed but emerges and changes with the understander's experience, as if through a 'conversation'.

Knowledge or understanding is intersubjective, and meaning is always constituted intersubjectively. The individual lives and works among and with other people. Even in solitary confinement (his predicament being a consequence of the activities of particular people) or on a desert island (where he is conscious of the absence of 'civilisation' or of company), his interests – whether brooding or working – involve his relationships with, and understanding of, other people and of social institutions. Understanding is also 'prejudiced', shaped by one's social history. One's upbringing, education, and so on, are social processes. It is almost impossible to conceive of an individual who does not 'share' her understanding with other people, unless she has never lived in the company of others.[4]

The idea of a double hermeneutic of social science rests upon just this conception of understanding as constitutive – that understanding is interpretation and interpretation is a process of creating meaning. Accepting a double hermeneutic in the 'observation' of human conduct means acknowledging that all knowledge, not just the understanding of other people, is *Verstehen*. To the social scientist who is interested in explaining my conduct, the meaning of the phrase, 'I prefer my house to the new one down the road' depends as much on his interpretation or understanding of things – why the phrase is significant, what it means to him, whether he has reason to pay attention to my utterances – as it does on his understanding of me and why I made such a remark. The double hermeneutic defines an epistemological and ontological 'relationship' between the theorist and his subject matter which sets apart the social and natural scientist. Both are engaged in *Verstehen* but, since the former interprets the activities of other people, the answers to his questions – what are they doing, why are they doing it – depend on his understanding of their understanding of 'social reality', of the meaning they ascribe to their activities. A first-person perspective recognises the interpretative interrelationships associated with the double hermeneutic and the term 'subjectivism' is particularly apposite when applied to the first-person perspective.

The issue of the relativism of subjectivism also needs to be clarified. The term 'relativism' denotes an epistemology that asserts that knowledge is relative, based on the individual's culture, experience, or other circumstances, and the term is often used in a pejorative sense. A conventional view is that at the farthest extreme of relativism lies solipsism, where the individual's world is essentially private (see O'Sullivan 1987: 23–35, on different models of relativism and a critique of epistemological relativism). The subjectivism of modern hermeneutics in particular is criticised as relativist, and the implication is that the subjectivist is bound to end up having to defend a solipsist position.

It is not difficult to appreciate the nature of this type of criticism against subjectivism but it is based on a twofold misconception. The first is the idea that there is a dichotomy between objectivism on the one hand – held to be the true epistemological basis of science – and subjectivism on the other. Because objectivism is right and natural, subjectivism is wrong and unnatural. Second, the espousal of subjectivism puts one on to the continuum of 'degrees of relativism' which ends with solipsism, whereas objectivism means absolute objectivity and precludes solipsism. A subjectivist can never claim objectivity and any subjectivist position is necessarily not far from solipsism. It is this sort of view which regards subjectivism as nihilistic.

First let us consider the matter of a dichotomy between subjectivism and objectivism. The caricature of the individual who is unable – because his experience is private or subjective – to communicate with others, is common to critiques of subjectivism. From an objectivist standpoint, each individual is a solitary observer of the world out there. Knowledge is acquired by observation. Each observes what is happening out there independently of others, and then communicates what he knows. To do so, he needs to 'translate' the observations into a language that means the same to everyone. Without a purely referential neutral language with which to describe the sense-data to one another, it follows that individuals have no means of ensuring that others really understand what the world and their experiences of it are like.

In fact, this reasoning is a product of the Cartesian ideal and of the belief that there could be a neutral and objective language with which to describe the world as-it-really-exists, out there. Individuals' subjective experience and understanding condemns them to solipsistic isolation only because the epistemology of objectivism fails to account for the intersubjective nature of all understanding and the fact that people 'share' their social world. Following Bernstein (1983) and others, my position is that the concern to provide an objective scheme is a misplaced one. Descombes (1985: 55) suggests that 'one cannot abolish the category of fact without abolishing also the category of interpretation; the words "fact" and "interpretation" get their meaning from the contrast between a fact and an interpretation of this fact'.

The dichotomy between subjectivism and objectivism is a false one. The contributions of hermeneuticists such as Habermas and Gadamer, in the course of the past thirty years, offer a possible resolution of what appears to be an essential tension between objectivism and subjectivism. The dichotomy is a consequence of the legacy of Cartesian science which claims that scientific knowledge is, or should be, universally valid, and is inherent in Rorty's (1980) conception of an 'epistemologically-centred philosophy' which has characterised virtually all philosophical thinking. The subjectivism–objectivism divide is a consequence of efforts to 'ground' our beliefs by demonstrating that they correspond with what things are really like. The promise of science, in the Cartesian mould, is to provide that grounding, but once it is recognised that science, as a human activity, is interpretative, and that it cannot sustain the claim to provide objective knowledge, the tension between subjectivism and objectivism is not so much resolved as disappears.

The problem that the advocacy of interpretative understanding means a lack of objectivity, has plagued subjectivists themselves. Scholars who held that *Verstehen* is a necessary basis of theories of social science bore the responsibility of assuring a sceptical and sometimes hostile scientific community that the theories yielded objective knowledge (see the discussion of Husserl's position in the next chapter). One can see from the considerable effort that they devoted to this task, which is also evident in the writings of Austrian economists, that the responsibility was an onerous one. Their efforts to 'prove' the objectivity of subjectivism had a constraining effect on the construction of a subjectivist scheme, necessitated by circumscribing the scope of interpretative understanding. The issue of subjectivism and relativism is important in clarifying the epistemological and ontological relationship between the theorist and his subject matter associated with the first-person perspective, and is a thread running through the analysis of the evolution of interpretative understanding in the next chapter.

Also relevant to clarifying the implications of a subjectivist theory is the role of the mind in explanations of people's conduct. Subjectivism is sometimes viewed, misleadingly, as taking account of the minds that 'lie behind' individuals' activities. Attributing to *Verstehen* the connotation of 'exploring the structure of the human mind', which is a position adopted by some Austrian

74

economists,[5] is as unjustified as arguing that *Verstehen* is rooted in psycho-analysis. A subjectivist methodology does not require, nor does it involve, any attempt by the theorist to put himself 'inside a person's head', or to specify the 'contents of her mind', in order to understand that thoughts, ideas, and experiences underlie her activities and to explain how they do so.

Subjectivism applies empathetic understanding to provide insight into human activities. The theorist is interested in how a 'typical' individual under 'typical' circumstances – for example a manager who is involved in under-taking an investment – understands, or constitutes, the problem of 'under-taking an investment'.[6] What is the 'world' of the investment decision-maker like? In what issues is she interested? What are her relationships with other people and how do these relationships have a bearing on what she does? Answers to questions such as these require a framework of categories and concepts, some of which are a result of reflecting on and attempting to understand empathetically the way in which others would constitute their circumstances. The ability to do so is the fact that empathetic understanding is part and parcel of cognition. It is not necessary to have been an industrialist and to have made investment decisions in order to understand the predica-ment of someone who is one and who makes these types of decisions – to understand, for example, what sorts of factors the industrialist is likely to consider. With reference specifically to Weber's work, Freund (1972: 98) states that 'interpretative sociology is not in the least concerned with enumerating the psychic and physical manifestations and elements which accompany, or even result in, meaningful goal-oriented behaviour'. There is certainly no presumption that a subjectivist approach to analysing investment decisions requires a knowledge of psychology or an ability to specify the 'contents' of a decision-maker's mind.

I now want to examine more closely the nature of a subjectivist approach to social theory, and the implications of a methodology based on a first-person perspective, by considering the evolution of interpretative subjectiv-ism associated with modern hermeneutics. This takes us into a realm of theory that the economics profession still regards as highly unorthodox; some economists find it distasteful even to consider such issues. It is appropriate at this point to comment on the attitudes of scholars towards, and their increasing acceptance of, a subjectivist position.

Initially, support for subjectivism was found only amongst a few social scientists, and subjectivism was narrowly regarded even by its protagonists as pertaining solely to the methodology of the social sciences.[7] They contrasted the subjective element in these sciences, associated with purposeful action, with the objectivism of natural science. Later, in the middle decades of this century, when positivism was at its height, subjectivism was almost entirely repudiated even by social scientists. According to Bernstein (1983: 27):

The prevailing attitude at the time among professional social scientists was that their discipline was now on the secure path of becoming a genuine natural science of individuals in society, a natural science that differed in degree and not in kind from the rest of the natural sciences. Progress in the social sciences . . . required adopting and following those methods, procedures, and criteria . . . that had proven so successful in the natural sciences. They therefore scorned 'interpretive sociology', with its appeal to 'subjective meaning', *Verstehen* . . . and such concepts as empathy and interpretation.

Social scientists who remain wedded to a positivist-empiricist conception of 'doing science' still treat subjectivism with scepticism and sometimes scorn, and regard subjectivists as misguided (see the arguments of Abel 1977). As Dallmayr and McCarthy (1977: 78–9) put it,

> those defending the methodological unity of the sciences typically proffer a rather low estimate of the importance of *Verstehen* for the logic of the social sciences. It is either rejected as un- or pre-scientific, or analysed as a 'heuristic device' that, while useful, belongs in the anteroom of science proper.

Such views, however, may be on the way out. Today, the hermeneutical tradition, derived from Max Weber and his predecessors, forms an important ingredient of a much more broadly based discourse on existentialism. According to Dallmayr and McCarthy (1977: 9), the shift from treating understanding as a method of social enquiry – the 'prerogative of individual cognition or consciousness' – to 'a basic attribute of man's existential condition or *Dasein*', is largely attributable to Heidegger. Paradoxically perhaps, Popper's *Logic of Scientific Discovery* – a robustly empiricist work – led the way in fostering the idea that scientific practice involves conjecture and that the scientist constitutes the problems that interest him (see Orkin 1979). In so doing, it subverted the positivist ontology of problems and relationships that exist in the world out there. An upshot of post-modernist philosophical debate is that it is now respectable to treat science as subjective, not objective; as ideas that are created, communicated, and interpreted within a community of people. The reformation of science as epistemology to science as hermeneutics is by no means complete and, perhaps, never will be widespread. Its significance from the point of view of this book, however, is enormous. Subjectivism is out of the closet. It is now a serious subject, worthy of the attention of philosophers of the top rank.

There has thus been a major shift. Initially regarded with disdain by the majority of philosophers and scientists, subjectivism was seen as the domain of certain social scientists who believed that their subject matter either could not, or should not, be studied by the methods employed by their natural-scientific counterparts. Today it is acceptable to return to the tradition which began as the attempt to justify a separate method for the *Geisteswissenschaften*, in order to answer questions about the ontology and epistemology of science *per se*.

APPENDIX TO CHAPTER 4

In view of the fact that each involves a defence of subjectivism from a different methodological position and that this leads to considerable confusion, it is appropriate to comment on O'Sullivan's (1987) view of subjectivism and to compare his methodology with my own. While our interests overlap, on matters of methodology there are fundamental epistemological and onto-logical differences between us.

O'Sullivan supports a 'subjectivist-interpretive' approach against the 'objectivist-behaviourist' one that he identifies as the purported foundation of mainstream economic theory. Like me, he regards it as inappropriate to attempt to build mainstream economics on objectivist foundations because its subject matter is human conduct. He identifies the subjectivist-interpretative approach as 'the only philosophically defensible approach to the human sciences' (O'Sullivan 1987: 161). So far we seem to be *ad idem*. 'Subjectivist-interpretative' to O'Sullivan, however, means a methodology based on Husserlian phenomenology, with the claim to objectivity which Husserl demanded, and believed was achieved through the process of phenomeno-logical reduction (see O'Sullivan 1987: 13–14; 175–85). Thus, in Rorty's terminology, O'Sullivan propounds a view of (social) science as epistemology, rather than as hermeneutic, but calls his methodology subjectivist.

O'Sullivan disapproves strongly of the sort of relativist position associated with modern hermeneutics (O'Sullivan 1987: 26–30), whereas in my view – adopting arguments associated with Gadamer – recognising the relativism of all understanding and knowledge is a major consideration in understanding how individuals understand and is central to subjectivism. A further point of divergence between our methodological positions is that O'Sullivan appar-ently also advocates a methodological dualism in respect of the natural and social sciences, whereas my position is that all science is understanding and is interpretative, although social science involves a double hermeneutic. What is problematic, in separating my approach from O'Sullivan's, is that we both treat subjectivism as originating from the Weber–Schütz tradition but I call mine subjectivist and hermeneutical and – in opposition to Husserl – I reject the idea of grounded knowledge, or that subjectivism is capable of yielding objective knowledge (see Chapter 5).

This indicates how much confusion and uncertainty surrounds the meaning of subjectivism. Clearly my reading of Weber's contribution, as set out in the next chapter, is at odds with that of O'Sullivan. I emphasise the hermeneutical and 'relativist' leanings of Weber, and believe that Schütz's work, much more than that of Husserl, belongs in a similar category. Schütz (1977) does not stress the ability of transcendental phenomenology to yield knowledge which is apodeictically certain, nor is such certainty essential to Schütz's object which is to apply a phenomenological philosophy in order to explicate the individual's life-world. Schütz is 'saved' from a relativist position (especially a solipsist one) by his emphasising that the individual constitutes her life-world intersubjectively; i.e. it is a world that 'exists' intersubjectively.

In the light of the difficulties in separating our approaches based simply on a superficial description of their methodologies and antecedents, it seems to me that the distinction between a first-person and third-person perspective is valuable in resolving different methodological positions. Like neoclassical and Austrian methodologies (both of which O'Sullivan classifies as subjectivist-interpretive as against the advocacy by neoclassical theorists of an objectivist methodology), O'Sullivan's methodological position is consistent with the epistemology of a third-person perspective. Understanding is grounded in a given reality out there. The epistemology, and associated ontology, stands in stark contrast to the continual unfolding – the knowing differently, rather than knowing more about the world out there – that is associated with experience in the hermeneutic circle and is at the root of the first-person perspective.

What I find particularly perplexing is O'Sullivan's characterisation of neoclassical economics as 'subjectivist-interpretive' with a 'teleological mode of explanation'. He says that the 'unmistakably interpretive character of economic theory ... arises from the pervasiveness and centrality of the "optimization" or "maximization" principle to all economic explanations' (O'Sullivan 1987: 74). The puzzling part is that in neoclassical theory no one does any interpreting. Both theorist and agents confront a given world consisting of a complete set of things that exists out there. O'Driscoll and Rizzo's (1985, see ch. 2) suggestion that neoclassical theory constitutes a 'static' form of subjectivism appears to be based upon a similar, faulty premise. In their view it recognises 'tastes' or 'preferences', which are subjective notions, as the basis of individual choice, but individuals are assumed to have given tastes so the subjectivism is static. The ontology of the third-person perspective, however, pronounces all elements in the scheme, whether tastes, prices, or commodities, to be objects or things in the world, that really exist independently of what people think, believe, or do.

Noting that O'Sullivan, as well as O'Driscoll and Rizzo, classify Austrian economics along with neoclassical theory as subjectivist (though the latter regard Austrian subjectivism as 'dynamic'), Mäki's (1990: 294) ideas about the nature of Austrian economics may help to resolve the paradox associated with both of their interpretations of neoclassical theory; namely that an objectivist epistemology contains subjectivist notions. Mäki characterises Austrian economics as 'ontic subjectivism' combined with 'ontological objectivism' (see also Chapter 6 below).

5

INTERPRETATIVE
UNDERSTANDING

Hermeneutics is no longer conceived as a subdiscipline of humanistic studies or even as the characteristic Method of the *Geisteswissenschaften*, but rather as pertaining to questions concerning what human beings are. We are 'thrown' into the world as beings who understand and interpret – so if we are to understand what it is to be human beings, we must seek to understand understanding itself, in its rich, full, and complex dimensions. Furthermore, understanding is not one type of activity to be contrasted with other human activities. . . . Understanding is universal and may properly be said to underlie and pervade all activities.

(Bernstein 1973: 113–14)

THE EVOLUTION OF *VERSTEHEN*

The crux of this chapter is the relationship between the theorist and his subject matter. The object is to clarify the first-person perspective of subjectivism, as contrasted with the third-person perspective of positivistically inspired equilibrium theories, by examining how the conception of interpretative understanding (*Verstehen*) has altered within the subjectivist tradition. The changes are associated with different views about the nature and task of social science and, in particular, about the objectivity of social science. They also signify different views of the relationship between the theorist and his subject matter, and the analysis will help to identify the different views, and to contrast the relationship inherent in earlier forms of subjectivism with that of modern hermeneutics.

My interest is solely in 'mainstream subjectivism', the tradition of *Verstehen* that includes phenomenology, and in the work of contemporary hermeneutical writers that leads to the radical rejection of the epistemological basis of positivist science. The analysis specifically ignores contributions, such as that of Talcott Parsons, which make an effort to assimilate *Verstehen* into a positivistically inspired methodology. Because my standpoint is that subjectivism offers a serviceable, advantageous, and constructive foundation for social theories, there is no further reference to

79

the methodological arguments for rejecting subjectivism. I will, however, consider the criticisms of subjectivism levelled by subjectivists themselves at their predecessors or contemporaries, whom they believed had somehow gone astray or who had failed to see the implications of their arguments.

The subjectivist tradition of interpretative understanding has its origins in the early nineteenth century, in the writings of Friedrich Schleiermacher (1768–1834) and later Wilhelm Dilthey (1833–1911), though Freund (1968: 93) attributes the invention of the 'method' of interpretative understanding to the historian Droysen, 'round about 1850'.[1] Dilthey was the first philosopher to argue for a separate method of the social sciences, employing hermeneutics, based on the role which interpretive understanding plays in these sciences. These early precursors of modern hermeneutics advocated a notion of *Verstehen* as 'neutral understanding'. They regarded *Verstehen* as a distinctive characteristic of the social sciences and as the essential determinant of a separate methodology of the social sciences, but as a notion which nevertheless would contribute to an objective explanation of the phenomena under consideration. In the following quotation, concerning the nature of Dilthey's contribution, Warnke (1987: 2, emphasis added) points to a similarity of outlook between positivists and the initial efforts to develop a theory of *Verstehen* out of the tradition of textual exegesis. (See also Bernstein 1983: 112–13.)

> Dilthey had tried to establish the autonomy of the logic of the *Geisteswissenschaften* or of ... the investigation of social norms, practices and institutions. That is, his desire had been to illuminate the difference between the structure of these sciences of *meaning* and the natural scientific explanation of events based on the formulation of theoretical frameworks and discovery of causal laws. Nevertheless he conceived of both kinds of study as *objective* sciences; the point of both was to develop a *neutral understanding* of social or human phenomena, an understanding *that would be accessible to all interpreters or observers* from whatever historical or cultural vantage point they might inhabit. The positivism of the mid-twentieth century differed only in denying any distinction in the logics of the natural sciences and *Geisteswissenschaften*.

Individuals responsible for promoting the concept of *Verstehen* have long desired to represent the sciences of meaning as objective, on a par with the objectivity of the natural sciences. Like Dilthey, most subjectivists have struggled with the problem 'that viewing the social sciences as a continuation or refinement of the self-understanding developed in ordinary experience leaves them prey to the same self-deceptions to which ordinary life is subject' (Warnke 1987: 34). Bearing in mind that earlier subjectivists held to the objectivity of social science and feared the problem of relativism identified here, it is instructive to consider Max Weber's position. Although addressing himself to the objectivity of social science and taking care to preserve its *Wertfreiheit*, his arguments take *Verstehen* further away from an objectivist position, the subtlety of which is lost in his epigones. Examining Weber's views provides a useful bridge from the ideas of his predecessors to a hermeneutical reading of all scientific discourse that is associated with Gadamer's critique of objectivism and with Rorty's (1980) analysis.

When considering Weber's standpoint on the position of the theorist as observer and interpreter of human conduct and also on the objectivity of social science, it is important to heed Bernstein's argument (1976) concerning the interpretation of Weber's position. Weber's sociology is probably known to most English-speaking scholars through Parsons's translation and explication (M. Weber 1964). Parsons's work, however, reveals a strong positivistic influence that is apparent in his description of the theorist as 'observer', quoted in Chapter 1. Referring to Parsons's predisposition, Bernstein (1976: 252, n. 26) adds that

> Parsons's own biases have influenced his presentation of Weber and have affected the way in which a generation of mainstream social scientists have read and interpreted Weber. . . . Weber saw clearly . . . that an adequate social theory must not only examine causal relationships. . . . We are only beginning to realise how Weber was much more profound and perceptive about these issues than those who progressed beyond him.

Much of Weber's writing can be seen as a struggle against a narrowly conceived methodology of science which was becoming more and more dominant and which would culminate in logical positivism. What he objected to was a dogmatic and rigidly prescriptive approach to science which also refused to acknowledge differences between the natural and social sciences. His open-minded approach produced a fundamental defence of subjectivism in social science, though Weber was adamant that the subjective basis of social science was not in conflict with the need for social scientists to produce objectively valid knowledge.[2] Examining the issue of objectivity in social science Weber (1977: 26–7), provides a point-by-point comparison of the methodology of the natural and social sciences. He rejects the view that a psychologistic explanation of social phenomena – reducing them to psychic conditions – is desirable, and that, if pursued, would give the analysis of social life a solid grounding, comparable with the objectivity of mechanics.

Weber's argument (see 1977: 27–30) that the task of explaining social phenomena is not assisted by the search for causal laws, rests on the consideration that the events or phenomena in which the scientist is interested have a 'significance' to individuals based on an underlying 'value-orientation' which individuals have towards cultural events. When he speaks of the 'cultural significance of a phenomenon' – and Weber provides the example of exchange in a monetary economy – he is saying that the phenomenon is not just a thing in the world which exists out there, but it has a meaning to individuals as a means to ends which they pursue. It has a subjective meaning or significance, based on the individual's appraisal of it in a particular role.

It is not difficult to see Weber's hermeneutical leanings in these arguments, and I view them as a foretaste of modern hermeneutics. It is the appraisal by individuals of phenomena that gives them their significance and allows their nature, function, and importance to be understood. If we were to take away or to overlook the meaning that phenomena have for individuals – their value-orientation – the phenomena would not be of interest to the social scientist. It is the cultural values of things that makes them social phenomena and it is the interpretation of their significance in a social context which determines both how and why the social scientist is interested in them. As meaning depends on context, so significance is specific to a particular period of history. In order to explain phenomena, social theory must reveal what significance they have for individuals in particular circumstances.

It stands to reason that an understanding of significance at a particular time or place cannot be gained through abstract, formal causal relationships nor can it be sought in universal analytical laws. Regarding these arguments, Weber states (1977: 30–1, emphasis added):

> An 'objective' analysis of cultural events, which proceeds according to the thesis that the ideal of science is the reduction of empirical reality ... [to] 'laws', is meaningless. ... [B]ecause knowledge of cultural events is inconceivable except on the basis of the *significance* which the concrete constellations of reality have for us in certain *individual* concrete situations. In *which* sense and in *which* situations this is the case is not revealed to us by any law; it is decided according to the *value-ideas* in the light of which we view 'culture' in each individual case. ... The transcendental presupposition of every *cultural science* lies not in our finding a certain culture or any culture in general to be valuable, but rather in the fact that we are cultural beings, endowed with the capacity and the will *to take a deliberate attitude towards the world and to lend it significance*.

What is particularly important, if this is a valid interpretation of Weber's ideas,[3] is the hint at the end of the quotation – which certainly foreshadows the position of Husserl and phenomenologists and after them hermeneuticists – that significance does not reside in things; it is constituted by the individual. Something has significance because the individual deems it so. So an explanation of the phenomena of the social sciences requires an understanding of the way in which problems or situations are constituted by individuals.

Weber's exposition contrasts sharply with the ambitions of determinism and its complete scheme of things. He points out that to try to embrace, or to analyse, all aspects of 'reality' would be impossible. Freund (1968: 39) attributes this conviction to Weber's adherence to the spirit of Kantian philosophy, that '[r]eality is infinite and inexhaustible'. Weber's position, one could argue, is that understanding – linked as it is to the meaning that individuals attach to phenomena as means to ends – 'unfolds'; it involves an ongoing process of interpretation over time. This perspective is the antithesis of a comprehensive 'world view'. For Weber, the fact that the theorist always approaches problems in a particular historical context and at a particular time, guided by particular value-ideas, is why a subjectivist approach always yields a partial view and why the findings of social scientists are in some respects always relative, despite being subjected to rigorous analysis.

An important difference between these arguments and the 'neutral (or objective) understanding' of nineteenth-century hermeneutics is that Weber's arguments constitute the emergence of a notion of *Verstehen* embracing a relativist position. The central role, in orienting understanding, of the individual's historical or cultural perspective and his particular interests, is identified by modern hermeneutics. From this vantage point, the inevitable 'relativism' of interpretation as a consequence of the individual's 'situatedness' is the essence of subjectivism. So Weber's arguments prefigure Gadamer's idea that the observer, or 'analyser', who is born into and immersed in a tradition and culture, is already 'thrown' into the world. Meaning and significance are only constituted through a pre-existing, pre-judged, 'understanding' (see Bernstein: 1983: 142; Warnke 1987: 82–91).

Weber makes the point (Weber 1977: 31) that 'knowledge of cultural reality . . . is always knowledge from *particular points of view*'. What is treated by the researcher as important or trivial is not determined by the facts of the situation, but by the 'evaluative ideas with which [the specialist] unconsciously approaches his subject matter . . . [selecting] . . . a tiny portion with the study of which he *concerns* himself' (ibid.: 32). In modern hermeneutics, the relativism of understanding is not something to be apologetic about or to be avoided, but something upon which to capitalise and to build in order to gain insight into the individual's understanding and the circumstances of decision-making. Explaining Gadamer's position on the importance of recognising the 'prejudices' that shape the individual's understanding, Bernstein (1983: 128) states that '[t]here is no knowledge without *preconceptions* and *prejudices*. The task is not to remove such preconceptions, but to test them critically in the course of inquiry'.

We can legitimately infer that the epistemological and ontological implications of Weber's subjectivism place him at a considerable distance both from the Cartesian objectivism that is associated with modernism and positive science and from the subjectivism of nineteenth-century hermeneutics. In Weber's work, interpretative understanding begins to reveal an epistemology where nothing is certain, where it is impossible to 'test' the validity of one's understanding because each individual has a different perspective on things. This of course seems to raise an enormous problem. Unless scientific knowledge is grounded and is intersubjectively valid, who is to say whether the theorist's interpretation and understanding is correct? Is it not true that in accepting Weber's arguments all explanation would have to be treated as either equally valid or equally arbitrary, since there is no objective, correct explanation? In a similar vein, if individuals' decisions merely reflect the way in which they constitute their worlds, what are the possibilities of people making the correct decisions? How do we know whether individuals base their decisions and conduct on a correct understanding, or whether they are simply mistaken in their (subjective) assessments of any situation?[4]

Questions like these arouse considerable disquiet in scholarly circles and most scholars would reject the modern hermeneuticist's standpoint that the questions are misguided. The hermeneuticist's position is that no one necessarily knows what to do, or what to make of a particular situation. If these questions involve a presupposition that, by having the right information, people could make decisions which are objectively the best, they are certainly misguided. No one has the third-person perspective that is needed to take demonstratively superior decisions.

OBJECTIVE-SUBJECTIVISM

By contrast, confronted with the apparent dilemma of recognising the subjective nature of experience and of wanting to provide a grounded theory of individual conduct, based on more than private experience, scholars have offered various 'solutions' for grounding subjectivist theory. It is useful to review these 'solutions' in order to explain the problems associated with them and also why modern hermeneutics repudiates them.

One approach, associated with exploring and explicating the rationality of behaviour, holds that experience is conditioned by psychological or mental characteristics and these, in turn, might have a physiological origin. In this way, psychology (and perhaps physiology) 'grounds' a theory of decision-making, providing the assurance that there is something real – in the form of, say, dispositions towards different goods – behind capricious human conduct. Traits, or even the physiological structures that 'cause' perception, provide a scientific objective basis for, and explanation of, human conduct. This is a 'solution' that Weber explicitly rejects (see also Freund 1968: 40–1, 115–16).

Subjectivists espousing the application of *Verstehen* have usually adopted a different approach in order to show that it is possible to determine what constitutes a valid interpretation (of a text) or what represents an optimal decision. Taking various forms, it involves the idea that 'behind' the individual's subjective experience of the world is a structure, which the theorist discerns and can refer to, which shapes people's experience and knowledge. Experience itself is grounded in something real out there. Alternatively, there is a 'real world' against which the individual's experience is tested. The theorist draws a distinction between the reality that exists independently of the individual's ideas (see Mäki 1990: 294) on the one hand, and the world as the individual experiences it on the other. Although experience is not always a good guide to action and the individual may be uncertain about what to do, in principle she can find out what she ought to do so that her actions are in concert with the dictates of the situation as it really exists. Thus the real world acts to circumscribe the range of feasible action. In a similar vein, the social-institutional context of action is regarded as a 'constant', or substructure, providing the parameters that determine the limits within which individuals can operate. Initially, the individual may not realise what things are really like, but over time her knowledge will come to mirror the reality of the world and then her actions will be optimal, conforming to the objective circumstances of the situation.[5]

The common denominator in all these efforts to demonstrate how experience is grounded is that individuals, or their conduct, and the world in which they reside are treated as separate entities. To the theorist, the individual with her motives and historical-cultural perspective confronts a set of circumstances. Over here is the individual; over there the cultural world which has meaning to her. Situated somewhere 'outside' all of this, the theorist has knowledge of the world which is different to the world as individuals see it. Unlike them, the theorist can see the whole scheme of things. On the one hand he has insight into the individuals and what they know, but on the other hand he can 'see' the reality of the entire structure of the world against which the individuals' activities stand out in relief and to which their more limited understanding refers.

Methodologically, the requirement that a theory based on subjective experience should provide a proper representation of reality arises from, and is satisfied by, the epistemological-ontological prescription that people live in a pre-given world 'out there', albeit one conditioned by historical-cultural circumstances and in which certain things have meaning to them. Such a scheme is purported to be subjectivist because individual action is based on what people know and their understanding, but at the same time the purported subjectivism is not an obstacle to obtaining a faithful depiction of social world and for determining whether conduct is optimal, because the scheme ultimately refers to a world that exists beyond individuals' understanding, which the theorist can comprehend.

I will refer to theories that claim to take cognisance of individuals' understanding while allowing the theorist access to a real scheme of things, as attempts to achieve an 'objective-subjectivism'. Just as it emphasises the contradiction in efforts to ground interpretation, the term draws attention to the inconsistent way in which the two elements of the double hermeneutic are treated. Individuals understand and theirs is a subjective viewpoint. The theorist knows and his is an objective viewpoint.

Perhaps the most unsatisfactory aspect of schemes that claim that understanding is grounded, is that they involve some form of epistemological dualism. The theorist's knowledge of the world is different from that of ordinary individuals, not just because he has an expertise in analysing social situations, or because he has a theory that facilitates a particular discourse, which the ordinary, untrained person does not possess. Objective-subjectivist schemes fundamentally deny that there is a double hermeneutic in explaining 'social reality' for they ignore, or gloss over, the theorist's position as an understander. The theorist has immediate 'access' to the structure of things as they really are, and his reality is different from that of the people whom he observes. How or why he should have a superior, more sophisticated understanding is not explained. In any event, the theorist is assigned a special role and by virtue of his epistemological-ontological privilege, he is not an observer in the ordinary sense of someone understanding the activities of his fellow humans.

An objectivist language and methodology necessitates this special sort of knower and the discussion above reveals that his epistemology and ontology is a third-person perspective. All approaches that recognise interpretation and incorporate understanding into explanations of individuals' conduct, but which also propose to provide a neutral, or objective, frame of reference for judging the veracity of interpretation and the appropriateness of conduct, assimilate this epistemology and ontology. In fact it only requires the rider that the world that exists beyond understanding is complete, so individuals could potentially find out all about it, to lay the foundations for a determinate equilibrium theory based on understanding. The significance of objective-subjectivism for economists today is that it characterises Austrian economics.

The question, though, is: what does *Verstehen* mean within an objective-subjectivist scheme? A rational individual is someone whose actions reflect the reality of the world out there and, in order to act rationally, the individual must know what the world is like and understand the meaning in things. Social phenomena in the world have meaning as means to ends, and through the process of interpretative understanding the individual comes to understand the meaning that things have. Understanding consists of transferring what happens in the world to the apprehension of the individual.

At most these theories involve a single hermeneutical element in the recognition that individuals understand, but the problem is that that understanding is not central to explanations of what people do. Indeed, the implication is that individuals themselves cannot trust their understanding and always need to go beyond it, to the real world, in order to be sure that they are doing the right things. The third-person perspective not only undermines but also destroys the explanatory role of subjective understanding. *Verstehen* becomes just something that people do – a mechanism that they use – in order to access to the meaning of the world out there, which by implication is their true object.

It seems that the very efforts to ground a subjectivist theory lead to the abandonment of the endeavour to understand what understanding is about.

In order to ground the theory it is necessary to demonstrate that there is more to the world than the individual's understanding of it; that understanding is not self-contained but always refers to something beyond understanding itself, beyond what is actually understood. Thus theorists who espouse the cause of subjective understanding in social science, but who also want to ground the theory, are in the predicament of having to conclude that interpretative understanding is not very useful either to individuals or the theorist. For the former it is an insufficient basis from which to act, or to decide, for it may lead to the wrong decisions being taken. For the theorist, without recourse to the underlying scheme of things that exists outside of individuals' understanding, it is not possible to explain human conduct and to show that conduct does have a rational basis.

THE *VERSTEHEN* OF PHENOMENOLOGY

It was the contributions of phenomenologists in general and Schütz (1972) in particular that, breaking with objective-subjectivism, set the course of subjectivism towards the modern hermeneutical position with a radically different concept of *Verstehen*. The suggestion that phenomenology undermines objective-subjectivism by casting doubt on the ability of social science to yield an objective view of the world, may be received with scepticism and needs to be substantiated. As explained in the Appendix to Chapter 4, this is one of the main points of difference between my position and that of O'Sullivan (1987).

One reason for scepticism is that Husserl regards transcendental phenomenology as a method capable of yielding knowledge that is apodeictically certain (see, however, Warnke 1987: 34–41). For Husserl, access to the structure of things that lies behind individuals' understanding is gained transcendentally, by 'bracketing' out the world of everyday experience through phenomenological reduction. From his point of view, by 'showing' that there is a real, unchanging structure at the core of the individual's subjective perceptions of what is, this process furnishes phenomenology with an objective basis.[6]

Yet in phenomenology the world is not pre-given. What the individual understands or knows is what she actively 'constitutes' in her consciousness. This marks a radical departure from the spirit of earlier subjectivist thinking. Although Husserl tried to find a way out of the dilemma posed by the relativity of individuals' life-worlds, postulating a world of 'transcendental subjectivity' beyond the different life-worlds constituted by the ego, the last are relative to the individual's historical and cultural circumstances. In addition, since for Husserl the natural sciences are projects that arise out of the circumstances of the life-world, science is inevitably situated in history. In his words (Husserl 1970: 332; see also Warnke 1987: 36), '[n]atural science is a culture, [and] it belongs only within the cultural world of that human civilization which has developed this culture and within which, for the individual, possible ways of understanding this culture are present.'

Where Husserl provides the concepts and methodology of phenomenology, Schütz's goal is to apply these to the social sciences. The notion of the life-world, which is central to Schütz's phenomenology, was introduced by Husserl (1970) right at the end of his life. In exploring how the individual constitutes the life-world, Schütz makes an important contribution to the formulation of a subjectivist scheme.[7] Schütz adopts the position that Weber left his notion of subjective meaning ill-defined and unexplored (Schütz 1972: xxvii). Schütz uses phenomenological categories, including Husserl's notion of 'internal time-consciousness', or Bergson's *durée*, to examine *Verstehen*, the constitution of meaning and experience, and the concept of action. The conceptual tools that Schütz develops are valuable in explaining decision-making, especially his increasing emphasis on the importance of social relationships and the intersubjective nature of the life-world (see Dallmayr and McCarthy 1977: 219–20).

Explanations of the phenomena of the life-world are rooted in the constituting activities of the individual and, for Schütz, the life-world into which individuals are born is a shared social world of contemporaries and associates. He states this succinctly (Schütz 1972: 32):[8] '[E]very act of mine through which I endow the world with meaning refers back to some meaning-endowing act ... of yours with respect to the same world. Meaning is thus constituted as an intersubjective phenomenon.' In this respect Schütz's approach represents a substantial and welcome departure from the subjectivism of his predecessors who overlook the reciprocal nature of social relationships and of understanding. Earlier formulations of the problem of subjective understanding have the individual as an interpreter of what is happening out there, rather than as someone who is aware of, and influenced by, his relationships with other people.

Modern hermeneutics disposes of the problem of relativism, which as we have seen was a vexed issue for subjectivists, by emphasising the intersubjective nature of understanding. It is really only once this is recognised that the difficulties faced by earlier generations of subjectivists over the problem of relativism can be clearly appreciated. Treating the individual as a solitary figure, who interprets a world that exists around him but who lacks the social relationships of family, colleagues, and business associates, obviously opened them to the charge of relativism and perhaps of solipsism.[9]

For Schütz, time, as *durée*, is an inseparable element in constituting meaning. Analysing experience in the life-world, he argues that '[a]ll action takes place in time, or more precisely in the internal time-consciousness, in the *durée*. It is duration-immanent enactment' (ibid.: 40). The individual, immersed in activity or engaged in the process of constituting meaning, is a stream of consciousness with a temporal element. The awareness of duration is only achieved, as Schütz puts it, when we 'turn back', or 'reflect', on that stream (ibid.: 47):

> As long as my whole consciousness remains temporally uni-directional and irreversible, I am unaware ... of any difference between present and past. The very awareness of the stream of duration presupposes a ... special kind of attitude toward that stream, a 'reflection'.

Consciousness, however, is of a 'world that is at every moment one of becoming and passing away' and as such is always being constituted, never completed (ibid.: 36). In the constituting process,

> meaning is a certain way of directing one's gaze at an item of one's experience. This item is thus 'selected out' and rendered discrete. ... Meaning indicates, therefore, a peculiar attitude on the part of the Ego toward the flow of its own duration' (ibid.: 42).

What is experienced is the present, but action involves projection; so consciousness – the present – has an orientation towards the future.[10] Constituting is a constant shifting of consciousness, or interest, of becoming aware of different things which are then one's experience. In the constituting process thoughts turn to the future with which experience of the present is bound up.

The *durée* gives an additional dimension to the 'situatedness' of experience and understanding. Earlier I suggested that the constitution of meaning is always within an intersubjective, cultural-historical context. Now we recognise that understanding has a more personal and temporal dimension. The individual's experience is constituted through her own focus or interests, which involve her relationships with other people, as she 'directs her consciousness'. Meaning changes as her perspective alters in the light of experience. Where there was uncertainty there is additional insight; doubt and scepticism give way to hope. Where only recently the prospects seemed good, there is now a feeling of despair. It is the nature of being-in-time that consciousness and meaning are part of the temporal sequence, and we cannot help but understand differently in the light of experience.

This brief examination of Schütz's contribution to interpretative understanding brings the discussion to the point where the meaning of *Verstehen* begins to intersect with the ideas of modern hermeneuticists and I now want to examine their subjectivism. These are the ideas most closely associated with the emergence of the epistemology and ontology of the first-person perspective. They lead to the complete rejection of attempts to ground understanding, treat knowledge as hermeneutical, and provide the foundation of a thoroughgoing subjectivism embracing the relativity of understanding.

VERSTEHEN IN THE FIRST-PERSON PERSPECTIVE

The relatively short history of social science, characterised by the desire for an objective social science, is replete with examples of attempts to ground theories in order to escape the charge of relativism: that social theories which incorporate individuals' perceptions or understanding into explanations of human conduct necessarily treat knowledge as relative to the individual. According to Gadamer, however, the concern with relativism is only the result of being indoctrinated with Cartesian objectivity. On that mistaken view, relativism means uncertainty about whether we have arrived at the truth, and whether our understanding is correct. Science must dispel doubt. But the Cartesian ideal is a deception and is a consequence of turning away from understanding. Reflecting Gadamer's views, Warnke argues (1987: 32–3; see also Bernstein 1983: 36–7) that social scientists who seek universally valid knowledge, and who wish to put the inferences which they draw beyond doubt, look at the social world from a false perspective. They fail

> to distinguish between two different kinds of doubt: the doubt that arises in the course of life and a methodologically sanctioned doubt. In life itself certain experiences can cast doubt upon one's conceptions, prejudices and self-understanding. Such doubts can lead to further reflection, revision in one's interpretation of one's life or one's projects. . . . This kind of doubt is thus part of the connection between experience and understanding. . . . In contrast, the methodological decision to doubt all of one's experiences in advance – the strategy of Cartesian doubt – does not have its roots in life but is rather directed 'against life'.

The dichotomy between objectivism and relativism is a false one for, when the theorist attends to the nature of human understanding, it is appreciated that the world does not just exist 'out there' but that meaning is constituted, the constitution of meaning is intersubjective, and doubt is always part of understanding.

In its interpretation of the constitution of meaning, modern hermeneutics takes the notion of *Verstehen* beyond that of phenomenology, as Bernstein (1983: 137) reveals when he asserts that 'we are essentially beings constituted by and engaged in interpretative understanding'. This statement extends the phenomenological notion of meaning being constituted, because in the process of understanding (*Verstehen*) the individual not only actively shapes her 'view', but – as an understanding, interpreting, sentient being – is herself being constituted. A theory concerned with explaining human conduct cannot be grounded, in the Cartesian sense of having an objective basis, because understanding is not grounded, except in understanding, in history or experience.

> Understanding is universal in several senses. It is not just one activity which is to be distinguished from other human activities, but underlies all human activities. It is universal in the sense that nothing is in principle beyond understanding, even though we never exhaust the 'things themselves' through understanding.

This quotation is from Bernstein (1983: 144). When he says that 'nothing . . . is beyond understanding', he means that understanding is all there is: knowledge is understanding (and reflects a particular perspective). From this point of view existence is a hermeneutic circle of understanding,[11] in which the individual is constituted by her understanding. We do not come to know more, but in the course of time we understand differently, and so the 'things themselves' are never exhausted. Uncertainty and doubt are part of life – of existence in the hermeneutic circle – and of understanding. A subjectivist theory of conduct, concerned with how people make decisions, must reflect the doubt and uncertainty that people feel, but at both levels of the double hermeneutic.[12] For just as individuals are constituted in their existence in the *durée*, so too is the theorist in the process of understanding their activities.

These arguments need to be examined in their proper context of Gadamer's explication of the hermeneutic circle. In that context the consequences of this reasoning are as devastating for the 'old' subjectivism (the belief that interpretative understanding can have an objective foundation) as the hermeneutical turn has been for the positivist-empiricist view of science as epistemology, completely rejecting the Cartesian search for certainty. The methodology of 'old' subjectivism is turned upside down and the idea of *Wertfreiheit* in social science loses its foundation.

Recognition of the hermeneutic circle – of the interrelationship between part and whole – is attributed to Dilthey who credits the formulation to Matthias Flacius, a Lutheran working at the time of the Reformation (Warnke 1987: 5). In rejecting Catholic teaching as a guide to the meaning of the Bible, Flacius had to create its meaning from an understanding of the individual parts. But in order to understand the parts it was necessary to be guided by, and to have an understanding of, the work as a whole. In this context the circle appears to be a vicious one and that is the way it is most often been treated (Bernstein 1983: 133). To the theorist who wishes to ground understanding, the characterisation of the hermeneutic circle as vicious may seem to be a just one, for it appears to be one more example of the relativism of understanding, which a sound theory must seek to avoid. Bernstein, however, argues that the circle is 'seen as such only when judged by the mistaken and unwarranted epistemological demands for empirical verification – the appeal to some "brute data"' (ibid.: 134). He goes on to note (ibid.: 135) that, in general, references to the circle of understanding are '"object" oriented. . . . No essential reference is made to the interpreter, to the individual who is engaged in the process of understanding and questioning, except in so far as he or she must have insight, imagination . . . and patience to acquire this art.'

An important distinction is drawn here. On the one hand there is the idea that the circle applies to what exists 'out there', to things which have an independent existence in the form of, say, books, works of art, societies, or traditions. On the other hand, there is the idea that the circle is what interpretation is about, that its 'existence' is bound up with the understander and her understanding, and that to understand is to do so within the context of a hermeneutic circle. The distinction is a vital one from the point of view of a subjectivist methodology for it identifies and serves to separate two conceptions of the position of the theorist, each embracing a different meaning of the concept of *Verstehen*. The one is that associated with the objective-subjectivist position discussed earlier. The other is the first-person perspective, involving a double hermeneutic where each level of the double hermeneutic recognises the social, intersubjective nature, and 'relativism' of understanding.

The hermeneutic circle, the interrelationship between whole and part in the process of interpretation, is seen to be not just a problem or puzzle that applies to, say, texts or works of art, but is the essence of all understanding. An appreciation of the circle, 'clarifies the relationship between the interpreter and what he or she seeks to understand' (Bernstein 1983: 137). What she seeks to understand concerns the activities of other people – friends, colleagues, suppliers, managers. The individual – whether the theorist or the subjects whose activities are of interest – brings to the process of constituting her history, culture, tradition, language, and understanding of other people. These shape the meanings that she ascribes to particular phenomena, events, and activities. But in the light of experience, and especially through her relationships with other people, the prejudices that shape understanding are themselves changed.[13]

Understanding, in this view, is always relative, not only from one individual to another, but also – allowing for hyperbole – from moment to moment.[14]

The important conclusion is that the relativity of understanding is what understanding is about; it cannot be otherwise. The conceptual schemes of social science should recognise this and enable the implications to be examined, including the many questions related to the nature of the communication, co-operation, and other interrelationships among people. Once the hermeneutical nature of experience is understood, and the idea of science as a hermeneutical activity is grasped, subjectivist social theory, in the fullest sense of the word, becomes the basis for examining the methodology of science rather than natural science providing the paradigm for social science.

I have now shown that the meaning of *Verstehen* has undergone a considerable change as subjective understanding has been re-interpreted at successive points in the evolution of a subjectivist paradigm. Initially the notion of understanding emphasised strongly how the individual attached meaning to events that were seen to exist out there. In this incarnation, subjectivism treated individuals as 'producers' of actions, the meanings of which (including their motives) could be understood by others, and the purpose of *Verstehen* was to do just that. Interpretative understanding was what individuals, the objects of the theorist's investigations, did to the actions of others out there. The theorist's position, as observer and explorer of social life, remained unaffected by the application of *Verstehen*: the theorist was a neutral or objective observer.

With the emergence of phenomenology, the emphasis shifted to highlight the constitutive and intersubjective nature of meaning. To constitute the meaning of phenomena it is necessary to understand the motives of others whose activities are interwoven in what is 'intuitively' a social world. In modern hermeneutics *Verstehen* is not about recognising and clarifying people's motives: it is about the nature of, and also the obstacles to, intersubjective understanding. Interpretation is the essence of understanding, of being-in-time. *Verstehen* is not understanding you, but is my understanding of you and everything else. In interpreting, I not only come to understand you; I come to understand. My perspective is shaped or transformed by understanding, which takes me further.

The starting point of a subjectivist methodology is that explaining conduct means understanding how individuals understand. In adopting a first-person perspective, however, *Verstehen* encompasses the theorist as well and involves the recognition, as well as a clarification, of the double hermeneutic of social studies. By exploring their activities, the theorist makes people part of his world. He engages with them in understanding and they become part of his hermeneutic circle. The first-person perspective thus acknowledges the ubiquitousness of the intersubjective nature of understanding as the foundation of a subjectivist methodology. The theorist brings the individuals into his sphere of understanding. Like those people, he is engaged in a continuous hermeneutical process which involves moving from particular to general and back again. The notion of a discourse, in which ideas are exchanged and evaluated and positions reassessed, provides the analogy for the hermeneutical view of individual conduct and the theorist's condition. At the 'start', he interprets the problem in a particular way and, in the course of his enquiry, he understands differently and his questions and focus change.

IMPLICATIONS FOR SOCIAL SCIENCE

The question that remains, after exploration of the epistemological and ontological foundations of a subjectivist scheme, is: how does the language of hermeneutical subjectivism shape the theories of social science? Although the ramifications are discussed in Chapter 7, I want briefly to distinguish between what is 'lost', or has to be abandoned on the journey from the older to the newer subjectivist paradigm, and also what is gained.

What is lost is not inconsequential. One implication of this post-modernist view of scientific activity is that there is no value-free science. With the abandonment of *Wertfreiheit*, the distinction between positive and normative science, so much a part of the modernist paradigm, falls away. Taylor (1977: 130), in noting that a science which is developed within the context of the hermeneutic circle cannot be *Wertfrei*, suggests that such an idea is 'still radically shocking and unassimilable to the mainstream of modern science'. The thrust of hermeneutical subjectivism is that understanding is personal in that it concerns the individual's – which includes the theorist's – interests and experiences in the *durée*. It is also prejudiced in a way that no scientist can avoid. One's perspective is literally pre-judged. Prejudice is re-created and perhaps revised over time, but understanding remains prejudiced. Social scientists, like everyone else, bring these prejudices to their enquiries. Their questions also reflect the value-judgements of a community of colleagues who condemn or sanction a particular type of research, set norms and impose standards, or establish conventions to which scholars must adhere.

Many social scientists will be unsettled by the idea that embracing a first-person perspective means abandoning an objective basis of theory. We have seen that some subjectivists have sought the best of both worlds. Recognising the importance of interpretative understanding for theories intended to illuminate social reality, they have tried to assure themselves, and others, that their theories are truly scientific and do not paint the theorist into a corner of relativism. They will surely wish to anchor understanding to something firmer and more permanent than ideas that are formed in an ongoing 'conversation'. Those who are sceptical of modern hermeneutics (including Rorty's interpretation of Gadamer's work), and who are concerned that it represents a position of irrationalism, will find ample support. Warnke draws attention to the idea that Gadamer's exposition of the hermeneutic circle is an attempt to move beyond objectivism and relativism, and this is also the position adopted by Bernstein (1983). These authors and others, nevertheless, express their concerns about placing too radical an interpretation on modern hermeneutics – one which undermines any attempt at grounding the theory (see Warnke 1987: ch. 5).

I cannot here resolve the question of whether abandoning the quest for an epistemology, as Rorty intends that we should, is irrational. The ramifications are undoubtedly enormous, and the question has implications for the foundations of social norms (see O'Sullivan 1987: 26–7). My conviction is that, through modern hermeneutics, the sort of position which Rorty adopts constitutes a powerful challenge to conventional views of the distinction between the natural and social sciences. In addition, the iconoclastic stand against the conventional wisdom removes barriers to an examination of the foundations of knowledge and understanding. By pointing to the discursive nature of understanding, the position that theorising occurs within a historically based hermeneutic circle is an appealing one. Adopting the view of science as hermeneutic means accepting that the scholar is open to, and receptive of, new ideas.

One of the least admirable aspects of modernism is the dogmatism that accompanies its claim to offer the path to truth and knowledge. The methodology itself is chauvinistic and denies adherents the opportunity to question its foundations. Because modernism was transformed from methodology into ideology, it came to represent a rejection of the rational ideal of scholarship. A hermeneutical conception of scientific discourse offers the prospect of restoring a sense of enquiry and challenge to methodology, where before the only things worth investigating were the scientific problems themselves.

For the social sciences in particular an important consequence of adopting a first-person perspective is that the narrow individualism of economic theory is supplanted by an emphasis on social interrelationships. Although both the natural and social sciences recognise that each successive generation of theorists, as Newton put it, 'stands on the shoulders of giants', positivism cultivated the idea that all that was necessary to discover the truth was for someone, in isolation, to observe what goes on out there. The advance made by Popper consisted of recognising that science was not discovery in isolation but in critical discourse. Hermeneutics, of course, emphasises that what we learn, we learn in a social context, through discourse.

In the social sciences, the narrow individualism covers both elements of the double hermeneutic. The third-person perspective has underpinned the idea of an isolated individual who is hardly aware of the existence of others. This caricature is particularly strong in economics, where the agent has no relationships with other people except through impersonal 'market forces', as a supplier, distributor, or anonymous consumer. He communicates indirectly, through the medium of 'market signals'. Hermeneutical subjectivism, the basis of a first-person perspective, recognises that understanding is intersubjective, and so must establish who the others are who 'share' the world of the individuals whose activities are of interest to the theorist. Why does the individual consider them to be important; what is the nature of the relationships; and what sorts of roles do they play in influencing his activities?

The recognition of the intersubjective nature of understanding, juxtaposed with the nature of understanding itself in the hermeneutic circle, requires the theorist to attend to the nature of the discourse between individuals at both levels of the double hermeneutic. How do individuals communicate? How well do they do so? To what extent do they understand each other, and why do they do so? Coming as these do on top of the linguistic turn in analytic philosophy, such questions point to exciting areas of study for all the social sciences.

What is needed are the conceptual tools that can be applied in order to investigate decision-making and conduct and to understand 'social reality'. Austrian economics is described as a subjectivist scheme and my immediate object is to examine the subjectivism of Austrian economics in order to determine whether it is compatible with the epistemology of a first-person perspective and furnishes the tools of interpretative understanding.

6

AUSTRIAN ECONOMICS
AND SUBJECTIVISM

One knew there was much wrong with modern economics, but one did not yet know how to put it right. It was necessary first . . . to figure out what difference this 'Austrian perspective' made for understanding the real world. To the much asked question 'What is Austrian economics?' there was simply not a ready answer.

(Vaughn 1990: 402)

AN INTERMITTENT HISTORY

The Austrian and neoclassical schools of economics are exact contemporaries, both having been built upon the contributions of protagonists of the catallactist revolution of the 1870s. Although often seen alongside Walras and Jevons as a founder of catallactic economics – the 'marginal revolution' – it is now conceded that, methodologically, Menger (from whom the Austrians trace their descent) is some distance from his contemporaries as regards his eschewal of equilibrium and other considerations (see Gram and Walsh 1978; Jaffé 1976; Shackle 1972b; Streissler 1972). One obvious methodological difference is Menger's spurning of mathematics. Jaffé (1976: 521) quotes from Menger's correspondence with Walras and states that the former

> declared his objection *in principle* to the use of mathematics as a method of advancing economic knowledge. . . . For the performance of this task what is required . . . [is] a method of process analysis ['the analytic-compositive method'] tracing the complex phenomena of the social economy to the underlying atomistic forces at work.

This quotation is also suggestive of Menger's objection to the use of the concept of general equilibrium, which is documented by Streissler (1972).[1] By opposing a positivist-empiricist methodology and having an interest in problems that lie outside the scope of mainstream theory, later generations of Austrians are also regarded as having taken a different route to their neoclassical peers.

What is it that sets the Austrians apart and how far apart are they? The answer to the first part of the question appears straightforward. In the course of what has become known as the 'Austrian revival' that began in the mid-1970s, we find that Austrian theorists emphasise subjectivism as their main distinguishing characteristic. 'Austrian economists', Kirzner (1976b: 40) says, 'are subjectivists' (see also Hayek 1955a: 31; Lachmann 1977b: 28; Littlechild 1978: 19; O'Sullivan 1987: 152–5).

Vaughn's question in the epigraph to this chapter, however, alerts us to the consideration that the issue may not be entirely clear-cut. For much of the last century there has been a tendency to view Austrian contributions, such as those of Hayek and to a lesser extent of Mises, as part of a rather undifferentiated body of economic theory. This is a characteristic of Robbins' influential *Essay* (1949) which was, and still is, regarded as defining the scope of modern economics (a variant of Robbins' definition appears in nearly every textbook). On closer reading, and especially on examining Robbins' sources, however, it is clear that the views that helped to shape Robbins' definition were confined to a fairly small group of Austrian economists (see Addleson 1984a).[2] Hicks (1976b: 214, n. 13) confirms that Austrian and neoclassical theories are not easy to distinguish. 'The Lausanne and Austrian versions of catallactics are by no means identical. . . . But it is noticeable that as time has gone on, these versions, at first distinct, have grown together.' His view is that many modern writers do not readily identify a well-defined Austrian paradigm, but 'draw upon Menger and upon Walras in equal measure'. Mises (1969: 41) also holds that by the 1920s Austrian economics had been absorbed into mainstream theory.

Is Austrian theory really different? A particular difficulty in deciding whether it is, is the lack of clarity about what Austrians mean when they describe themselves as subjectivists. Some scholars have even expressed doubt about the accuracy of the subjectivist label. Boehm (1982: 43) says that '[a]t the risk of being stamped on for heresy I venture to propose that there are some important obscurities in the thesis that Austrians adhere to the principle of subjectivism'. Mäki (1990: 294) goes further, suggesting that Austrian economists are objectivists, basing his justification on a realist interpretation of Mengerian economics. For me, in search of a subjectivist framework to give substance to a first-person perspective in order to explore human conduct, these issues are particularly important. Does Austrian economics provide this framework? Answering the question sheds further light on the relationship between Austrian and neoclassical economics. By establishing that Austrian subjectivism entails a third-person perspective it becomes clear why the relationship between Austrian and neoclassical economics remains unresolved both within and outside Austrian circles and why Austrian economics is not really an alternative to mainstream theory, certainly not the sort that we are looking for.

Using an approach with which the reader will be quite familiar by now, I am going to examine the epistemological and ontological foundations of Austrian subjectivism. In order to do so, however, it is necessary first to identify a characteristic Austrian subjectivist methodology and this is not an easy matter. In principle the task ought not to be difficult, because the investigator can draw on a number of methodological treatises written by Austrians. From Menger's *Untersuchungen* [1883] (1963), through Mises' various methodological contributions (see Mises 1958; 1960; 1978) including his *magnum opus*, *Human Action* (1949), to Hayek's *Individualism and Economic Order* (1948a) and *The Counter-Revolution of Science* (1955a), and Lachmann's *The Legacy of Max Weber* (1970) and *The Market as an Economic Process* (1991), unlike their mainstream counterparts who have tended to take their own methodology for granted, Austrians have continually sought to clarify their methodological positions.

The difficulty in identifying a definitive 'Austrian position' is that, since its beginnings, Austrian economics has experienced mixed fortunes and because the school has enjoyed only sporadic support throughout its history there is an inevitable lack of continuity of ideas. After the eclipse of the 'Older Austrian School', comprising Carl Menger and immediate followers like Friedrich Wieser and Eugene von Böhm-Bawerk (see Mises 1969; Kauder 1957; White 1977), the school enjoyed a brief but conspicuous resurgence in the 1930s. Various factors led to the subsequent decline of the school's fortunes (see Coats 1983: 95–6) which experienced a reversal only in the mid-1970s and since then Austrian economics has gone from strength to strength.[3] In the Austrian revival, when the ideas of the leading members are being re-evaluated, a variety of methodological views is in evidence and there is substantial debate about the extent to which Austrians do share a common approach (see, for example, Lavoie 1991b; Caldwell and Boehm 1992).

The reviewer of neoclassical theory is on fairly safe ground in addressing 'orthodox', or 'mainstream', economics particularly in its modern, and modernist, 'axiomatic' embodiment identified in Chapter 2. Because of its dominance as the language of economic theory and its long history, there is a conventional notion of what constitutes neoclassical economics. This is not so with Austrian economics. While the leading Austrians share the conviction that the social sciences require methods that differ from the modernist methodology of natural science, a brief review of their diverse circumstances and of the different philosophical influences upon each of them exposes the problem of identifying a well-defined, 'orthodox' Austrian position. Even establishing who belongs to the school is not a straight forward task.[4]

Menger is often regarded as an Aristotelian and methodological essentialist (Hutchison 1973: 18), although this designation is now being reassessed.[5] Menger's task, certainly in *Problems of Economics and Sociology* (1963) in which he clarified his methodological position, was to defend a theoretical science of economics against the attack of Gustav Schmoller, the main figure in the German Historical School (see Bostaph 1978).

In Mises' work the dominant theme is that economics is a branch of praxeology, the method of social science. Praxeology provides the formal framework in which human action is rendered intelligible and at the heart of the method that Mises advocates is his claim that individuals have an *a priori* understanding of the categories of action. With his emphasis on *a priori* knowledge, Mises is viewed by various authors as a neo-Kantian (Lachmann 1982: 35–6; B. Smith 1990) who faced the problem of protecting economics, as a social science, from positivism. Richard Ebeling (*pers. com.*) has expressed the view that Mises' ideas also draw from phenomenology. Alfred Schütz was a member of his *Privatseminar* held at the Austrian Chamber of Commerce, and Mises' conception of the 'essence of action' is derived from Husserl.

Both Hayek and Mises were refugees from Nazism. The former, however, had support for his ideas from a group of economists at the London School of Economics where his work first attracted real attention. In the 1930s in England, Hicks suggests that Hayek had a popularity to rival Keynes (see also Boehm 1992). Mises lacked the support of a devoted audience, having moved from country to country. When he settled in the United States, he was not accorded any great esteem and he wrote for a largely unknown audience. This may account for the polemical character of much of his work.

Later generations faced different problems and adopted different methodological standpoints. Lachmann (1970), seeing Weber as a kindred subjectivist spirit, asks Austrians explicitly to adopt *Verstehen* as a basis of Austrian theory. While there is little evidence of Weber's direct influence on earlier generations of Austrians, Lachmann's position is that there is an affinity between Weber's views on methodology on the one hand, and the general flavour of Austrian subjectivism on the other. This affinity is evident in both the rejection of modernism by successive generations of Austrians and in an interpretative element in their contributions, which began with Menger. The last few years have seen a sprinkling of efforts, by individuals who find Lachmann's arguments compelling, to marry Austrian economics with phenomenology and hermeneutics (see Ebeling 1986, 1991; Lavoie 1986, 1990, 1991b). How well does the interpretative coat fit Austrian subjectivism?

THE BASIS OF AUSTRIAN SUBJECTIVISM

In order to analyse the subjectivism of Austrian theory, the issue I want to address is how Austrian economics portrays the relationship between the theorist and his subject matter. Recognising the double hermeneutic of social science, dealing with this issue means considering how the theorist 'sees' or understands things and then examining how the individual and her knowledge or understanding is portrayed. By examining the contributions of some of the main Austrian scholars, my object is to identify a conventional Austrian methodology and epistemology and then to look more closely at the Austrian conception of the individual in economic theory. In the light of my contention that the methodological positions of Austrian theorists sometimes diverge widely, in referring to a conventional Austrian methodology I will unfortunately inevitably caricature individual contributions and also ignore important differences between them.

O'Driscoll and Rizzo (1985: 1–2) provide an excellent definition of Austrian subjectivism which, as a starting point for analysing that brand of subjectivism, is worth quoting in full.

> On the most general level, subjectivism refers to the presupposition that the contents of the human mind, and hence decision-making, are not rigidly determined by external events. Subjectivism makes room for the creativity and autonomy of individual choice. Dealing as it does with the individual mind and individual decision-making, it is also intimately related to methodological individualism. This is the view that overall market outcomes ought to be explained in terms of individual acts of choice. Thus, for the Austrians, and for subjectivists generally, economics is first and foremost about the thoughts leading up to choice . . .

What are the origins of Austrian subjectivism, and how does it differ from the hermeneutical subjectivism explored in the previous chapter? Menger is regarded as one of the great economic thinkers. Is it correct to view him as a proto-subjectivist?

The evidence of Menger's subjectivist leaning revolves around his 'atomistic', 'compositive', or 'causal-genetic' (see Silverman 1990: 70–1) method – which today would be referred to as methodological individualism (Hayek 1973b: 8). The elements out of which the 'complex phenomena' of economics evolve (Menger 1950: 46–7) are the 'individuals and their efforts, the final elements of our analysis, [that] are of an empirical nature' (Menger 1963: 142, n. 51). The 'goods-character' and value of things in exchange – things that are capable of satisfying an individual's needs – are derived from the needs (*Bedürfnisse*) themselves, and the individual's knowledge of the ability of the good to satisfy a need (see Menger 1950: 52). The classification of goods (as first, second, third, or higher order) depends on the good's proximity, in the production process, to being able to satisfy a need (ibid.: 55–67). This proximity, in turn, hinges on the individual's *knowledge* and 'is nothing inherent in the good itself and still less a property of it' (ibid.: 58).

Such considerations – whether something is a good and its classification as being of a high or low order – which constitute the foundations of Menger's conceptual scheme, are taken as evidence of subjectivism in that they indicate an evaluating and appraising human mind at work. According to a modern Austrian interpretation of subjectivism, 'social phenomena . . . [are] the outcome of human action guided by plans (even though these often fail) and *prompted by mental acts*' (Lachmann 1986: 23). In Menger there is that element which O'Driscoll and Rizzo refer to, in their definition quoted above, as 'room for the creativity and autonomy of individual choice'. Milford (1990: 218) draws attention to this.

> Menger perceived the economic agents not as passive, but as active, problem solving individuals. He depicted a world in which individuals do not simply react to their changing surroundings in a passive way [as one would interpret the agent of neoclassical theory to do] but try to discover new possibilities. . . . These individual agents continuously solve problems and . . . they will err in this process.

Seeking out new possibilities is also the essence of Kirzner's (1973) formulation of the entrepreneurial element in human action. Entrepreneurship, meaning an 'alertness to new opportunities for profit', is regarded as a characteristic of the agent in Austrian theory from Menger to Mises and beyond.

While Menger's classification as early subjectivist is associated with the conception of subjectivism as a theory that recognises an active human mind at work, this notion of subjectivism is an unconventional one viewed next to the tradition of *Verstehen* in phenomenology and hermeneutics. Boehm (1982: 43–4), warning of the proliferation of definitions of subjectivism in economics, identifies various notions 'entertained in the literature by economists of very different persuasions'. Although a number of Austrians, especially those writing during the last twenty years, do associate subjectivism with the tradition of interpretative understanding that gained stature and credence through the work of Weber (Lachmann 1970), Austrian subjectivism on the whole does not correspond with the subjectivism of hermeneutical or interpretative understanding.

The consequence is an apparently paradoxical situation where Menger is seen by some as a 'subjectivist', while Mäki (1990) classifies Mengerians (and Austrians) as objectivists. Arguing that Austrian economics is realist,[6] Mäki explains how the apparent contradiction between the self-characterisation of Austrians and his own classification can be resolved. The reconciliation is achieved by understanding Austrian economics as a combination of 'ontic subjectivism and ontological objectivism' (ibid.: 294).

> *Ontic subjectivism* says that the economy is at least partly constituted by individual's subjective valuations, expectations, purposes, etc. *Ontological objectivism* says that the economy as the object of economic theories is unconstituted by those theories and exists independently of them.

As I will try to show, this combination is compatible with the epistemology and ontology of a third-person perspective where individuals and their mental acts form part of the workings of the economy. Explanations of economic phenomena, such as prices and investment decisions, should take account of 'mental acts' including the formation of expectations, but to the theorist these are all things that form part of the world that he observes out there.

An additional and useful dimension to understanding Austrian subjectivism is found in Mäki's (1990: 308) suggestion that the Austrian conception of the 'agent' – *homo agens*, or acting man (to be contrasted with the neoclassical notion of *homo oeconomicus*) – belongs to 'folk psychology'.

> Folk psychology is the conception of human action deployed by ordinary folk and also by scientists in ordinary life situations. This conception is formulated in a framework of minds with thoughts, emotions, desires, motives, intentions, beliefs. Within folk psychology, human action is explained and predicted as an emanation from these mental entities. Indeed mental entities are the ultimate explainers; they are not to be eliminated in favour of something else, unlike some radically materialist approaches that seek to substitute neurological or computational accounts for the intentional accounts of folk psychology.

Reference to 'ordinary life situations' in the quotation indicates simply that Austrian economics depicts action as a manifestation of thoughts, motives, and expectations. It does not mean an interest in exploring the 'life-world', or world of 'social reality', in the manner suggested by Schütz; for whom doing so entails understanding how the individual constitutes the life-world. In general, Austrians make no commitment to do this.

THE THEORIST AND OBJECTIVE-SUBJECTIVISM

According to Lachmann (1977f: 261–2) the task of Austrian economics 'is to make the world around us intelligible in terms of human action and the pursuit of plans'. How does the Austrian theorist make the world intelligible; how does he 'see' the world; and, in particular, what is the epistemology and ontology of Austrian theory?

Plans, knowledge, expectations, and motives are manifestations of a human mind and are things that *exist* in the world. In order to explain economic phenomena in terms of human action, the Austrian theorist's task is to relate what is happening out there (the observable phenomena of the social world such as markets and prices) to the mental acts of people out there – the choices, the expectations, and plans – that give rise to the observable phenomena.

Subjectivism, here, refers to the fact that different people, or different 'minds', possess different 'facts' and work differently, picking up different bits of knowledge and applying it in different ways. Because the knowledge which each one has is different, they make different plans. In the course of time they also acquire new, and different, knowledge. Their minds work differently, so they 'interpret' the world out there differently and as a consequence they continue to do different things. The knowledge that is acquired and the expectations that are formed through mental acts do not correspond in any determinate way with what happens out there; there are no known functional relationships linking the individual's knowledge and expectations to the world out there. So knowledge and expectations are described as subjective and the methodology is identified as subjectivist. Yet people do not conjecture, interpret, or understand. They are not active constituters of their worlds but are 'acquirers' of knowledge which comes from somewhere out there.

This is the objective-subjectivism discussed in the previous chapter. As revealed in Mises' (1949: 18) description of the two worlds or 'realms' that are known to the theorist, the theorist confronts both an 'external world' and an 'internal world' of the mind – associated with the formation of expectations and the acquisition of knowledge – observing each and relating one to the other.[7]

> Reason and experience show us two separate realms: the external world of physical, chemical, and psychological phenomena and the internal world of thought, feeling, valuation, and purposeful action. No bridge connects – as far as we can see today – these two spheres. Identical external events result in different human responses, and different external events produce sometimes the same human response. We do not know why.

The world is a system out there that consists of minds, with their associated activities and things. Making the world intelligible involves linking the observable phenomena (things) with the mental phenomena (plans, which also exist in the world) that give rise to them, and then drawing inferences about the system. The distinction between the external and internal worlds is an important aspect of the epistemology of Austrian economics which embraces the mind, and its associated 'doings', as objects. Ontologically, the internal world is private and subjective but it exists and, to the theorist, it is part of the world out there. Other things that happen in the world are known to depend on events in the internal world; so, for example, when knowledge – which belongs to people out there – changes, people do different things and prices change. In this interpretation of how the theorist 'understands', he represents a peculiar type of observer who has a particular way of understanding. It is important to clarify how the theorist 'sees' the world and the notion of understanding that is involved.

Even though some Austrians may not associate themselves with the *a priorism* of Mises' methodology, O'Sullivan (1987: 160) notes that *a priorism* of some sort is present in the work of 'all the Austrians', and *a priori* categories seem to be important for the process of 'observation'. These include the category of action itself, involving means and ends, as well as manifestations of the alert human mind, such as plans, expectations, and knowledge. Their *a priori* nature provides the means of 'understanding'. Watching people buy and sell shares or build a factory, and 'understanding' stock market activity or investment decisions, means 'seeing' knowledge and expectations at work. The individual is purposeful and chooses means to specific ends; that is human action. What he does depends on his 'stock' of knowledge or the expectations he holds. The *a priori* existence of knowledge and expectations – the internal world – is necessary to explain why particular actions are observed.

Based on this 'understanding' the theorist can pose questions about the relationships amongst individuals or, specifically, their plans. Are these compatible or incompatible? If what is observed is people competing, then the plans are incompatible. Are the expectations of different individuals convergent or divergent? If what is observed is speculative activity, then the expectations are divergent. In the light of these questions conclusions are drawn about the consequences of action for the state of the world. The actions will lead to an equilibrium or will induce other people, with divergent plans, to revise them.

The epistemology is that of the third-person perspective. The world is 'given', though it is not necessarily all directly observable. Some of what exists, the mental phenomena, are only known as *a priori* categories, known through introspection, but known to all. As Mäki's (1990) arguments suggest, there is a presumption that all the phenomena that economists seek to explain – such as money, prices, entrepreneurs, or pieces of machinery – have a real, unambiguous existence. Except for asserting that the categories of action are known *a priori*, Austrian economics does not ask how or what the theorist knows or observes. Four examples from Austrian theory serve to illustrate this.

Menger (1950: see ch. 5) treats prices in much as the same way as neoclassical theory does. Prices manifest the subjective values that people place on things that they exchange. Menger's object is to explain how prices are related to individuals' valuations. Both prices and values are things that exist in the world and the theorist's task is to show how they are linked. There is no recognition of either the theorist or the actor as an understander, interpreting prices or price changes. In Lachmann's (1978a) analysis of the 'capital structure', the theorist's object is to explain changes in the structure of capital, with reference to values, expectations, and plans. Changes in production plans affect the values of individual pieces of capital making some worthless because they no longer fit into an overall structure, but the existence of a structure, as something that is in the world, is taken for granted. The theorist is not interested in how people think about plant and equipment; whether the idea of the capital stock as a complete system is a meaningful one to the businessman making production or investment decisions, or to anyone else. In the case of the structure itself, the 'value orientation' which Max Weber ascribes to individuals' understanding of social phenomena is missing.

Similarly in Austrian theory money is a social institution, but there is no recognition that it may have meaning for people and that this meaning may change in the course of time. Money exists in terms of people's plans to

105

transact, without reference to their understanding of institutions and the confidence, or lack of it, that they have in institutions or in other people. Such understanding is, however, implied in a notion like Keynes' 'liquidity preference', revealing that Keynes' explanation of the effects of monetary policy has at its base an understanding of how individuals understand. Implicitly recognising the hermeneutic circle of understanding, liquidity preference suggests that a person's confidence, or 'state of mind', influences what she does. People do not just have expectations about the future. The confidence that they have shapes their assessment of prospects and of the desirability of holding different asset portfolios. Moreover understanding and confidence is intersubjective. People's outlook and decisions depend on their assessment of what others think, or of what they think others are likely to do.

The absence of *Verstehen* is also reflected in the Austrian notion of entrepreneurship. Entrepreneurship is a consequence of gaps that exist in the market out there because plans do not 'dovetail' (Kirzner 1973). Plans exist in the world and when these plans do not match there are gaps to be exploited. The entrepreneurs are individuals who are predisposed to find such gaps. These individuals are 'alert to price differentials' as things that can be found in the world. Contrasted with the hermeneutical view of the enterprising individual who built his business on his ideas about the requirements of shoppers in the neighbourhood, the Austrian entrepreneur identifies gaps that exist between different people's plans. A person, for example, is not a struggling, out-of-work actress, seeking some way of making a living, relying on her friends and other 'social connections' or contacts, and 'making' her own opportunities. Motives and social relationships are not a party to explanations of entrepreneurship; prices in the world out there tell the entrepreneur where opportunities exist. If we view these examples as illustrating how a typical Austrian theorist sees the world and what he knows, as far as this knowledge is concerned the Austrian scheme is not hermeneutical.

THE CONCEPTION OF THE INDIVIDUAL

This general characterisation of the epistemology and ontology of Austrian subjectivism is important as a backdrop to the next task of examining the other aspect of the double hermeneutic: the individual and her understanding. What is the concept of an individual? What role does she play in the scheme of things? How and what does she know? In order to deal with these matters it is necessary to examine separately the views of some of the foremost Austrian writers because in espousing different philosophies each treats the individual somewhat differently. I will deal with the ideas of Mises, Hayek, and Lachmann, with the object of identifying a general conception of the individual in Austrian theory. There seems to be sufficient common ground among the different writers to permit this and I will argue that the conception of the individual and her role in life is essentially the same in Austrian as in neoclassical economics.

Even though he acknowledges an intellectual debt to Menger, the foundation of Mises' methodology is his conviction that praxeology, the deductive science of human action, is *a priori* valid and its axioms are 'self-evident truths' (Mises 1978: 11–21). Mises' *a priorism* has made his methodology a subject of extensive debate and it probably has more detractors than supporters amongst economists and philosophers, though not necessarily amongst Austrian economists. Because I am concerned with the epistemological implications of Mises' methodology, I will not scrutinise the methodology but instead refer the reader to some of the more recent assessments of it.[8]

Mises' concept of action (1949: see especially 92–8) is similar to Weber's notion of economic action (M. Weber 1964: see especially 158–64) and probably owes much to the latter. However, Mises' analysis of action – choosing means to attain 'given' ends – will appear quite orthodox to economists. Individuals are not omniscient, they have to speculate, and they make mistakes, but otherwise they appear to be quite good, rational agents who would maximise if their essential condition permitted it. They choose in accordance with a subjective and changing scale of preferences which they have (Mises 1949: 94–5, 118) and their actions are geared to removing uneasiness (ibid.: 97, 120).[9] Substitute 'increasing utility' for 'removing uneasiness', and add the idea of the attainment of an equilibrium (a determinate outcome), and Mises' analysis bears a striking resemblance to the neoclassical theory of choice. It is important to acknowledge, though, that Austrians have repudiated the Paretian idea of a complete preference field (see Rothbard 1956).

In considering the role of equilibrium in relation to Mises' conception of human action, it might appear at first that equilibrium is of little significance. Mises does not postulate that individuals' activities are equilibriating and people are not in a position to optimise – which in his terms would mean removing the most uneasiness. Mises, however, holds that equilibrium is an indispensable notion when analysing action and he states (Mises 1949: 245) that

> [t]he only method of dealing with the problem of action is to conceive that action ultimately aims at bringing about a state of affairs in which there is no longer any action. .... Action thus tends toward a state of rest, absence of action.

Furthermore, in order to understand how an economy works, it is necessary to resort to the 'imaginary construction' of an 'evenly rotating economy' (which is essentially a stationary state, although Mises (1949: 251–2) objects to equating the two notions and of a 'final state of rest' (general equilibrium). The evenly rotating economy serves as an *argumentum a contrario* (ibid.: 251) in order to highlight the differences between the imaginary and real worlds;

while the final state of rest identifies the direction in which 'the market' would go if it were not perpetually disturbed. The market 'is always disquieted by a striving after a definite final state of rest' (ibid.: 246). For someone trying to explain human action, the assertion that a notion of general equilibrium assists the theorist is an odd one indeed. Paradoxically, Mises is saying that the theorist needs a conception of a scheme of things that is complete and, indeed, one that is in equilibrium, in order to understand the real, changing world out there.

Mises does not see himself as an equilibrium theorist for, according to him, the difference between orthodox, 'mathematical' (equilibrium) economics and 'logical', praxeological economics is this: the former postulates a determinate outcome and makes equilibrium its centrepiece; the latter is concerned with processes and treats equilibrium as makeshift (Mises 1949: 352–3). Mises regards the difference as significant because logical economics recognises the importance for explanations of human action of time and uncertainty, whereas mathematical economics does not. Yet in respect of the epistemological bases of the theories, there is not a lot to separate the mathematical and logical approaches as Mises conceives them. Logical economics still implies that the individual confronts a world out there, which reveals opportunities to him, but which he can never quite grasp in its entirety. Contrasted with neoclassical theory, either the individual is not 'given' complete knowledge or the world changes anyway, so there are always unexploited opportunities. And, because he never gets exactly what he wants and his uneasiness is never fully removed, there is always scope for action.[10] Tendencies towards equilibrium are never allowed to assert themselves in human conduct, but in order to explain human action the world has to be conceived transcendentally[11] as manifesting tendencies towards equilibrium.

This brief discussion of his position supports my contention that Mises does not embrace subjectivism as interpretative understanding of individuals' understanding. His 'language' is the epistemology and ontology of the third-person perspective. Individuals and their conduct are in the world. The individual (over here) forms judgements about the world (over there). The task of social science is to connect economic phenomena with individuals' judgements: to explain what happens in the world as a consequence of the fact that people form judgements and have expectations. The object is to explain the conditions under which action takes place, but not to understand, or to obtain insight into, action itself. The theorist observes the action taking place out there and, in order to explain it, has to superimpose on his observations various *a priori* categories as well as a conception of tendencies towards equilibrium.

Mises' 'subjectivism' rests on judgements and expectations. These are part of an ('internal') world that is separate from another physical world. Taking cognisance of the existence of judgements and expectations, the theorist recognises that the physical world out there means different things to different people. But he cannot establish why it means different things or what it means, because to do so would involve going beyond observation and *a priori* categories to an understanding of individuals' understanding. The upshot of this approach, as Lachmann (1982: 37) puts it, is that for Mises subjectivism really means 'no more than that different men pursue different ends' and Lachmann also notes that at times Mises' position borders on behaviourism (ibid.: 38). This is ironical because praxeology was supposed to serve as an alternative to the positivist methodology of science which behaviourism exemplifies, and because behaviourism is the epitome of an attempt to construct a modernist, non-subjectivist explanation of conduct. Yet the following quotation certainly bears out such a view and illustrates the enormous gap between Mises and the subjectivism of modern hermeneutics. Mises (1978: 37) states that 'valuing' is

> man's emotional reaction to the various states of his environment, both that of the external world and that of the physiological conditions of his own body. Man distinguishes between more and less desirable states. . . . He acts when he believes that action can result in substituting a more desirable state for a less desirable.

Does this approach to the concept of valuing and decision-making go beyond neoclassical theory? There is no hermeneutic, let alone a double hermeneutic, of social science. The theorist confronts a world, and his understanding of it is given *a priori*. Individuals are objects that possess certain properties, such as the ability to value. Endowing them with such characteristics does not alter, or disguise, an objectivist epistemology.

In common with the work of Mises, Hayek's work reflects the idea that individual conduct has to be studied against the backdrop of equilibrium. Indeed, the notion of equilibrium features even more prominently in Hayek's economic writings. Though he pioneered the analysis of epistemological issues in economics, Hayek (1948c) takes it for granted that an equilibrium framework is the proper context in which to pose questions about what individuals know and how they acquire knowledge. As this brief analysis shows, the demands of equilibrium severely constrain the scope of any epistemological enquiry.[12]

Milgate (1979) credits Hayek with having conceived the notion of inter-temporal equilibrium (see also Petri 1978). In his earlier writings Hayek held that the task of economics is to explain the unintended or 'undesigned' consequences of human conduct. His is a Walrasian conception of decen-tralised market activity exhibiting coherence, in the form of a co-ordinated equilibrium solution. Co-ordination emerges out of the myriad of independ-ent decisions made by individuals, where no such co-ordination was intended. One analysis of Hayek's economic writings (O'Driscoll 1977) presents his contribution under the title, *Economics as a Co-ordination Problem*. Rather than just wanting to show the logical possibility of equilibrium, Hayek's interest (e.g. 1948c, 1948f) is in showing how equilibrium is related to individuals' decisions or plans.

Although he refers to the subjective nature of social science (Hayek 1955a: 28, 29–30), as with Mises, Hayek's subjectivism has to be congruent with a conception of the economy as a series of equilibriating (and possibly disequilibriating) forces at work. As such Hayek's scheme complies with the epistemology of conventional Austrianism. Economists, unlike natural scientists, should attempt to take account of 'what men think and or do about [things] . . . [t]he views people hold about the external world' (Hayek 1955a: 23). Yet economists do not attempt to understand those views, nor do individuals themselves understand their 'worlds'. That different people have different views is pertinent to the analysis of conduct, but it is a given. For Hayek the important issue is that the market system produces coherence from these divergent views. The theorist's task is to explain how this happens.

In his 'Economics and Knowledge', Hayek (1948c) contributes to that task and it is significant that his explanation of the co-ordinating process rests upon a dual epistemology (see Addleson 1984a: 514–16). There is one world view for the theorist and another for the individuals whose decisions are the object of study. The theorist's is the characteristic third-person perspective. He can discern the equilibriating forces at work and knows about the whole scheme of things. Individuals on the other hand cannot grasp the entire picture. Each has a limited view but, in order to ensure that his plans succeed, is concerned to discover 'the facts of the situation' and to find out what the world out there is really like. A central question to Hayek is how and through what mechanisms does the individual's knowledge come to correspond with the facts of the world out there? This, more than any aspect of the analysis, identifies an objectivist epistemology and a third-person perspective.

Like most of his fellow Austrians, Hayek finds the Walrasian notion of equilibrium unsuitable as a cornerstone of economic theory, which is about individuals and their activities. While clearly not rejecting the concept of equilibrium *per se*, he regards Walrasian equilibrium as static and holds that an apposite notion of equilibrium is one that can be applied to the individual's plans. Hayek takes the view that any notion of equilibrium which involves different individuals with their own plans is problematic unless it can be shown how their plans become consistent. At the level of the individual, a notion of equilibrium is derived from an understanding of conduct. Individuals live in a changing world which, via the activities of other people and their access to resources, imposes constraints on each of them. In the light of this, in order to be able to carry out her plans, each person has to try to ensure that her different activities are compatible, that her plans are internally consistent and conform to the changing constraints imposed by conditions in the world. If she were to achieve this, her actions would be in equilibrium, and in order to try to make her plans internally consistent and compatible with the constraints she faces, she has to find out what the world is like.

Hayek warns that as observers of individual conduct, we need to recognise that only actions that are part of a single plan can be treated as equilibrium actions. This assertion indicates that he conceives of plans and also the observation of action in a particular way; that Hayek's epistemology and ontology reveal the observer as a third-person perspective, and that his conception of rational decision-making echoes Mises' idiosyncratic approach to human action. According to Mises, the postulate that people act rationally is true *a priori* (Mises 1949: 18–20). To be able to draw inferences about the rationality of action, based on observations of individuals' actions, all actions must be part of the same plan. If the actions are not part of the same plan, they may appear to the observer to be contradictory and to refute the rationality of action. This is because the goals of one plan, on one day, are not the same as those of another plan formulated on another day.

In analysing this argument, the crucial issues which reveal the epistemological and ontological underpinnings of both Hayek's and Mises' positions are the questions: how do we 'observe' action and what does it mean to say that all actions form part of a single plan? Actions are apparently things that exist out there in the world and the inference I draw is that both Hayek and Mises conceive of 'plans' as not unlike a set of Paretian indifference curves. The reason for this inference is that in juxtaposing the criticism that Walrasian equilibrium is static with the conditions that must be fulfilled in order to be able to judge whether an observed action is rational, what Hayek seems to imply is that Paretian curves are essentially suitable for describing plans and representing the 'choices' available on a particular day; however, in the light of changes taking place in the world, people confront different circumstances, so the curves change over time. Orthodox 'static' analysis fails to recognise that plans have a time dimension and that the individual's knowledge and actions change over time.

The statement that equilibrium actions must be part of the same plan also suggests that a plan is something that exists in the world like a set of curves or a blueprint indelibly created on paper. This interpretation is consistent with the way plans are conceived in Austrian economics. A realist conception of a plan with 'elements' and 'shape' is clearly identified in Lachmann's statement (1970: 31) that '[i]n social theory our main task is to explain observable social phenomena by reducing them to the individual plans (their elements, their shape and design) that typically give rise to them.'

Hayek's logic is impeccable. If equilibrium of the individual means that her actions are consistent and if those actions are planned, they must form part of a single plan. But the notion of planning that is compatible with this logic has nothing to do with how a person plans or with what a planner understands by planning. Hayek, and more generally the Austrians, conceive of plans as things that are complete systems, within which different 'actions' can be consistent. Each part of the plan has a counterpart in an action (another thing) out there. Thus every observation of an action – and it is not clear what this means unless actions are conceived as discrete objects – is the observation of a piece of plan being carried out.

Hayek's notion of equilibrium of the individual reflects the epistemology and ontology of the third-person perspective as much as any other notion of equilibrium. Equilibrium, even that of the individual, requires a transcendent conception of the scheme of things. An interest in equilibrium constructs means turning away from understanding (*Verstehen*) and from insight into planning and choice. My standpoint on this matter is quite bluntly that there is no role for a notion of equilibrium in a hermeneutic or subjectivist theory. If we are interested in explaining human conduct, we cannot go along with Lachmann (1986: 140–1) who argues that '[e]quilibrium has its legitimate uses' and that the notion of equilibrium is unambiguous when it refers to actions that are 'under the control of a single mind'.

As the final stage in my perusal of Austrian subjectivism I look to the 'radical subjectivism' of Lachmann – what he calls 'the subjectivism of the active mind', and find that this does not change the nature of Austrian subjectivism but extends its scope as Lachmann intends.[13] That extension involves incorporating the subjectivism of plans and expectations, in addition to knowledge, which he views as the mainstay of Austrian subjectivism. What does the subjectivism of plans and expectations mean in terms of the way these are conceived? In the following quotation (Lachmann 1970: 30), his reference to 'comprehensive surveys' echoes Hayek's ideas discussed above.

> One trait distinguishes all cultural phenomena from natural ones. When men act they carry in their minds an image of what they want to achieve. All human action can be regarded as the carrying out of projects that are designed to give effect to imagined ends. . . . To act at all, men have to make plans, comprehensive surveys of the means at their disposal and the ways in which they might be used, and let their actions be guided by them.

Plans, expectations, and knowledge are things that co-exist within the individual. Together with the actions in which each person can be observed to be engaged, the unobservable plans, knowledge, and expectations define the individual. Each individual acquires particular knowledge, forms particular expectations, and makes particular plans. Different individuals have different, and sometimes divergent, expectations. As the individual 'changes' – as she has new experiences of the world – so her knowledge and expectations change. The theorist has a duty to reflect the existence of knowledge, expectations, and plans in his scheme because they are an essential part of the individual and what she does. Just as the economist would fail in his duty to provide a satisfactory theory if he did not recognise and take account of things like prices, so he must also build in plans and (sometimes divergent) expectations. Plans and expectations are a part of the world, even though they cannot be seen, and they are the 'causes' of observed actions. The theorist understands that individuals have plans. It is this that makes the theory a subjectivist one, incorporating the Weberian notion of *Verstehen*.

However, in the conceptualisation of these attributes of the human mind and in the 'explanation' of human conduct – which involves relating the activities of individuals, their knowledge, and expectations, to an ongoing 'market process' – the epistemology is that of the third-person perspective. The world exists out there as a system that contains both equilibriating and disequilibriating forces. It consists of individuals who themselves experience a world 'around' them and respond to changes with new knowledge and revised expectations. The individuals have 'active minds' in that they translate ('interpret') what is going on around them and what will happen beyond them in time, but they do not themselves constitute their worlds through their understanding. Their responses to what is happening in the world are not always consistent, with the result that there are ongoing changes over time which are manifested in 'the market as an economic process' (Lachmann 1986). As a consequence of viewing the scheme of things as something that exists out there, this conception of the market process as a bounded course of affairs is as much a view of a complete system as any notion of general equilibrium. At an epistemological level, what separates the market process from general equilibrium is the question of what – rather than how – the theorist knows. The postulate of a market process involves an assertion that the theorist does not have knowledge that would enable him to isolate and to measure equilibriating and disequilibriating forces and, therefore, to tell which way the process is going at any time. Because the process is not determinate, the theorist may never be able to acquire the knowledge that he would need to establish either the nature or magnitude of equilibriating and disequilibriating forces.

In summarising these arguments I have certainly not done justice to the varied and extensive contributions of Mises, Hayek, and Lachmann, leading lights in the Austrian School. I have tried to show that within a somewhat ill-defined 'conventional' Austrianism the transcendent epistemology and ontology of the third-person perspective is dominant. In the work of these writers, both the theorist and the people who are the object of his enquiry see the world in much the same way as it is portrayed in mainstream economics. Depending on one's standpoint, the language of Austrian economics may be richer than neoclassical theory as a basis for describing conduct, but the language derives from the same conception of the scheme of things. Although the language of Austrian economics is less 'mechanicalist'[sic],[14] the two schemes offer similar types of explanations of human conduct and this is not a coincidence. The epistemology and ontology directs enquiry in the same way. Austrians generally eschew the idea that people are able to optimise; but in relation to neoclassical economics the reasons why people act are essentially the same, and they are guided by the same 'external' considerations. Explanations of individual conduct are sought in taking advantage of opportunities for profit or for attaining greater satisfaction, revealed in the relationships between prices or costs and revenues, out there. We have already seen that equilibrium features prominently in Austrian theory. Its presence there points to the incompatibility of Austrian (objective) subjectivism and the first-person perspective.

THE NEED TO MOVE ON

The form of subjectivism associated with conventional Austrian theory is problematical and has been supplanted by the subjectivism associated with the hermeneutical turn in science. At a time when positivism is in retreat, it is appropriate that the Austrians, who fought a spirited battle against it when positivism was at its height, should move on. I am sure there are Austrian scholars who accept this assessment and feel constrained by the methodology outlined in this chapter, although, no doubt, there are also those who would not share my enthusiasm for a theory based on interpretative understanding.

Though there are others, especially among the younger generation of Austrians, who fall into the former category, Lachmann's work certainly does. Even his earliest contributions are characterised by a desire to extend Austrian – and economic – theory and to forge links with economists and others outside the Austrian tradition. His discussion of 'subjectivism of interpretation' (Lachmann 1986: see ch. 3, especially 54–5) shows a commitment to a hermeneutical approach (see also Lachmann 1991). Indeed, a reformation of Austrian theory based on hermeneutics is under way, for Lavoie (1991b: 9) points out that there is already a small group who have broken with the standard Austrian methodology. They champion hermeneutics and 'advocate bold revisions to traditional Austrian economics'.

Much of the work associated with the Austrian revival in the past two decades in fact represents an attempt to break with orthodox, neoclassical theory and methodology. The difficulty, however, has been knowing where to go and how to get there, as is clear from discussions about how and why the emphasis on a market process changes the nature of economic theory. If, as is generally the case, the notion of a market process is constructed on the foundations of equilibrium and optimisation (a third-person perspective), the introduction of the concept of a market process *per se* does not change the nature of the theory. This is where the classification of methodological approaches as involving either first- or third-person perspectives and an understanding of their respective epistemologies and ontologies proves its worth by helping to provide direction to Austrian theorists.

In addition to showing that there is a methodological affinity between Austrian and neoclassical theory, which is much greater than first meets the eye, the identification of the two methodologies helps to establish why Austrians who are opposed to the methodology of mainstream economics may be dissatisfied with the objective-subjectivism distilled out of the work of Menger, Mises, Hayek, and others. The distinction between first- and third-person perspectives is also helpful as a pointer to where subjectivists ought to look in order to develop a genuine alternative to orthodox economic theory. My object in the next chapter is to consider the ramifications for Austrian economics, and for economics in general, of adopting a first-person perspective.

7

IMPLICATIONS OF
INTERPRETATIVE
UNDERSTANDING

TOWARDS A FIRST-PERSON PERSPECTIVE

Austrian subjectivism, reviewed in the previous chapter, is prefaced upon a Cartesian desire to show what the world is really like. It is characterised by an 'external world' that is independent of individuals and their experiences. There is one real world, though individuals' experiences of it may differ. Determinism, if not central, is at least an important motif in Austrian contributions which emphasise the significance of equilibrium in one way or another. Determinism means that the world out there can be grasped and represented in its entirety. Whether it is Hayek's (1948f) interest in the unintended consequences of conduct, or Mises (1949) referring to the need to explicate the conditions of an 'evenly rotating economy', or Kirzner (1973, 1985), analysing the implications of entrepreneurial activity or Lachmann reflecting upon the character of the market system (1986: see 'Appendix'), in each case, as with neoclassical equilibrium theory, the object of the enquiry is an entire scheme of things. Objective-subjectivism combined with determinism ensures that the theory cannot accommodate interpretation or understanding.

The first-person perspective, which engages understanding at both levels of the double hermeneutic, eschews an ontology of things that exist in the world. The individual is not some*thing* oriented towards a given world out there. Understanding something means making it part of one's being or of one's awareness. Understanding is personal, reflecting the understander's interests of the moment, and prejudiced, coloured by her interests and beliefs. The focus is thus the individual's world, which she constitutes through being conscious of things and doing things. The individual breathes meaning into her world which is co-extensive with her thoughts, changing as her interest, or perspective, changes. The first-person perspective also eschews an epistemology of 'completeness'. Meaning is temporal, tied to experience in the *durée*. From moment to moment the individual constitutes her understanding in terms of her interests and purposes and continually reconstitutes her understanding with her experience of, for example, people and their attitudes.

In addition to being personal, understanding does not entertain an ultimate goal, such as a state of rest, or removal of all felt want. Hence 'tendencies towards equilibrium' are extraneous to the first- person perspective as is the idea of an all-embracing 'state of the world'. To paraphrase Leitch (1988: 200), man is thrown into an endless interpretative existence; there is never closure. Equilibrium demands closure in the form of a complete scheme.

Having identified epistemological and ontological differences between Austrian and interpretative subjectivism, an answer to the question, 'How do we get from the objective-subjectivism of Austrian economics to interpretative understanding and the first-person perspective?' is now reasonably clear-cut. Embracing interpretative understanding requires adopting a different epistemology and ontology. The difference between Austrian objective-subjectivism and hermeneutics is not in what the theorist or individuals know (for example, what there is in the world or what the world out there is really like), but in *how* they know. A scheme based on interpretative understanding must begin with questions that conventional Austrian theory glosses over. How does the theorist, or an individual, 'observe' or understand? What does 'knowing' mean? Because, in a sense, everyone understands differently, the intersubjectivity of knowledge cannot be taken for granted. Understanding, though intersubjective, is not universal, but depends on the understanders and the extent to which they share a common basis of understanding and interpretation, and why their interests coincide. These are issues that have to be investigated. To what extent do individuals 'share' understanding? Why and how do they do so? What are the relationships between people and social groups who understand differently and what are the implications of their differences in outlook?

Aspects of some of these issues are considered in the second part of the book, in examining the nature of investment and location decisions. Dealing with the decisions of individuals in their capacities as managers of industrial undertakings provides an opportunity, for example, to examine the relationships between individuals in their business lives and to assess how these relationships influence their plans and decisions. In the main, however, the exploration of these questions is a long-term goal of a hermeneutically based social science and will have to await the efforts of scholars to formulate social theory from a first-person perspective.

My focus here is on the consequences, for economic theory and for Austrians, of pursuing a hermeneutical approach. At the end of Chapter 5, I discussed certain implications for social science of adopting the language of hermeneutical subjectivism, noting that the first-person perspective leads to the abandonment of *Wertfreiheit* in science and also of the possibility of grounding one's theory. I noted too that, happily, the notion of individualism undergoes a substantial change in the context of a hermeneutical scheme and the narrow individualism which characterises economic theory is replaced by an approach which deals with the individual in her intersubjectively constituted social life-world. In considering the consequences of adopting a methodology involving a first-person perspective, for convenience I will continue to use the conventional Austrian position as a basis of comparison, and to focus on four sets of issues that are especially relevant to that position. These issues and the implications of a first-person perspective, however, are of consequence to all economists. The ones with which I will deal are: the question of *Wertfreiheit*, a notion which Austrians – like most social scientists – endorse; the notion of equilibrium; individualism, which is a cornerstone of Austrian methodology; and the matter of prediction in economics, for there are Austrians who hold that economic theory should be capable of yielding some form of prediction.

RELINQUISHING *WERTFREIHEIT*

Wertfreiheit and interpretative understanding belong to two different conceptions of the scheme of things. Each is the product of a different epistemology and ontology. *Wertfreiheit* belongs to the positivist conception of science as observation and classification. It rests on the notion that the scientist must, and can, maintain an arm's-length relationship with his subject matter, so that he does not bring his own prejudices, values, and moral precepts to bear in observing phenomena and drawing inferences or conclusions about the relationships that he is investigating.

The rejection of a value-free theory, bound up with the question of grounding the theory, rests on twin assertions, each of which is found in the work of Gadamer. The first is the idea that the scholar or scientist does not arrive to undertake his theoretical investigations with a clean slate, but is 'thrown' into the world and, therefore, into his research. In addition, understanding – within the hermeneutic circle – is an open-ended process of interaction: a dialogue or conversation. The theorist is involved both as participant – who is influenced by it – and as creator of the conversation, and so are the people who interpret the work, supporters and critics alike. These people, on whom the propagation of scientific thought depends, are also thrown into the world.

Kirzner (1976c) offers a useful overview of the principle of *Wertfreiheit* and an appraisal and defence of its application to Austrian economics. He highlights the embodiment of the principle in Mises' definition of economics, a definition that has become the standard definition of the subject matter of economics, and is more commonly attributed to Robbins (1949). That definition is generally interpreted (note my emphasis), as 'the science which studies human behaviour as a relationship between [*given*] ends and [*given*] scarce means which have alternative uses' (Robbins 1949: 16). The spirit of the Robbins–Austrian definition is inexorably bound up with the adoption of a third-person perspective. Although Mises (1949: 92) argues that '[m]eans are not in the given universe; in this universe there exist only things', in the context of an economic theory constructed around Robbins' definition it is impractical to treat means and ends as anything other than things that simply exist in the world. In this definition, all matters that are of interest to the interpretative understander – why individuals choose to do certain things; how they make their choices; what exactly it means to choose ends or means – are ruled out. They are defined away partly because, in order to maintain his value-free standpoint, the economist should not be interested in the nature of the ends that people choose.

A flaw in the sort of defence of *Wertfreiheit* in economics that Kirzner offers is the failure to recognise that the hermeneutic circle applies as much to the readers, or people interpreting the work, as it does to the author or theorist himself. Gadamer argues that it is entirely misleading to suggest that the theorist should distance himself and his beliefs and values from his analysis because understanding is always prejudiced. Even the injunction to 'bracket out' beliefs and prejudices reflects a prejudice about what is a 'good' or 'appropriate' scientific method. But even if the theorist should try to do so, he would still face the problem of how the audience is going to interpret what he has to say. He can neither ensure nor insist on their understanding being value-free. Moreover it is the community of theorists together with their interpreters who contribute to the formulation and survival or demise of 'scientific knowledge'. The communities of people who 'do science' – Thomas Kuhn's 'invisible college' – are extensive and their relationships, both within and between these social groups which have a bearing on people's positions, are complex.

A work, constituted intersubjectively, is reinterpreted as the hermeneutical conversation among specialists and others leads to new insights and to different ways of understanding it. The passage of time, the *durée*, is important to how the meaning is constituted. Accepting the principle of a value-free science means either that there is only one real interpretation of any work or that different interpretations are attributable to factors (perhaps ones like neural pathways) which are known to be independent of the individual's beliefs and value-judgements.

Wertfreiheit is only compatible with misplaced efforts to view the world from a third-person perspective and, in maintaining this principle, the theorist is precluded from understanding. Relinquishing the principle broadens the scope of economic theory immeasurably. The radical suggestion of abandoning the principle of a value-free science leads one to investigate the sorts of issues to which I have already referred: how do people – including scientists – understand; and who shares a common basis of understanding? Although the need to do so may seem foreign to Austrians and to economists in general, in arguing that these are necessary tasks of economists and more generally of social scientists, I am in fact doing no more than reiterating Hayek's (1948c) entreatment to them to explain how individuals find out about the facts of the world. This is also the sort of question that Hahn (1973a) has posed and, as I suggested in Chapter 3, it is quintessentially hermeneutic. For the Hayek of 'Economics and Knowledge', as for Hahn, equilibrium is the natural domain of economists and their questions refer to gaining knowledge about the (real) world out there. From a first-person perspective the questions appear somewhat similar. What do individuals know about the world? What do they treat as facts? How do they agree on what constitutes 'the facts' of any situation? Although the epistemological and ontological connotations are entirely different, both equilibrium theorists and hermeneuticists seem to agree that these are questions that need to be asked.

REJECTING EQUILIBRIUM

Despite the appearance of various notions of equilibrium in the contributions of virtually all Austrian economists, throughout the history of the school their attitude to the relevance and the role of equilibrium has been one of ambivalence: some readily embrace the notion, others feel that equilibrium is not without its problems. General equilibrium is rejected by most Austrians, but equilibrium of the individual is seen to be important, and there is substantial, if tacit, agreement that market equilibrium – Marshallian partial equilibrium – is a useful notion. Lachmann explores the role of equilibrium in many of his contributions, but in a recent work (1986) conveys something of the dilemma confronting the theorist whose interest lies with interpretative understanding but who wishes to find a place for equilibrium in economic theory (see also Lachmann 1977b: 37–8). Lachmann holds that '[e]quilibrium of interaction between individuals, households and firms, i.e. between different *minds* is clearly a problematic notion'. He goes on to argue (1986: 141–2), however, that

> [e]quilibrium has its uses. For all that has . . . been said, it would be quite wrong to conclude from it that all use made of the notion of equilibrium outside the sphere of action of the individual must be illegitimate. Marshall's partial equilibrium concept is a striking counter-example . . .

Equilibrium is not relevant to the epistemology-ontology of the first-person perspective, so economists have to choose between equilibrium and understanding. Equilibrium designates a complete scheme, a self-contained system with clearly designated parts and well-defined interrelationships; a set of things that exist and can be known without interpretation or understanding. Whether that system constitutes an economy, or a market, or the plans of an individual, makes no difference. It is also immaterial whether the theory postulates an equilibrium outcome or a process where equilibriating forces are dislodged by their continual interaction with disequilibriating ones, or even 'pattern co-ordination' (O'Driscoll and Rizzo 1985: 85–8). The identification of particular forces as equilibriating and others as disequilibriating is still the third-person notion of a system of things that exists out there. Recent debate on the implications for economics of time and uncertainty produced the view that the state of the world is one of *dis*equilibrium, where tendencies towards equilibrium exist, but are continually thwarted by unexpected changes (see Rizzo 1979b). Because it persists with the idea of an all-embracing cosmology – a complete world or system – this reasoning is as much a product of a third-person perspective as any notion of equilibrium.

In arguing that an equilibrium scheme takes as 'given' the very things – such as the concept of the market – which a theory of interpretative understanding must explain, I am once again echoing a view expressed by Hayek (1948f: 93). How do individuals constitute 'the market'? What does the notion mean to them? How does one person's understanding of 'the competition' – of who is competing with whom – differ from that of another? What are the implications for the competitive strategies which each formulates? In response to the potential criticism that rejecting equilibrium amounts to 'throwing out the baby with the bath water' – which is Hahn's argument (Hahn 1973a, 1973b) – in the second part of this book, I want at least to indicate that economists have much to say without equilibrium but, because he is using a different language, the matters that interest the social scientist are very different. The idea that equilibrium is indispensable stems from the view that the only good economic theory is one that follows the canons of positive science, and that there is only one sort of 'explanation'.

A question that naturally arises, though, is whether some concept of co-ordination involving the activities of different people is not necessary in any social theory. Any theory that explains the activities of individuals must reflect the intersubjective, social nature of decision-making and conduct. In order for people to carry out their plans, is it not necessary for them to ensure that these plans are co-ordinated with the plans of others, just as conventional Austrian theory suggests?

In answering this question, bear in mind that the emphasis of Austrian theory, and the sorts of questions which Austrians as well as neoclassicists ask, falls on the consequences of 'given' interrelationships rather than on an understanding of what these interrelationships are and what they mean to the individuals themselves. The problem of 'interdependency' for the objective-subjectivist is the Hayekian and neoclassical one of whether, and how, co-ordination occurs and also whether different actions are, or become, compatible. As we now know, these questions are prefaced upon the epistemology-ontology of the third-person perspective, and only make sense if we treat the plans of individuals as concrete things in the world. Then we look upon different plans as forming a system and ask whether and how the different parts fit together. The emphasis of Austrian theory is exemplified by Kirzner's theory of entrepreneurship (1973, 1985) which gives prominence to the co-ordinating role of the entrepreneur.

The object of a hermeneutical approach, by contrast, is to understand the nature of the interrelationships and social interaction among people and how this bears upon their plans and the decisions that they take, as well as the successes or failures of their endeavours. This does not imply that success means integrating different plans, as if these were parts of a jigsaw puzzle, or that the criterion of failure is not being able to meet some objective, external optimum. Freed from the constraints of a 'systems view', which stipulates that plans form a system and deals with the conditions that are necessary to ensure that the system is fully integrated and complete, a hermeneutical approach enables social relationships to be examined more fully. In planning business activities, as in all facets of life, individuals require the co-operation, participation, involvement, and assistance of others. One of the important tasks of interpretative understanding is to explore how people understand and make use of institutional arrangements in order to get things done.

The specialised businesses and other institutions which organise, manage, and orchestrate the activities of different parties are legion. They range from auctioneers, banks, lawyers, and consultants of all kinds, to advertising and other elements of the marketing function, and even include 'business lunches'. Lobbyists exist in order to ensure that legislators and others take into account their clients' interests when it comes to formulating, amending, opposing, or approving legislation.

A function of middlemen in a distribution chain, or of various types of intermediaries such as brokers and agents, is to 'bring together' potential buyers and sellers or lenders and borrowers. The more successful they are at doing this, the more money the intermediaries will make. Often, as in the case of merchants, these enterprises fulfil other functions as well (see Hicks 1969). But whether one focuses on the role they play in holding reasonable stocks so that retailers are able to replenish their shelves at short notice, or holding a range of goods from different manufacturers, or in being able to purchase in bulk because they supply a large number of retailers, they facilitate the production and distribution activities that involve a number of people and businesses. A conceptual framework that enables the theorist to examine these institutions and arrangements is surely desirable, even though that framework does not include an equilibriating function.

Explaining where and how relationships have to be managed or co-ordinated depends, first, on recognising the mutual interests of individuals. Business activities involve mutual or common interests, even though some-times people's interests converge (in the cases of buyers and sellers) while at other times they diverge (as in the case of competitors).[1] The people who have a mutual interest in each other's business are not confined to the same industry or market as these are conventionally defined nor, in a world of 'global competition' and transnational corporations, even to the same country. Though economics is largely silent on these matters it is important to discover how relationships are established and are managed in order to maintain ongoing, successful partnerships or other contractual affiliations. In order to do so we have to understand the business relationships. Who are the customers, suppliers, subcontractors, partners, subsidiaries, or competitors? Who is 'the opposition'? Current as well as former business interests may influence plans, as might the individual's views about possible future relationships with particular parties. How important are these relationships to the individuals concerned and how central to their plans?

I have more to say later about the meaning of competition, and the failure of economists to provide a proper theory of competition which discloses the rivalry that is at the heart of competitive conduct. Since interpretative understanding is the foundation for getting to grips with all these issues, traditional economic theory has not been able to do so. That such considerations have been disregarded or overlooked because they have no place in a scheme with a third-person perspective, speaks of the poverty of equilibrium economics when it comes to explaining the business of business. The business of people in business is as much about building and maintaining social relationships as it is about making money. Sometimes the fostering of these relationships will be at the expense of more profits or a larger turnover. And of course they are not all financially based contractual relationships but involve social obligations in the widest sense, including kinship and authority. These are things about which economists ought to have something to say if they wish their claims regarding their ability to explain the market economy to be taken seriously. To do so it is necessary to understand how others understand. Far from regretting the need to jettison equilibrium, my view is that those who look to economics to explain social phenomena will come to regard the legacy of equilibrium theories as a minor one.

RECONSIDERING INDIVIDUALISM

These remarks take me directly to the next issue, that of individualism in economic theory. A first-person perspective is naturally a form of individualism but it is not the individualism of either mainstream or Austrian theories. As a cornerstone of Austrian theory, methodological individualism appears to have two sources. One is an affinity for eighteenth-century liberal, social and political philosophy found, for example, in the work of Hayek (see Hayek 1948c; Barry 1979: ch. 1). The other, the more strictly methodological one, is seen in Mises' praxeology (Mises 1978, 1949: Part 1 on the praxeological method), which has been influential in shaping modern Austrian economics. In arguing that methodological individualism is troublesome, it is the form of individualism associated with economic theory that is at issue, not the idea of 'seeing' things from the individual's perspective.

I have two principal objections to the Austrian conception of individualism, both of which stem from the particular conception of the praxeological method. Praxeological reasoning is only applicable to, and can only explain, action that has meaning in that it reflects individuals' purposes – their attempts to use means to attain particular ends. Economics, therefore, is

123

concerned only with 'rational' – i.e. conscious, deliberative – action. Other forms of behaviour based on habit or a response to stimulus, are not intelligible to the praxeologist. What is more, 'collective' entities like the firm or the government exist as intersubjectively constituted 'meaning structures', and what they do can be explained only in terms of the activities of individuals who work for, or belong to, them.[2]

The first problem with the Austrian conception of individualism is raised by Hodgson (1986: 215). His concern is that 'there is no adequate differentiation between actions which are carefully planned and others, such as habits'. The tenet that the limits of praxeology lie in the area of rational action means that economists can, or should, have nothing to say about people's habits, customs, conventions, or routines, and how and why these forms of conduct are important. Because there is no distinction between planned and habitual conduct (the latter is not part of economics), the misleading impression is gained that the individual plans meticulously all her activities and, what is more, does so in isolation. The resulting view of conduct suggests that individuals do try to maximise and are always guided by intricate and carefully laid plans which they have formulated in splendid isolation from the rest of humanity. Epistemologically, this is not unlike Pareto's approach discussed in Chapter 2.

The second problem with Austrian individualism, to which I alluded in the previous section, is that it is excessively 'atomistic' and fails to take cognisance of the social nature of action, including the importance of social institutions. Hayek (1948b) refers to the individualism of neoclassical theory – a conception of the individual-as-mechanism associated with Cartesian rationalism – as a 'false' individualism, and Hodgson (1986: 219, n. 1) notes that it deprives the individual of any sense of 'agency'. In spite of Hayek's contention (1948b: 6) that 'true individualism' is primarily a theory of society, an attempt to understand the forces which determine the social life of man' (emphasis omitted), there is little in Austrian economics which can be described as relating to the social life of man. Much like neoclassical theory, and for the same reasons, it abstracts from social relations.

A few examples serve to illustrate this. The Austrian theory of money – of how it evolved and its role (see Menger 1950: ch. 8) – as well as the analysis of speculative markets (Lachmann 1986: 10–11, 125–7) and of other social institutions, expressly recognises the interaction of individuals; but their interaction is indirect and anonymous[3] – through (rather than in) markets – and their impersonal 'relationships' are based only on perceived market opportunities and on price signals. The problems here can be attributed to a combination of methodological precepts and I need to discuss the whole matter at some length.

One contributor to the Austrian conception of the individual as an isolated figure is that both according to praxeology – where the explanation of economic phenomena is achieved by spinning out the implications of a few self-evident theorems – and in terms of what Hayek (1955c: 38–40) calls the 'compositive method' of the social sciences, nothing much matters beyond individuals' choices. As noted in Chapter 6, the compositive method has been associated with Austrian theory since Menger (see Hayek 1955a: especially 38–9). This method proclaims individuals' actions, or choices, as the basic building blocks of social phenomena, and explaining social phenomena means showing how actions, plans, expectations, and knowledge give rise to them (see Lachmann 1977c: 152–5 for an account of the compositive method). Another contributor is the pervasive influence of the implicit third-person perspective which rules out discussion of people's motives. Motives belong to the language of interpretative understanding and without them neither friendship, trust, filial duty, nor loyalty to the company, or to one's country, can form part of the explanation of conduct. It is motives such as these, however, which identify the social nature of conduct.

The individualism of Austrian economics is also a reaction to, and rejection of, collectivism. This is particularly true of Hayek's contribution (e.g. 1955a: 55–9), which is marked by a tireless crusade against collectivism and also against central planning which was seen as a corollary of collectivism (Hayek 1948a: chs 7, 8, 9). Mises (1936, 1972) is also a strong opponent of collectivism (see also Lavoie 1985). Apart from throwing individualism into sharp relief, the rejection of collectivism seems to have two sets of implications.

The first, which causes little trouble and is less relevant here, is a critique of macroeconomics based on the argument that the notion of an aggregate social welfare function, conceived as a basis for policy, makes no sense; one cannot produce an aggregate of individual's preferences (see Kirzner 1976c).[4] The second implication, however, is more problematic, for it seems to me that the rejection of collectivism is linked to the rejection of a role, and especially an explanatory role, for institutions. In Austrian economics, institutions exist as products, and often unintended products, of human action but they do not shape individuals' activities, or their decisions. As Hodgson (1986: 220) puts it, '[t]he inclusion of social structures and institutions in the moulding of human action, appearing both as partial explanations and things to be explained, would be inconsistent with work of methodological individualists such as Hayek'. Hodgson (1986: 222) goes on to say that 'the socio-economic and institutional environment has a significant effect on the kind of information we receive, our cognition of it, our preferences, and thereby much of our behaviour'.[5] Hermeneutics goes considerably beyond this critique of methodological individualism which still contains the idea of the individual as a passive recipient of information about the institutional environment.

For the modern hermeneuticist, understanding is always in terms of our relationships with other people – our colleagues, associates, friends, or immediate family – the people whose interests we have in mind because they have a bearing on the things we are doing at the time. Although the individual is rightly the protagonist of a subjectivist theory, the individual's 'world'

– the life-world as he understands it – is always constituted intersubjectively. I support the contention that collectives, or 'wholes', as Hayek sometimes refers to them, cannot have motives, and that an explanation of collectives' activities means understanding the motives, objectives, or activities, of the individuals who manage, or are associated with, the institutions. Yet Hayek's views are too narrow. We understand collectives and ascribe meaning to them, as social institutions and organisations, according them an existence and a role both of which are separate from the people who manage the institutions or who are associated with them as employees and members. More than this, the very identity of an individual – Wendy the marketing consultant, or John who belongs to a football club – is bound up with his or her affiliations with institutions and social organisations. We constitute identity, which signifies the individual's individuality, as a social phenomenon, and how we do so is partly a matter of understanding institutions as entities with their own identities, not just as collections of individuals.

Institutions are constituted through social interaction as part of the life-world and their very purpose and existence is established in the context of social interaction. The individual's understanding of institutions is interpretative understanding and individuals attribute characteristics to institutions – such as stability, reliability, honesty, inefficiency, corruption – which are not associated with specific people in the institution. How they view the institutions has a bearing on what they do, or do not do. It is because institutions might be expected to survive beyond the life-span of the average individual, and have an existence that is independent of their present owners, managers, or employees, that their managers can undertake long-term investments 'by' the institutions. Similarly, it is her trust in the banking system, probably learned from others, rather than in the directors of a particular financial institution (who in any event are probably not even known to her), that encourages the individual depositor to place her life savings on long-term deposit.[6] Or it is a belief in the inefficiency of the postal service that leads her to insure her parcel or to send an important document by special courier, rather than entrusting it to the vagaries of the mail?

Mises argues that 'social entities have real existence' and 'determine the course of human events' (Mises 1949: 42). At one level his view is that it is desirable to highlight the importance of institutions in an analysis of human action: 'Methodological individualism, far from contesting the significance of such social wholes, considers it as one of its main tasks to describe and to analyse their becoming and disappearing, their changing structures, and their operation.' This statement, however, makes no reference to integrating an analysis of institutions into an explanation of action; and his epistemology makes such a goal irrelevant. On a number of occasions Lachmann has made a case for providing a role for social institutions in Austrian theory (see the second essay 'On Institutions' in Lachmann 1970; also Lachmann 1986, 1991). Austrian individualism confounds this object,[7] at least in a manner that would enable the analysis of institutions to be integrated into an explanation of individuals' understanding and thus into the explanation of individual conduct. Understanding people's activities, what they are doing and why, involves an understanding of institutions – from religious to business – and of how individuals themselves understand the social nature of institutions.

In different circumstances the individual is a churchgoer and a businesswoman, though sometimes the two activities, and her motives regarding these, are not entirely separate. As economists we are particularly concerned with the individual and her 'business environment', but the analysis of decision-making in later chapters shows that the individual's 'business' decisions cannot, and should not, be divorced from her other social relationships. By taking cognisance of individuals' understanding of institutions and their changing consensus at different times about whether to rely upon particular institutional arrangements, the theorist concerned with problems of social interaction adds an important dimension to economic theory. For, as Hodgson argues (1986: 222),

> if we were to believe that action was entirely the result of constrained but otherwise free individual choices, then we may be quickly drawn to the conclusion that a great number of people are stupid, irrational, evil, or insane. In contrast the institutionalist view leads us to emphasise that much of this behaviour is moulded by factors outside the individual concerned, and it leads to a greater respect for that person in his or her predicament, as well as a more fruitful and less simplistic explanation of those actions themselves.

Hodgson's view is not compatible with interpretative understanding, for to him the institutions exist 'outside' the individual and, presumably, are things in the world to which an individual responds. What is important, nevertheless, is the spirit of his argument, and his recognition of the role of institutions in shaping conduct is entirely congruent with the individualism of a first-person perspective.

ABANDONING PREDICTION

Some economists set great store by the ability to build models that have predictive capabilities. Prediction, as the term is used conventionally to mean forecasts based on the discovery of underlying regularities within a system, is not part of the language of interpretative understanding, for prediction is prefaced upon knowledge of the behaviour of the system as a whole. The questions of whether a hermeneutical view of science supports prediction as a goal of science, and of what prediction means in the context of a philosophy which holds that the quest for certitude is misplaced, raise a number of thorny issues. My interest is in the issue of prediction in the social sciences. Although these more general concerns are pertinent, there is a sense in which they are distinguished from my main concern with an appropriate language for social theory by the matter of whether a modernist methodology of orthodox economics has ever been compatible with prediction as understood in terms of the deductive-nomological model.

In arguing that economists who embrace interpretative subjectivism have to give up the possibility of predicting, it could be held that they have never possessed that ability anyway, and that their efforts at predicting were 'illegitimate' (see Coddington 1972; Katouzian 1980: ch. 3; McCloskey 1983; O'Sullivan 1987). Economists' predictions are not based on being able to claim that certain phenomena fall under particular covering laws, but rely on discovering regularities in historical data explained, perhaps, by models that postulate theoretical relationships among variables. If the data 'fit' the relationship postulated by the model, the forecasts are based on statistical relationships found to exist in historical data (see Caldwell 1982: 22).

Although they hold a variety of positions on prediction in economics – some rejecting outright the possibility of prediction and others arguing that a form of prediction is possible – Austrian economists have emphasised explanation, as opposed to prediction, as the main purpose of economic theory.[8] There is certainly no presumption amongst Austrian theorists of the symmetry of explanation and prediction, which is a feature of the 'covering law' notion of explanation associated with positivism (see Chapter 2 above).

Caldwell (1982: 122–3) provides an overview of a general Austrian position on what he identifies as the two most important uses of the term 'prediction' in economics: forecasting and the testing of hypotheses. He explains that Austrians reject forecasts as 'nothing more than summaries (with projections) of certain recent statistical regularities' (ibid.: 122), and he sets out the reasons why Austrians reject both the need for, and ability of, economists to test hypotheses. Caldwell is probably correct in his identification of the general Austrian position on prediction, though there are differences of opinion on the matter and this is where the lack of a well defined, commonly held Austrian methodology and theory is revealed.

Characteristically, Mises (1949: 117) adopts the position that praxeological knowledge – the *a priori* categories of understanding – 'makes it possible to predict with apodictic certainty the outcome of various modes of action'. 'Prediction' here applies purely to logically necessary relationships which Mises treats as the basis of knowledge. When it comes to practical 'quantitative matters', all that individuals have to go on is understanding, which is the 'only appropriate method of dealing with the uncertainty of future conditions' (ibid.: 118). Lachmann, too, reveals extreme scepticism about the possibilities of prediction (1950, 1986: 140), taking the view – one that he shares with Shackle – that the task of economics is fundamentally 'backward-looking' (Lachmann 1986: 32, 1977e: 89). Its purpose is to explain what has happened rather than to predict what will happen. At the other end of the spectrum of views, Hayek has argued for some time (see Hayek 1967b, 1975) that economics permits 'pattern predictions' of 'the kinds of structures that could be formed from the available kinds of elements' (Hayek 1975: 8). Pattern prediction finds support from O'Driscoll and Rizzo (1985: 27) who introduce 'favourable relevance' as an analogous, but not identical, notion.

A taxonomy of different positions on the issue of prediction is less important than the epistemologies which those positions reflect. Though their reasons for doing so differ, possibly because they subscribe to different philosophies, all these authors repudiate a modernist methodology. Even when they support some form of prediction, this support does not stem from a belief that economics has been able to identify empirical regularities or underlying mechanisms at work, or that it is the task of economics to do so. It is one thing to establish a general position on what Austrians reject, but another to discern a middle ground in terms of what they accept. It would be useful to be able to say that these positions represent differences between those who are more, and those who are less, hermeneutically inclined. On a general reading of their work, one would put Hayek and Lachmann into the former position but, on the question of prediction, the two are fairly far apart.

I believe that Austrian theorists are not particularly concerned with prediction; nor do they wish to be. Somehow, since they espouse a view that the world is not determinate, prediction should not really be part of the picture, but the epistemology associated with the conceptual scheme that they employ always directs thought back to questions about prediction. They take the view that the world should be conceptualised as a whole, and as one that exists out there. From this effectively third-person perspective it is difficult to conceive of 'knowing' without a counterpart 'predicting'.

The unpredictability of human nature is one of a number of reasons put forward by C. Taylor (1977: 128–9) to deny the possibility of 'exact prediction' for the science of interpretation. His position is certainly worth considering, as he argues that 'only if past and future can be brought under the same conceptual net can one understand the states of the latter as some function of states of the former, and hence predict' (ibid.: 129).[9] An implication of this argument is that because the individual is transformed in the *durée* (she understands differently with the passage of time), past and future can never be brought under the same conceptual net.

A first-person perspective, however, both provides a different, compelling argument as to why prediction is precluded as a goal of social theory, and gets to the heart of the epistemology and ontology. From a first-person perspective there is no sense of a general scheme of things against which to formulate predictions. Predictions are based on the idea that as the world works in a particular way, and in order to predict it is necessary to know the system and the relationships which operate within that system. Because that is not the way in which the individual constitutes her social world, it is not in the nature of a first-person perspective to ask questions that presuppose a 'systems view'. The type of explanation that is sought through interpretative understanding is different, and the issue of prediction is simply irrelevant. Prediction, like equilibrium, demands a determinate, closed, or complete system and is prefaced upon a third-person perspective.

Early on I described the third-person and first-person perspectives as incommensurable. The question of prediction and understanding (or, rather, prediction *versus* understanding) illuminates the divide and indicates the two mutually exclusive options which are available to the theorist. By formulating his scheme, as neoclassical theorists do, from a third-person perspective, he might be able to discern those regularities that are a basis for prediction. The cautionary note is sounded because, considering the arguments above, the nature of his subject matter probably precludes prediction. From this standpoint, however, he will not be able to explain individual conduct, which is beyond his epistemological 'grasp'. The alternative, first-person perspective, is congruent with interpretation, but precludes prediction.

To the subjectivist, understanding is all and is all there is to understand. Nothing is beyond the open-ended hermeneutic circle of interpretation, an ongoing dialogue of finding out. Prediction defeats understanding and the hermeneutic circle, for it implies that the scheme of things out there can be known in its entirety. We need to know all the possible options in order to be able to predict which will occur. Lachmann (1986: 152) is correct in saying that 'prediction ... would mean that the growth of knowledge has, at least for the time being, reached its end'.

We can, and must, conjecture about what may happen. We are conscious of the future because the things in which we are engaged today, or now, point us ahead in the *durée*, in the same way that they may take us back in time, thinking about activities and social relationships in the past. In thinking about how someone may respond to a suggestion or request, it is natural to rely on an understanding of that individual's character or habits. The expectation that a person will do something is a belief that he will act 'according to type'. It is a conjecture, which does not replace unknowledge with knowledge. I hope, or think, that he will do something, but I am still uncertain. It is entirely appropriate to fall back on one's experience of other people. If they act according to expectation, well and good; but judgements about what others will do are not 'predictions' as the term is used in positive science. A conjecture is not a belief that I have discovered in his conduct some underlying mechanism or law. If the person does not do what I expect, I may be surprised or disappointed and will certainly put it down to experience, but I will not seek to revise a theory of behaviour, as if my surprise were evidence of the violation of some important rule or postulate concerning the inter-relationships and the workings of a system.

Individuals are creatures of habit. I will argue in due course that activities are not necessarily guided by well-thought-out plans. Knowing and understanding people's habits can stand us in good stead, enabling us to embark on courses of action with high hopes, and even a 'fair degree of certainty', that we are doing the right thing. None of this, however, presupposes a third-person epistemology, the knowledge of a complete system and its mechanisms that would make it possible to predict. A third-person epistemology, quite literally, is beyond understanding. Throughout history people have been able to make decisions without being able to predict. Decisions are based on experience and judgement, not on knowledge of what will happen. They take account of what we think might happen, and do not involve the certainty that only specific things can happen. This is the only basis we have for making decisions, and fortunately it seems to work quite well.

Part 2

8

MODELS OF INDUSTRIAL LOCATION

DECISIONS AND LOCATION THEORY

In this, the 'applied' half of the book, my object is to explore how the two languages of social theory 'explain' decision-making. The exercise will help not only to identify the limitations of the third-person perspective but also, and more importantly, to illustrate what it means to adopt a first-person perspective. While my interest lies in business decisions of all types, I will use the issue of industrial location and location decisions as the vehicle for pursuing both objectives. The theory of industrial location is unfashionable amongst economists today, although it is less so with industrial geographers who have continued to develop a 'behavioural' theory of location, and it is as well to explain my reasons for using it.

One important reason is that in the economic theory of location we find a well-developed theory, about decision-making, which is built upon neo-classical foundations. Orthodox theorists sometimes adopt the position that neoclassical equilibrium theory is not about practical problems (see, for example, Arrow and Hahn 1971: vi–viii). In the case of location theory, however, such arguments carry little weight, since the formulators are certainly of the opinion both that their frameworks are serviceable and that their analyses have a direct bearing on the problem of finding suitable locations for industrial undertakings. In order to show why determinate optimisation models are wholly unsuited to the task of explaining decision-making it is necessary to have an example of such a model to dissect. The economic theory of location meets this need.

The theory of location was developed in two phases. There is the orthodox, neoclassical, or traditional theory and a later behavioural approach, associated with industrial geography. By examining both types of location models, the object of this chapter is to reveal how the location theorist 'sees' the world and specifies the location problem. After reviewing and assessing these models and the conventional ideas about decision-making in the next three chapters, I then examine the 'location problem' from a manager's point of view. Far from reviving or revising the theory of location, this analysis, which

135

highlights the intersubjective, social nature of business life, and hence of business decisions, shows that the location problem evaporates when treated in the context of how the manager understands.

I hope to show that the conventional and well-ingrained idea that managers have to find optimal locations, which they do by analysing spatial economic data, is a fiction created by applying the modernist language of economic theory to business problems. The ontology of positivism identifies the world as a set of things out there, so locations, too, are things in the world. As a rational agent, the decision-maker must search through the entire set of locations, separating the good ones from bad ones until he finds the best. That is one story told by one language of theory. The issues look completely different, however, when we adopt a language that recognises that individuals constitute business problems, and enables us to explore how they do so. Then, not only do we find that optimising has no bearing on the way in which managers understand, but also that the question of location may be irrelevant to their investment decisions. In rejecting a commonly held view that optimisation theories are an appropriate way of explaining people's business activities, I will also deny that these models have a value beyond their role as conundrums or logical puzzles.

NEOCLASSICAL LOCATION THEORY

Models of the location of economic activity had begun to be developed in the first half of the last century. At that time it was the location of primary producers, especially agricultural production, that attracted the attention of writers like von Thünen [1825] (1875), who was interested in formulating a scientific theory of rent and in analysing the spatial configuration of production. In the light of both the growth of manufacturing that occurred in European countries in the second half of the last century and the social changes that accompanied this growth, it was problems associated with the location of manufacturing activity that later directed the economic theory of location. Neoclassical economics, as the orthodox theory of the time, provided the methodology and conceptual tools for developing location theory. Alfred Weber [1909] (1929) presented the first systematic treatment of problems of industrial location in a contribution that marks the foundation of modern neoclassical location theory. This theory is carried on through the work of many authors, notably Palander (1935), Lösch [1939] (1954), Hoover [1948] (1968), Greenhut (1956), Isard (1956), and D.M. Smith (1971).[1]

Lloyd and Dicken (1972: 1–2) identify the particular problems with which location theory is concerned. They note (ibid.: 3) that although economists generally steer clear of spatial considerations, there has, nevertheless, been an ongoing interest in 'the construction of *general principles* and *theories* that explain the operation of the economic system in space. . . . The central concern is the search for the explanation of general locational tendencies and patterns.' D.M. Smith (1971: 5) specifically alludes to the role of decisions in location theory.

> As the participants in a specific industry make their location decisions, selecting some places for development in preference to others, an areal distribution pattern emerges. . . . Attempting to understand industrial location patterns, and the individual decisions embodied in them, constitutes the fundamental task of the field of inquiry which is [industrial location analysis].

Interest in the spatial arrangement of economic activity thus boils down to a concern with two interrelated sets of problems: the issue of the spatial patterns of industrial or economic activity, and also what causes, or determines, the pattern. The quotation also confirms that the theory is an attempt to understand location decisions. I will deny unequivocally that it is capable of doing so.

Neoclassical location theory explains the location problem in the following way. Location decisions are made by firms. The firm is generally viewed as small because, like the archetypal perfectly competitive firm, it is treated as a price-and-demand-taker (see Stafford 1972: 189). The firm is also generally regarded as a single-plant operation, although it is difficult to understand why. A firm is merely some thing that exists through its 'pure economic relationships' with other firms, suppliers of resources, and customers. There is no sense of the firm as an organisation, as a manager or other employee would understand it, with implications of control and authority based on individuals' relationships with one another and their understanding of others' requirements, as well as of their own competencies and authority. D.M. Smith (1979: 38) identifies the 'traditional focus' of location models as a factory 'viewed in isolation from other elements of the space economy and society, except for sources of inputs and destinations of outputs. Its individual economic success (usually the level of profitability) is the sole operative criterion of performance.'

Choosing a location means optimising, subject to constraints. The difference between location models and other neoclassical models of 'choice' is that, in the former, the optimisation problem has a 'spatial' dimension. The spatial element means that the things that are relevant to the firm's 'decision' – resources, other firms, customers – are arranged, or scattered, on a grid in Euclidean space. The firm has to 'choose' the optimal position in space in the light of prescribed assumptions. The factors which constrain the firm's 'choices' differ from model to model.

Some models focus on the role of resources, including transport costs, in the location decision, while ignoring the locating firm's relationships with other firms. Other models may highlight the importance to the location decision of the market for the firm's product. Sometimes firms 'act' to minimise costs, so their proximity to suppliers and raw materials is important, while revenues are treated as constant in space. In other models, which focus on the demand for the firm's output, the object of the exercise is to maximise revenue, so the distance from the market is crucial and it is assumed that costs are spatially constant. Some location models also represent the firm's spatial relationships with other economic units in a predefined market area on the basis that its location in relation to customers, as well as to other firms, has a bearing on the firm's sales and revenue.

The core of location theory is the standard 'axiomatic economics' identified in Chapter 2. The agent is a rational optimiser who must 'choose', but in the face of a different set of constraints to those faced by agents in non-location models. There are 'tastes', 'resources', and 'technology' in the optimiser's world, but now wherever he 'goes' in Euclidean space, either costs or revenues, or both, are different. The values of all variables have a 'spatial' dimension – varying with their distances from points within a system of axes.

From one generation of theorists to the next, this approach to location problems leads to the evolution of more complex models, reflected in the concepts and types of relationships that the theorists seek to explain. The early models tend to focus on the importance for location of one set of factors, say costs of production. Later generations of writers, such as Lösch (1954) and Greenhut (1956, 1963), combine different approaches, which means that in their models firms have a number of objectives which determine location. In some cases, for example those of Weber (1929) and Palander (1935), the authors make use of a partial equilibrium framework and deal with the location of a firm or with one market area. In others, a general equilibrium approach is adopted, where the interrelationships and the problems and patterns of location embrace the whole economic system.

Neoclassical location-decision models are capable of almost infinite variety by the addition, removal, or changing of assumptions. The differences between models are to be found, for example, in assumptions about the nature of competition, whether perfect or imperfect; the nature of the demand curve facing the firm; whether the markets are points or areas; the 'shape' of the market area; and the spatial distribution of resources.[2] A feature of the models, however, is the similarity of the core of each contribution: the way in which the location problems are conceived and the concepts and relationships such as cost and revenue functions used to analyse the problems. These clearly identify their theoretical foundations as neoclassical and link all the contributions to a single paradigm.

It is interesting that most writers, going back to the earliest years of location theory, criticise the models of their predecessors for their lack of realism, or for over-simplification, which is seen to limit their usefulness in one way or another (see, for example, D. M. Smith 1979: 38–45). My position is that, in terms of explaining what a location decision is and how it is made, adding or changing assumptions makes no difference. The nature of the location decision, as an optimisation problem that involves selecting points in Euc-

138

lidean space, is determined by the methodology of neoclassical location theory. The epistemology and ontology of orthodox theory defines the nature of the location problem and this is what prevents the theory from providing insight into decisions. Massey is one of the few scholars to have recognised that the epistemological underpinnings of location theory are important and circumscribe its usefulness. In what amounts to a far-reaching critique of the orthodox theory,[3] she argues (Massey 1979: 58) that

> the most important problems of industrial-location theory exist at an epistemological level. . . . [T]he theory as a whole lies firmly within one major, overall 'paradigm'. None of the changes in direction in the historical evolution of industrial location theory has produced a re-formulation at such a basic level.

MAPS AND LOCATION PROBLEMS

In order to examine the implications of these foundations I will begin by considering how the location problem is cast. Suppose that you are able to conceive of the world as a whole, that your conception is of a world that exists out there somewhere, and that you find it appropriate to represent important aspects of this world as a 'map' on a rectilinear system of axes in two-dimensional Euclidean space. Included in your knowledge-as-map image is knowledge about various pieces or elements of the world that exist out there. One set of information is labelled 'industrial activity' and includes elements like firms, resources, and markets. You also represent the different bits of information in this set as points on a grid. Each piece of knowledge that you have about the world out there – each firm and each of its suppliers, as well as its sources of labour and its market – has its place and is identified by its co-ordinates in Euclidean space.

Viewing the world as you do, if you were asked to describe how to locate a firm, your response would surely be in terms of finding a suitable place on the map. Asked if there are any other issues pertaining to manufacturing activity that interest you, the question of how and why industries 'fall' on the map – the spatial pattern – may also arouse your curiosity. But these two issues appear to exhaust the types of questions about location that one could ask someone who conceives of the world as a map.

In the neoclassical theory of location, the location problems take precisely this form. They do so because that is how the language of neoclassical theory requires the theorist to represent the location decision-maker's knowledge and world view. Neoclassical theorists endowed location decision-makers with 'spatial knowledge' of the values of economic variables at different points on a map. They did so, apparently, because they believed that making location decisions required this sort of knowledge. In the location models, market areas and other economic variables are things in the world, and are what people 'see' when they make 'decisions'. Because the agent's knowledge corresponds with observable things in the world, it is practical to represent 'spatial knowledge' on a map, as patterns or points in Euclidean space. This formulation is entirely consonant with the epistemology and ontology of neoclassical theory. Both the world-as-map image and the allied conception of the location problem, that of finding an optimal point in space, exemplify the third-person perspective.

I attribute both the belief that location decision-makers require spatial knowledge, and the form that the knowledge of agents takes, to a combination of two sets of factors. One is the geographer's traditional interest in maps. The other is the paradigm of positive science that has shaped the geography of enterprise, no less than other disciplines. A modernist methodology represents knowledge as something that exists out there, and in keeping with the ontology of positivism it has a physical quality. Because 'space' – as distance and area – is a part of the world out there which the theorist can observe, the agent, too, can have spatial knowledge. What more logical way to represent the spatial elements of the world than as a map? Positivism and maps have had a powerful influence on geography up to the present day.

In order to illustrate the influence of positivism, I refer to a well-known contribution to the study of people's 'images of places'. According to Gould and White (1974: 46),

> [h]ow men perceive their physical and social environment is a crucial question for the contemporary human geographer. It is also important for the way it directs the geographer's attention to other areas of the human sciences in which environmental questions are rapidly emerging.

To explain perception, these authors look to behavioural psychology, with its objectivist epistemology and ontology. The metaphors that they use to describe perception crop up again in this chapter in the analysis of the framework used by industrial geographers to explain location decisions. Their description runs in terms of information from the environment (out there) that 'impinges' on the individual, whose mind 'filters' the information. In this description of perception, the theorist has no interpretative understanding (*Verstehen*) of human conduct and the individuals themselves do not interpret and understand. The individual, as well as his 'mind', is a thing that exists in the world out there, perception being determined by how the mind records events which are also things in the world that exist outside the mind.[4]

Looking at the influence of maps on geographers' views of space, Forer (1978: 233) identifies the map concept of space as 'absolute space *par excellence*: static, independent of the objects within it and unrelated to the processes occurring about it'. Arguing (ibid.: 231) that among geographers 'the fundamental definition of space has received scant attention', he adds that 'many usages of space in geography are inspired by a static absolutist viewpoint. Absolute space is exemplified in our infatuation with maps and isotropic plains' (ibid.: 233).[5] The map concept is completely compatible with the 'static absolutist' viewpoint, the third-person perspective, which characterises neoclassical theory.

The map metaphor of spatial knowledge is in fact an apt metaphor for the third-person perspective. It is also misleading if we interpret it to mean – as neoclassical theorists would have us do – that someone who has a map image of the world also has complete 'spatial knowledge' regarding distances and areas, and could usefully apply this knowledge to find an optimal location. In rebutting neoclassical location theory, there are two notions that need to be challenged. One is the idea that map-knowledge of the world is a sufficient basis for optimising in space. This is dealt with immediately below. The other, the theme of later chapters (see especially Chapters 12 and 13), is the view that the locator of a factory needs, and uses, this type of spatial knowledge.

For the positivist, who has to sustain the illusion that the theorist (as well as the agents of social science) possesses a third-person perspective, maps are seductive. They seem to depict complete systems both in the sense of what is constant and unchanging and what exists on its own, independently of a knower. A map appears to capture the essence of a whole world out there, an idea that is central to a determinate scheme.[6] The surface of a map is continuous and, speaking metaphorically, the observer can travel back and forth over, or 'through', the entire scheme. In this way, all points on the map, all elements of it, appear to be simultaneously present. No point takes priority over any other one because there is no recognition of an observer's interest or his spatio-temporal horizon in the *durée*. It also appears to be possible to compare all points in respect of some criterion, such as their distance from one particular point, in order to find out which point is optimal. The relative values of those variables that are functions of their positions in space can be compared at every point.

As a metaphor for complete certainty, the map image of spatial knowledge appears to offer a representation of all possible spatial interrelationships. Location theory postulates that this is the sort of knowledge that the locator of a business requires and assumes that the possessor of the knowledge is capable of calculating an optimal set of interrelationships. Where will he find the data that he needs? The answer is on a map; a map image of the world would seem to be the perfect tool for anyone who has to optimise 'in space'. In fact the map image is such an important metaphor for determinism that neoclassical theory employs map analogues to represent all choices, not just 'spatial' ones. So it is not just geography which lends itself to the use of this image of knowledge. The formulation of the location problem in economics merely mirrors the formulation of all decision problems in neoclassical theory.

The ontology of the third-person perspective encourages mainstream economists to illustrate 'decision-making' in graphic form and agents' 'knowledge' of the options that are available for choice is typically represented as points on a plane. For the positivist, decisions involve picking out things that exist in the world. The complete set of things available for choice is translated into a 'map', a diagram describing a rectilinear system of axes in two- and sometimes three-dimensional space, where all options and data germane to the problem of choice are visible as points in Euclidean space. This convention applies to all optimisation problems or all aspects of 'choice', from the decisions of consumers that involve finding the optimal combination of goods to purchase, to the selection of optimal production techniques involving different combinations of inputs.

The 'choices' that exist in the world are translated into indifference curves, isoquants, or – in location theory where 'space' matters – isodapanes, lines of equal cost or expense (see Alfred Weber 1929: 102–4 and Figure 8.1 below).[7] The optimising agent responds to observable changes in prices by finding new points on his preference map, each of which corresponds with a set of resources, or goods, or production quantities in the world itself, which he would then have.

In some formulations of the optimisation problem the values of variables are 'dated'; they are given time subscripts to identify the 'period' to which they belong. Location models add a 'spatial' dimension to the variables, but all the models embody the same epistemology and ontology. The use of a map to depict the options available for choice in location theory actually represents the concurrent application of the geographer's conception of spatial relations and the neoclassicist's metaphor for 'knowledge'. By picking the preferred point on a map which shows the values of variables at different points, the locator establishes the economic optimum and also identifies the best 'spatial' place on which to put the factory (the optimal physical location).

Forer's remark (1978: 233), addressed to geographers, is just as applicable to economists who have been seduced by a particular methodology into accepting the metaphor of the map as a suitable representation of decision-making: 'Faced by the seductive utility of Euclidean space we have allowed an interest in maps to become an obsession.' Much of this half of the book is devoted to establishing how the third-person perspective and the map-image of the scope of choice is thoroughly misleading. It disregards the interests and understanding of the knower at both levels of the double hermeneutic. In location theory, as with other variants of this formulation of 'decision-making', it is assumed that everything is in the world, and therefore in the map, and is accessible and means the same to everyone. No consideration is given to the map-user's understanding and what the map means to her in the context of her understanding.

From a hermeneutical standpoint the agent constitutes her world. The world and knowledge does not exist out there, in some ready-made form, waiting to be mapped in two-dimensional space. For the same reason, the map-user does not, and cannot, treat a map as an image of the world capable of yielding up the knowledge she requires in order to make decisions. Just as she interprets a work of art, so the individual constitutes her understanding of a map by 'interacting' with it. What a map means depends on the individual's interests. A visitor to a city, who wants to get to the airport, probably requires a different sort of map of the same area to someone who lives there and wants to locate a particular address. Even if they had the same map they would read it differently. The person who knows the city and uses the map frequently, understands the map differently in the course of time and takes certain things for granted, ignoring details and perhaps whole parts of the map which, however, help the visitor to get her bearings.

Unlike the neoclassical theorist as positivist 'observer', a map-maker does not take the user's understanding for granted. Presuppositions and conventions used in drawing a map regarding scale, projection, and the date of publication are articulated in order to guide the user. The reason being that different people, not familiar with the conventions, might misinterpret the map, or might not be able to make any sense of it. By the time the user needs it, the map may have become outdated in that changes that have occurred since it was devised make it unreliable or perhaps even useless.

Producing a map is just as much a matter of interpretative understanding as reading one. The features that a map conveys are those that one or more people have selected and decided should appear. Maps are based on social conventions, which are not necessarily universal and which can and do change over time. Compare a map drawn by an eighteenth-century explorer with a modern one. Both incorporate not just the 'objective knowledge' of the people who drew them, but their ideas, as a product of the social milieu of each, of what users ('readers') would expect to find. Where the early explorer had no knowledge of what he was supposed to depict, he would conjecture about what he would expect to find – 'here be dragons'. In part any map is conjecture, but conjecture influenced by social circumstances, by beliefs, the nature of scientific analysis, and the quality of the measuring instruments that are available. Like a work of art, a book, or any human activity, a map is the product of two sets of interpretations or 'understandings' – those of its creator (the map-maker) and the reader.

It is one thing to argue that individuals interpret maps, that interpretation is a process of understanding in the hermeneutic circle, and that the possession of a map does not mean that the individual is directed to an optimal state of affairs – as if this were something that existed unambiguously in a world which the map reproduces in whole. As far as location theory is concerned, an additional and in some ways more practical question that remains is whether – allowing for her need to interpret it – the locator of a business could *benefit* from having a map. Are the sorts of things that matter to her, as a 'location decision-maker', spatial ones, concerning distances or areas, so that they could be represented on a map? Is this the type of knowledge that she needs, or is the map metaphor of the choice of location a complete misrepresentation of what location decision-making is about? If so, what is a location decision?

These are hermeneutical questions about how the individual understands, and they cannot be answered by neoclassical theory. What is certain is that the third-person perspective absolutely subverts our understanding of what it is to make a location decision. Schütz (1943: 131–2) describes how different individuals, including an 'expert' brought up in the city, a stranger to it, and a cartographer, understand a city. He paints a stark contrast between a first-person perspective and the ontology associated with the map image of spatial knowledge. Referring to the expert, Schütz says (ibid.: 131) that he

> will find his way in its streets by following the habits he has acquired in his daily occupations. He may not have a consistent conception of the organisation of the city, and, if he uses the underground railway to his office, a large part of the city may remain unknown to him. . . . [The] . . . centre will usually be his home, and it may be sufficient for him to know that he will find nearby an underground line or a bus leading to certain other points. . . . He can, therefore, say that he knows his town, and, though this knowledge is of a very incoherent kind, it is sufficient for all his practical needs.

Notice that Schütz makes no reference to spatial relations, but emphasises the subjective nature of understanding. The centre is merely the area from which in the expert's experience everything happens. The city is 'defined' by his own interests and lifestyle, and his understanding of institutions is important in his daily life. Knowing where to catch a bus is more important than having a map or specific information of the route from one place to another. Placing these ideas in a hermeneutical context, the individual's city does not exist out there. What he knows, and how he knows it is what he makes of it. The 'structure', or the way he thinks about it (which need not have spatial connotations), reflects his interests, habits, work and family relationships, and many other things. Schütz also highlights the incoherent and inconsistent nature of knowledge compared with the comprehensive and well-structured world view associated with the epistemology of the third-person perspective (compare Aangeenbrug 1968; Barr *et al.* 1980; Gould and White 1974; Huff 1960).

So, in re-examining the location of industry, as I do in later chapters, it is necessary to question the entire narrative of the economics of location, starting with the idea that individuals possess and use a map image when they make location decisions. I will show how a first-person perspective, which identifies the knower as constituting her understanding, fashions our view of decision-making, and will compare this explanation with the narrative of orthodox location theory. The issue that I now want to consider concerns the appeal of neoclassical location theory. Even industrial geographers, who are generally critical of it, have not entirely dispensed with neoclassical location theory. The question is: where does its attraction lie? An answer not only helps us to understand why these sorts of models continue to be used, but also provides an insight into the thinking that has influenced the formulation of the behavioural approach of industrial geographers, which is supposed to be a more realistic framework for analysing industrial location.

THE ATTRACTION OF ORTHODOX THEORY

In the first instance the attraction of neoclassical location theory is a reflection of the dominance of neoclassical economics and through this of the pervasive hold that modernism has had on the methodology of the social sciences. With regard to the particular problems of industrial location, two considerations underpin the appeal of mainstream theory. One concerns positive attributes of the theory itself. The other involves the conviction that alternatives to neoclassical economics either appear to be completely out of reach or are too problematic to warrant further effort in their development.

A typical assessment of the contribution of neoclassical theory but also of its limitations, seen from the perspective of industrial geography, is that of Lloyd and Dicken (1972: 136).

> In effect, we have been looking at the behaviour of a very special kind of human being, one who is generally known as *Economic Man*. For many purposes he is an extremely useful individual. Economists have built highly sophisticated economic models around him and, similarly, we have been able to describe how the spatial form of the economic system would appear if the individuals ... were to behave perfectly rationally.

It is claimed that despite simplifying and unrealistic assumptions, scholars, including geographers, cannot do without the type of framework that neoclassical location theory provides. Adams (1970) explains why economic man is an 'extremely useful individual'. Reviewing a two-volume work by Pred (1967, 1969), Adams (1970: 260) demonstrates the geographer's commitment to the neoclassical framework and, more importantly, provides an indication of why that attachment exists.

> Pred finds the present body of geographic location theory unsatisfactory because it is based for the most part on two sets of unrealistic simplifying assumptions, namely economic man and static equilibrium. However, the use of simplifying assumptions such as these is standard practice in the social sciences and must remain so.
>
> It must be recognised that one cannot deal with the total complexity of reality all at once. ... One is guilty of oversimplification if one forces more weight on the conclusions than the assumptions will permit them

to bear. It is oversimplification that deserves to be attacked – not economic man and static equilibrium. Their limitations are well known but they continue to be used because they provide useful insights and because most attempts so far to make economic man more human and dynamic have become hopelessly bogged down in the complexities of reality.

I take these as representative views. In order to answer the question regarding what 'useful insights' the theory has provided, it is actually necessary to understand what Adams means when he says that alternative approaches have become 'bogged down in complexities'.

Like the notion of 'realism' discussed in Chapter 1, 'excessive complexity' is not in itself an appropriate criterion for rejecting one approach or theory in favour of another. 'Modelling man' is a complex exercise and, if the object is to construct useful theories in order to understand human conduct, it may be impossible to avoid these complexities. The theories of sciences like genetics and astrophysics are so complex that the layman cannot understand them, but this does not make them unsuitable or provide grounds for rejecting them. Behind Adams's sentiments, and also supporting the appeal of neo-classical location theory, is an unarticulated view about the type of complexity that is acceptable and about the criteria that make a good theory.

Both of the preceding quotations point to the desirability of a simple and elegant theory or an aesthetically acceptable framework. One of the virtues of natural science, in the often-cited example of classical mechanics, is that it 'fits together' flawlessly and a few universal laws explain the phenomena. The relationships make up a self-contained system and apply to the entire system and the theory is robust, yielding predictions which can be tested and which stand up to testing. Positivism endorses all these as criteria that comprise a good theory and this is what is meant by 'simplicity' when social scientists are called upon to avoid getting bogged down in complexities. Theories that neither offer precise solutions nor permit propositions to be rigorously tested against the evidence are best avoided. So, if neoclassical or a deterministic theory is abandoned, what would be left?

Viewed in terms of its ability to reproduce the scheme of things as elegant, two-dimensional, spatial models (the appeal of determinism), the orthodox theory of location is an aesthetically pleasing conceptual framework. This is especially apparent in the maps of isodapanes which originated with Alfred Weber, and in the symmetry of the location patterns derived by Lösch. Both are reproduced here as Figures 8.1 and 8.2, to illustrate the aesthetic of location models. The appeal of these models also lies in their apparent coherence and analytical rigour (the appeal of modernism). Preferences for locations are converted into well-defined topographical relations, and the essential symmetry produced by 'pure' locational forces is revealed. There is none of the 'fuzziness', 'imprecision', or 'complexity' that one usually associates with human conduct, and scholars who pursue this paradigm are not bogged down in metaphysical arguments. The models supposedly disclose the highly structured and logical design that is behind the manifestly uncoordinated activities of businesses. Presumably this is the way orthodox economists like to think of an 'invisible hand' at work. The problem, however, is that the models do not reveal anything about location decision-making. Webber (1972: 8) states that location theory is 'a theory of location patterns, not of individual decisions', but it is not even a theory of *location* patterns, just abstract relationships. Because the third-person perspective is misleading in terms of how people understand location matters, it also fails to explain location patterns such as the geographic spread of firms.

When it comes to understanding why people like particular theories, aesthetics, which is quintessentially prejudiced, certainly plays a role. Positivism lauds the role of mathematics in scientific explanation and makes a virtue of 'neat patterns', but it precludes consideration of the consequences of using a language which lends itself to this particular aesthetic. It appears

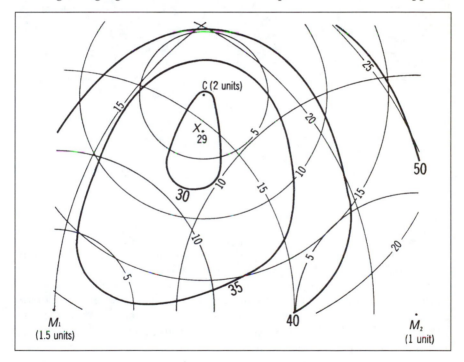

Figure 8.1: The Weberian location problem with isodapanes. 'Lines of equal transport cost (isodapanes) are constructed around [two material sources] M_1 and M_2 and the consumption centre, C. The costs of moving, M_1, M_2, and the final product are summed for each location to derive lines of equal transport cost from which the minimum cost location, X, may be found.
Source: Webber (1972). Reprinted by permission of MIT Press. Copyright © 1972 by M.J. Webber.

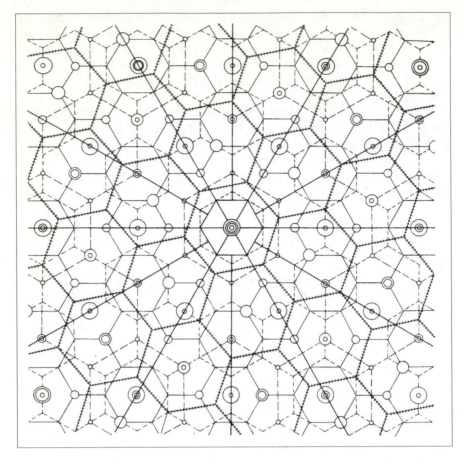

Figure 8.2: The theoretical arrangement of market centres and market areas according to Lösch.
Source: Lloyd and Dicken (1972: 24). Reprinted by permission of HarperCollins Publishers, Inc. Copyright © 1972 by Peter E. Lloyd and Peter Dicken.

to me that neat patterns are all that sustain neoclassical optimisation models, and we surely require more of our theories than this. The ability of a theory to satisfy our intellectual curiosity, or to help us to understand, and to do so in a way that we find persuasive, is at least as important. Neoclassical theory, as illustrated by industrial location models, fails to do this.

THE BEHAVIOURIAL APPROACH

The evolution of the neoclassical line of location theory probably ended in the late 1960s, possibly with the work of D.M. Smith, which is still based on a conventional framework. At that time, geographers, dissatisfied with neoclassical location theory, began to develop new models of location decision-making under the umbrella of 'industrial geography'. The theory of decision-making adopted for this purpose was developed in the field of behavioural psychology, so I will also use the term 'behavioural' location theory to identify this approach.

Industrial geographers have attempted to redress shortcomings of the orthodox theory of location and to formulate a 'more realistic' approach to location decision-making. A substantial body of literature now exists around a number of basic themes.[8] Advocates of the behavioural approach differ in their assessment of the value of neoclassical location theory. Carr (1983: 391–2) explains that various behavioural writers 'rejected Weber's traditional position as the theoretical basis of industrial geography' (ibid.: 392). On the other hand, there are those who regard aspects of the earlier theories as useful to industrial geographers. Carr concludes that 'although industrial geographers deposed Weberian theory . . . the theory was not rejected totally, but limited to certain topics where its application was considered justified' (ibid.: 392).

To many of its advocates, the behavioural approach is supposed to extend orthodox theory by relaxing some of the restrictions imposed by 'unrealistic assumptions', and by including considerations beyond purely economic relationships (see Hamilton 1974b: 4–5). The lack of an explicit theoretical framework for industrial geography, however, is a theme echoed in a number of evaluations of this literature (see, for example, Carr 1983: 386; Hamilton 1974b: 3; Harrison *et al.* 1979: 337; Hayter and Watts 1983: 173).

In surveying this literature, I will deal only with the definition of the scope of the theory and its explanation of location decisions. The questions that I want to answer are: how does the behavioural approach of industrial geography extend the scope of neoclassical location theory, and does it remedy the methodological shortcomings of the latter? In order to answer the last question, I will examine the methodology of the behavioural approach.

According to Downs (1970: 68), this approach

> replaces the black box concept of man by a 'white box'. Thus more realistic assumptions about the nature of man, drawn largely from other social sciences, are employed, and mean that the basic schema for analysis is no longer environment/spatial behaviour, but environment/ man/spatial behaviour. Man therefore becomes an intervening variable, and in this behavioural formulation is a significant, if not crucial variable.

He adds (ibid.: 69) that these more realistic assumptions are 'more . . . adequate expressions of man's nature'.

In making man a 'crucial variable', the behavioural approach focuses on the decision processes in organisations, drawing on models of decision-making and industrial organisation in social psychology (Katz and Kahn 1966) and the work of Simon (1952, 1957, 1959, 1960); that of March and Simon (1958) on organisations; and Cyert and March (1963), McNee (1960a, 1972), and Wolpert (1964) on the firm and decision-making. Figure 8.3 illustrates the matter that is at the heart of this approach. It is a model of the policy and decision-making structure of a large organisation out of which location decisions emerge.[9] These diagrams are described (Townroe 1969: 16) as treating 'the question of the choice of location for industrial investment as essentially a process of decision-making under the stimuli of factors internal and external to the . . . firm' (I have omitted one of Townroe's original four diagrams. The figure is meant simply to illustrate the type of model that characterises the behavioural approach).

This model treats decisions as occurring within a self-contained, policy-making system which exists in the firm and links the firm with its environment. Decision-making is a lengthy iterative process, with individuals at different levels investigating a myriad of different factors to ascertain the nature of problems caused by the impact on the firm of events in the environment. Decision-making is analogous to following a flow-chart of the company's operations. The flow-chart identifies the types of decisions that have to be taken about each of the operations and the model proposes that location decisions may eventually emerge out of this system. As decision-makers evaluate and review different parts of it, they may classify a problem as one of location. 'Pressures' emerge for a change in space and these may, after further consideration and another set of iterations involving consideration of the firm's overall management policy, lead to 'pressure' to find a new site.

Industrial geographers do not attempt to answer the question of what constitutes a location decision. This type of decision is a response to particular types of pressures that impinge on the firm, and the structure of decision-making determines the nature of the response. The interest of industrial geographers, and the location problem with which they are concerned, is in how 'pressures', either from inside the company or outside in the 'environment', produce responses through the decision structure which may or may not result in a new location being selected. Information, which exists out there in the world, is received as 'signals' which, when processed, may give rise to pressures to change the firm's space. The decision structure traces the organisation's response as part of a system to such pressures, and the theorist's interest is in how the system 'fits together' to reveal the operation of the decision structure. The enterprise is an optimising entity, but it does so within a particular structure which determines what types of responses are appropriate, and it is subject to various constraints such as those imposed by existing relationships or 'linkages' with other firms. These factors limit the range of possible solutions which the system can produce.

Mechanical analogies are a feature of the theories of cognition and perception that were developed in the 1950s and 1960s under the umbrella of

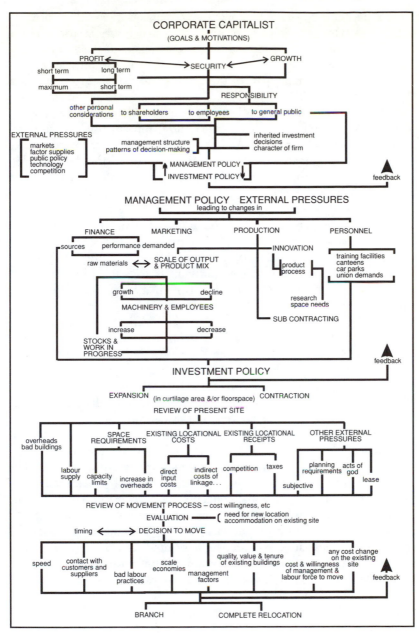

Figure 8.3: The behavioural approach to the process of decision-making and the choice of location. Adapted from Townroe (1969, 1971).

Source: Adapted from three diagrams by P.M. Townroe (1971) – The Development and Environment of Management Policy, Pressures for Change in Space and The Pressures for a New Site. Copyright © 1971 by Centre for Urban and Regional Studies, The University of Birmingham.

behavioural psychology and which, like most branches of social science, fell victim to some extent to the form of positivism which was in vogue at the time. Decision-making is conceived of in a mechanistic way. Feedback processes, 'filters' and 'channels' of information, 'stores' of knowledge, and 'searches' for information are part of the language of that theory (see Lloyd and Dicken 1972: ch. 8). The 'real world' is transformed into an 'image' which the individual or firm has. The following quotation from Katz and Kahn (1966) in Dicken (1971: 428), 'explaining' how information is acquired, typifies the discourse of behavioural decision theory. 'Systems can react only to those information signals to which they are attuned . . . [they] . . . develop their own mechanisms for blocking out certain types of alien influence and for transforming what is received into a series of code categories'.

In neoclassical theory, agents have a comprehensive set of preferences which determine their 'choices'. The behavioural approach gives them social and economic characteristics to which 'perception and preference are functionally related' (Downs 1970: 69), and perceptions determine behaviour. Like the agents of neoclassical theory, individuals are guided by a desire to 'obtain the "best" location in terms of optimum management satisfaction compatible with public policy. [Although t]his location is . . . not necessarily the economic optimum derived by [neoclassical] location theory' (Townroe 1969: 16). The problems which individuals confront exist in the world out there. The theorist has no understanding and to him individuals are things in the world, except that now they have 'minds' which enable them to process information that is transmitted and received from the world out there. The epistemology and ontology of the behavioural approach is still that of a third-person perspective and an understanding of how decision-makers understand the 'problem of location' is just as much beyond the behavioural approach as it is beyond neoclassical theory. The behavioural approach merely adds a set of concepts to the list of 'givens' that pertains to neoclassical models. The system is influenced not just by individuals or firms, but by their interaction with an environment. So additional concepts are needed to account for the interaction. These are the decision-making structures of organisations, the information or signals that individuals receive, and the procedures for decoding signals, i.e. what goes on in people's 'minds'.

Like the models of neoclassical economics, the behavioural approach also professes to describe a complete system, but a system which is centred around a decision-making mechanism. In behavioural location theory, the system consists of the company's decision-making procedures, the environment within which it operates, and the interaction between the procedures and the environment. Explaining location decision-making in an industrial organisation means describing the interrelationships among the firm's structure, its place in the environment, and its decisions. The internal procedures of the enterprise are deemed to be important, says Steed (1971: 324), because '[f]rom the viewpoint of the enterprise, the identification of its relevant environment is a function of two general variables: first, the internal resources and procedures or operations of the enterprise; and second, the qualities of the management team.' It is the 'relevant environment' that influences why, how, and where, the firm locates.

In neoclassical theory, the reason that firms have – if one can call it that – for choosing a location is to minimise costs or to maximise profits. This has nothing to do either with the firm's operations or with its management's motives. The 'reason' for choosing a location is to be found in the objective circumstances regarding costs and revenues that exist out there in the world. By contrast, behavioural location theory recognises that location problems arise from the firm's activities and that location decisions have to be integrated with those activities. In fact, industrial geographers postulate that they are made in the context of the firm's investment decisions (see, for example, North 1974: 213–14), an approach which I follow in later chapters. The problem is that the third-person perspective does not permit us to appreciate the nexus between activities, the identification of problems, and decisions that are taken. In order to do so, it is necessary to understand how individuals understand.

Compared with the epistemology of neoclassical theory, that of the behavioural approach is puzzling. In neoclassical economics the third-person perspective is applied consistently in defining both the theorist's and the agents' 'knowledge' of the world. Agents know about what exists out there – other agents' preferences, technology, and profit opportunities – through prices. There is one world, but because different agents have different preferences they are predisposed to respond differently to price signals. The behavioural approach, however, postulates that the theorist's 'understanding' is fundamentally different from that of decision-makers. The theorist knows of the complete scheme of things, whereas the decision-makers have only a partial view. Only part of what really exists in the world gets through the 'filter' that is the human mind.[10] The theorist, therefore, has two types of knowledge. First, there is the knowledge of the 'objective environment' (Lloyd and Dicken 1972: 138) – the world 'out there' in its entirety. Second, he also knows of the individual's 'filtered' knowledge of *part* of the objective environment.[11] Why and how the theorist should know more than any individual, who only knows her 'perceived' environment, is a question which is neither posed nor answered. This dualism of knowledge makes the epistemological foundation of the behavioural approach even more problematic than that of neoclassical theory and, putting all my other criticisms aside, refutes the claim of industrial geographers to construct a more realistic theory of location decisions.

A further problem related to the third-person perspective, which lays bare an entire decision-making structure but fails to reflect the interests of the individuals making the decisions, is that there is no way of establishing how and why particular factors do, or do not, play a role in the decisions that are made.[12] The model builders caution that the elements in a decision structure are not equally important, and that in particular cases some elements are immaterial, but there is no means of explaining how or why some are likely to be more important than others. Without an understanding of decision-makers' interests and their social relationships, one can only say that in a particular case these proved to be the important ones.[13]

Although the behavioural models are no better than the neoclassical ones at helping us to understand what a location decision is and how it comes to be taken, it is instructive to see how industrial geographers actually describe location decisions, and then to compare their descriptions with these formal models. A number of writers describe the decisions as being taken within the context of the individual's 'horizons', based on her experience, interests and objectives (see, for example, McDermott and Taylor 1976; North 1977); but the formal models nowhere reflect the significance of the individual's interests. In this vein, Carr (1983) reproaches industrial geographers for failing to recognise the individual's perspective and horizons (i.e. that the 'location problem' reflects the individual's own interests). He argues (ibid.: 389) that researchers misunderstood the purpose of the profit maximisation construct in neoclassical theory. As a result, they attempted

> to 'prove' satisficing behaviour when the idea of proving it or profit maximization are both meaningless. One of the aims of these satisficing studies was to provide evidence against the idea that an industrialist would consider every possible location to find the proper profit-maximizing location – an unrealistic belief for a school of thought arguing realism!

The canons of modernism compel the theorist who is modelling decision-making to produce a highly formalised conception of how things work. Writers who simply wish to describe location decisions, however, are under no such obligation. No one has justified the discrepancy between the descriptions of decision-making and the models. Is it that the formalism of the models is supposed to circumvent the 'complexity' of location decisions? Unfortunately, because it makes no reference to how individuals understand the 'location problem', this formal language also proves to be an in-surmountable obstacle to our understanding of that problem. In the next chapter, treating location theory as a narrative in order to establish what it reveals about decision-making, I elaborate on the incongruities between the way we understand decision-making, and how formal economic models represent it.

9

LOCATION THEORY
AS A NARRATIVE

'Uncertainty', so often completely forgotten, or regarded as a 'trim-ming', by economists, is something that it would be disastrous not to introduce into administrative theory at the outset. If money revenue is the businessman's sole aim, cost, as well as revenue, is always some-body's uncertain, fallible estimate or projection of future prices and is a 'function' of that particular person's mind. If the first approximation allows us to forget this, it becomes a 'vicious abstraction'.

(Thirlby 1973: 206)

INVESTIGATING THE NARRATIVE OF THEORY

I have indicated my dissatisfaction with the approaches to the location problem of both the behavioural and neoclassical theories of location. There is a sense that the accounts of how firms find a suitable location that are to be found in these theories, both of which entail a third-person perspective, are wrong. I propose to clarify this by investigating how the theories explain location decision-making. The basis for doing so, for establishing the criteria against which the theories will be assessed and for determining where the explanations are unsatisfactory, is our understand-ing of decision-making. As social beings, who make decisions and spend both our business and family lives with other people who do so, we have first-hand experience or understanding of what decision-making is about. By treating location theory as a narrative and examining that narrative, I will ask whether the story accords with our understanding, or how it deviates from our comprehension of how decisions are made.

In order to treat economic theory and specifically location theory as a narrative, it is necessary to articulate what is left implicit in the formulation of the theory. With the exposition of location theory in Chapter 8 as the starting point, the object now is to highlight aspects of the two approaches to location that provide insight into what a discourse, conducted within the parameters of a positivist methodology, reveals about the world and, ultimately, about decision-making. The picture

155

which emerges should also serve as a foil against which to compare a subsequent analysis of decision-making based on interpretative understanding and a first-person perspective.

For various reasons it is appropriate to approach this task circumspectly. At the outset it is probably wise to defend the legitimacy of this task. Am I attempting to wring out of economic theory more than it is intended to yield? Economic theory is not normally viewed as a narrative. In its older, traditional guise, science investigates, explains by discovering relationships, and predicts. Theories are the tools for pursuing these tasks and it is not their purpose to tell a story. So there may be social scientists who balk at the idea that theory should be treated as a narrative, but it is a view of theory embedded in a post-modernist, hermeneutical conception of science. The rationale for this view is that theories – the languages of science – are one of the means by which social and other scientists conduct a discourse.[1] The theories themselves reveal how scientists understand and describe phenomena. Even where the double hermeneutic is only implicit in descriptions of agents' behaviour, the social sciences also contain an account of how the individuals, whose conduct is under scrutiny see, or 'relate to', the world. Thus, theories are not neutral languages for classifying phenomena, but are the basis of discourse in scientific communities. It is important to ascertain the nature of that discourse and to establish what it reveals both about the communities' views about science and about how they understand and explain – how they 'see' the world.

A second reason to be cautious when wanting to treat location theory as a narrative about decision-making, is the potential criticism that it is inaccurate to ascribe to these models the task of explaining decision-making. I may be trying to find content that is not meant to be there. Some economists would hold that axiomatic neoclassical theory is not meant to explain or to describe people's conduct, but I have argued that this cannot be said of location theory. Location theorists assert that they are interested in 'real life' problems. Whether their formal language actually enables them to engage these problems, however, is a different matter.

These issues notwithstanding, the question of whether it is legitimate to look to location theory for an explanation of decision-making is also somewhat clouded by the consideration that there are important differences in the neoclassical and behavioural conceptions of the location problem. As the two sets of figures in Chapter 8 reveal, the theorists are interested in different sets of issues and it is important to be aware of these differences. In keeping with the spirit of neoclassical equilibrium theory, the problematic of traditional location theory is that of constrained optimisation. A locator has to optimise by assessing the values of economic variables which are a function of their position in Euclidean space. Optimising means selecting the right place on a map. The theory does not question or investigate the goal of selecting an optimal point in space. It is taken for granted that this is what a rational agent does when confronted with what is self-evidently a 'spatial economic problem'. The object of the theory is to 'explain' what constitutes an optimal spatial position for a firm to occupy, and so the key ingredient of these models is the specification of values of the relevant economic variables and how these vary in two-dimensional space.

The behavioural approach, by contrast, shifts the focus to the decision process in an attempt to model the way in which large firms behave. Here it is simply taken for granted that if the nature of the problem warrants it, if the problem turns out to be classified as a location problem, the firm will select an appropriate location in the light of both its economic relationships with other firms and the values of economic variables. The firm is a constrained rational optimising entity. What has to be 'explained' is the decision procedures of firms. These take the form of particular structures within the firm which process the firm's data and determine how locations are selected.

Where neoclassical theory can be said to be preoccupied with the nature of the data on which optimal calculations are based, the behavioural approach is absorbed with the calculating procedure itself and takes the nature and source of the data for granted. Geographers construe the behavioural approach as an attempt to reveal the planning procedures of firms. While, on a conventional interpretation of the subject matter of neoclassical theory, we could say that it is concerned with the ingredients of location decisions.[2] If, like most social scientists, we regard these as models of individual behaviour, what do they tell us about individuals and their worlds?

KNOWLEDGE, PREFERENCES, SPACE, AND FIRMS

In reconstructing neoclassical models of 'choice' as a narrative, with the object of revealing the idiosyncrasies of the narrative, the way to set about doing so is to consider the implications of the ontology of the third-person perspective that decisions rest on objective 'data'. In terms of this ontology, the data on which decisions are based exist out there. When the decision-maker 'chooses' in order to optimise, the knowledge which she needs exists in the world and is public, in that it is potentially available to everyone and anyone. Many consequences follow from this. One is that individuals are able to compare all the alternatives that are available to them, or to 'search' until they find an optimum. Finding an optimal location is no different. A decision must be made by comparing alternative locations.

Since everyone potentially has the same access to knowledge, one implication of this ontology is that they should all have the same ability to exploit economic opportunities, which raises the question of why some firms end up choosing less profitable locations. Orthodox economic

157

theory has never successfully tackled the problem of business failure and cannot do so from a third-person perspective. The most common explanation is that losses are caused by overcrowding, when too many firms 'enter the market'. In response to this unsatisfactory account, the question is: why do people not learn, either from their own experience or from others, to exercise caution and not pursue elusive 'opportunities'? Why do they not learn that 'a profit opportunity which is available equally for everyone is in fact available to no one at all' (Richardson 1973: 14)? Richardson's argument is a devastating critique of the idea of public knowledge and is fatal for determinism, for it means that decisions, even those concerning 'known' opportunities, are based not on knowledge of things out there but on conjecture about whether perceived opportunities will last and about what other people may do.[3]

An investment is always something of a gamble that others won't beat us to it, and that the market will still be there. The decision to pursue a particular line of business rests on the manager's *belief* that there are people who will buy her products, or her *hope* that she will be able to produce at a lower cost than other producers, or perhaps some of a thousand other factors that have little to do with profits and costs. These decisions have nothing to do with actually having 'found' an opportunity that is objectively and certifiably better than all others. Decisions can only be based on a conjecture and hope, such as a hope that this is an appropriate place for a factory. Conjecture and expectation always leave room for doubt. Doubt is part of the predicament of the decision-maker in the *durée*, and it is important that theories of decision-making should reflect this, not banish it by invoking an inappropriate epistemology.

Behavioural theory tries to skirt the awkward implications of public knowledge, touting as a 'more realistic' formulation of perception the argument that people perceive the environment differently and receive different pieces of information from the real world out there. This does not alter the ontology of public knowledge and it does create an equally awkward problem of epistemological dualism, where the theorist-'observer' and the decision-makers have radically different world views.

A notable and puzzling aspect of the narrative of neoclassical location theory, which after all is meant to be about the location of firms, is the absence of any account of firms themselves. I raised this point in Chapter 8 and will reconsider it in Chapter 12. The criticism applies to the whole of neoclassical economics, not just to location theory, and is an indication that, in general, mainstream theory has no interest in decision-makers, either individuals or firms (though Marshall's economics is something of an exception). Instead, the theory focuses on the phenomena that arise out of exchanges between economic units as well as on the objective circumstances under which the adjustments to these market relationships occur:

prices and quantities demanded and supplied, revenues and costs, numbers of firms.

We would search the theory in vain for clues about the firm as an institution, organisation, or administrative unit. Similarly, we know nothing of why employees do things. The firm exists to produce in order to optimise, though what induces it to optimise is not explained. It appears merely to be programmed to pursue profits that are defined to exist out there. In this respect it is not even the activities and interests of the firm itself, its shareholders or employees, that cause things to happen or have a bearing on why they happen. External factors force production in one direction or another and the mystery of location theory is why firms are 'looking' for suitable locations.

The behavioural approach provides an essentially similar narrative although, in the 'pressures' that induce an investment, this approach gives firms a 'reason' for locating. The formal models of the behavioural approach identify the firm as a series of interconnected activities but do not depict an organisation. There is no attempt to establish people's interests, or to describe the channels of authority, or how organisational politics affects the relationships between divisions and how it impacts upon their growth and expansion. One would imagine that, since this approach deals almost exclusively with large multidivisional and some-times transnational operations, these matters could hardly be overlooked. Certainly it would seem to be important to reflect on the bureaucratic nature of the large firm, including its implications for policy-making, but again there is no recognition of motives, of personal or sectional interests, or of how conflicts of interest between individuals and parties affect the choice of location and how disagreements are resolved. Neither of the approaches tells us anything about the people who work for the firms, as if this were completely immaterial to the 'interests' of firms.

Another consequence of the ontology and epistemology of the third-person perspective is that the very thing location theory was intended to illuminate – the spatial element in economic decisions – is elusive. Although we infer from the definition of the location problem that decision-makers have to deal with problems in Euclidean space, the theory itself has nothing to say about what space is, what it means to individuals, or how they perceive it. Space, like everything else, is part of the data and to agents it has no form. Little has been written by economists about the concept of space as such, but as a property or component of things, the treatment of space in neoclassical theory is analogous to the treatment of time, so it is worth considering what time is supposed to mean to agents.

Shackle, in particular, has examined the notion of time in neoclassical theory (see especially Shackle 1958, 1959, 1969, 1974).[4] He emphasises that time – the mathematician's concept of time as extension, or as a continuum (which is the only notion compatible with the third-person perspective) –

is a purely formal notion that bears no relationship to the experience of time, i.e. Bergson's concept of the *durée*. Shackle is supported in this by Hicks (1976b). When, as Schütz puts it, we 'turn back' and reflect on our being-in-time, we are living a hermeneutic circle and are conscious of changing interests and different insights. The only way a neoclassical agent would recognise the 'passing of time' is that the values of variables are different. Time has passed because prices are higher at t_2 than at t_1, and so on. In his complete determinate world, however, he would be able to know beforehand what the values were going to be. The agent would have no sense of a future and would not be able to conjecture, nor could he experience surprise or disappointment.

Like time, space is also a purely formal notion, with no connection to experience. The change from one spatial point to another is marked by a change in the data, or a change in the data marks the difference between one spatial point to another. The only way an agent would know that he was 'somewhere else' would be because economic variables, such as wages and revenues, had different values. As a result, if there were two points located the same distance from markets of the same size, and from identical sources of raw material, with the same costs of production at each, firms would necessarily be attracted to both points in the same degree; they would be unable to tell the points apart.

Because 'preferences' generally take centre stage in neoclassical theory as determinants of purchasing decisions, it is perhaps somewhat surprising not to find spatial preferences in location models as 'explanations' of people's preferences for different points in space. The reason why preferences are not given an explanatory role appears to be that 'firms' not individuals are the locators, and firms do not possess preferences and do not need to. It is the objective circumstances of the world, in the form of costs, revenues, and profits at difference places, that determine the firm's activities including its location, not individuals' 'subjective' preferences.[5]

One can argue that this way of looking at business decisions is misleading, and that it is entirely inappropriate to ignore the decision-maker's interests or point of view. Yet the omission of spatial preferences from location theory cannot be seen as a loss, because the Paretian idea, now firmly embedded in economists' thinking, that people possess a comprehensive computational scheme for making selections among any number of things that they confront in the world, is nothing less than bizarre. Even if it is only treated as a metaphor, this conception is inappropriate; and on these grounds I reject the notion, which is a central element of the narrative of the behavioural approach, that people possess coherent and internally consistent systems for making decisions. In behavioural decision theories, people come equipped with mechanisms for 'decoding' the 'signals' that they receive from the environment out there, while organisations possess decision structures which serve the same purpose.

The way in which behavioural location theory deals with people's perceptions of spatial considerations, and how these affect location decisions, has much in common with the Paretian conception of individuals as possessors of built-in schemes for expressing preferences. The perception of spatial relations is an important topic in industrial geography, which also informs other areas of interest, such as industrial linkage studies.[6] With few exceptions – Forer's (1978) contribution is notable in keeping an open mind about alternative approaches to the conceptualisation of spatial perceptions – the analysis of spatial perception shares the conceptual underpinnings of the behavioural theory of decision-making. This means it draws from a positivistically inspired behavioural psychology (see, in particular, Downs 1970).

In these studies of businesses' spatial perceptions, unlike in the neoclassical framework, map space is not pre-eminent, and it is held that 'management teams . . . may not perceive and learn of the space economy . . . in terms of Euclidean or geographic space but in terms of more abstract hierarchic space' (Taylor 1978: 1171). Yet the individual still possesses a 'mental image' of spatial relations (see Barr *et al.* 1980: 870), which has a concrete structure and form. This is exemplified by the assertion of McDermott and Taylor (1976: 326, emphasis added), that the earlier contributions to perception 'give no indication of the *structure of the image* that management has of places within this space. Yet the nature of the image will be extremely influential for decision making and locational choice'. So, although the individual's perception of space may not be of Euclidean space,[7] he has a 'mental image', postulated to be a two-dimensional areal picture, that he can call up in a corporeal form to make 'spatial decisions'.

Many of the flaws in these conventional explanations of how location decision-makers are supposed to see things, including the question of how 'space' bears on location decisions, are disclosed in reviewing Schütz's ideas about people's images of the city (see Chapter 8 above). If the people who make the decision to build a factory are going to be working for the firm in its new premises, they know that they will go to work or will live in a particular *place*, or they will be making a decision that will affect where other people will live and work. Factories are not 'located in space'. People find places desirable because they are an easy commute or because of the neighbourhood, but the third-person perspective cannot accommodate individuals' personal ('prejudiced') appreciation of different places, whatever influences their views. A person's interest in, or attachment to, a particular place may be due to a number of factors nearly all of which concern her relationships with other people. These may be business relationships with colleagues and suppliers, or they may be social relationships that involve friends, people who share an interest in cultural activities, or people of the same religion.

These considerations reveal once again how a third-person perspective obstructs understanding. Because it fails to provide any insight into the intersubjective nature of understanding, it also fails to illuminate the way in which interpersonal relationships influence decisions. In order to explore the importance of these relationships we require an epistemology that allows us to reflect what Polanyi (1973) terms 'personal knowledge' as the basis of understanding and decision-making.

In this regard even the behavioural approach, which purports to have something to say about the way decisions are made, is unable to offer any justification for a decision-maker's interest in particular places and is equally remiss in dealing with interpersonal relations. In industrial geography, when the need for a new location is indicated by the decision process, people embark on searches for suitable locations but without any preconceptions about where to look, about what places might be suitable, or who might be able to help them in their search.[8] Actually, when people make decisions, they are wont to ask for advice. They do not typically conjure up two-dimensional images of spatial relations with implicit or explicit economic values built into them. Experience is of a social world, shared with friends, acquaintances, and colleagues, who pass on bits of information and who know of other people who might be able to assist. A social theory that does not include these considerations in the story that it tells about how or why things happen, is a poor theory indeed.

RISK, DOUBT, AND UNCERTAINTY

An aspect of the narrative of location theory that is well worth exploring is what firms do when there is uncertainty about the values of variables. How do firms 'decide' and 'act' under uncertainty? Location theorists have not given much consideration to uncertainty or how to deal with it, but other neoclassical theorists have, and Webber (1972) attempts to add uncertainty to location theory, employing what have become standard approaches.[9] The story that is told is that decision-makers who are uncertain determine the probabilities of different outcomes and use these to calculate an optimal location given the uncertainty. The use of probability theory as a refuge for the uncertain decision-maker is entirely a consequence of the third-person ontology of determinate theories. Equally, an appreciation of the ontology and an awareness that decisions are not made from a third-person perspective, which we owe to modern hermeneutics, reveals why it is completely illegitimate to apply probability theory in this context.

Uncertainty, or doubt, is associated with being-in-time. Uncertainty means not knowing; or, as Shackle puts it (see for example 1983), it is 'unknowledge'. When we are uncertain we form opinions, or expectations, or take a view on what might happen. In other words, we conjecture. In the *durée*, I am uncertain about everything beyond what I am conscious of at present. Circumstances to which my plans and decisions 'point', are not in some sense pre-existing, out there, and waiting to be revealed. The future is entirely 'open' because I will constitute it. My understanding then will depend on what I as well as other people do now, and on my interests at that time. What I now think of as the future, I will constitute by my interests and activities later on. What I 'learn' in the interim, thus how I understand later on and how I constitute events in the future, depends on my interests now and what I do now. For all these reasons the future is not knowable. It is not *there* to be known until I constitute it. I can think about various possibilities, and I may expect that someone will do something that I look forward to, or I may hope that a particular event which I would like to avoid will not come to pass. Yet I am always in doubt, and therefore uncertain, about the things on which I am pinning my hopes.

It is with regard to such arguments that Shackle (1972a: 27) says '[t]ime is a denial of the omnipotence of reason'. He is referring to the supposed ability of the agents of mainstream theory, who possess complete knowledge, to optimise by 'reasoning' about the alternatives that they face. Shackle holds that this notion of rationality applies to a timeless world where everything that is 'going to happen' has already been 'foreseen'. 'Time', however, 'divides the entirety of things into that part about which we can reason [the past], and that part about which we cannot [the uncertain future]'. I would add that the orthodox notion of rationality not only concerns an epistemologically complete and therefore timeless world, but it presupposes an ontology that specifies that reasoning means identifying, enumerating, classifying, or ranking, some of the complete sets of things that make up the world out there.

Any notion of time that is employed in a determinate scheme must not interfere with a requirement of the third-person perspective that knowledge is in every sense complete. This is why the notion of time that is endemic to neoclassical theory is the purely formal notion of extension or mathematical transformation but is not the notion associated with experience, in terms of which we distinguish between future and past. In both the comparative-static and dynamic formulations of neoclassical theory, the configuration of 'events', such as prices or expectations at t_1, are transformed into a different configuration at t_2, and that at t_2 into the configuration at t_3, in some predetermined way, through dynamic equations, for example, that specify how events evolve over 'time'. Because the transformation is mechanical and the mechanisms are known, any one 'period' contains the seeds for events in all 'future' periods, and the completeness that is associated with determinism is sustained.

The only form of 'uncertainty' that is compatible with the third-person perspective is risk, related to the statistical probability of different outcomes of, say, a game of chance or human life expectancy. For the roulette player the 'future' is not open; he is not able to constitute that part of his future that is the outcome of the game. The rules of the game, the properties of things, and laws of physics, define and limit the outcomes. Because only specific things can happen, the probability of their occurrence can be calculated. The scheme of things is complete, or can be treated as such. The more often the roulette wheel is spun, the more knowledge is gained about the probability of any outcome occurring. A probability statement is knowledge of the workings of a system and once we have knowledge we are not uncertain. It is perfectly legitimate to apply probability theory to these problems but they are not characterised by uncertainty, only risk, and these are not like most business problems. The difference, explained in Chapter 13, is that most business problems, such as investment decisions, are not about elements of a system with various outcomes, each of which can be specified.

The problems that encompass the location of a factory, for example, pertain to people's understanding. They are problems concerning interpretation, including someone's interpretation of how other people understand or of what they think. Such problems are open-ended, in that the nature of the problem depends on how people constitute their worlds. It is practical to know and to enumerate the possible outcomes of a game of chance, but I submit that an answer to the question 'Will the competition put a product on the market before we do?' or 'Will the next generation of computer users want a new operating system?' is always a conjecture. The answer is, we do not know, we are uncertain. There is no *set* of outcomes from which the most likely one can be identified, moreover whatever views people hold today may change tomorrow.

To approach uncertainty from the point of view of statistical probability, as neoclassical economics does, is to attempt to conflate the incommensurable languages of the first- and third-person perspectives, which involve different epistemologies and ontologies. Orthodox theorists confuse what Shackle terms 'two opposing and discordant meanings' of probability. Expectations, as conjecture, belong to the language of interpretation and understanding. Risk, and statistical probability, pertain to a scheme of things that is complete. Probabilities are parts of a class of outcomes which, in turn, is consistent with a complete, self-contained system of things from which a sample of outcomes can be drawn. Expectations are subjective feelings or beliefs, based on personal experience, and there is no basis for determining how likely it is that one's expectations will be fulfilled. Uncertainty is not removed through experience or by 'acquiring knowledge', for the future always remains open, to be constituted in understanding. Doubt is a part of life and of understanding.[10]

It is not possible to add uncertainty to a determinate scheme because uncertainty is at odds with the epistemology and ontology of the third-person perspective. For this reason, Webber's (1972) attempt to do so, in respect of location theory, goes badly awry. He is familiar with some of Shackle's work and with the work of Knight, whose seminal contribution (Knight 1933) introduced the distinction between risk and uncertainty to economists: indeed, discussing the mathematical theory of probability as a means of modelling 'uncertainty', Webber (1972: ch. 5) actually highlights the distinction between 'risk' and 'uncertainty'. Yet he fails to respect this distinction. Citing various sources, he adopts the position (ibid.: 95) that uncertainty is either impossible to incorporate into any theoretical framework, or that there is really no difference between risk and uncertainty. Having disposed of the important issues by dismissing them, the way is now clear for him to apply probability theory to situations of uncertainty and so perpetuate a problem which Jefferson (1983: 122) highlights in the following quotation.

> Despite the pervading mist of uncertainty there is a deeply embedded desire in human nature to impose order on disorder ... to speak and act as if we had knowledge where it cannot exist; to seek firm answers and 'optimum' solutions as if uncertainty were eliminated. There is thus a tendency to live in a pretend world where by ... introducing and using techniques, claiming systematic approaches and objective assessments, people can come to believe that their capacity for sound decision-making is far more robust than is the case.

Webber is only partly correct in his assessment of the difficulty of working with the notion of uncertainty. It is not that uncertainty cannot be incorporated into *any* framework. To explore uncertainty a scheme based on interpretative understanding and a first-person perspective is required, but uncertainty will not fit into a deterministic scheme, which is the only sort that location theorists know. On the other hand, the conditions of risk, under which probability statements can be meaningfully assigned to events, do not apply to the problems of human conduct in which location theorists are interested.[11]

As described by Shackle (1972a: 17–18), conditions of risk pertain to 'a concrete, existing and delimited system' (a 'complete system' in my terminology) and, 'as a *sine qua non* of [the existence of such probabilities there must be] some underlying stability and invariance of the system being described'. Using the case of an investment decision to exemplify problems that involve an understanding of human conduct, in the quotation below Shackle explains how these differ from situations of risk, and he illustrates the distinction I have drawn between the two different types of problems. In situations of risk the number of possible outcomes is finite and the frequency ratios of the different outcomes sum to unity. In contrast, the total discounted value of a series of projected future earnings on an investment is a conjecture. The expectation of a particular outcome may be an 'educated guess', but it is a guess all the same (see Chamberlain 1968: 40).

> Many different numbers of pounds [Sterling] . . . can be entertained as possibly representing [the discounted value of projected future earnings]. The cost of [acquiring the machine] may also of course in some degree be uncertain. But if one or both of the two amounts is uncertain, what is it to be compared with what?
>
> To be uncertain is to entertain many rival hypotheses. The hypotheses are rivals in the sense that they all refer to the same question, and that only one of them can prove true in the event. Will it, then, make sense to average these suggested mutually exclusive answers? . . . Moreover, the average can be a weighted one . . . . There will be a temptation to call such weights probabilities. But what is their source? . . . The various hypotheses or contingencies to which frequency ratios are assigned by statistical observation are not *rivals*. . . . All of them are true, each in a certain proportion of the cases with which, *all taken together as whole*, the frequency distribution is concerned.
>
> The probability which can be assigned to one of many rival hypotheses is a 'subjective' probability, it belongs to . . . "a language for expressing personal judgements".
>
> (Shackle 1972a: 19–20)

The narrative of location theory, like that of the rest of neoclassical theory, is thoroughly misleading when it comes to dealing with uncertainty. A theory that aims to provide an understanding of how people understand and make decisions, cannot assume away doubt or ignore how decision-makers cope with uncertainty. When the future is clouded by political instability or great economic upheaval, it is difficult even to conjecture either about what people are going to do or about business conditions, so any investment plans are shelved. At other times, decision-makers take steps to insulate themselves from adverse circumstances that might affect their activities. Some institutional arrangements serve this purpose. While not removing uncertainty, they help to cope with the consequences of not knowing what will happen. Institutions, such as insurance and particular market structures,[12] help to mitigate the effects of unexpected changes. Maps and contingent plans can assist in novel situations.[13] One of the factors that contributes to coping with uncertainty is the firm's location and the business community that 'surrounds' each manufacturer. In general, the larger that community, the greater the sense of security that a location provides. Location decisions involve investment in plant and equipment and have long-term implications. It is therefore important that the conceptual framework that aims to explain these decisions is able to recognise uncertainty for what it is. Rather than trivialising the concept or rendering it nugatory, there is a need to explain how and why uncertainty influences decisions.

ISSUES TO CONSIDER

In Chapter 2, I referred to Coddington's advice that in order to assess the usefulness of a theory one has to be clear about what relationship it has to its subject matter and to ask 'whether the conceptual framework is adequate to sustain the intellectual tasks that we set ourselves'. Though it may have been the object of the theorists to do so, and though the scholars who produced the theories may have thought they were doing so, location theories do not explain how location decisions are made nor do they reveal what a location decision is. The methodology that gave rise to these theories does not constitute a language for explaining decisions. These are grounds enough for rejecting the theories.

My task, then, is to suggest how social scientists might set about examining the nature of decision-making. The pervasive influence of modernism means that the efforts to formulate models of, say, business decision-making employ an unsuitable methodology. I will review these models briefly in Chapter 10. My main aim in the remaining chapters is to outline the route which a subjectivist theory might follow in examining the nature of planning, decision-making, and choice. In order to answer questions about how decisions come to be taken and why certain decisions are taken, we have to understand how the decision-makers themselves understand. How do they constitute the problems to which their decisions refer? By adopting a first-person perspective, social scientists can obtain insights into what it means to make a location decision and how location decisions are made.

Since the conventional models tell us nothing at all about how individuals understand, an interpretative approach must address the question of whether the people who are responsible for the firm's location think about 'spatial issues', or spatial relations, such as the distance from one place to another, or the number of potential suppliers within a particular area or radius. Are these the sorts of issues which bear upon their plans and decisions? If they are, the choice of location might be aided by a map or by understanding the types of areal-economic relationships which dominate traditional location theory. Or are such considerations largely irrelevant when it comes to the location of a factory?

The answers really depend on an answer to the prior question of whether locations are actually chosen. Is the siting of a manufacturing facility an important element in the planning process undertaken in a business organisation, as opposed to being an incidental aspect of the decision to invest in a plant? If locations are chosen, then how are they chosen? When people decide to invest in a factory, do they think in spatial terms or constitute the problem as a spatial one? Questioning whether locations are chosen may seem absurd because each industrial undertaking has a location and someone made a decision about the location, either to build or to buy a factory at a particular place. Yet this does not mean that the location was examined to see whether anything could be gained by putting the factory in a different place, or whether the location was analysed to ascertain whether the factory was appropriately positioned in relation to suppliers, to buyers, or to a transport route.

Using an interpretative approach, I aim to substantiate that the people who are contemplating an investment do not pay much attention to the issue of location. The investment decision is the context in which location matters may come to be considered, and the people who are responsible for planning investments or for ratifying investment plans, may not be particularly concerned with 'spatial issues'.[14] In terms of explaining how decisions are made, it is important to understand the context of location problems, as the individuals themselves understand them, and this means that investment decisions should be the focus of any analysis of location issues.

Explanations of a firm's location cannot start with the assumption that the location is of singular importance, let alone the sole consideration that led to the factory being established at a particular place (Rees 1972a: 204, makes a similar point). The pre-eminence of the location problem is a consequence of the epistemology and ontology of the third-person perspective which entirely undermines understanding by pigeon-holing different types of knowledge. Knowledge is a thing that can be divided into many different pieces. One component is spatial knowledge, and if there is spatial knowledge inevitably there are location decisions in the world to which this knowledge applies. If the issue of location does come to the fore in the planning of an investment, the analysis of investment decisions must reveal why it does, and how location issues fit into the overall planning of an investment.

Even when it is clear that someone gave considerable thought to a location, the location need not have been selected from amongst a number of potential sites, as location theory presumes. If we reject the narrative of neoclassical theory, the question is whether decision-makers evaluate the prospects of locating at more than one possible place. Consideration of the circumstances surrounding the identification of an investment opportunity ought to cast light on whether locations are chosen. In adopting an interpretative approach to decision-making, I will highlight the importance of the social context of investment decisions and the significance of social 'networks' in creating new business opportunities (see Chapters 12 and 13). If, as we would expect, those networks also play an important role in the identification of investment opportunities, they may well influence the location of the business. The more that the people planning an investment rely on the advice and information of others, the less likely they will be to make comparisons of possible alternative locations.

In the context of how locations bear upon investment decisions, a further matter to be resolved concerns the basis, or criteria, on which a location may be identified. How do people go about 'finding' the site? Do they pay attention to the sorts of spatial relationships that characterise the economics of location? Are the relative labour costs at different places, or the number of competitors within a particular area, likely to be important? Even if they are taken into account, does an investment decision stand or fall on economic considerations? Because of the inability of standard theories to enlighten us about decisions and how they are made, it is clear that if we wish to understand these problems we have to use new approaches and to start afresh. In the next chapter I begin to outline how we should go about this task. Although later chapters do no more than provide a rough sketch of decision-making from a first-person perspective, it will be apparent that as we gain an understanding of decision-making, so we also repudiate the conventional account of how economic factors determine what firms do.

10

DECISIONS ABOUT THINGS
IN THE WORLD

MODELLING BUSINESS DECISIONS

A likely answer to the question of how a planner, or the manager of a business, approaches the location of production facilities is that he does so in the course of planning an investment. The decisions that have a bearing on a firm's location are matters that have to do with managing production capabilities: whether it is worth acquiring new production facilities; whether to rationalise or reorganise what already exists; whether to reduce the production capacity; or to extend the existing facilities. So in order to comprehend the nature of location decisions, it is necessary to understand investment decisions. Understanding why such activities are contemplated means examining how particular individuals – the managers and planners – assess their situation. Senior management may have decided to diversify in the light of exceptionally strong growth, or to rationalise when faced with declining profitability, or they may have decided to buy out the competition. Each of these decisions will have different implications for the location of production facilities.

Decisions to build a new factory, to purchase one, or to extend existing production facilities, will be regarded by the people managing the organisation as 'strategic'; as part of the process of planning which shapes the organisation itself and how and where it does business.[1] Strategic plans might revolve around all or some of the following: diversification into new markets; restructuring the management of the enterprise; or developing alternative distribution channels for products. Measured in terms of the financial capacity of the company, the consequences of strategic decisions are usually costly. Because they may result in changes in the way an organisation is managed, or may involve an upheaval as far as the production activities are concerned, strategy formulations are likely to be accompanied by a large-scale planning exercise involving various people or departments in the organisation. By studying the 'character' of investment plans – the circumstances under which they are made, the nature of the plans themselves, and the sorts of considerations which bear upon the way in which the decision-maker thinks about an investment – my object is to throw light on how locations

170

come to be identified and the sorts of factors that direct the 'choice' of a location.

What is a logical starting point for studying business plans and decisions? The answer, it would seem, is to go to the literature on business decisions and to investigate the models of investment decision-making as well as models of other types of business decisions that are found in this literature. That is where I propose to go, albeit briefly. For, noting the ubiquitousness of positivism in all branches of social studies, it does not come as a surprise that the modelling of business decisions is governed by positivistically inspired methodologies which are inappropriate for that purpose. It is desirable, nevertheless, briefly to examine these models in order to see what they say about decision-making and to identify their limitations in the light of my critique of the third-person perspective. Although it is necessary to understand the nature of investment plans and decisions before re-examining the question of location, the following analysis reveals why the models of investment decision-making found in texts on business management fail to enlighten us on these topics.

Different approaches to business decision-making in management theory can be classified into two categories. The first are partial equilibrium models which purport to offer what I would call 'techniques' for making decisions. These are associated with disciplines such as marketing, managerial finance, and corporate strategy, and they profess to specify the logic for making effective, 'rational' decisions. In general, the epistemological and ontological underpinnings of the conceptual frameworks employed and the frameworks themselves are not made explicit, but they are the same as those of neoclassical theory. The contributions define an 'optimal decision' in the context of different 'business problems', and they identify the conditions associated with optimal decisions. (See, for example, Weston and Brigham (1975) on financial decision-making and compare Kotler (1971) on marketing decisions.) The second category serves a somewhat similar purpose, that of specifying what constitutes an optimal process of decision-making. The foundation of this behavioural theory of decision-making is behavioural psychology – the same conceptual scheme associated with behavioural location theory – and the foundation is often explicitly identified. These contributions sometimes examine the psychology of decision-making on the premise that, if he understands this, the manager – whose primary role is to manage people – will be more effective in his role. (See, for example, Hogarth 1987.)

Neither category approaches decision-making from the point of view of the individuals involved by asking how they understand the problem at hand. The problem is taken to be 'there', existing in the world, and decision-makers have to solve it in an optimal way. In both categories the spirit of modernism is very strong and its tenets (as identified in Chapter 2) are plainly visible. Models of financial decision-making, for example, rely extensively on mathematical formulations of the decision problem and they frequently appeal to probability theory as the foundation for determining the outcomes of 'uncertain' events. Implicit both in the application of mathematical models and in the use of statistical probabilities is the idea that the decision-making problem pertains to a complete, or closed, system that I have associated with the third-person perspective. A fundamental premise is that the decision should be viewed in the context of a system, which can be specified in its entirety, and all the possible results or outcomes can be determined, if only on the basis of the probability of their occurrence. Behavioural theorists also use experiments to test how individuals make decisions or form judgements.

PARTIAL EQUILIBRIUM MODELS

Examples of partial equilibrium models of business decision-making can be found in the area of managerial finance, which consists of an assemblage of such models rather than an integrated theoretical scheme. Like neoclassical theory, the focus of modern corporate or managerial finance is optimisation. In this case, the object of each model is to solve a partial equilibrium problem by determining an optimal asset portfolio or by finding the optimum capital budget – 'the level of investment that maximises the present value of the firm' (Weston and Brigham 1975: 257). For each problem there is a technique which should be applied, say, to identify an optimal investment portfolio by allocating a sum of money among a portfolio of assets with different streams of expected returns with which are associated varying degrees of risk.

The definition of the capital budgeting problem is clearly governed by the language of the third-person perspective. The investment decision is about maximising 'risk-adjusted returns'. It is presupposed that there are specific, clearly identifiable, distinct, alternative investment opportunities available to the firm. Streams of earnings from each investment are estimated for various dates in the 'future'. The magnitude of the earnings is 'uncertain' but their probability distributions are known. For each investment, the object is to find a suitable risk-adjusted rate of discount which can be applied to these earnings to estimate a present value. This exercise identifies which investment yields the maximum present value and, by comparing that value with the cost of each investment, which are the profitable investments. (See Beenhakker 1974, 1975) on this standard approach to modelling investment decisions.) Planning in this context means defining all relevant aspects of the world in order to find the best combination of elements. The nature of the planning procedure leads one to understand that there is a 'correct' estimate, or at least a good estimate, of future earnings, and there is an optimal solution to the investment problem. Optimising involves the assumption that a limited number of 'states of nature' can occur out there. The modeller is required to be able to identify and to scrutinise closely all of them, or at least the most probable ones, in determining an investment or decision strategy.

In each of these models the object of the decision-maker is to grasp all relevant aspects of the world, in order to find a solution to the problem in the particular concatenation of events out there that has developed or, that, according to estimates of statistical probabilities, is most likely to develop 'in future'. An important implication of the formulation both of the problem and the method for finding a solution is that the world consists of pieces or parts, some of which – such as 'the market' or 'expected annual net earnings' – are germane to the problem at hand. The statement of the problem implies that it is practical to establish what parts of the world are relevant to the problem, to isolate these from the other parts, and to find a solution by careful scrutiny, measurement, and assessment of elements of the problem.

This formulation of the problem, including the exercise of attaching specific figures to different streams of earnings under various assumptions – for example, about market growth potential and levels of interest rates – in order to optimise, clearly identifies the epistemology and ontology of the third-person perspective. If we were to look at these models as prescriptions for decision-makers, the procedures which they recommend that decision-makers should follow, such as estimating future earnings on a specific project, are strictly beyond the comprehension of an ordinary planner, as she thinks about what lies ahead and considers prospects. The procedures do not correspond at all with her understanding in the *durée*, and the reason is that there is a radical difference in both the epistemology and ontology of 'thinking about' on the one hand, and 'optimising' on the other. Postulating that there is an optimal, determinate solution to allocating a sum of money, and that people can estimate the solution, is a third-person conception pertaining to an entire scheme of things.

To illustrate that the planner or decision-maker is not capable of understanding in the way in which the models prescribe, consider whether it would be possible for a planner to follow the advice for making rational decisions. The decision-maker is instructed to evaluate investments in terms of their expected outcomes. What is the 'outcome' of a proposed investment? Would anyone be able to say when the outcome had been attained? The decision-maker is supposed to optimise, but is she able to specify her objective, and how would she do so? What does it mean to maximise profits? Is it 'higher than average profits' that she should look for, or 'an acceptable level of profitability', or 'a better than average return'? What do such 'goals' mean? How would we know when, or whether, the decision-maker had achieved her objective? The answer to the last question is that we would not, unless she tells us that she thinks she has achieved it and we accept her interpretation.

All the 'advice' to planners which these models contain is based on the idea that profits and streams of earnings are things that can be found out there, and the counsel about what to do to be a good decision-maker only makes sense in the context of an ontology that treats the world, or the problem, as pertaining to a complete set of things that exists out there. From the first-person perspective, which is the comprehension of an individual engaged in her day-to-day activities, such injunctions are baffling. They cannot be acted on except in terms of different individuals' prejudiced interpretations or perceptions and conjectures. Profits or earnings can only be measured *ex post* and then they are reported (that is, interpreted), using accounting conventions and practices. To a degree, profits are what the reporters want them to be. They depend on the conventions that are chosen and, when it comes to 'measuring' a charge against gross profits such as depreciation, this is again someone's estimate or interpretation. Whether reported profits are deemed to be 'high' or 'low' is also an interpretation, over which there will be at least some differences of opinion. Are we taking a short- or long-term view? With what are the profits being compared and with what should they be compared? Should actual returns be compared with the 'estimates' made at the planning stage, which were necessarily conjectures, prejudiced by circumstances and the experiences of the planners? Should they be compared with the (interpreted) published results of other firms? The interpretative nature of estimates and comparisons also highlights their social dimension. For example, the conventions themselves and their use, including the decisions about which conventions are the 'right' ones to apply, depend on intersubjective understanding.

BEHAVIOURAL MODELS

Referring to problems with the types of models that I have described, Simon (1979: 66) notes that 'economic behaviouralism' is rooted in psychology and was 'brought into economics to handle certain problems that appeared not to be treated satisfactorily by the [other] situational approach' to modelling the firm. The object of the behavioural approach to decision-making is to consider the nature of the process of decision-making rather than optimising situations. Simon was instrumental both in developing the behavioural theory of decision-making and in applying it to problems of economics and of business (see Simon 1952, 1957, 1960).[2] How does it treat the process of planning and decision-making? Does it provide a more satisfactory treatment than the situational approach?

As the analysis of location problems in Chapter 8 reveals, behavioural decision theorists see decision-making as a process, with a definite structure. Their object is to identify both the structure and the process by which the decision-maker 'grasps' the world out there, in order to show what constitutes an efficient decision-making process and whether the decision-maker uses a process that is 'procedurally rational'. The decision-making process is identifiable as a self-contained entity and the process is analogous to the operation of a mechanism.[3] In addition, the process exists within a system of events and circumstances which also form the closed, self-contained, 'external world' of the decision-maker.[4] The decision-maker responds to events in the world, which happen in a mechanical way, by having to calculate the probability of their occurrence.

The behavioural theory of decision-making postulates a scheme of things that is no different from that of neoclassical theory and the partial equilibrium models of business decisions. Simon calls the rationality associated with the optimising agent of neoclassical economics 'substantive rationality', which 'is viewed in terms of the choices it produces' (Simon 1987: 26). Behavioural theory is concerned with 'procedural rationality', which refers to processes; while substantive rationality emphasises outcomes or results. 'Behaviour is procedurally rational when it is the outcome of appropriate deliberation. Its procedural rationality depends on the process that generated it' (Simon 1979: 68).

Taken at face value, the definition of procedural rationality as behaviour that is 'the outcome of appropriate deliberation' (ibid.: 69) is liable to mislead because there is no indication of the third-person perspective associated with optimising behaviour. Yet procedural rationality does involve a third-person perspective and its ontology is identical to that of orthodox economics. Knowledge is 'grounded' and refers to things out there. The scheme of things out there is complete, although the individual's knowledge of what is out there may not be complete. Simon's statement (1987: 27) about the context in which procedural rationality is relevant identifies the epistemology as the third-person perspective.

> If ... we accept the proposition that both the knowledge and the computational power of the decision maker are severely limited, then we must distinguish between the real world and the actor's perception of it and reasoning about it. That is to say, we must construct a theory (and test it empirically) of the processes of decision. Our theory must include not only the reasoning processes but also the processes that generate the actor's subjective representation of the decision problem ... [5]

The various 'problems' that are used to illustrate procedural rationality all fulfil the ontological requirements of a third-person perspective. Examples cover 'computational efficiency' (Simon 1979: 69) related to cognitive processes associated with solving 'problems' such as playing chess, completing puzzles, and betting in games of chance. The very nature of each of these problems lends itself to determining a solution, in terms of a procedure or course of action that is demonstrably superior to others. They are problems which can be thought of as closed or complete, and one of their features is a definite outcome, or outcomes. A puzzle is solved or it is not; a chess game is won, lost, drawn, or abandoned.[6] The 'states of nature' and the choices that can be made are finite in a game of chess, and at any one time are constrained by clearly defined and agreed rules. Bearing in mind that the game of chess is understood and, like all understanding, an understanding of chess is prejudiced, the outcomes and permutations can be established independently of what a particular person decides or thinks. The chess player, whoever he is, can only make certain moves and achieve certain outcomes within the framework of the rules and objectives of the game.

Although they would deny that business decisions are any different, hence the argument that understanding how people play chess provides insights into business decisions (see Simon 1979: 83), the fact is that the problems that behavioural theorists choose to study are deliberately chosen, or defined, to fit their methodology (compare Keirstead 1972: 161).[7] This is well illustrated in the application of probability theory to these problems in order to deal with situations where the decision-maker 'faces uncertainty'. In recent years especially, the behavioural theory of decision-making has focused a good deal of attention on decision-making under uncertainty (see Kahneman *et al.* 1982; Hogarth 1987: ch. 5). In behavioural theory uncertainty is not, as in ordinary language, a general 'state of mind'. Uncertainty does not refer to one's doubts, but is a feature of the world. Uncertainty exists out there and means that specific things – individual instances or cases – are not clear. There will be a particular profit or a particular revenue, but what it will be is unclear. Thus, Kahneman and Tversky (1982: 507) state that '[a]t all levels of biological complexity there is uncertainty about the *significance of signs or stimuli* and about the possible consequences of actions' (emphasis added).

Probability theory is seized upon with enthusiasm to show how decision-makers cope with 'uncertainty'. The point to be emphasised is one that I made in the previous chapter. It is perfectly legitimate to use probability theory to solve the puzzles, games, and riddles which comprise the problems of 'decision-making' in positivistic theories. These 'complete worlds' effectively replicate the third-person perspective. All the possible outcomes can be established or identified and the problems are amenable to the application of statistical probability. But they are not problems characterised by uncertainty as that term is understood, for example, by the manager of a business and specifically by one who is concerned with planning an investment.

The failure to comprehend that in this scheme there is no uncertainty only risk, is a source of considerable confusion among scholars and leads to absurd conclusions, as illustrated by Zeckhauser's (1987: 257) reasoning. Having introduced the distinction between risk and uncertainty, he has no option but to conflate uncertainty with ignorance. His dilemma is that, by his own definition, uncertainty refers to situations where probabilities are unknown. Yet behavioural decision theory permits decision-makers to determine the probability of anything and everything happening, so uncertainty must refer to situations where people are simply ignorant and have not taken into account, or have not calculated, the probability of the event. Certain 'states of the world', as they exist out there, have not been considered. In support of this reasoning, Zeckhauser (ibid.: 258) provides a marvellous illustration of the third-person perspective: 'even if one thinks for a very long time, one can only identify states of the world that capture, say, 90% of [all] *the possible outcomes*' (emphasis added).

There is an important epistemological distinction between ignorance and uncertainty; between what is not known to some, and what cannot be known by anyone. Ignorance means to be unaware or uninformed, and refers to situations where some individuals know, while others do not. In most cases, with time and effort, ignorance can be overcome. Uncertainty, which pertains to plans, applies at a particular moment in the *durée*, when we are thinking about doing something and need to commit ourselves. The significance of being uncertain is that at that moment, when we want to do so, we cannot find out what is going to happen. And later, when we can find out, the opportunity has passed; it is too late. Uncertainty is the doubt that the individual associates with an 'open' future and it can be neither removed nor overcome.

To illustrate the distinction between ignorance and uncertainty, let us suppose that most of the people who work in my office do not know how to set the timing on a car, but could probably learn to do so fairly quickly; they are ignorant on this matter. One of my colleagues is not mechanically minded and we are uncertain about whether he could acquire the skills. Until he actually undergoes instruction and demonstrates aptitude, we are all *uncertain* about his ability. The uncertainty represents a state of 'unknowledge', which no one can change or 'remove' before this person is put to the test. Even then the test may prove to be inconclusive, so that the uncertainty remains.

To argue that uncertainty, which is in the nature of all business decisions, can be expressed as so many degrees of probability associated with each of a number of outcomes is doubly misleading. As Shackle points out, the argument presumes that there is a specific, finite number of outcomes (implying a closed system) which has been determined in advance, but to know of the possible outcomes is to have knowledge of the system as a whole. The other, and in a way the more telling critique, is that the idea of degrees of probability implies at least that the decision belongs to a class of similar identical events. To estimate the probability the decision-maker must be able to recognise this decision as belonging to a class, must identify the class, and must know, or be able to estimate, the frequencies of the outcomes of the events in the class. Again, all this presumes the existence of a complete world and that business decisions are about things that exist in the world which presumably can be identified and classified as if they were different species of animals. The application of probability theory to business decisions implies that every decision always has a counterpart somewhere else or at some other time. No one has explained whether, or how, decision-makers recognise the class of events in order to establish the probabilities, because the narrative of behavioural theory has no place for recognition, in the sense of understanding.

For the behaviouralist as for other positivists, there is no problem of understanding or interpretation. The world is an agglomeration of things that can be observed and each agent possesses means of identifying, classifying, and estimating these things.[8] Behavioural theorists are prepared to admit that 'the laws of probability theory do not apply to all variants of uncertainty with equal force' (Kahneman and Tversky 1982: 519), but efforts to work with other notions of uncertainty are hampered by the epistemology of the scheme. An individual is either uncertain or he is not because he knows what will happen. He is not more, or less, uncertain. In the course of time, he can know about things about which, formerly, he was uncertain. This is an essential aspect of the conception of the individual as being-in-time, and of understanding as interpretation in the hermeneutic circle, associated with a first-person perspective.

The treatment of expectations in these orthodox approaches to decision-making is as unsatisfactory as the treatment of uncertainty, and is a corollary of the notion of 'uncertainty' itself. Expectations are envisaged as detailed pictures that individuals have about specific events or phenomena that already exist, or will exist, in the world out there. Expectations, conceived as mental images, are the counterparts of the probabilities that people hold about events. Since probabilities refer to specific things happening, so expectations are representations of the things to which the probabilities refer. Consider the following statement about decision-making (Hogarth 1987: 101).

> [I]n many – if not most – realistic situations, people are ambiguous concerning the probabilities of events that can affect outcomes. . . .
>
> In the Einhorn–Hogarth ambiguity model, people are assumed to assess ambiguous probabilities by first anchoring on some value of the probability and then adjusting this figure by mentally simulating or imagining other values the probability could take. The net effect of this simulation process is then aggregated with the anchor to reach an estimate.

This view of expectations, notably in the notion of assessing 'ambiguous probabilities' (which is an oxymoron), serves as a good illustration of how plans are depicted from a third-person perspective. In both behavioural theory and business management theory, the tendency is to treat plans – which direct the firm's future activities – as models or blueprints. Regarded as things that exist in the world, it is not difficult to view them as capable of being represented in a physical form and also as exact descriptions or representations of what people should do.

THE RECEIVED VIEW OF PLANNING

The following extracts are from a work by Le Breton and Henning (1961: 5) which is intended to guide planning in, and the management of, business enterprises.

The attainment of a given goal will be best achieved by first devising a precise plan of action. This will begin with a clear statement of the objectives of the plan. When an enterprise-wide plan is formulated, the objective of the plan may be a near duplicate of the objective established for the enterprise. . . .

The finished plan will contain a recommended course of action and a statement of required resources. . . . Depending on how detailed a plan the marketing manager might wish, this plan could contain reference to hundreds of items.

. . . Two additional facts should be emphasised. Within each major plan, reference is usually made . . . to the functions organizing, staffing and controlling. . . .

The second significant fact is that as a plan is prepared, it will often require the creation of new policies or the redefinition of existing policies.

In these extracts the organisation is depicted as a complete system and the plan encapsulates that system in its entirety. The different approaches to business decision-making identified above share this conception of both the organisation and plans. The plan also constitutes the basis on which the system is optimised. As the plan is formulated so the system must adjust, adding here, removing there, until it fits together 'properly' and matches the plan of which the organisation is a replica.

The reason why plans are conceived in this way is again revealed by understanding the third-person perspective, which explains why economists, too, are seduced by the metaphor of a plan as a complex and comprehensive blueprint for action. As an example, here is an economist actually explaining decision-making to an audience of non-economists. Johnston (1967: 61–2) begins a radio talk with an anecdote about a holiday-maker who has to choose between saving his wife from drowning or getting into the pub at opening time. The economist elaborates on this in terms of utility functions and values, adding that the imaginary problem

introduces most of the basic elements of real decision problems. There is first of all the set of possible decisions or actions; there is secondly the set of possible outcomes or results; there is thirdly the network of relationships connecting decisions and outcomes and finally, associated with every action is a 'cost', and with every outcome a 'value'.

Real decision problems are characterised by a 'network of relationships connecting decisions and outcomes'. We find this compelling metaphor repeated by Lachmann, who is rightly critical of neoclassical formalism, and who argues that plans should form the nucleus of subjectivist economic theory, the task of which is to 'make the world . . . intelligible in terms of human action and the pursuit of plans' (Lachman 1977f: 261; 1977g: 47). He states that 'plans and the meaning the planners attach to them are things that matter and must be included in every attempted explanation of [economic] processes' (Lachmann 1970: 7) and that the focus on individuals' plans provides 'a new starting point, based on the method of interpretation, for a theory of action . . . inspired by the Weberian notion that action derives its meaning from the mind of the actor' (Lachman 1970: 9). How are these plans conceived? Plans are 'a mental picture of the situation in which [the individual] will have to act' (Lachmann 1977h: 75) they constitute 'comprehensive means-ends frameworks'.

> At any moment the actor's mind takes its orientation from (but does not permit its acts to be dictated by) surrounding facts as seen from its own perspective, and in the light of this assessment decides on action, making and carrying out plans marked by the distinction between means and ends. . . . Interaction as reflected in market events is always interaction between individual plans. Each stage of a market process reflects a mode of such interaction.

Lachmann's statement above (1986: 4), that market activity represents interaction between plans, can be misconstrued. It suggests that plans are things that exist, concrete in substance and with definite form. Perhaps they are a less permanent manifestation of Paretian indifference curves. Thus, 'economic agents meet in markets, each with his own plan that constitutes a co-ordinated means-ends scheme, and find that these plans are not consistent with each other' (Lachman 1986: 56).[9]

The main difficulty in overcoming the misconception of planning as a process of formulating models or blueprints of the world is that, although there is a great difference between a plan of action and an architect's drawing, the epistemology-ontology of the third-person perspective conflates their meanings. All plans are things in the world that mirror precisely other things in the world. Plans are about things that are yet to happen, but both the plans and the things they describe are as real as anything else out there. Because events are determinate, we can tell what is going to happen or can estimate the probability of events. Knowledge has its counterpart in pieces of the world, so plans represent pictures of the world as it will materialise in the 'future'. In the same way that knowledge is either complete or incomplete, so plans are either more or less accurate; or good or bad representations of reality. And, as knowledge changes, bits can be removed from plans and new bits added.

Modernist social theory has handed down the erroneous idea of the plan as a single, comprehensive, unequivocal description of things to be done. This conception continues to dominate social and business theories and to prescribe how a rational person ought to think when he has to come to a decision. The notion is, however, a figment of the imaginary third-person perspective and is a product of a scheme that is negligent towards interpretation or understanding. Leaving the troublesome third-person perspective behind, my object now is to investigate the nature of plans and decision-making from a first-person perspective. This means asking questions about how plans are constituted: questions that deal with how individuals understand and what they know when formulating their plans.

11

PLANS AND DECISIONS
AS UNDERSTANDING

Businessmen do not always 'calculate' before they make decisions, and they do not always 'decide' before they act. For they think that they know their business well enough without having to make repeated calculations; and their actions are frequently routine.

(Machlup 1946: 524–5)

THE NATURE OF PLANS

What is a plan? Le Breton and Henning (1961: 5) offer the following advice to the business decision-maker. '[T]he attainment of a given goal will be best achieved by ... devising a precise plan'. Previous chapters have identified what prompts this sort of advice, but neither you nor I know what to make of it. Try to follow such advice in daily life, whether in business dealings or at other times, and the difficulty we face is knowing what constitutes a 'precise' plan and a 'given goal'. Indeed, just what are our goals?

It is practical to draw a precise plan of a house, or to make a precise measurement of a table or of the rainfall in winter, and if someone instructed me to do so I would understand what he meant. Like all (social) activities, questions of how detailed the plan should be, or whether the measurements are accurate, are of course matters of interpretation, and there may not be unanimity or even substantial agreement about my interpretation. There may even be discussion about whether something is a desk not a table, and which are the winter months. On the other hand, advice to draw up a precise plan of action, which refers to the individual's intentions and endeavours and which consequently juxtaposes 'precision' with interpretation and understanding, is misleading and probably meaningless. Precision is part of an epistemology-ontology of things that exist in the world and plans are not such things; plans and purposes are understanding. Objectives are not things out there but pertain to my constituted understanding of what to do, because it is worth doing or because it is necessary for me to do.

182

Suppose 'precision' is interpreted practically to mean either 'detailed' or 'accurate'. When would the plan be sufficiently detailed and how is its accuracy to be decided? What level of accuracy will ensure that a plan is 'accurate'? What criteria are appropriate for assessing accuracy and who is going to specify these criteria? At least as important is the question of what purpose would be achieved by devising more detailed plans. If my aim is to 'clear my desk' so that I can go away on vacation, would it help me if I laid out a plan of my activities minute-by-minute for the next week? Will an hourly or a daily plan be more beneficial, and what should the plan encompass? Should I try to ensure that no one in the office gives me work during the week? Should I have my car checked to see whether it is likely to break down on the way to work during the next week? Should I plan not to sleep at all so that I will have time to deal with matters that require urgent attention if they arise? Perhaps my best option is simply to find someone who is willing to handle any important work that I am unable to finish before going away and to deal with any urgent matters that may arise while I am away.

Plans are thoughts in the *durée*. Planning means thinking about what we would like to do or are required to do, and about how to do what we want to do or need to do. Sometimes, indeed most of the time, there is no more to planning than this. Plans, as aspects of consciousness, are not clearly delineated, distinct ideas which stand out in relief from the rest of conscious thought or have a defined scope or 'shape'. Nor are the objects of planning – our aims or goals – well defined, robust, and clearly identified, in the way that the positivist ontology of things-in-the-world suggests.

Planning is not a discrete process in the sense that now an idea or goal develops, next it is translated into a plan of action, then at a specific time which is determined in the plan, it has an outcome. Schütz (1972: 45) refers to Bergson's notion of the *durée* as 'a continuous coming-to-be and passing-away of heterogenous qualities'. Later (ibid.: 51), he says that 'the "Now" is a phase rather than a point, and ... the different phases melt into one another'. While these phrases have a somewhat metaphysical ring to them, they capture the idea of an evolving and changing understanding (*Verstehen*), of being conscious of different things, or having different interests. The shifting focus of thought marks the passing of time, but our interests, plans, and their evolution are not identified in the *durée* as such but only, as Schütz (ibid.: 19) describes it, by self-reflectively 'isolating [action] . . . from the flux of experience and consider[ing it] . . . attentively'. As beings-in-time, we do not think to ourselves, 'I have a goal', 'now I must formulate a plan', 'I am now planning', 'now I have completed this plan and can set my next goal'. Rather plans are part of our interests, our awareness, and our doings.

The procedure of considering plans self-reflectively reveals the passage of time in the *durée* as an ever-evolving awareness or consciousness that is associated not so much with sudden realisation, or with new ideas continuously brimming up, as with a 'firming up' or 'crystallising' of ideas; of becoming aware that this is, or is not, the thing to do. Possibilities or options are turned over, not necessarily as clear-cut alternatives but as rather vague ideas about what to do, and why something is worthwhile. Gradually a plan emerges, never as a fully fledged 'structure for action', but as ideas about what to do and how to do it. Ideas never really solidify; they do not amount to a coherent entity which contains detailed inter-connections. Instead, different concerns are given attention. Something now is of interest, then attention is turned to something else as one's interest changes. This is the nature of understanding and of constituting meaning in the hermeneutic circle.

Experience involves contact and discourse with associates, friends, colleagues, and family. Being-in-time is a social existence and plans as well as purposes originate in our social being-in-time. I have stressed that understanding is intersubjective. Plans, though personal in that they reflect the individual's interests, are inherently social. Our interests – whether getting up for work, going to work, setting up a meeting, taking a lunch break, ordering spare parts, or writing a book at home – concern and involve other people. These others are more or less directly involved in our activities, in that we have their requirements, interests, habits, and attitudes more or less clearly in mind as we go about our lives. Even though, at a particular moment, we might not be thinking of others, or of their 'participation' in our interests of the moment, the interests of others always bear upon our own interests and plans. Our social interaction shapes our interests. As understanding is constituted and reconstituted in the *durée*, so are purposes and plans.

The social nature of activities, and the fact that in daily life people co-operate or collaborate to do the things they want to do, is one reason why it is sometimes desirable to formalise plans. People meet to discuss objectives and plan their attainment and later they meet again to discuss the progress of their plans. The more that hinges on the outcome of the plan, the more complex the tasks – in terms of the number of people involved, the number and nature of activities (whether routine or out of the ordinary), and the more costly the operation – the more likely it is that the activities will be designated in a formal plan. Business enterprises are formed around collaborative activities and the need for people to co-operate in order to produce goods or services for others. Many business plans are thus formalised and managing bureaucratic hierarchical organ-isations in particular requires the formulation of formal plans, as part of the process of communicating with other people. But it would be wrong to infer that such plans represent comprehensive blueprints, or take on the character of 'structures' for action. They are never complete guides to action or to decisions and a formal plan is just one way in which people communicate with one another in order jointly to achieve goals. It is important to realise that a plan is just part of the process of communication between people and groups and, in order to understand how plans work or how people get things done, we also have to understand the complex nature of social interaction in organisations, including the many levels of discourse that characterise a person's life in an organisation.

In use, a plan is understanding, which means ideas and thoughts about procedures that should be followed and things that need to be done to attain goals that are necessarily vague and ill defined. Decisions are taken on the basis of these ideas. Businesses want to 'improve their profitability', 'increase their turnover', 'improve productivity', or 'increase their market share'. Even the desire to reduce the reject rate to less than 1 per cent of output is a goal that could be achieved in various ways. Each of the many possible courses of action would have considerably different implications for people in the organisation and for the way in which production is managed. It would be inconceivable to try to formulate a plan which would replicate what should, and will, happen in order to reduce a high reject rate. In explaining the decisions that are taken and also what people do to achieve these purposes, it is necessary to understand the meaning that they ascribe to the goals themselves, their understanding of others' plans, and how and why they interpret them as they do.

An individual's view on whether a course of action appears to be feasible, attractive, or impractical, depends on that decision-maker's interests. Plans are assessed against the extent of the decision-maker's involvement in the matter, including perhaps her personal financial stake, her perspective on the problem and the firm's situation, and her assessment of its prospects. Although it is her job as managing director to make a decision, her recommendations may well depend on whether she is applying an accountant's or personnel manager's experience to the problem. Her inevitably prejudiced judgement might hinge on any of a number of different factors, not least her relationships with other people, from colleagues to shareholders or customers. In the course of this prejudiced assessment, which may also reflect the decision-maker's assessment of the reliability or motives of the people who did the planning, documents are interpreted and used selectively. The decision-maker may have to choose between incongruent recommendations, or may find that the positions which individuals hold on the feasibility or desirability of a project may be at odds. In such circumstances it is necessary to compromise or else to reject certain interests in favour of others. None of this can be planned.

Even after the 'go-ahead' for a particular venture has been given because someone with authority thinks that it is going to be worthwhile, any plan will be reshaped in the interests of various people. Plans actually evolve, perhaps long after the basic procedures are established, not 'growing' but changing, influenced by people's social interaction and their evolving discourse which is part of this interaction. It is very difficult to say that this is what the plan is or this is where it began or ended, as there are no clear-cut beginnings or well-defined endings in the *durée*. New projects emerge from what people are already doing. The company might have been successful and grown rapidly, or its sales might have dwindled. Depending on what happened, the people involved understand differently, and their plans and the courses of action they pursue will be different. This description of the continuous nature of planning and decision-making in the *durée* is supported by the account of Williams and Scott (1965) of the nature of investment decisions. The purpose of their research was to 'examine . . . particular decisions in the . . . general context of the firm's policies and procedures' (ibid.: 11), but they were not easily able to find suitable projects to study because '[m]any projects were so closely related to previous and subsequent investments that it would have been impossible to study them in isolation'.

Le Breton and Henning (1961: 7) are correct in asserting that planning and deciding are different. They see decisions as resolving 'conflicting alternative choices'. Making a decision involves reaching a conclusion, settling something, or making up one's mind. A plan, in their view, has three characteristics: the future, action, and the idea that the course of action will be taken by the planner or by someone designated by him. But they also make the important point that decisions are taken throughout a planning process and are 'inextricably interrelated to planning'. There is no conscious distinction between the two. The threefold classification of plans, decisions, and actions, that is so much a part of social theories of decision-making, is comfortably accommodated in positivistic methodo-logy, where each of these is conceived as a definite entity in the world, coming into being in sequence, in response to some 'pressure'. A problem arises out there and the individual has to respond to it, so she makes a plan to deal with it, takes a decision, following a logical 'path' if she is 'procedurally rational', and then does something. The classification is unhelpful, however, when the object is to explore how the individual constitutes her world. Treating the classification as a rigid sequence that *exists* in people's minds – with the implication that they are conscious of doing something called planning, then of deciding, and finally of acting – is misleading.

Schütz (1972) provides valuable insights into the nature of decision-making and his analysis is a landmark in the development of a subjectivist paradigm. Yet his conception of plans is also apt to mislead because it implies that these are formulated as definite and coherent images, 'pictures' of a future state of affairs, as the following passages reveal. '[T]he analysis of action shows that it is always carried out in accordance with a plan more or less implicitly preconceived' (ibid.: 59). It is a characteristic of conscious action that (ibid.: 63)

> before we carry it out, we have a picture in our mind of what we are going to do. This is the 'projected act.' Then, as we do proceed to action we are either continuously holding the picture before our inner eye (retention), or we are from time to time recalling it to mind (repro-duction). . . . This 'map-consulting' is what we are referring to when we call the action conscious.

Schütz explains (ibid.: 63) that 'actions are conscious if we have previously mapped them out "in the future perfect tense"' and his exposition suggests that projection amounts to mentally rehearsing the action. While not denying the idea of 'projection' – it is the sort of notion associated with thinking about the 'quality' of an investment that we are about to undertake – I want to avoid the impression that the project amounts to a complete mental picture, or a blueprint, of the 'completed action'. Such implications are at odds with the spirit of Schütz's phenomenology and are in conflict with the understanding of how individuals constitute their understanding in the hermeneutic circle.[1]

Not only are 'projects' (in Schütz's sense) the individual's personal understanding, but most plans we make are of the type associated with the following statement: 'I plan to be at the office by 8.30 and to see my first appointment at 9.00.' Getting to the office is simply a matter of routine. Much of the time, if plans are made at all, we are hardly conscious of this. A considerable part of daily life consists of routine activities that are more or less habitual.[2] The 'projected act' does not presume that activities – mine and other people's associated with my getting to the office – are mapped out; that the individual is conscious of checking the clock, picking up her briefcase, walking through the front door, going down the path to the car, opening the gates, and so on. Nor does the notion of projection presume that she thinks about what other people will be doing that may delay, or facilitate, her departure. Planning to be at the office by 8.30 means little more than making a mental note to leave in time to get there by 8.30.

Busy with our activities, immersed in the *durée*, thoughts evolve; we have ideas and identify problems. Planning is part of this process of 'being conscious' and plans may evolve slowly or, as suggested, the need to do something is merely noted, or perhaps we are struck by a thought about a way of overcoming a snag that has arisen. The line between planning and deciding is difficult to draw and is certainly not at the forefront of con-sciousness in our daily activities. Planning, generally, is without a time dimension. The activities in which the individual engages merely continue. It is only by 'stepping out' of the *durée*, through the act of self-reflection and of turning consciousness in on itself, that there is a sense of having 'planned' or of having decided.

Like the idea that plans, decisions, and actions are identifiable and form a definite sequence, the contention that plans and actions are observed is also a creation of the third-person perspective. Of course we do not observe other people planning, deciding, and acting. We understand what they are doing in the context in which we encounter them, a context shaped by our relationships with others, as friends, or colleagues, or family. Unless they tell us that they have decided to do something, or are working on a plan for some purpose, or we are sitting down together to draw up a plan, the fact they may be planning or deciding is unknown and is mostly irrelevant. What matters is our interaction in the *durée*. Either we are doing things together – such as having a game of golf, taking a tea break, resolving a crisis, planning a luncheon – or my activities are directed towards meeting your demands, taking cognisance of your request, and so on. This 'social existence', the intersubjectively constituted life-world, is the cradle of understanding, the *fons et origo* of thought and activity.

SOCIAL RELATIONSHIPS AND PLANNING

Planning, whether it is done by one or many people, is a social activity and plans are constituted intersubjectively. In addition to the people who do the planning, there are those for whom a plan is intended and who will use it and also those who, one way or another, are going to be involved in the planned activities. They may be consulted or instructed about what they will do. The planner and decision-maker rely on advice, assistance, and information. Sometimes it is consciously sought but it may be acquired serendipitously. What goes under the heading of 'the provision of information' is to a large degree institutionalised, in that the planner has both formal and informal contacts. These may range from business associates to family members to fellow golfers. Institutions such as estate agencies, banks, or computerised online databases, provide specific information and, sometimes, specialists are called upon to undertake 'feasibility studies'.[3]

For reasons related to their methodology, economists have neglected social relationships,[4] but the question of the decision-maker's associations, the nature of these relationships, and how they influence her, are important in understanding the process of planning and decision-making. Because they serve to illuminate factors that bear upon decisions, these are issues that I must address. What is needed, first, is a means of conceptualising social relations, a framework in terms of which the decision-maker's relationships with others can be examined. Then it is necessary to establish which relationships are important to the investment planner. In his 'social world', which associations have a bearing on his decisions and why do they do so?

In order to conceptualise the social interaction associated with business decisions, the categories provided by Schütz (1972) are fruitful. His analysis of social relationships is particularly suited to my object of exploring the first-person perspective because he examines social interaction from the point of view of how people constitute social relationships; that is, how they understand these relationships.[5]

Discussing the individual's awareness of other people, Schütz states (1972: 140) that

> I not only consciously experience you, but I live with you and grow old with you. I can attend to your stream of consciousness, just as I can attend to my own, and I can, therefore, become aware of what is going on in your mind. . . . You and your subjective experiences are not only 'accessible' to me . . . but are taken for granted by me . . .

He adds that there is a 'complicated substructure' in our interpretation of other individuals of which, for most of the time, we are unconscious, but the 'deeper layers' are brought to light as soon as we contemplate others' motives or directly question them about their intentions or aspirations. Even in the shared 'Here and Now', the *domain (or realm) of directly experienced social reality* (ibid.: 142), we have different relationships with our contemporaries who share this *'Mitwelt'*. There is a group of people with whom each of us is most intimate, which we might think of as an inner circle of associates, and which may include family and friends and work associates. Others, consociates, are part of our *Mitwelt* but are hardly known to us at all. We may have little understanding of their interests and habits and little insight into their motives and, indeed, may have no need to understand them.

Schütz also distinguishes between the individual's *'Umwelt'* and his *'Mitwelt'*. The former is the 'world of directly experienced social reality' (ibid.: 30), the latter consists of contemporaries who surround my world, who live in the world *'with'* me but who do not live *'through'* it as a matter of direct experience' (ibid.: 142). These people are referred to simply as 'contemporaries' (*'Nebenmenschen'*). They are people whom I do not have occasion to meet, or with whom I do not come into contact, although at some or other time I may do so. The importance of the distinction is that (ibid.: 142–3),

> living with my fellow men, I directly experience them and their subjective experiences. But of my contemporaries we will say that, while living among them, I do not directly and immediately grasp their subjective experiences but instead infer, on the basis of indirect evidence, the typical subjective experiences they must be having. Inferences of this kind, of course, can be well founded.

Schütz identifies another category, a *'Vorwelt'*, or world of predecessors which is separate from old, or past, relationships with people who were, or still are, contemporaries in the individual's *Mitwelt* (ibid.: 207). A predecessor is someone 'in the past not one whose experiences overlap in time with one of mine' (ibid.: 208). The significance of the *Vorwelt* is that, in interpreting the activities of predecessors, 'there is no open horizon towards the future . . . there is nothing as yet undecided, uncertain, or awaiting fulfilment'. Finally, there is also a social world of successors (*'Folgewelt'*).

Now, as Schütz points out, there is a fundamental epistemological distinction between the individual's insight into the circumstances of the *Umwelt* on the one hand and the *Mitwelt*, *Vorwelt*, or *Folgewelt* on the other. Knowledge of the *Umwelt*, based on experience, is our understanding or interpretation of lived-through events. Using terms coined by Max Weber, Schütz refers to this as '*observational*' understanding, while our ability to understand and to explain the actions of our contemporaries, or for that matter our predecessors or successors, is based on '*motivational*' understanding (ibid.: 30). The theorist who wishes to explain investment and location plans is concerned to understand the life-worlds of business decision-makers. The theorist's understanding is motivational understanding which is 'not tied to the world of directly experienced social reality' (ibid.: 30). But, and here the significance of the double hermeneutic of social science is once more apparent, his interest is the lived experiences of the managers of business enterprises and how these decision-makers' experiences bear upon the things that they do. This motivational understanding Schütz calls 'genuine understanding of the other person' (ibid.: 111, emphasis omitted).

At the heart of modern hermeneutics is the problem of understanding how the individual understands. Explaining business decisions means asking how the decision-makers constitute their worlds, or how they understand and resolve the problems at hand. In doing so, the theorist, concerned with his *Mitwelt*, is interested in the planner's *Umwelt*, identifying the social relationships that are important to her in her role as manager, and establishing why and how particular relationships pertain to decisions that are taken. In so doing, however, he must necessarily bring those planners into his own sphere of understanding and examine their activities from his own prejudiced perspective. My object in the next chapter is to examine the social circumstances of managers in order to throw light on investment decisions and ultimately on the issue of choosing a location.

DECISIONS AS JUDGEMENT

The conception of decision-making associated with a third-person perspective is as ingrained as it is unsatisfactory. The story behind that conception is that agents each possess a list of well-defined alternatives, of things that are out there in the world, from which they select the one that will be best for the firm. Each acts independently and the criteria that they use to optimise are economic ones. By contrast, in coming to understand the individual's 'situation' – her understanding that is the context of her business decisions – I have stressed the importance of being-in-time and of the social nature of business activity, both which are characterised as the interpretative existence that is the hermeneutic circle of discourse with others, conscious thought, and conjecture. Focusing specifically on the person who is planning an investment, what does this discussion imply regarding the nature of decision-making?

Making their decisions in the *durée*, investment planners have no recourse to 'facts of the situation' as a basis for their decisions. So what ensures the success of an investment? Ultimately, the people who buy the products. Whether they do so depends on what the business does to produce and to market a product that they regard as an 'attractive' offer; but it depends on many other things besides. These cannot be planned for, or even defined or established today, except in the vaguest of terms which are of no value to a decision-maker. For example, the success of the venture will depend on what the firm and its competitors do in the course of time. The likes and dislikes of potential customers matter, and perhaps their attitudes towards environmental issues will have a bearing on things. Technological developments that occur, and changes in weather patterns, may impede or assist the firm's success. If its markets are international, developments in the field of international relations as well as changes in economic policies may have an impact on the firm. Finally, as Hayek (1967c) explains so well in an 'off the record' discussion (which is notable because it does not try to cloak an explanation of purchasing decisions in a fanciful model of consumer choice), what people buy probably depends as much on social influences – peer group pressures, fashion, custom – as it does on firms' efforts to persuade them to buy. Enumerating the different factors that make a product successful, however, does not resolve in the decision-maker's mind the question of whether to undertake an investment, and no amount of searching will yield information on these matters that will settle the question. It will only be possible to find out about any of them in the course of time.

We are back to the implications of the hermeneutic circle. When it comes to deciding whether something ought to be done, whether a project may succeed or whether a failing business is beyond the point of rescue, the decision must be a matter of judgement. Judgement is not grounded, except in personal experience. Even when the 'measuring rod' of profits and losses enters the picture, personal judgement is always the final factor in determining whether to continue to roll over a loan, support a new rights issue, commit money to an expansion of a subsidiary, or to cut inventory levels.

It is important not to jump to the conclusion that because decisions are subjective they are therefore arbitrary. On the contrary, in spite of having to rely on their feelings about what to do, or about whether this is or is not the right way of going about things, the individuals who make these types of decisions probably give considerable thought to the matters at hand. When decisions are not routine, they will weigh up the matters at hand in order to do what they consider to be worthwhile or appropriate, and they will try to judge consistently when dealing with other matters at different times. It is of the essence of judgement that it reflects one's prejudices, not only in that it is a matter of how the individual understands, but also because decisions exercised at a moment in the *durée* must necessarily reflect the decision-maker's assessment at that moment. The manager who has a background in human resources may well give weight to factors that the accountant does not consider. When siting a factory, the person who has personal knowledge of a place will judge it differently from a stranger who lacks personal experience but who has a list of pros and cons that someone else drew up. The stranger's assessment, too, may be different when he has had an opportunity to speak to an 'expert'.

In the theory of search, orthodox economists have nurtured the view that the uncertainty associated with decisions can be resolved before coming to a decision.[6] By diligent searching, the 'quality' of which can itself be assessed against an algorithm for optimal search behaviour, the decision-maker can eliminate, or overcome, the judgemental aspect of reaching a decision. In early formulations, the idea behind search theory was that agents confronted a random distribution of prices and had to find the particular parts of the distribution that were relevant to them. Later, the theory required them to estimate an unknown, but unchanging, distribution of prices using Bayesian analysis (see Lippman and McCall 1976). All this was supposed to make for more realistic models of decision-making because it did away with the postulate of perfect knowledge and made explicit the costs of acquiring information. That search theory, and the economics of information, is based on the epistemology and ontology of a third-person perspective is clearly indicated by the conditions under which Bayesian analysis applies: that things that matter in making decisions – in this case prices – are all in the world out there and form an unchanging distribution. Because the world of search theory is a closed, complete system, it is possible for individuals, eventually, to find out what all the conditions are like and to optimise.[7]

From the point of view of the individual constituting a plan of action in the *durée*, it is inconceivable to search for any solution, let alone an optimal one. She may certainly gather information, or may ask others to do it for her, but does she have enough? Is it worth trying to obtain more information? There are no hard and fast answers to the questions. The information that she obtains does not, in itself, direct her towards the 'right' answer. It may help her to form an opinion, suggesting that circumstances are not yet opportune for a particular course of action. But – in contrast to the conventional story associated with determinate schemes where there is a fixed 'amount of knowledge' in the world – all she can 'acquire' are ideas, suggestions, clues, or possibilities. What she makes of the information is obviously a matter of interpretation.

These arguments justify the value that is attached to experience. Orthodox economic theory would have nothing to say about experience because it is not a notion that the third-person perspective can accommodate, except as 'acquired knowledge' which anyone can acquire. The quality that is valued by peers and associates and that gives the possessor authority, or makes her an 'expert' and is considered a *sine qua non* for appointment to positions of responsibility, however, is not something that can be found in the world and that is potentially available to all. Experience belongs with Polanyi's concept of personal knowledge.[8] Experience is about the transformation of the individual in the *durée*, the 'dialogue' of the hermeneutic circle of interpretative, prejudiced understanding. Gaining experience means that in the course of her activities the individual understands differently. She 'tests' her understanding, prejudices, and preconceptions, and these are shaped or revised. Because decisions are judgements, there is no substitute for experience – for having had exposure to, and 'internalised', similar situations.

The problem for managers who have to make investment or location decisions is that they rarely have the necessary experience to identify what is or is not likely to prove worthwhile, or to identify a good place for a factory, or what needs to be done in co-ordinating activities associated with the investment. This is why decision-makers rely on the advice of experts – not because the latter have the knowledge to optimise or to be able to determine what will happen, but because of their experience. Large organisations are conservative and, with funds at their disposal, hiring experts is a practical way for managers to try to satisfy themselves that they are doing the right thing.[9] The expertise may be found among specialists within the firm, or management consultants and other advisers who are contracted for a particular project. They bring different perspectives on the matters at hand. When consultants make their recommendations, it is their experience with other companies that they draw on, including what they have learned from other people about why and where companies have been successful. Their advice reflects a current view of what has been successful both locally and abroad and, for this reason, it often has an element of faddishness about it.[10]

The received view of planning leads to the conclusion that allowing personal prejudices to 'get in the way', or relying on the advice of others without 'finding out the (real) facts for oneself', is irrational and undesirable. The decision-maker is supposed to look for the right answers and calculate the best solutions as if the future course of events could effectively be reduced to numbers today. The consideration that plans – and knowledge – are understanding helps to clarify the nature and significance of the personal element in decision-making, which modern hermeneutics takes to be the essence of decision-making. The decision-maker relies on well-established contacts and trusted sources because he has only his own and others' experience to guide him. Decisions reflect feelings, including one's faith in a colleague. Which means that I rely on that person's advice but disregard the information provided by someone else.

Machlup's views quoted at the start of the chapter certainly convey something of the flavour of a first-person perspective on decision-making, and their implications may be more significant than he himself realised. There is little point in businessmen doing calculations before they make decisions, because what is going to happen can only be conjectured. When it comes to making decisions, they do indeed know their business – from experience.

The significance of the arguments set out in this chapter is that they put an end to the idea that, in making decisions, managers can, or should, seek to optimise shareholders' returns, or to minimise costs. Such advice stems from the premise that the goals that firms pursue, including these ones, are things that can be found in the world out there. For those economists who find the narrative of neoclassical theory appealing, the disconcerting implication of my arguments, as we will see, is that 'economic factors' – the values of variables such as prices and costs which dominate the orthodox theory of 'decision-making' – may not be at all relevant to making investment and other decisions.

12

INVESTMENT DECISIONS

To fail to bring the planning stage to the surface ... allows, by default, the emergence of the view that the large organisation operates under a single planning mind, and, by not looking into the nature of the organisation's authority relationships, allows to persist, if it does not propagate, authoritarian views of a very naïve order. The persistent '*he* will adjust his output ...', *he* will do this and *he* will do that, coming from teachers and students alike, is extremely irritating and provoking to anybody who has made a disciplined inquiry into these matters. (Thirlby 1973: 206)

THE ISSUES

Kenneth Boulding describes the neoclassical firm as 'a strange bloodless creature without a balance sheet, without any visible capital structure, without debts' (quoted in Penrose 1959: 11, n. 2). These are not mere gaps in neoclassical theory, which can be filled. Their absence betrays a fatal affliction of the third-person perspective: its complete indifference to people's histories or social circumstances, as a way of understanding their situations, revealing their social obligations and commitments, and thus of explaining their activities and their decisions. The seeds of a plan, while they 'look forward' in a sense, also refer to a past: to how things have been going, to ongoing responsibilities, and to contractual obligations. This is an area in which the third-person perspective is utterly misleading. The agent of neoclassical theory is constrained only by his 'budget', which requires him to tailor his 'choices' in the face of the prices imposed by the activities of others. Whatever he does, there is always a huge range of options open to him. By implication, with each 'decision' the agent begins with a clean slate.[1]

In order to gauge the potential for a conceptual framework involving a first-person perspective to address problems of planning and decision-making, I must show that it is practical to gain an understanding of how decision-makers understand those problems in which we, the theorists and

195

interpreters of others' activities, are interested. In addition, our efforts must contribute to our understanding of the problems themselves. I intend to do both, but wish to emphasise that it is unrealistic to expect too much of what is essentially an exploratory exercise into developing a hermeneutical approach to social problems. I will have accomplished my goal if I can point out how an investigation of decision-making from the standpoint of interpretative understanding might proceed. With these provisos in mind, my object is to clarify the nature of investment decisions, and I will then go on in Chapter 13 to discuss the location decisions of business enterprises.

My point of departure is that explaining investment decisions requires an understanding of the importance of managers' motives, circumstances, 'histories', and their understanding of firms' past and present positions. These factors shape each manager's understanding of his social circumstances and they are integral to an explanation of the decisions that managers make. The chapter aims to link motives and circumstances to investment decisions, showing how individuals' motives and their appreciation, or interpretation, of their circumstances have a bearing on the identification of investment opportunities, and how taking account of their motives and circumstances offers useful insights into investment decisions.

Recalling the discussion in previous chapters, I look upon investment opportunities as ideas born in the *durée*, in the process of taking stock of or assessing the current situation, as part of the individual's ongoing 'dialogue' which involves other people and constitutes the hermeneutic circle of understanding. Investment opportunities emerge – perhaps, as no more than a fleeting thought about some possibility – in a way that makes them a product of the moment, as the situation is 'grasped' or 'read'.[2] This 'reading' is the planner's understanding. Understanding means that the individual assesses events in terms of her experience of business conditions, places where she has worked, and people whom she knows. Experience is the source of prejudice, in the sense of previously established judgements. The individual has opinions about people; they are regarded as unfriendly, or industrious, or trustworthy, as the case may be. Understanding also means being conscious of one's ongoing commitments to other people. Each planner has her own *Umwelt*, consisting of friends, business associates, and others, from whom she might come to hear about business opportunities. The individual has views about which of her social obligations and business relationships are important, which should be fostered, and which are not worth maintaining. She also has insight into the business and has formed judgements about her prospects for advancement and about the success of a competitor's marketing campaign. Ideas about investments are always embedded in one's prejudiced understanding and they always derive from the social context of that understanding. My first task is to consider how the manager's *Umwelt* bears upon the identification of investment opportunities.

LARGE AND SMALL ENTERPRISES

The nature of our social relationships – our *Umwelt* – is influenced by our work environment, and therefore by the type of organisation in which we work. People's experiences differ from organisation to organisation and their experiences are influenced by the social relationships that they form. The way in which the organisation is structured and managed affects these relationships. Thus, in analysing the social context of business decisions, I propose to divide decision-makers into two broad groups with the justification that the daily lives – the social business worlds – of people who work in large, typically bureaucratic firms are generally very different from those of the managers of small firms. Treating the social worlds of all managers alike would obscure factors that are important in understanding their conduct.[3]

It is important to note that the categories 'large' and 'small' which I propose to employ are only indirectly related to conventional measures of size such as employment or turnover. They refer to whether managers operate in a hierarchical, bureaucratic environment (see Torrington and Weightman 1985: 32–4) normally associated with bigger industrial undertakings, or whether theirs is the experience of the autonomy and flexibility of managing a smaller concern. The defining characteristic of the smaller organisation (also noted by Torrington and Weightman 1985: 31–2) is that, in contrast to its bureaucratic counterpart, it has an 'entrepreneurial culture'.[4] In Chapter 7, I referred to individuals' interpretative understanding of institutions. The characteristics discussed by Torrington and Weightman are ones which are understood by people involved with large and small businesses, and are qualities that they ascribe to the different types of institutions.

For the purpose of examining managers' investment and other decisions, it is the relationships between people in the firm and between them and other individuals with whom they associate that is of interest, rather than the size of the firm *per se*. Yet, to the extent that there is a rough and ready link between the structure and the 'culture' of the firm on the one hand and its size and structure which influences social relations on the other, size seems to be a practical a means of categorising firms so as to highlight the social relationships that are the points of interest. By the same token, defining 'small' and 'large' firms in practice is not necessarily straightforward, and in order to classify firms, or more particularly to describe the circumstances of the individuals who work in them, it is really necessary to understand the social structures of different organisations.[5]

From a practical point of view, it is not immediately obvious whom we would single out as the investment decision-makers in large organisations. Discovering who they are may require not only an investigation of each specific organisation, but also of the sort of intimate knowledge of the organisation and its *de facto* structures of authority that come from substantial experience in the organisation. Williams and Scott (1965: 21–3) describe investment decisions by large companies. Their position is that where and with whom the idea originates determines who becomes involved in assessing an investment proposal. Certainly individuals at the highest levels within the company will become involved, sometimes to ensure that the proposal has adequate patronage before it is formalised. Wright (1964: 36) does not add much to the picture of who makes decisions, other than to say, 'we are dealing with an individual who is occupying a position at the upper management level'. At the stage of approving or endorsing the commitment of resources to a particular project, the people involved will certainly be senior managers. In larger companies, however, planning may be carried out in different departments and between the head office and divisions of the company. Without some knowledge of management structures and the recognition that there are both formal and informal channels of authority, communication, and decision-making, it will be difficult to determine who they are and what positions they hold. By contrast, identifying the planners and decision-makers in small companies should prove easier because there are few senior managers and the whole activity may rest upon the shoulders of one person – the owner or chief executive.

Besides the practical difficulties of establishing who makes plans and decisions, there is a further *caveat* regarding the distinction between managers of small and large firms. The distinction may be useful for certain purposes, but the 'ideal type' is a concept that has to be handled carefully and the idea of a typical individual in typical circumstances is not without its problems. Clearly the requirement is that the ideal types that are employed should serve to illuminate those aspects of individuals' conduct that we wish to examine.[6] At the same time, we have to guard against the particular classification concealing important differences in the circumstances of individuals within each group, which it is necessary to identify and to emphasise in order to explain their decisions.

Bearing these qualifications in mind, my contention is that the character of a large firm, as opposed to a small one, influences the relationships between people in terms of the nature of their associations as well as the variety and types of people with whom they interact. So we must look to the social circumstances of people within the two types of organisations, identifying what contributes to these circumstances and explaining their significance for the outlook of planners, or for the way they constitute business problems, and the decisions that are taken. I will begin by examining the position of the manager in a large organisation and then deal with his counterpart in a small firm.

MANAGING IN A LARGE ENTERPRISE

The senior manager of a large organisation is sensible to his structured work environment. He is part of a 'team' (see Penrose 1959: 45–9) and is required to participate in meetings, planning groups, and motivational seminars with colleagues who represent the rest of the team. A considerable part of his day-to-day activities is spent with his associates fulfilling this function. As a 'team player', his independence and the scope for pursuing personal goals is limited. His superiors and other colleagues expect that the decisions that he takes will fit in with the organisation's goals and requirements, and he understands that this is expected of him. 'Corporate loyalty' is encouraged by the fact that the career prospects of a senior manager depend almost entirely on review and assessment by his superiors and peers within the firm, based on performance-related criteria such as profits, sales, or turnover. The manager's views regarding the organisation's requirements and goals will be shaped by the attitudes of superiors, perhaps the managing director or chairman, to whom he is accountable and others to whom he has a responsibility or whom he respects and whose attitudes he admires.

A corollary of the structured environment is that planning and making important decisions is usually a collaborative effort. In all aspects of his job, including the planning function, the individual typically can, and does, rely on a substantial number of people, including support staff, to assist him. By virtue of the structure of the organisation and the specialisation of functions within it, our individual's jurisdiction is relatively limited when it comes to making decisions and is confined to matters that fall within his designated area of authority in the organisation. One of the consequences of being in a niche within a well-established large organisation is a sense of security, and perhaps even complacency, about one's position. There is a popular conception that conditions of employment in large corporate organisations are secure. Torrington and Weightman (1985: 34) state that the predictability of the institutional setting 'provides a secure environment for the employee and a clear line of safe career progression'.

The most important reason for the apparent greater security of individuals within the large enterprise may be that, compared with the small firms described below, large firms are felt to be on a sounder financial footing.[7] The value of a company's assets itself normally enables its management to secure access to credit but, in addition, the large company probably has many options for meeting financing requirements. Besides the banks, a listed public company may make use of the stock exchange, issuing its own shares and debentures. All these factors contribute to the firm's ability to raise money on demand. Its financial standing also derives from its position in the marketplace. With a diversified product line and a wide distribution network, perhaps including foreign markets, the firm is somewhat insulated against both domestic business cycle fluctuations and changes in local market conditions. Losses or declining sales sustained in one area or in a particular product line represent only a percentage of turnover and profits, and can be absorbed by the company's performance elsewhere. In terms of its relationships with suppliers, the large firm does not necessarily suffer if a single supplier fails to deliver or goes bankrupt. In all probability, because of the volume of business, it has a network of suppliers, with whom it has well-established business relationships, who can be called upon if circumstances require this.

These arguments do not mean that the managers of large businesses are insensible to the uncertainties of the 'environment' and the vagaries of the market. What they do mean is that the large business organisation has the resources to weather a volatile business environment, or even to withstand temporary setbacks, such as the effects of a failed investment, better than the smaller manufacturer.

For various reasons, managers within the large organisation are likely to be conservative in their attitudes towards the 'risks' (used in its colloquial sense) of doing business. Conservatism is reinforced by the consideration that, in most cases, there is little opportunity to give expression to personal motives and only limited opportunity for personal gain from taking risks if the venture is successful. For, accompanying the security experienced by a manager in a large organisation, is a lack of autonomy characterised by having to fit into a particular structure: being assessed on one's role as a 'team player'; being constrained by the structure; and feeling what is described as a 'lack of creativity'. It is frequently asserted that this type of organisation stifles resourcefulness and does not reward ingenuity.

The existence of substantial fixed assets also engenders conservatism by forcing the managers of a large organisation to operate within fairly narrow limits. From his perspective, as he assesses possibilities in the *durée*, decisions taken in the past have committed the company to certain products and markets, and there are well-established business relationships, brands, and customer loyalties which have to be maintained and supported. These significantly circumscribe the nature of the business and the individual's autonomy or freedom of action. If the large firm also has a substantial amount of long-term debt, the manager's main responsibility will be to maintain continuity of the firm's activities and operations and to ensure the continued use of these assets in the future. Appreciating these conditions, the manager recognises that he does not have much scope for departing from what have become the established practices and policies of the organisation.

The broad financial base of the large firm also means that decision-makers are not pressured into seizing opportunities. Especially for senior people, the penalties associated with having made what turns out to be the wrong decision are probably greater than the rewards of making what proves to be a successful one. Managers are secure in their positions and at senior levels will probably receive a substantial remuneration package without having to pursue what they perceive as risky, but perhaps high-yielding opportunities. The individual manager's ability to 'stick his neck out' and to depart from well-established practices, or to venture into new areas of business, is also circumscribed by the emphasis on corporate norms, which is a feature of such organisations. Major decisions probably have to be ratified by a board, which means that in order to gain acceptance a proposal has be supported by people with different outlooks and interests. The need to convince a group of people with diverse interests of the acceptability of a project in itself suggests a bias towards conservatism and restraint, partly because compromises will be needed to avoid conflicts of interest that are bound to arise, and partly to resolve those conflicts that do arise.

The shareholding of a large company, which favours financial conservatism, also promotes a generally conservative outlook amongst its managers. The main shareholders are likely to be other large companies, whose own financial interests will be served by a share portfolio that yields good, stable, and sustained returns, rather than the sort of volatility of earnings that may accompany high-risk ventures. That the investment advisers of the major shareholding companies select their portfolios with these considerations in mind is evidenced by their preference for blue chip shares.[8] A further moderating influence on the activities of senior managers in larger companies is that public listed ones in particular operate in the public domain, and are subject to the scrutiny and censure of the financial press.

All these arguments support the somewhat paradoxical idea that the large industrial organisation, which is generally financially secure, typically leans towards conservatism in decision-making. In terms of our object of understanding how particular investment and location decisions are made, this conservatism and its consequences are most important. People are designated to undertake feasibility studies, and the decision-makers – those who have the final say over whether or not the investment goes ahead – will want a detailed assessment of the 'risks' and uncertainties associated with any proposed investment.[9] Almost all those involved in the decision-making process in the large organisation will be from within the organisation. Planning is a 'team effort', but since the team consists of insiders, perhaps with diverse interests, there may be conflicts of interest that have to be resolved in formulating the plans. Because of the size and diversity of the organisation, there is a potential for conflicts of interest whenever there are policy changes, so Nelson and Winter (1982) set considerable store by 'routines' for managing large organisations. They hold that an aim of managers is to maintain, as routines, policies that people accept. The large firm is a coalition of people and the need to sustain routines – to avoid departures from the tried, trusted, and accepted – imparts a further element of conservatism to the culture of the organisation.

> [A] contemplated action otherwise sensible both for the organisation and for the member taking it may have to be rejected if it is likely to be interpreted as 'provocative'. . . . The result may be that the routines of the organisation as a whole are confined to extremely narrow channels by the dikes of vested interest. Adaptations that appear 'obvious' and 'easy' to an external observer may be foreclosed because they involve a perceived threat to internal political equilibrium.
>
> (Nelson and Winter 1982: 111)

These arguments suggest that people's views about financial or profit considerations will not be a primary motivating factor in investment decisions.[10] Rather, decision-makers will be preoccupied with the 'internal' implications of strategic investments on a diversified company: the effects on divisions, management, and power structures, shareholders, and on the perceptions of these people. I propose that the circumstances of the 'environment', including the traditional economic determinants of investment such as the cost of capital, wage rates, and exchange rate variability, will be less important to the decision-makers. If the risks appear to be high, an investment proposal will simply not be ratified; large firms do not have to grab at chances. Wherever possible, decision-makers will try to adopt courses of action which give them flexibility, so that there is a better chance of rectifying problems that might arise. The substantial financial resources of the large enterprise may even encourage planners, prompted by the conservative environment in which they work, to plan for 'worst cases' or at least to adopt a moderately pessimistic, rather than an optimistic, outlook.

'Building in' flexibility to plans is liable to increase the cost of an investment by requiring more – or more expensive – resources, allowing for longer lead-times, or perhaps acquiring more capacity than people expect to utilise. These are costs which a large organisation will be better able to afford. In the next chapter I explain that the location of production facilities is a factor that may give the firm greater flexibility.

THE MANAGER OF A SMALL FIRM

In contrast to the picture that I have painted of the circumstances of managers of large firms, two sets of factors will typically set apart the individual and her life within the smaller manufacturing operation. One is the extent to which the individual's *Umwelt* consists of people outside the organisation for which she works, and for this reason her business associates are less likely to be employees of the same organisation. They may not even be in allied businesses, but may simply be acquaintances. The other is the relative lack of security of individuals in a small organisation, perhaps especially felt by people in management positions.

Apart from the skills of those directly involved in the manufacturing process, from supervisory positions upwards, there is not a great deal of management expertise in the small firm. This means that each manager is also a good deal less specialised and has less administrative support than her counterpart in the large industrial organisation. As a consequence, in their business relationships, managers of small organisations place relatively more reliance on people outside the organisation compared with their counterparts in larger organisations. This reliance extends from obtaining specialised services (functions such as book-keeping, machine maintenance, and catering may be contracted out) to generating new business. Because senior people in a small organisation carry wide-ranging responsibilities and have little opportunity to delegate within the organisation, their reliance on outsiders and the trust they place in some of these people may be particularly strong. Out of necessity perhaps, the business relationships of these managers are likely to extend to a wider spectrum of people than the managers of larger enterprises. For the former, too, the distinction between business and social relationships is likely to be less clear-cut.

Her business has a small asset base and is regarded as risky, so financial institutions will not grant the manager of the small firm the ready access to credit that is available to her large-company counterpart. Not only is the cost of credit likely to be lower for the latter, but the large company has a wider range of financing options open to it. The small manufacturer may have to look to unconventional sources of credit, possibly paying higher rates of interest. One possibility is to turn to networks of friends and family to provide her with the capital that she requires.

Godsell (1990: 35) defines a 'network' as a business relationship 'with more than one strand to it. Not just a straight supply and demand relationship, but something based on friendship or kinship, on religious affiliation or geographic location or simply affinities dating back to childhood'. If these types of relationships characterise the way that small firms do business, this definition gives tangible meaning to the concept of '*Umwelt*' as applied to the managers of these firms. Godsell also notes that networks can be 'organic' and inherited because the associates are family or belong to the same ethnic or religious group, or they can be 'functional' because they are 'consciously developed'. The reasons why such networks exist and are forged are entirely understandable. They may assist individuals or groups who feel marginalised by, or are subjected to discrimination within, a broader community, or who lack the resources, such as some form of collateral, to borrow money and conclude other transactions with institutions that will conduct their business only around formal contracts. Networks provide skills, capital, and business contacts for small businesses that are struggling (see various contributions in Greenfield *et al.* 1979).[11]

For a small-business manager – as opposed to her corporate counterpart – the people who comprise her network play a bigger role in, and have a relatively greater influence on, her decisions. The reasons are twofold. People who are not employees of the company simply play a bigger part in her life. In addition, since the manager of the small business has to spend much of her time keeping the business going, she will rely on word of mouth and the opinions of other people to keep her informed about matters that affect her business. Investigation will probably reveal that the distribution channels of a small manufacturing business are a social network. The relationship with buyers is not a strictly business-like one. Credit terms are flexible, the customers are people whom the manager meets regularly and with whom she socialises. She may even live among them in the same community. In addition to keeping the business going, this also serves to keep her informed of customers' requirements, which is important when operating in a niche market, as small businesses typically do. It is thus likely that in many cases, when investment opportunities arise, these have been identified by outsiders: friends, family, or business associates.

Another important aspect of the life of the manager of a small manufacturing firm is her concern with, and efforts towards, ensuring that the business remains liquid and survives. The high 'mortality' rate among small business is well documented (see, *inter alia*, Kennedy 1985; Larson and Clute 1979; Meredith 1977; Storey *et al.* 1987) and is hardly surprising. These firms face a variety of problems compared with larger businesses. The small volumes and product ranges of small manufacturers mean that they do not have the ability to offset losses in one market against a satisfactory performance elsewhere. They probably face stiffer competition because entry into the market niches occupied by smaller concerns is relatively easy, there being few barriers to entry such as high start-up costs and technological superiority. They do not possess the capital easily to withstand the sorts of changing market conditions associated with the business cycle and macroeconomic policy, such as a reduction in aggregate spending and rising interest rates. Because of its tenuous market position, the small business also has difficulty in coping with a deterioration in its relationships either with its suppliers or its customers. Limited inventories, and being one of a number of suppliers to a larger concern, make it difficult to retain business in the face of unexpected problems, such as a machine breaking down or a strike by the work force. Small-scale manufacturers that supply large firms may find it difficult to secure long-term contracts if the large firm uses short contracts as the pretext for regularly reviewing the prices of its suppliers, and uses the threat of nonrenewal to ensure that the small supplier accepts the pricing structure which the former demands.

The manager of a small independent manufacturer thus spends a considerable part of her time coping with problems that arise, worrying about finding new business opportunities, and maintaining existing contracts. The corollary of this aspect of business life is that the decision-maker does not have much occasion to evaluate alternatives nor does she have the luxury of waiting to see whether something better will turn up. She has to seize those opportunities that do arise, seeing herself and her company as being at the mercy of 'the market' and 'economic forces', with little ability to influence the conditions under which she trades. In order to compete, she has to find opportunities to reduce costs, perhaps by paying lower than average wages, or by eliminating some, or all, of the stages in a distribution chain. What is more, ensuring the survival of the small firm is not only a matter of self-esteem; in many cases, the manager's personal assets are tied up in the equity of the business because her access to external funds is limited.[12]

This account helps to clarify the position of a manager faced with expanding her production capacity. The firm's present capacity is a consequence of decisions circumscribed by limited finances as well as other factors such as a small niche market. In view of the need to generate business in order to remain solvent, the small firm will have difficulty in controlling its expansion. If it is doing well and capacity limits are reached, the manager of a small firm considering a new investment will again have little cause to deliberate and to choose. Even if, in the circumstances, the management decides to move the entire operation from one place to another, the decision is most likely to be taken in the light of the assessment that 'this is the only thing for us to do'.

MOTIVES FOR INVESTING

Asking why managers undertake investments may seem absurd and the answer self-evident. The problem, however, is that motives are missing from the economist's usual account of investment decisions because the third-person perspective does not need them. Optimising agents pursue, or respond to, opportunities that exist out there in the world. Modernism offers the excuse that motives do not matter in a scientific theory.[13] If necessary, empirical studies prove that markets work, and people behave as if they are profit or utility maximisers.[14]

The absence of motives is yet another instance of how orthodox theory subverts our understanding of the organisation and operation of the institutions of a market economy in a subtle but pernicious way. Without any direct reference to individuals' motives, we are left with the impression that the 'motive' of firms is to optimise profits. This, however, is an erroneous view of what managers do and why they do it. Optimising behaviour concerns the solution of puzzles, not business decisions. I have stressed that optimisation is impossible except for someone who has a grasp of the complete scheme, or who believes he does. The pursuit of profits *per se* is illogical unless one knows what profit opportunities exist out there, or believes that one does. Managers concerned with investment decisions know and believe neither, but, heeding Thirlby's views quoted in the epigraph to this chapter, without an understanding of their motives we are liable to end up with a completely misguided conception of why 'firms' do things.

'Motive' means 'a factor that induces a person to act in a particular way' (*The Concise Oxford Dictionary*, 1990). What factors induce people to act, specifically to undertake investment decisions? What are their motives? Asked these questions, and assuming that their responses are frank, managers might furnish a variety of answers to both. Motives include personal gain ('this looks like the opportunity that will make me a millionaire'), opportunism ('if this plan succeeds I will be able to gain control of the company'), or animosity associated with company politics ('this will give me the leverage to force the chairman of the other division to resign'). The desire to own her own business, or to be her own boss, may be paramount, so when an opportunity presents itself – almost irrespective of what it appears to offer by way of financial returns – the individual may seize it. Similarly, some may see a business opportunity as a means of escaping from poverty, or of getting out of a family business. Or, with an eye to retirement in a few years, the town and its setting may be regarded as especially suitable. A desire to overcome the problems of an unruly workforce or to avoid the effects of a change in government policy – from stricter pollution control measures to higher corporate tax rates – are plausible motives behind particular investments. Some decisions, no doubt, are a consequence of attempts to stave off bankruptcy, and others are based on the desire to become the dominant force in the industry or to have a foothold in a growing market.

The need to understand motives necessitates a hermeneutical approach to human conduct, and any discussion of motives takes us straight to the social nature and context of conduct. If an analysis of people's motives is going to prove useful, it is desirable to be able to generalise about what motivates decision-makers, and this is anything but straightforward. Motives are personal and particular and the question is how to reconcile this with the requirement that theory is general, for a first-person approach must feature motives in explanations of decisions. The answer to the question lies in the double hermeneutic itself. The theorist, as a decision-maker, has an understanding of how others constitute problems and of their motives.

The people who comprise a person's *Umwelt*, and also to an extent his *Vorwelt* and *Folgewelt*, are those with whom his interests overlap. Their requirements, habits, motives, or attitudes matter in some way, either in terms of what he is doing or what he plans to do. Some individuals set criteria that he must meet, while others are associates or people with whom he does business.

Some he can count on for support, others are viewed as rivals. His relationships with them will vary accordingly. With the object of considering why people undertake investments, my approach is to regard motives as interwoven with the individual's social circumstances. Whose interests the planner or decision-maker considers, and his feelings about how important it is to take cognisance of other people's motives, are influenced by the type of social relations that he forms. Here again the distinction between large and small manufacturing firms is useful for characterising the social circumstances of a 'typical' decision-maker.

Conventional wisdom suggests that planning and decision-making in the large organisation reflect the 'interests of the organisation'. The recognition that conduct is circumscribed by an emphasis on corporate norms supports the idea of corporate loyalty and a commitment to 'the company's interest' as important motives behind investment decisions. This view seems to be confirmed by the consideration that to most people, both inside and outside the firm, the corporate senior manager remains an impersonal name and title. When he meets with people from outside the organisation to do business, he is the representative of the firm. His presence as an individual is almost incidental; on another occasion someone else may represent the company. People do business with the *institution*, and it is the reputation of the institution that matters when financing and similar considerations are at stake.

The idea that corporate objectives guide the strategic decisions taken in large bureaucratic firms may, however, be misleading, when the formal and impersonal nature of relationships within such organisations are viewed in conjunction with other factors. Lately, the literature on strategic management recognises a multiplicity of interests within the large organisation (see Child 1972; Connolly *et al.* 1980).[15] According to Connolly *et al.* (1980: 216), because groups within the organisation have different interests, they will assess its performance in various ways using different criteria. A multiple-constituency view repudiates the sort of authoritarianism that Thirlby, in the quotation introducing this chapter, attributes to neoclassical theory. Stockholders, senior managers, employee unions, and customers, may espouse divergent views of what the organisation's goals should be, and there is no requirement that these groups and others should, in any particular setting, have reached a negotiated agreement or formed a dominant coalition that generates operative goals.

The institutionalisation of planning in the large organisation brings different groups into an investment planning exercise. Individuals are seldom party to the whole planning process and no one understands the plans as a single, unified, coherent entity. These points, and the consideration that different groups may have different ideas about the purpose of the planning exercise, are conveyed by Williams and Scott (1965: chs 4, 7). Planners know little about what the others in the organisation think. They are not aware of any 'corporate objective' and do not try to identify one. Those who put together a proposal intend the document to meet with the approval of whoever has to make the decisions. The planners' views on what is required will be shaped by directives, usually from senior management. So the 'interests of senior management' – members of the board of directors, or possibly the chairman or managing director – as interpreted by the planners, have a major influence on the formulation of an investment proposal. The planners will seek advice and make recommendations incorporating views that they think top-level managers will find appropriate or conducive to their own (i.e. the senior managers') thinking.

Various interests are supposed to be represented by the people on the committee charged with making a decision on whether or not to proceed with the proposed investment. What criteria will they use? Probably, with different considerations in mind, they will try to reach agreement on whether the investment is the 'right thing at this time'. This, of course, gives them considerable scope to do as they please. Does 'the right thing' mean the project is expected to be especially profitable, or will it enhance the company's image? Will it give the company a leading position in the industry, or improve its competitive position? These rather vague and ambiguous notions mean that there is neither an unequivocal sense of purpose nor a well-defined corporate goal behind the acceptance of an investment plan.[16] If the plan has to be debated, or if there is behind-the-scenes lobbying because differences of opinion or divergent interests make it difficult to arrive at a decision, then rhetoric and political alliances, rather than economic or financial considerations, will play an important part in the decision. It is at this point that particular individuals, by virtue of their positions of authority or their powers of rhetoric, may be in a position to serve their interests by convincing others that the course of action which they want to pursue is the 'right thing for the company'.

'Strategic' investment and location decisions are guided by people's convictions. They can reflect the interests of particular individuals rather than those of 'the company'. Given that individuals' motives matter and that interpersonal relationships influence their outlook and decisions, what remains of traditional business goals such as profitability? Even if people do not consider these, won't the 'invisible hand' of the competitive market ensure that firms are 'weeded out' if they do not give high priority to economic factors? To preserve a coherent argument, I would prefer to defer discussion of these issues until we have completed the analysis of decision-makers' motives and have been able to draw general inferences about firms' locations. Clearly, economic factors are not irrelevant when it comes to making investment decisions, but I will argue that there are serious flaws in the key components of the received view: namely that profits or costs are what really matter in making decisions; that the market, when it works properly, ensures that only the firms which choose the most profitable investment opportunities survive; that pursuing maximum profit is the 'right' or 'natural' thing to do; and that anyone who does not try to maximise profits is irrational.

Now, what can we say about the motives of the manager of a small manufacturing firm? It is a commonly held view that the motives of managers of small firms reflect personal ambitions and goals. Although personal motives may be the main factor behind the initial decision to go into business, my earlier analysis has stressed that, having done so, these individuals are largely at the mercy of their social and business milieux. From identifying investment opportunities to obtaining distribution for her products, the manager of a small firm will not have much opportunity to weigh up options. She almost always has difficulty in securing adequate financing. This individual may well find that financial constraints necessitate certain courses of action, and preclude others, in order to satisfy her bank manager or creditors. A further curb on her 'freedom of choice' is the constant need to attract business, to retain customers, and to gain new ones. Such considerations certainly circumscribe her activities.

I have argued that her most important business relationships are forged with people outside her firm. In considering how they bear on her activities, the personal nature of the relationships is important. In a small manufacturing concern, the senior managers are the firm, and their ability to make their way depends on their own reputations and how they, as individuals, are perceived by others. Given that she has considerable competition, either actual or potential, in the market niche in which she operates, the inference is that the small-business manager's success depends on the network of relationships that she cultivates and how well she maintains it. To do so, she may have to go out of her way to meet the wishes of customers or to satisfy the requirements of suppliers of materials or of finance.

IDENTIFYING INVESTMENT OPPORTUNITIES

The question that I want to consider in the final section of this chapter pertains to both large and small firms: how are these considerations relevant to the identification of investment opportunities and to the decisions that are taken? Where do investment opportunities originate, or how are they identified? Finally, what are the motives for undertaking the investment?

As a rule, only a few small-scale endeavours can be considered as new business ventures which literally start from scratch and even then the people involved have a history which shapes the project. The capital costs alone of a large-scale venture necessitate that any proposed 'new' firm has established antecedents. Banks, prospective shareholders, or investors need a record of doing business as an indication of the likely success of the venture. As far as small companies are concerned, in many cases the manager who is considering undertaking an investment will be going into this business for the first time, though she may have been involved in other businesses before. On the face of it, she has considerable latitude in what she does, how she does it, and where she does it, being constrained neither by decision-making/power structures within an organisation, nor by a history of commitments to particular products, markets, or even employment practices and social programmes.

The circumstances of the managers of small businesses appear to resemble the description of the agent in orthodox theory and, especially, the entrepreneur associated with Kirzner's work (see 1973, 1985). Does the small manufacturer search for 'profit opportunities' and perhaps locations? The answer is no; her own history matters in identifying and pursuing opportunities – the skills she has, where she worked or grew up, who she knows, her knowledge of financial matters. While the culture, structure, and practices of a large business place their managers under certain obligations, the things that the manager of a small business considers to be obstacles to her plans, and even the opportunities that she identifies, are perceived as personal opportunities or problems. Her plans reflect *her* circumstances. She asks: how can I deal with this matter? Is it worth my while to do this? Who do I know who can help me? Will they have sufficient confidence in my ability, or honesty? Other people, to whom she goes for advice or for financial assistance, base their dealings with her on an assessment of her competence, honesty, or enthusiasm.

When contemplating the investment opportunities of the small firm and how they arise, these considerations have to be seen in conjunction with the fact that the *Umwelt* of the small-business manager consists of a social network – people who are not employees of the firm. How then do investment opportunities arise? They emerge from the current activities of the business and its existing contractual obligations. Few investments in small manufacturing firms represent absolutely new starts, for example where the individual has an idea, designs the product, builds or rents factory space, and purchases new machinery to manufacture it. Much stands in the way of carrying ideas through to fruition, and her lack of experience in running a successful business will be an impediment to obtaining funding from financial institutions (see Meredith: 1977: 22). She might find people – including friends and family – who will finance the business on unconventional terms. Such financiers, who may insist on a share in the business, are not business associates in the conventional sense and really represent part of a social network.

We can postulate that many investments in small businesses involve the purchase of existing operations, even when the manager is going into business for the first time. The factors that lead to such investments fall into two categories, and each category has many permutations. In one case the individual herself identifies the opportunity, which probably comes to mind as a result of her employment at the time. As a sales representative, for example, she realises that one of her major customers requires a specialised finish to the product that she supplies. In the other category, someone in her social network – an associate, friend, or family member – alerts her to a business opportunity. In each case, whether it is a new or existing business that is the individual's starting point, we understand that the investment opportunities that she considers are narrowly circumscribed. There is limited scope for choice, except with regard to whether or not she should proceed with the idea.

In the large enterprise, the identification of investment opportunities and the sorts of investments that are contemplated can be traced to managers' understanding of the 'history' or circumstances of the organisation including their perceptions of relationships among people in the organisation. All the factors considered earlier in the chapter in describing the circumstances of managers of large firms may have a bearing on how the investment opportunities come about and, subsequently, on the decisions that are taken about realising the investment plans. These factors include financial security, that success in managing a large enterprise is measured by sustained progress and performance, that decisions taken by a committee or a board require consensus and compromise, and that managers are conservative. All these considerations support the claim that 'routines' are important in large organisations (Nelson and Winter 1982) and we may infer that new projects that will be considered, including ones based on new products formulated in the research and development department, are viewed as providing 'natural' or evolutionary growth for the organisation.

Investment proposals will be for projects that are believed to complement existing activities and, therefore, to fit into the firm's already extensive sphere of operations. They may include products that extend the existing range and that build upon the same technical and marketing expertise; or investments that extend or consolidate the firm's existing markets. Similarly in the case of mergers and acquisitions, a major consideration will be whether the demands placed on people can readily be dealt with by drawing on the experience of the present management. This means that in a large firm managers do not 'search' for investment opportunities. These are 'created', in that they emerge from deliberations about the firm's current position and future prospects: its financial position and market share, its competitive position in a global market, its management or regional structure, the impact of technological developments or of labour relations.

The consideration that investment opportunities are identified and defined in the deliberations of people about the performance, structure, or future of the enterprise, is reinforced by the role of experts in the planning process. Investment decisions will usually only be taken after discussions with a range of people both inside and outside the firm. These include specialists in a variety of fields, from structural engineers to merchant bankers, and associates and acquaintances with knowledge of, or an interest in, particular products, markets, or countries. Specialists are hired for their experience. An investment plan defies being treated as a self-contained problem and, when faced with many imponderables, a sensible approach for planners is to look for 'recipes' to follow, which help to transform a novel situation into something of a routine one. One way of accomplishing this is to adopt methods and practices that have been tried elsewhere and have been shown to be successful. Consultants are often hired in the hope that they can provide a recipe. With their wide experience, it is expected that they will be well placed to identify 'strategies for success'. It is understandable, then, that even firms in different countries pursue the same general business strategies. A consequence of using specialists is to narrow the approach and options which are considered in planning an investment.

I hope that these arguments provide pointers to how we might go about examining the way in which decisions are made. They have surely also drawn attention to the futility of attempting to construct a theory of decision-making around the epistemological and ontological requirements of the third-person perspective, as exemplified by neoclassical theory. The consequence of not being able to reflect the intersubjective, social nature of business decisions, including the identification of investment opportunities, is an erroneous view of the sorts of choices and decisions that people make and how they make them. This brief attempt to understand the investment decisions of people in both small and large firms affirms that investment opportunities are firmly rooted in the *experience* of managers and other people, rather than existing somewhere out there. While the nature of the planning process in the organisation indicates that the people concerned identify specific rather than general opportunities for investing and, coupled with these, they have specific ideas about how to undertake the investment.

Broad as they are, the arguments provide a *prima facie* case for questioning the conventional wisdom about the role of expected profits, costs, and revenues in investment decisions. Based on these arguments we should not be surprised to find, when we actually discover how particular investment decisions are taken and what factors 'convinced' the people concerned that this was what should be done, that estimates of anticipated returns, or of costs and revenues, did not come into the picture. I have more to say on this in the remaining chapters, but first I want to consider the implications of the analysis of investment decisions for industrial location, for I believe that the analysis gives fairly clear pointers to how the 'location problem' is treated by decision-makers in both small and large firms.

13

UNDERSTANDING
AND LOCATIONS

HOW LOCATION THEORY MISLEADS

My suggestion that the economic factors which mainstream theory identifies as the determinants of investment may have little bearing on decisions to invest, presents an obvious challenge to conventional approaches to decision-making and, as I now propose to show, to the economic theory of location outlined in Chapter 8. Acknowledging that location problems will arise when the managers of manufacturing businesses are planning investments, we are in a position to answer the question: what does it mean to 'choose a location'? After presenting a general critique of the theory of location and a revisionist view of what location decisions are about, I will consider what choosing a location means from the point of view of managers of both large and small firms. Regarding the role of economic factors in location and investment decisions, the middle section of the chapter deals with the basis of the contradiction between the arguments of orthodox theory and those that flow from a hermeneutical approach. In the third section I use the earlier arguments to illustrate the faulty logic behind industrial relocation policies, with the object of adducing why these policies failed to influence the geographic pattern of industrial location. I will begin with a brief re-capitulation of the story told by traditional location theory about how firms' locations are chosen. This serves both as a reminder of the content of the theory and as a foil for the revisionist view.

What is a location or an investment opportunity? A modernist methodology represents knowledge of the world, and therefore the scheme of things, as a set of elements. The subject matters of the different social sciences are sets of separate things – economic, sociological, psychological – that are observed to exist out there in the world. Locations are some of the economic things that exist out there and are distinguishable as to their qualities. Apparently both the theorist and the agent can – or should be able to – tell a good location from a bad one. The same is true of investment opportunities and firms. Each of these things exists separately out there in the world, as do costs, revenues, and profits.

Associated with each firm, but as separate entities, are investment opportunities and location possibilities – the things that are available for 'choice'. Each of the investment opportunities has particular characteristics, such as its internal rate of return, return on equity, or profitability, which themselves are conceived as real things that co-exist with each investment and which vary in some systematic way with the values of other things, such as interest rates, time, or prices. Similarly, each location has particular characteristics in terms of costs and revenues. Although a multitude of costs and profits exists in the world, these are clearly and unambiguously associated with each of a large number of investment opportunities and locations. By inspecting the investment opportunities and locations it is possible to estimate the costs and profits associated with each, and therefore to decide which investment opportunity and which location is the optimal one.

What is a location decision? Somewhere in the world out there are agents looking for locations. The object of each is to find an ideal location and the way they do this is to search for one. What they concentrate on are the values of economic variables at different points in Euclidean space, their searches being directed towards things out there. The things out there in the world, which attract firms to particular points in Euclidean space, are the reasons why firms choose their locations. The 'data' on which location decisions are made are also out there in the world and are potentially available to everyone and anyone. Decision-makers all possess knowledge in the form of a 'map' of an area which itemises the values of economic variables at different points. These factors determine costs and revenues at each location and therefore establish the best location.

Decisions are made to achieve clearly identified interests of a firm which, as a thing in the world, is a distinct, whole entity.[1] Each firm possesses a ready-made scheme, with definite objectives, for solving location (and other) problems, and has definite linkages to other firms. All the linkages make up an identifiable, self-contained system, which represents part of the data that decision-makers have to evaluate. Their choices, such as whether to minimise costs or to maximise revenue, are independent of the firm and its activities, though each firm has to take advantage of 'opportunities' which are found out there. Finding an optimal location is an end in itself and is the result of comparing the characteristics of alternative locations against predetermined criteria. The best location for the firm is the one that scores more highly than alternatives in terms of criteria such as costs or sales. These are the considerations that matter when choosing a location. Decision-makers do not, and should not, have personal attachments to, or preferences for, places.

I have already argued that it is this conception of the scheme of things that encourages and underpins the mathematical formulation of economic and other social problems. It is also the means of separating economic, sociological, psychological, and political problems, on the grounds that each of the sciences deals with a separate, clearly identifiable set of elements out there in the world.

The features of orthodox theory that are highlighted in this summary, we now know, are not capricious aspects of a theory of decision-making. The story that the theory tells is congruent with the language of determinism and the entire conceptualisation of the location problem in orthodox theory is attributable to the third-person perspective. The conventional account of the location problem is a fiction and is an effective illustration both of how the language of theory influences the way in which we look at the world and of just how much the epistemology and ontology of determinist schemes is at odds with the way in which people understand, or think about things. But the modernist paradigm has a hegemonic influence in science, and social scientists who have been inducted into that paradigm may well believe that the language of modernism is the appropriate one and that the scientist's conventional way of looking at the world is the correct way, and possibly the only way.

From the standpoint of an individual's understanding – the epistemology and ontology of the first-person perspective – the compartmentalisation of the world into definite and clearly defined categories and subjects, and its coincidental representation as a set of things that are observed to exist out there, both of which are characteristics of determinism, is mystifying. The decision-maker understands the firm and its location in terms of people whom she meets at the office and who do various things with, or for, her; also she understands the firm as an institution which imposes particular demands on her; as a job which offers certain prospects; as a place which has certain amenities or lacks particular resources; and so on. She has experience of social and business relationships, and of other institutions, that go with the job. This experience is shaped or prejudiced by the 'location' – the community and place where the firm is situated – as it is by the types of machinery and technology with which she is familiar, and by the extent to which aspects of the manufacturing process are subcontracted, or by her contacts with suppliers of raw materials. These are not things that are, or can be, separated from her conception of the 'firm', but are part of her understanding of the business.

It is in the context of this prejudiced understanding that she assesses prospects and identifies opportunities. She can conjecture about whether a new plant with a new technology (which someone has told her about) will help to improve the profitability of the firm or to reduce unit costs; but she cannot determine what effects this new technology will have on the 'bottom line'. Any calculations which she may make are just conjectures. In the same way that the consequences of technological innovations cannot be understood and assessed independently of the administrative competencies or even the good fortune of the management of an enterprise and of the operation of a particular production line, so the 'location' is not a point on a map. The

215

decision-maker does not have an investment (a thing over here) which she needs to put at an optimal location (something else over there). What she understands about a place, the people she knows and what they can offer, is the basis on which she identifies an investment opportunity worth pursuing. The particular project takes shape because of the way the decision-makers interpret the conditions or circumstances at which the production facilities are, or will be, located: for example, because of the quality of the financial services; the reputation for reliability of a potential supplier; the scenic beauty of the area; the supportive attitude of the local authorities; or the technical expertise of the local manufacturers.

When, as theorists interested in human conduct, we begin our investigation into location decisions, the people and firms whose activities we wish to investigate are not randomly scattered over the landscape. Nor are managers wandering around with maps that depict spatial economic relationships looking for investments and places to locate their factories. As the previous chapter has emphasised, their circumstances play a principal role in the identification of investment opportunities and the same is true of the location of the business.

Freed from the conceptual blinkers of the third-person perspective, we recognise an investment proposal as a possible course of action that planners are thinking about. What they think about is not 'proximity to other firms' or 'distance from the market' – at least not at the stage of conceiving an expansion, or takeover, or even a new product line. Those concepts are a product of the notion that people have knowledge of the values of variables and of relationships in Euclidean space, a notion which itself is derived from the positivist conception of things-in-the-world.

Factors such as 'proximity to other firms' are not what matters in determining whether an investment proposal succeeds. Because profit opportunities do not exist in the world, but the profitability of a business is a result of doing all the things necessary to make the business work, what matters, ultimately, is how the project is managed. When the investment opportunity is identified – 'this seems like a good business prospect' – proximity to other firms hardly ever plays a part in the identification of the opportunity: nor does the 'size of the market'. A firm's market is not something that simply exists in the world, which can be found by marking off a circle on a map. 'The market' will only exist *if* the investment is undertaken and *if* the managers do the appropriate things to find and to retain customers. Costs certainly have to be considered when setting up and running a business, but inventory management, advertising, and industrial relations policies, most of which are independent of where the firm is situated and which themselves affect the costs of production, are going to be at least as important as the costs of raw materials or the distance from the market (and hence transport costs) in contributing to the success or failure of the venture.

For both the person starting a small manufacturing concern and the

216

manager of a large industrial undertaking, the matter of locating the plant is hardly ever an issue. In each case the location is settled when an investment opportunity is identified. The location is defined by the nature of the investment itself and the circumstances surrounding the identification of each investment opportunity, or the location becomes apparent in the process of carrying out the decision to invest. The people who put forward an investment proposal already have in mind the place where the business will be situated if the project goes ahead, or the place is identified in the course of pursuing the idea, while making enquiries and conducting feasibility studies.

If planners do consider the matter of a location, this is likely to be a question of finding a suitable site in an area which has already been earmarked for the firm to expand, or to set up a new factory, and there is no reason at all why they should have 'spatial information' concerning costs and conditions at different places. Generally, planners who consider alternative 'locations' will be examining different types of operations, and the 'choice of location' is a matter of choosing one project over another. For example, uncertainty about the market potential of a new product may induce management to back a proposal for a smaller scale of plant which, because of lower smoke emission, can be situated adjacent to the company's existing factory close to the city centre. The possibility of adopting some other approach (a smaller plant, perhaps, or a number of decentralised plants rather than one integrated operation) leads planners to think about alternative 'locations'. It is the operations – not the location *per se* – that are important.[2]

We can be somewhat more specific about the factors that influence the location of investments undertaken by large firms. If an expansion of capacity is being considered and if it is practical to do so, the inclination of management will be to develop an existing site. Townroe (1971: 35) says, '[t]he normal pattern of growth is by building extensions . . . or by increasing the productivity of the existing floorspace' (see also D. J. North 1974: 242). The conservative outlook of large companies, together with the general desire to do those things that are least disruptive and do not lead to upheavals and uncertainty within the organisation, suggests that an extension of the existing plant will be most attractive. This satisfies the need for continuity, for example of relationships with existing suppliers and of a workforce whose capabilities are known, since supervisors, foremen, and other managers will be 'transferred' to the new facilities as they come on stream. Unlike a plant located some distance away, the senior management team can exercise more control over the setting-up, commissioning, and phasing-in of the extended facility; the phasing-in period being the time when problems most likely to affect production and the company's performance will occur.

For the large enterprise, with adequate financial resources and a conservative outlook, which is able to pick and choose investments, an alternative to developing existing sites is acquisition or merger. These present distinctly favourable strategies for growth. (See Penrose 1959: ch. 8 on why firms grow by acquisition and merger.)[3] With access to enough capital, there is no need to 'start small' or to embark on new ventures on a piecemeal basis. Buying up an existing, established firm has obvious advantages. The most important is that the business and its potential have been tested. If it is a successful firm that is acquired, the uncertainty of the venture is much reduced. I noted in the previous chapter that, compared with its smaller counterpart, the large firm has the resources to weather cyclical downturns and to wait out unfavourable market trends. In this context, as a strategy for expansion, the acquisition of a firm which has failed may be preferable to starting out with an entirely new operation. Drawing on the experience of new managers in order to put things right, such an investment may be 'safer' than a greenfield investment, because teething problems will have been overcome and the firm will have established relationships with suppliers and customers. Once a large enterprise owns a number of plants, much of its investment activity is associated with extending or reorganising production at these plants.

In none of these cases does the investment involve looking for, or even thinking about, a location. In an industrialised country with a large manu-facturing infrastructure, most of the activities of the bigger firms, as they expand or decline and have to rationalise their structures and production capacity, will involve investing in new plant and equipment and even new buildings on existing manufacturing sites. The reasons why the firms come to be there tend not to be found in a search for suitable sites, but in the decisions which lead to the acquisition or the sale of an existing business.

In the case of small firms, an investigation of the choice of location might appear more interesting if their investments involve the establishment of new firms rather than modifications or additions to existing plants. Yet this is probably not the case. More so than large manufacturing concerns, the small manufacturer's investment is tied to a particular 'opening' in the market; to the ability to identify and to seize an opportunity which is specific to a particular place, and which – in the case of fads, gimmicks, or fashions – may have a very limited life-span. The manager locates wherever she, or someone who knows her, 'finds' the opportunity. In general, small manufacturing firms do not constitute interesting case studies with regard to location decisions, as the individuals concerned are unlikely to do more than find premises to suit their purposes. Thus, while the issue of location is only incidental to the investment decisions made by managers of large companies, the managers of small firms hardly have occasion to think about the location at all. Indeed, it may not be inappropriate to treat the location of the small manufacturing operation as shaped by factors that are beyond the manager's control.

In the case of an established small business with large firms as customers, any investment decision taken by the manager will reflect the opportunities created by these customers. A small manufacturer who services various small customers, either distributors or manufacturers, also operates under significant constraints. Variability in the size and frequency of orders and erratic payments by her debtors place the manufacturer at a disadvantage in terms of planning the growth of her capacity. In addition, she may have to contend with business failures among her small customers.

Investment opportunities for existing small firms will involve incremental changes to the operation, mainly changes in capacity. When new products are added they are likely to be variants of those already being produced, which can be made without expensive retooling and without having to add entirely new production facilities. When she needs to find new premises, the manager will try to find something convenient, as close as possible to her present location, from where she can service her existing customers. If a large customer moves, she too may have to move. In general though, financial constraints, together with modest space requirements, will almost certainly mean the purchase or rental of existing premises, rather than a desire to build new ones, a point that applies equally to the individual embarking on a new venture by starting her own manufacturing concern. These views confirm the conclusion of industrial geographers that small manufacturing businesses offer little to interest the location theorist, but this does not mean – as geographers seem to imply – that there is no reason to study the plans, motives, and activities of the owners or managers.

In summary, far from being a centrepiece in the process of planning an investment, the issue of location, if it is examined at all by decision-makers or planners, is incidental or is influenced by particular considerations associated with the investment. As far as large firms are concerned, either in the identification of the opportunity or in deliberations about how to proceed, the location will usually have been 'decided' without much thought having been given to the matter of where that location should be. Searches and comparisons based on spatial considerations are superfluous. Either the location is implicit in the identification of an investment opportunity, or by the time the project has been planned the location has emerged from a consideration of factors such as the markets in which the product will be sold, the main source of supply of raw materials, the location of the major supplier of components, or simply because a consultant feels that it is a good place. In the case of small firms, the location and the business opportunity are generally inseparable. The firm is set up, or the owner goes into business, to take advantage of a niche market that exists in a particular geographic area. In view of her limited means and other considerations, the manager of a small business has difficulty in managing an expansion of capacity. Relying on 'outsiders' for ideas and advice and needing constantly to ensure that new business is available, the small-business manager simply avails herself of opportunities wherever she finds them.

ECONOMIC FACTORS AND DECISION-MAKING

This enquiry subverts the traditional account of both how and why locations are chosen. It denies the conventional view both of a search for business opportunities and of the primacy of economic considerations – costs, revenues, and profits – in the identification, or selection, of investment opportunities. Little was said about the actual motives of managers except for the short treatment in Chapter 12, but the view that motives are likely to be diverse runs counter to the customary notion that a high return on investment and the desire to maximise profits are the main priorities of the businessman. The analysis also contradicts the idea that decision-makers 'shop around', comparing alternatives before they make up their minds.

Various questions need to be addressed in order to clarify the challenges presented by this analysis. The most important one concerns the role of economic considerations in investment decisions. How are they relevant to the decision-maker? In order to answer this, I must first look to the source of the contradictory interpretation of decision-making. Understanding why there is this dissent over the role that economic factors play in investment decisions involves comparing the ontology of the 'investment problem' in conventional, positivistically inspired approaches to decision-making with the ontology of understanding or interpreting.

Orthodox economic theory purports both to provide a recipe for effective decision-making and to define the ingredients for doing so. The variables that are relevant to the selection of a best course of action are invariably economic. The pursuit of profits is necessary for the firm to function effectively in all spheres of its activities. In the pursuit of profits, costs and revenues matter. Location theory simply extends the logic of this argument. In the context of the third-person perspective, this recipe for making decisions is incontrovertible because the underlying postulate is of an entire or complete scheme of things that exists out there. As long as decision-makers can 'learn' all about what is out there, they can find out how it fits together and can find the optimum solutions to their problems. The epistemological and ontological foundations mean that every problem out there consists of many parts and has a best solution. But the ontology of the third-person perspective undermines our understanding of decision-making. The conventional view treats each investment problem as an entity, a complete system that exists out there. All the components of the investment problem – the interests of shareholders, streams of future earnings, 'the competition' – are capable of being identified and are 'given' as unambiguous and distinct elements. 'Considering the interests of shareholders in the light of opportunities for long-term growth', for example, means estimating, measuring, and comparing things as one would the ingredients of a cake.

There is, however, an essential difference, of an epistemological and ontological nature, between, say, ensuring that a cake has the right ingredients and deciding whether to undertake an investment, or deliberating on whether there will be a market for a product. Like all matters of human conduct that involve thought, finalising the ingredients of a cake is of course a hermeneutical activity. The ingredients and the measures have to be understood. Reading the recipe is understanding – a prejudiced, intersubjective dialogue in which language and culture plays a fundamental role. For example, the measures of volume, weight, and temperature are conventional ones. These conventions may be widely used and accepted, but they are certainly not universally known or incontrovertible.

The point about the cake problem is that it can be treated as 'self-contained'. It can be grasped in its entirety and it is appropriate to think of it as having a solution. Baking a cake, and for that matter playing chess or throwing a die, is analogous to a 'system' with an 'outcome'. We can establish through discourse whether the ingredients and procedures are correct, whether we have followed the recipe, and whether the result is satisfactory. The discourse associated with this activity only encompasses a single hermeneutic; that involving the baker and the cookery book writer, and perhaps other people who are called on to give their opinions about the procedures. As individuals who are assessed as psychologically 'normal' (by people also applying conventions of the time), we are not interested in – and, as far as I know, cannot be interested in – whether the cake thinks it has been baked correctly.

If we had to worry about whether the cake thought it had been baked correctly, or what the cake understands as a 'good cake', and to assess the merits of the cake's view on 'goodness' in relation to our own views, we would engage another level of hermeneutical discourse and this is precisely what we do when dealing with social problems. In economics in general, and in analysing decision-making in particular, the problems have a double hermeneutic because they are about how individuals understand or constitute their 'worlds'. Both 'deciding on an investment' and defining 'the market', for example, involve intersubjective understanding, but not just my understanding of how other people understand some*thing*. The problem is one of *understanding*. The market – not as a place, but as buyers or sellers – is a matter of what and how people understand. Defining a market for toothpaste, personal computers, or umbrellas means not only settling the matter with other economists, but knowing who the buyers and sellers are and how they themselves understand.

'The market' for a product consists of those people who, over a period of time, think, at a moment in the *durée*, that it is worthwhile buying a particular product. As far as a market analyst is concerned, implicit in this notion of a market are various conventions about a geographic area, the product itself, and possibly even about substitutes and competitors. Having resolved any controversies over these conventions, it may be feasible to ascertain what the market was yesterday. But no one knows what the market will be in six months' time, not even those who will then constitute the market, unless they have all already made up their minds. Whether the market will exist, and an estimate of how large it will be, can only be conjectured and, as thoughts in the hermeneutic circle, no measures of rightness or wrongness apply to conjectures. Unlike baking a cake, defining a market is not the type of problem where one can say: 'if you do this and take account of this and this, you will have determined the market; therefore these are what should go into a good estimate of the market, and if you do not take account of these you will have a bad estimate'.

So it is with an investment opportunity, which emerges and changes in the *durée* with the planners' circumstances and their understanding of others. 'Recognising an opportunity' implies that the person concerned believes he has a business proposition and can earn an income or make a profit, since that is what he needs to do to stay in business. He may even believe that it will be very profitable. His colleagues may 'see' things differently and convince him, for the time being, that he is unduly optimistic. Yet none can say 'for certain', or even on the balance of probability, that his is the right way of 'estimating' the investment opportunity, or that if one wants a good estimate of the opportunity these are the things to take into account. There is no means of measuring one view against another, whether they are views about different investment opportunities or just different people's views about the same investment prospect. The only basis for choosing one view over others is that we prefer this person's defence of his position, or we find his arguments more persuasive.

In this light a maxim such as 'managers must always consider the shareholders' interests when they make an investment', cannot serve as a guide to action in any practical sense. Suppose it is interpreted to mean that decision-makers should think about the effect of the investment on the company's dividend payments, and suppose the managers agree that they may have to cut the dividend this year but also believe that next year the dividend will be much larger. What should they do? Even the shareholders can only say whether they think they would sell their shares if the dividend was cut. Like management, they are uncertain about the consequences of undertaking the investment, and they do not know about all sorts of other unrelated considerations which will affect their desire to hold the shares.

For similar reasons there is no justification for saying that an investment decision *must* be based on an estimate of costs or returns, and it is an illegitimate use of statistics to argue that the decision-makers should calculate the probability of costs being high or low. The decision problem – do we have an investment opportunity and is it a good one? – is not a self-contained system of parts, in which some (economic) parts are more important than others. In the nature of the problem, we cannot say that certain factors must be given more weight or ought to be considered. No one can know, now,

222

what will be important or how important it will be. That depends on what other people think and do in the future.

What about 'testing' the decision in retrospect to see whether, by placing more emphasis on prices or by taking a longer-term historical view, there would have been better results? This notion is as much a product of the third-person perspective as the idea of optimising. We can say what we think might have happened if another course of action had been followed, but this is pure conjecture and no one knows, or can know, 'for sure'. Understanding is in the *durée*, and courses of action that may seem feasible or even desirable now, with the benefit of hindsight, did not occur to anyone then. The opportunities just did not present themselves. It is not possible, now, to go back and start afresh. The passage of time transforms us in the sense that we understand differently.

One does, of course, 'learn from experience' – drawing inferences, gaining wisdom, learning to be more cautious – but experience means that the individual judges differently when he comes to make a decision. Experience does not mean accumulating knowledge that will enable one to make better and better decisions over time. Each moment in the *durée* is another moment in the hermeneutic circle. The experience of a stock market collapse or of holding excessively large inventories during a cyclical downturn, may lead one to diversify an asset portfolio or to adopt another approach to inventory management. It will not necessarily prevent either capital losses or being over-or under-stocked. Paying more attention to economic factors the 'next time round' will also not improve the chances of doing the right thing, unless they happen also to be the right factors. That, however, one can only know with the benefit of hindsight when it is obviously too late to do anything about it.[4]

These arguments expose the fallacies in the received view of decision-making. Investments, no doubt, are made with an eye to what effect they will have on the balance sheet and the company's performance. Between a subjective assessment that prospects are highly satisfactory or are completely unsatisfactory, lies a whole range of possibilities that are acceptable and are accepted. Though in the end the investment must pay its way, and it must be believed that it will pay its way, there is nothing which suggests that an assessment of economic performance is, or should be, the bedrock of investment decisions.[5] It is certainly not the case that investments are undertaken because they are expected to earn the highest profits or because they are estimated to yield the highest return on investment.

It is often argued that it does not matter what managers want to do because 'competitive pressures of the market' require them to take cognisance of economic factors. Those who do not will be forced out of business. The literature on business management distinguishes between strategic decisions and operating decisions related to the day-to-day management of the business. It is in the realm of the latter, rather than in the decisions related to the acquisition of plant, that economic factors are likely to be considered. Management is certainly under pressure from various quarters to see that the firm does perform adequately. But there is no clearly articulated view of what must be done and no well-defined notion of 'adequate performance'. Managers have a great deal of latitude, even (at least for a time, and barring evidence of corruption) of justifying why they have not done very well.

The company's profitability, growth, or sales volumes can be maintained or improved in the short term by means which have nothing to do with the initial investment decision. An acquisition or divestment may have the object of improving the 'bottom line' in time for the next annual general meeting. When competition increases, the addition of new product lines, defending market share by a more intensive advertising campaign or through price discounts, and changes to the product specifications, are ways to try and improve the company's performance. Although in making operating decisions, managers pay close attention to the economic factors that have a bearing on their ability to do business, it is wrong to infer that neoclassical theory explains these decisions. The considerations set out here are as relevant to understanding short-term as they are to long-term decisions. Though managers monitor costs and turnover, they always have to interpret the situation and its likely implications. Motives, history, institutional arrangements, and obligations to others matter whenever decisions are taken.

Thus, for example, in contrast to the economist's time-worn tale that individuals are alert to, and respond to, price differentials, the knowledge that something is available at a lower price may not provoke any action. A purchasing manager who wishes to buy bolts is unlikely to search through a list of potential suppliers until he finds the firm that will sell him the items at the lowest price. He will not contact another firm selected at random; neither is he driven by 'price signals'.[6] His concern is whether the price is appropriate. To this end, he relies on his customary supplier, who is known to be reliable and to deliver promptly or to offer extended credit. The purchaser may 'shop around' from time to time, in order to confirm that the price he is paying is reasonable, but even if he feels that it is excessive he will try to get a better price from his customary supplier before considering new purchasing arrangements. In this example the question of what is 'reasonable' or 'excessive' is answered not only with regard to other prices, but also in relation to the trouble and inconvenience of changing suppliers and other such factors.

INDUSTRIAL RELOCATION POLICIES

The relatively insignificant role played by economic variables in investment decisions, and the reasons for this, may help to explain the almost universal failure of policies of industrial relocation or decentralisation (World Bank 1984, 1986a, 1986b). The formulation of these policies in many countries around the world seems to have rested on the traditional arguments of economics and location theory, that firms will choose locations that minimise costs or maximise revenues or profits. In order to induce them to locate at places which policy-makers select as points for new industrial growth, various financial incentives are offered to manufacturing firms.

Enthusiasm for these policies was strong in the 1960s and 1970s, and was often motivated by a concern about 'uneven spatial development'. Though the problem was only dealt with at a national level, it was perceived by Marxist economists as part of a broader, international problem of uneven economic development that was attributed to a relationship of structural exploitation between core areas – the industrialised ones with substantial economic activity – and underdeveloped peripheral areas. The aim was to create new 'poles' of growth to counter the concentration of industry in a few core areas.[7] The nature of the policies differed somewhat from country to country. Some, like Britain, aimed to revitalise areas in economic decline. Others, like Italy, intended to develop the most impoverished regions. Korea aimed at diffusing industry in spatial terms, decentralising it around the core metropolitan areas. In South Africa, the motivation was overtly ideological. The policy was intended to provide an economic base for the 'bantustans', or 'homelands', that were a central feature of Dr H.F. Verwoerd's scheme for 'grand apartheid'.[8] For our purposes, it is permissible to group these policies under the umbrella term of 'industrial relocation' because they share a common method of implementation involving the use of economic incentives to achieve a desired geographic pattern of economic activity.

In this section my object is to juxtapose the analysis of investment and location with the policies of industrial relocation. The scope of the enquiry is narrow. I am going to use South African evidence to draw the general points that I wish to make. The object is to challenge the economic rationale of relocation policies and to establish why industrialists are likely to prefer core locations in metropolitan areas over more remote locations.

Taking the theory of location at face value, one can appreciate why economic incentives form the main tool of relocation policies. If either their profits or costs were adversely affected by locating at designated growth points, industrialists would avoid these and would select their most preferred locations. In the nature of relocation policies, many of the designated areas are some distance from the main markets or from the sources of supply of materials and components. In the early stages of the development of growth points, industrialists who located there would also lack the benefits of economies of agglomeration which are associated with a large business community. In order to select these places at all, they would need financial inducements to compensate for the disadvantages. The principles behind the development of growth points are discussed by Dewar *et al.* (1984) and Dewar (1987: Section IV). The most compelling objection to relocation policies is that they are based on the assumptions that manufacturing businesses are mobile and that locations are determined by economic considerations. Both these assumptions are compatible with location theory, which implies that there is potentially a number of points at which a manufacturer can locate, and that the actual location is based on what is best for the firm from an economic point of view. So, if offered appropriate economic incentives, firms will easily give up one potential location in favour of another.

My analysis of investment decisions, however, suggests that neither large enterprises nor small manufacturing firms are potentially mobile. When they make an investment the managers of the large firms are constrained and influenced by their existing business activities. They have well-established and intricate relationships with other organisations and an out-of-the-ordinary location would affect these, particularly if that location was in the sort of remote area that the South African policy-makers intended it should be. Given the magnitude of the task of rearranging their distribution systems, finding new suppliers, and many other considerations, for the managers of large firms the inconvenience would outweigh benefits from financial incentives. They would, therefore, simply shun the policy. Small firms are either dependent upon niche markets or they are suppliers to larger businesses, which means that they locate where they find the business opportunities. Yet, unlike the large firm, the small one faces problems of finance and from this point of view they may find the incentives provided by government particularly desirable.

A number of separate surveys were undertaken of industrialists who made use of decentralisation benefits in South Africa (see Addleson *et al.* 1985; Dewar *et al.* 1984; Wellings and Black 1987). These focus mainly on the industries located in the bantustans, at 'growth points' which are often far from the main metropolitan areas. Employing criteria that are commonly used in industrial location surveys, each study investigates the reasons why industrialists chose their locations, and identifies the types of firms located at the growth points. The findings in all cases are remarkably similar.[9] Overwhelmingly the companies at these growth points were small, approximately two-thirds employing less than 250 people, although they belonged mainly to labour-intensive industrial sectors (see Bell 1983 on the classification of industries). In the survey by Addleson *et al.*, 82 per cent of the firms indicated that they would not have chosen the present location in the absence of the incentive package that was made available to them under the industrial decentralisation scheme. Most of the decentralised firms were relocations from a non-subsidised location, including some from countries in South East Asia (see Rogerson 1987), and only a few were entirely new operations.

In each survey, the majority of the companies indicated that they were dependent upon the incentives for their survival. Some of those which indicated that they would be profitable without incentives also stated that they would not remain at the location if the incentives were withdrawn. In any event, the typical decentralised manufacturer was small and on the margin of profitability, with limited prospects for survival unless he was subsidised. These are not characteristics that are likely to ensure the success of new growth points.

In spite of generous incentives, including transport rebates to compensate for having to move goods over greater distances, the industrial decentralisation policy was a failure. In line with the failure of relocation policies in other countries, by 1991 the South African government, on the recommendation of the Development Bank of Southern Africa (1989a, 1989b), scaled down the programme considerably.[10] Traditional economic arguments, which focus on costs and revenues, do not explain why so few companies – and almost no large ones – showed an interest in what were conceded to be extremely generous industrial decentralisation incentives. Together with the arguments that I have put forward about how managers make decisions, a critical examination of the surveys may shed some light on the matter.

While economists, drawing on public choice theory, may argue that the majority of decentralised firms are 'rent-seekers' (see Tollison 1982) that argument, though no doubt valid, does not account for the unwillingness of large companies to consider decentralisation. The reticence of managers of larger manufacturing companies even to consider the decentralisation option was confirmed in personal interviews with industrialists (Addleson et al. 1985). According to traditional theory, the absence of economies of agglomeration should not be a deterrent to any firms, as long as the incentives provide adequate compensation for this. Because the incentives were determined as a percentage of the total investment, or in relation to the number of people employed, there is no reason why large companies would not benefit to the same extent as small ones. Both the general reluctance of manufacturing firms to take advantage of the incentives and the types of the firms which actually responded to these inducements, support the view that investment decisions are not necessarily based on economic or financial considerations. In preceding chapters I have emphasised the importance of the individual's social relationships in his business and other activities. The tenor of these arguments was confirmed by an empirical study (Addleson et al. 1985) which I will use to spin out some ideas concerning social relationships and the issue of uncertainty, in order to help to resolve why industrial relocation policies attracted the wrong firms from the point of view of making growth points viable.

Firms that relocated to remote locations identified the absence of ancillary services, their inability to obtain both inventory and spares for their own machines on time, and the lack of contact with manufacturers' agents and sales representatives, as major drawbacks. For the manager on the look-out for new customers, the chances of finding them – through various contacts – are much greater in a large business community which is a 'pool' of potential contacts and business associates. The contacts between managers of private businesses and government employees are also important considerations. Taxes have to be paid, problems over the duties levied on imports need to be resolved, and zoning regulations or regulations governing environmental pollution may have to be challenged. Central government departments and organisations tend to be highly concentrated in a few of the main metropolitan areas. Having easy access to the small number of people in public service who are in a position to exercise discretion and to give a ruling on aspects of regulations, may be important to firms. This alone constitutes a sound reason for locating in a core area.[11]

The firms that did locate at growth points appear to have been those least in need of the support of a business community, a substantial number being more or less self-contained, small-scale, often craft-type operations, such as furniture manufacturers and weavers. These rely on local materials and could draw on the unskilled female labour from local settlements whose only alternative in the bantustans was to eke out an existence in poor conditions for subsistence farming. The decentralisation incentives, including subsidised loans, cover the firm's financing needs and this is particularly important to small firms. There is evidence of the abuse of the incentive system to the extent that some firms were able to make 'profits' without producing anything. Noting also that at growth points within the bantustans the cash subsidy per worker was higher than the very low monthly wage, one can readily infer that some managers or owners were willing to give up a normal business and social environment in order to obtain the incentives, knowing that they would simply close down when the subsidies expired or were withdrawn. The fact that the entire investment was heavily subsidised, that the equity in many businesses was nominal, and that premises were rented, made it easy for owners to quit without incurring costs. Fundamentally, the main motivation of the owners of these smaller businesses was rent-seeking. They had no desire to cultivate a business, to develop it by applying their managerial and marketing skills, but their object was to enrich themselves through the incentive system. Many undocumented stories, as well as numerous press reports, confirm that the people involved had substantial scope for doing so.

The firms that decentralised cut themselves off from a proper business and social community. Now, among the purposes that a large community of businesses serves is the sort of function which Richardson (1973) ascribes to 'oligopolistic' market structures, one which we can designate as 'helping to cope with uncertainties and the vicissitudes of business life'. Whether problems are caused by a supplier going bankrupt, a customer switching to a competitor, a machine breaking down, the need to deal with regulations affecting exports, or to find accommodation for the managing director of an affiliated company who has arrived from overseas, they are likely to be more easily resolved in a large business community.

I do not know whether senior managers ever think this way about the 'support' provided by the larger community; whether they are conscious of the role that the community plays in reducing some of the uncertainties of running a manufacturing business. Yet people who have managed businesses both in cities and in more remote areas certainly seem to find that it is easier to do so in a city.[12] Their attitude is that in the city more can be taken for granted, more of one's daily business life falls under the heading of 'routine', and managers even have 'recipes' for dealing with 'crises'. In remote areas, by contrast, individuals have to be self-sufficient to a greater degree than when working in a city. These arguments point to the incentive system either attracting firms that are essentially self-sufficient (such as the craft industries that do not have extensive business networks), or firms that do not need the business opportunities and 'security' afforded by a larger community, because the managers have no desire to maintain their businesses beyond the time when the incentives run out.

In the light of these considerations we can perhaps infer how managers may view central and remote locations and what this may mean in terms of the types of businesses that will be encouraged to relocate. From the planner's point of view, knowing about economic advantages of decentralised locations in the form of lower costs of land and labour, is one thing. What she is uncertain about are the disadvantages that a remote location may hold. With a central location, however, the situation is reversed and this is what makes the core location more attractive. The potential disadvantages are usually known and their consequences can be assessed, but the advantages of a large business community are uncertain. She is certain that services and social networks exist and that she can use them if she needs to, but she does not know whether, when, or to what extent, she might have to do so. An understanding of the perceived riskiness of different locations and what influences people's thinking provides another set of reasons why firms – especially large ones that are conservative, risk-averse, and that can afford to be selective – would shun decentralised locations. As far as large firms are concerned, being isolated from a business community in a remote location hides all sorts of potentially problematic situations, while the known advantages of these locations are relatively few and are small. The converse holds in the case of core locations. The known disadvantages are fairly small but the unknown advantages are potentially great.

Taking into account the discussion of how investment opportunities are identified by managers of both large and small manufacturing concerns, it is not difficult to understand why the growth of a city leads to a 'virtuous circle' of more growth and more business opportunities, and why the development of a country is associated with a limited geographic spread of industrial activity. Economic linkages, the focus of traditional theory in the form of agglomeration economies and the industrial linkage studies that are popular in industrial geography (see Gilmour 1974; Taylor and Thrift 1982a, 1982b, 1983a, Wood 1969), reveal little of the way in which relationships between businesses affect investment decisions. The reason is that the language of the theory is not appropriate for its purpose.

We need insight into how managers view their relationships with other people, or how they treat commitments between their organisation and other ones, and how they interpret policies. Understanding how managers understand their circumstances, what matters to them and why it matters, puts to rest the myth that firms can easily and successfully be moved to wherever policy-makers would like them to go. An interpretative analysis, which facilitates an understanding of how managers 'see things', also rebuts the view that 'uneven spatial development' is an aberration caused by 'market imperfections'. This conventional view is underpinned by a modernist ontology which treats all problems as things that are wrong in the world out there. Unequal spatial development, itself a creature of positivism and the planner's and social geographer's preoccupation with Euclidean space, is caused by inappropriate economic linkages between businesses – guided by inappropriate 'market signals' – as well as by other obstacles. By implication, these distortions can be removed or corrected with sufficient government spending. This will cause businesses to be spread evenly across the map and will be associated with an improvement in 'social welfare'.

This analysis, I hope, gives an inkling of the harm that is done when the language of theory is inappropriate for its purposes. The methodology of mainstream social theory makes it fundamentally unsuited to doing what social theorists need do – to understand how and what people understand. An analysis of location theory helps to identify the double danger of not being able to understand how people understand. One consequence, the result of being unable to appreciate managers' perspectives on their businesses and social relationships, is that the theory gives a distorted view of the effectiveness and repercussions of efforts to relocate industry. Another consequence, this time concerning the population at large, is the result of being unable to understand what people understand by their 'welfare'. The links, if any, between points on a map and people's welfare would seem to be tenuous at best, with a thousand other considerations, perhaps, having an impact on their quality of life as they see it, and being worthy of consideration in terms of what it would take to improve their circumstances. Positivism precludes the theorist from exploring how people feel about their circumstances. As borne out by the use of location theory to support industrial relocation policies, it is dangerous to formulate 'social policies' around conventional theories. Promising the dubious benefit of rearranging the spatial co-ordinates of industry and employment, decentralisation policies, instead, have been associated with an enormous waste of resources.

14

RETROSPECT AND PROSPECT

Received economic theory does deal with preference and choice, but in models which are strictly deterministic and which rest on simplifying assumptions which remove from the scene the distinguishing human attributes of individuality and imagination. It is small wonder that so many of our contemporaries spend their time in refining static and deterministic models and in displaying logical and mathematical virtuosity. One may admire, as one admires the expert who can do *The Times* and *The New Statesman* crosswords in a half hour, but one can hardly regard it as useful. It is only when we allow the imaginative process of decision-taking that we may hope to develop a new economic theory which may be helpful in our contemporary society.

(Keirstead 1972: 162)

LOOKING BACK

Keirstead's views, in the opening quotation of this chapter, reveal admirably the sterility of mainstream economic theory. Though written two decades ago and shared by a few economists, these views can hardly be said to have influenced the economics profession at large. One of the reasons, perhaps, is that although they identify how economic theory is deficient, criticisms of this nature, and there have been many over the years, have not gone far enough to enable theorists to understand why it is deficient. In order to do that, and to see why and where we have to begin in order to 'allow the imaginative process of decision-taking', it is necessary to go all the way down to the methodological foundations of social theory.

In a way, the nature of the predicament of orthodox theory has been known for a long time. Perceptive scholars like Hicks (1976a, 1976b) and Kaldor (1972, 1979) knew that the matter was somehow tied up with equilibrium. Others, like Mises and Hayek, took the view that there was not enough of human action in neoclassical theory. Both assessments were correct, but what was not understood is that the two issues are interrelated

231

as symptoms of a particular epistemology and ontology. Even today, those grappling with the crisis in economic theory have not appreciated the interrelationships between a determinate scheme, its epistemology and ontology, and the problems that the theorist is able to explore. So we find, for example, that Hahn attributes difficulties with the neoclassical scheme to the limitations of specific equilibrium models (i.e. those of the Walrasian or Arrow–Debreu type), but the intriguing and vital questions that he poses cannot be tackled by any equilibrium theory.

Recognising that the problems of neoclassical theory are hermeneutical, concerned with how decision-making is understood and represented, is an important step, not only for the insights that it offers but also because it helps to direct the theorist to particular questions which otherwise may go unasked. In investigating how an equilibrium theory represents the nature of the scheme of things, and in defining the associated epistemology of the third-person perspective, the book accomplishes two things. It reveals that neither the epistemology – the how and what of knowledge – nor the ontology of an equilibrium theory – the complete system, or world, that exists out there – have any bearing on the individual's knowledge – her understanding of her 'world'. Being able to trace the failure of economics to explain 'how things work' back to its epistemological and ontological foundations is important for another reason. It suggests that the limitations and the fates of all determinate schemes are interlinked and explains why that is so. All schemes which purport to explain human conduct but are concerned with systems or processes, and postulate that these have identifiable outcomes, involve the same third-person perspective and are equally unsuited to the task of explaining conduct. Problems that have plagued economists, such as dealing with time and uncertainty, are associated with the entirely erroneous methodological premise that a world, or parts of a social 'system', are known and can be grasped in their entirety. Although they may acquire a different gloss, the problems do not go away by reformulating the notion of equilibrium or by working with different concepts of optimising.

I have tried to show that, at least from the contribution of Max Weber onwards, there is a distinctive, subjectivist tradition involving attempts to develop a scheme with a different epistemology and, especially in the work of modern hermeneuticists, a different ontology. Defining subjectivism as an epistemology-ontology may help to remove some of the confusion surrounding the term, while the definition of the methodology of subjectivism as a first-person perspective lends coherence to what otherwise tend to be treated as dissimilar methodological contributions. I believe that a comparison of different contributions to social theory in terms of their epistemologies and their ontologies is particularly constructive in that it enables us to establish why subjectivism is a distinctive methodology. In the past, different approaches, seemingly with little in common, have gone under the heading of subjectivism. The distinction between first- and third-person perspectives confirms that 'subjectivism' often simply meant using a different set of terms, like 'mental states', in conjunction with the ontology and epistemology of objectivist theories.

Recognition of what is involved in the first-person perspective also helps one to unravel the methodological limitations of much of Austrian economics, the main contender for a subjectivist economic theory. Austrians have made a conscious effort to distance themselves from mainstream economics but it has not been easy to say why, or whether, there is a methodological difference between the contributions of particular Austrians and the neoclassicists. Understanding the methodological foundation of mainstream theory helps to show why this is the case, while the difference between the first- and third-person perspectives provides a means of orientation for those Austrian economists who, like Lachmann, recognise the severe limitations of neoclassical economics but have struggled to pinpoint the source of their dissatisfaction. I hope that my arguments also underscore the value of the contributions of scholars like Richard Ebeling and Don Lavoie who, in spite of strictures which academia places on younger scholars, have been forerunners in recognising the potential of hermeneutics to extend the scope of subjectivist economics and are willing to break with convention to obtain a deeper understanding of social problems.

A prevailing view about subjectivism, which would apply *a fortiori* to a hermeneutical approach, is that it may be appropriate for investigating individual cases but it is not suitable for constructing a theory, which ought to be general in nature. To some extent, this criticism is a hangover from the Cartesian desire for a comprehensive meta-framework and also from the deductive-nomological conception of explanation, where things are only explained if they are brought under the same covering law. Even when the term 'explanation' is interpreted differently to mean 'understanding' or 'gaining insight', however, an important virtue of any scheme that lays claim to providing insight is its ability to generalise. My examination of industrial location, in the context of firms' investment decisions, was intended in part to show that it is practical to use a subjectivist approach in a general way, to understand the circumstances and decisions of a wide range of people in business. More than this, by employing 'types' and casting decision-makers as managers of large and small firms, it is possible to provide insight into how different people think about problems, and how they act. The key is to establish appropriate types, and the typology is based on an interpretative understanding of the experiences, interests, and social relationships of the people concerned. In this case, it appeared that the institutional setting of their business lives could serve as a useful and convenient basis for developing the categories required, but one can envisage many other ways of grouping people for different purposes.

Some might see in the last point a shortcoming of a subjectivist approach, as viewed from the standpoint of the Cartesian ideal: namely that, applied to the subject matter of the social sciences, subjectivism does not lend itself to the construction of broad theories which are completely general, or comprehensive, in their scope. I can only begin to speculate whether economists will find that the analysis satisfies their curiosity and desire for 'an explanation'. In large measure the matter hinges on what people are prepared to accept as an explanation. While it may be true that mainstream economic theory is general, contrary to conventional wisdom I hold that it does not, and cannot, explain conduct.

A subjectivist analysis brings to the fore the social nature of planning, decision-making, and conduct, which the bogus epistemology-ontology of the 'omniscient observer' cannot appreciate and mainstream theory cannot acknowledge. An appreciation of the social nature of conduct depends on understanding the intersubjective nature of all activity and thought, and therefore on understanding understanding itself. It requires a subjectivist methodology to understand the 'dialogue' of the hermeneutic circle of understanding. What is revealed at the same time is that subjectivism is underpinned by an entirely different notion of individualism from that associated with a third-person perspective. The individual constitutes her world as a social world, and all her plans and activities reflect her relationships and dealings with others. The 'omniscient' agent of neo-classical economics is alone. Indeed it is a paradox of the third-person perspective that the theory would present the individual as something of a 'cog' in the economic machine, forced by the invisible hand of the competitive market to do what is in the best interests of her fellows. In the context of a complete scheme, however, she becomes omniscient and, to a great extent, omnipotent. Whatever she does reverberates through the entire system and, like a potentate, she has the 'power' to make an enormous range of 'choices', constrained only by her budget.

THE END OF ECONOMICS?

The positivist conception of the scheme of things, which has fostered equilibrium and optimisation theories, begins from a position which denies understanding. Its epistemological-ontological foundations obliterate the intersubjective, interpretative social existence of individuals in the *durée*. These theories preclude the possibility of understanding others and their understanding, or of showing how other people's activities bear upon our own interests.

The sorts of questions with which social science is engaged arise out of, and concern, people's understanding of their 'worlds', or circumstances. How do people do certain things? Why do they do them? What are the consequences? We do not pose questions like these because we want to find out what is happening 'out there' to individuals, or to a group, whose activities are completely alien to us, and who are divorced from our own lives and interests in that they have no bearing on us. On the contrary, we are motivated by a desire to understand the activities of others who share our social worlds and we want to do so *because* they share our social worlds. In short, we want to understand those activities because we want to understand ourselves.

Whether the problem is about Welsh coal miners, the crusaders, the global motor industry, a religious sect in Wyoming, the prospects for space exploration in the next century, poverty in Sub-Saharan Africa, Singapore's balance of trade, or the increased traffic flow in the neighbourhood, it is a problem that involves people's activities. These are people who 'share' our *Umwelts, Miltwelts, Vorwelts*, or *Folgewelts*. Their activities are relevant to our interests and when we understand their activities we do so in terms of our own interests and motives, whether this interest is intellectual curiosity, or arises from the need to pass an exam, to sell expert advice, or a desire to write a letter of complaint to the local newspaper. Our interest in the activities of others is to make our way in life, and also to help other people to make their way. Making one's way in life involves understanding, and that is what social theory is about. Understanding means understanding others, and understanding how they understand.

The title of this book states blandly that economists (but it should include other social scientists as well) confront the stark choice of either abandoning equilibrium or optimisation theories, or of foregoing the opportunity to develop an understanding of social problems. I hope I have succeeded in explaining why the language of determinism prevents the theorist from casting problems in a way that makes them relevant to the everyday circumstances and interests of people. From the tenor of the arguments, my views on which way the choice between equilibrium and understanding should go must be apparent. Theories born of the positivist paradigm are no more than intellectual puzzles.[1] That in itself means that they serve a purpose, or are relevant to our interests, but it is a very limited purpose. Orthodox economists themselves have shown an interest in understanding the conduct of others and mainstream theory will not do for this purpose. Unless there is a convincing argument that the third-person perspective offers more than a means of grappling with conundrums, I do not think social scientists have any choice but to abandon modernism.

This conclusion, however, places the reader in an awkward position if she has found herself agreeing with the tenor of at least some of the critique of neoclassical economics, and is perhaps sympathetic to some of the ideas regarding the interpretive nature of cognition and of science. Rejecting the whole of neoclassical economics, in which so much effort, not to say self-interest, is invested, is likely to be viewed as far too radical a step to take.

Besides this, the 'ungrounded' subjectivism that I am advocating may well be regarded as an unsuitable foundation from which to construct economic theory. Subjectivism is commonly, but erroneously, regarded as nihilistic. The inferences drawn from the analysis of investment decisions, since they apparently turn orthodox economic theory on its head, may reinforce this view. The reader is being asked to reject mainstream economics in favour of interpretative understanding, which in itself seems to spell the end of economics. If so, what is left? Are there no halfway positions, no compromises, between rejecting equilibrium theories and understanding individual conduct?

On the second of these questions, my standpoint is uncompromising and the reasons were spelled out early on. There are no halfway positions or compromises. The languages of equilibrium (the third-person perspective) and understanding (a first-person perspective) are incommensurable. It would, however, be most unfortunate to draw the conclusion that hermeneutics spells the end of economics. Here my standpoint is just the opposite. Neoclassical economics has reached an impasse, confirmed by the inability of theorists to deal with issues that are important to them and also by the admission of some that the language of this theory does not help them to understand practical problems. Subjectivism provides a way forward not only because it addresses directly those issues that are of concern, but also because it opens up new opportunities. At the moment neoclassical theory is not making progress, and I have identified the obstacle as the epistemology-ontology of the theory. A subjectivist approach is different and that is its strength; it does provide a means of bypassing the obstacle. As a conclusion, I will consider some additional areas where I believe it can be clearly and quite simply shown that subjectivism does provide the way forward.

It is certainly not appropriate to reject subjectivism out of hand as long as there is at least some agreement that the epistemology and ontology of neoclassical theory limit the scope of economic analysis. For then the question is not how to improve or to resurrect orthodox theory as an equilibrium theory, but what other epistemologies and ontologies are available and how they can be applied. Once this question is posed, we are looking at a type of theory that is completely different to the one with which we are all familiar. The new theory has to be evaluated by criteria other than those of modernism, because it is the foundations of modernism that are being discarded. It is then incumbent upon economists who agree with the substance of the critique of neoclassical theory, but who find hermeneutical subjectivism unpalatable, to put forward something different.

On the matter of the possibility of turning away from neoclassical theory, it is worth remembering that, despite the dominance of the modernist paradigm today, there are different types of economic theories, and that economists have turned their backs on the conventional wisdom before, for example when they dropped the classical paradigm in the aftermath of the catallactist revolution. They missed the chance then of turning from determinism to understanding. It would be a pity if they did so again. The effort invested in neoclassical economics certainly is enormous but mainstream economists who were true to their teachings would view this effort as sunk costs which should not influence future decisions. The hermeneuticist understands, however, that people continue to believe in or be influenced by what they have done in the past and, as shown by the 'successes' of different social sciences over at least a century, that scholars are drawn to theories that treat human activities as mechanistic and determinate. Yet it is worth noting that, today, in virtually all areas of social theory outside of economics, a post-modernist spirit seems to be taking hold, and with this the influence of determinism is waning.

LOOKING AHEAD

With the object of illustrating where hermeneutics could lead economists, and that this would be a desirable route to take, I want to highlight the inadequate treatment in neoclassical economics of institutions that are central to market economies. Neoclassical economics is indifferent to social institutions in the same way and for the same reasons that it neglects social relationships. From the point of view of her understanding, institutions and the individual's relationships with other people are interrelated. Orthodox theory lacks the capacity to examine her understanding of either, and those institutions that do appear, such as markets, firms, and money, have been denatured. So an understanding of institutions is necessary and a desirable end itself, but this requires an appropriate theoretical scheme. A study of institutions and their role in society involves hermeneutical questions. What do institutions mean to individuals, and how do the institutions 'fit' into their plans? How do people understand institutional changes, and what do they do in the light of the changes?

The desirability of making use of a subjectivist approach, when examining institutions, is illustrated by the problematic foundation of anti-trust or anti-monopoly legislation. Based on measures of competition that are informed by modernism, involving the size of firms and the structure of industry and relationships between the two, the legislation does not begin to come to terms with the conventional, and also the business manager's, meaning of competition as rivalry (Addleson 1984b, 1994). Why has competition policy been formulated as if competition were associated with the structure of an industry, or with the 'market form'? One answer is that this is the only sort of 'competition' that is compatible with the ontology and epistemology of neoclassical theory, which does not accommodate rivalry. Rivalry is understood by interpreting the relationships between people, or their attitudes to one another, and rivalry is the mainstay of competition. Unfortunately, in the light of the work of Cournot and others, the term 'perfect competition' came to be associated with what is, in effect, just a mathematical curiosity – a logical puzzle. States of affairs that did not meet the conditions of perfect competition (because there were fewer agents than the infinite number associated with perfect competition) were deemed to be less competitive, when in fact neither the former concept nor the 'imperfect competition' counterparts have any bearing on the notion of competition.

Legislators, who would have difficulty in deciding whether and to what extent rivalry is present or absent, presumably found a notion of competition based on something observable and measurable (assuming that the crucial problem of defining 'the market' has been solved) to their liking. Guided by economic theory, they accepted that competition was linked to the form of the market. What is the 'form' of the market? Under scrutiny from a subjectivist approach, even the market structure turns out to be completely elusive.

From a third-person perspective, which transcends understanding, the nature and size of the market is easily defined. From the first-person perspective of a competitor constituting his *Umwelt* and *Mitwelt*, and interpreting his relationships with other people, the concept of 'the market' or 'the industry' is anything but clear-cut. While anti-monopoly legislation fails to legislate about competition, criteria used in applying the legislation, such as 'market share', are conventional, often arbitrary notions[2] which may bear no relationship to 'his market', as each competitor understands it. Any estimate of his market implies an assessment of how other people's activities could impinge upon his own business. The notion of a market is intersubjective. It is constituted in terms of reciprocal relationships and involves consideration of the motives and ambitions of other people in relation to one's own. Even among manufacturers, competitive relationships are always in a state of flux, changing with the types of products being produced, and with advertising and distribution policies.

Problems similar to these apply to the way in which neoclassical economics treats the 'market mechanism'. For the most part the markets of neoclassical theory are as nondescript as 'firms'. Hicks tries to remedy this with his important distinction between 'fixprice' and 'flexprice' markets (see Hicks 1946). The economics profession has largely ignored the distinction because the type of market does not make a great deal of difference from a third-person perspective. Economists do not have the methodological means for understanding the predicaments of different people in different markets. Whether markets are of one type or the other is, of course, important to buyers or sellers. In flexprice markets they have to interpret price changes and also take a view – conjecture or speculate – on whether prices will move up or down in future. Whether they are farmers, gold mining companies, or foreign exchange buyers, they are speculators and there is an element of uncertainty that does not concern the ordinary consumer in the supermarket. The relationships between participants, contractual and otherwise, are different in each type of market. Ironically, even though this form of market is the stereotype for all markets, the very issue of the uncertainty of participants in flexprice markets, let alone the question of what this means in terms of how people try to 'get around' the problems and of how the markets work or fail to work, are beyond the purview of neoclassical theory.

The examples here illustrate that, in orthodox theory, an understanding of institutions is as much distorted and limited by the methodology as is an understanding of concepts like choice. In broad terms the task of economics is to help us to understand the many aspects of processes of production in society and of how those processes are managed. This also includes questions about the efficacy of both the processes and of their management. Traditional economic theory is not up to these tasks and its application to the social aspects of managing businesses – as institutions that undertake and manage production – has been ineffective. One unfortunate consequence of the use of equilibrium theory is that, at a time when the social institutions of many countries are undergoing radical change, in their formal theory economists have only the flimsiest of frameworks with which to explain or to advise on what factors are likely to promote, or to retard, the transition from one set of institutions to another.

I submit that we cannot build an adequate explanation of institutions on the foundations of a third-person perspective and, without this, economic policy is likely to be seriously flawed and so is the legislation that is informed by unsuitable theory. The examples above point to a major limitation of orthodox economics being its inability to reflect either the social context of institutions, and how this influences the way they work, or the social nature of the institutions, which come into being through the people's social interaction.

In looking ahead to the development of a hermeneutical economic theory, a virtue of this language is that it 'compels' the theorist to deal with the social nature and implications of human conduct. The problematic of hermeneutics is how the individual constitutes her *intersubjective life-world*. The first-person perspective not only brings the social dimension to the fore but also requires the theorist to look beyond the traditional boundaries of disciplines. As is illustrated by the examples used here, when we adopt a hermeneutical approach the object is to analyse a problem, such as industrial location, in terms of the way that the protagonists and other people concerned understand it. In doing so, we cease to view problems as strictly 'economic', and transcend the barriers between disciplines that modernism has erected. The epistemology and ontology of the third-person perspective are also the source of the idea that disciplines are self-contained: 'in that fully defined world out there are all the issues, and these problems are economic ones'. Understanding, however, is not compartmentalised into disciplines, although her understanding of theory influences the way the individual constitutes her world.

Thus, my answer to the question of whether the subjectivism of interpretative understanding spells the end of economics is assent only in so far as economics is regarded as a framework formulated from a third-person perspective. 'Economics', as we understand the term today, is an artefact of seeing and of trying to describe the world with the language of a modernist theory. With a different language we form a different conception of economics. A subjectivist theory does mark the demise of equilibrium theory and of orthodox economics. For many, there will be regrets at the passing of what has proved to be a durable, though not necessarily enlightening, conceptual scheme. Hermeneutics is the foundation of a different type of economics and provides a distinctive language for dealing with these problems. As a language that permits new and unorthodox questions to be posed, it rekindles the discipline, offering a means of augmenting the sphere of traditional economic studies and of revitalising interest in economic, or rather social, issues.

NOTES

1 TWO LANGUAGES OF ECONOMIC THEORY

1 'Modern hermeneutics' is examined in Chapter 4, in analysing subjectivism. I argue that the hermeneutical turn belongs to the tradition of philosophy that has come down from Max Weber's interpretative sociology through phenomenology.

2 Some philosophers see the contrast between the epistemological view and the hermeneutical view of science as establishing the foundations of the previous dualism versus monism debate. The reasoning is that the origins of methodological dualism lie in the idea of science as epistemology. Methodological dualism may be supported on the grounds that, as there are two sets of phenomena in the world, the physical and the social, two methodologies are needed to deal with them. People understand other people but not other objects, so the social sciences need to reflect this understanding.

3 I must emphasise that Hayek's interest lies in articulating the assumptions about knowledge and foresight, which are implicit in orthodox economic theory, in order to make *equilibrium* theory more serviceable. His view is that this body of theory consists of tautologies. If 'the pure logic of choice' – i.e. neoclassical theory – is to serve to explain, or to convey an understanding of, what happens in reality, then economists must clarify how individuals acquire that knowledge which the theory merely takes as 'given'. Hayek, who takes it for granted that the theorist views the world in terms of some sort of equilibrium, does not consider the epistemological implications of doing so.

4 Throughout the book terms employed in neoclassical theory and defined by that epistemology and ontology, but which are unrelated to the same word used in everyday speech, are placed in quotation marks in order to show that the meaning is different. Terms like 'choice' and 'decisions' acquire their meanings in the context in which they are used – the social interaction of individuals in the life-world. It is unfortunate that economists do not have a separate language to describe the things that agents do. The absence of such a language is a source of considerable confusion. For example, the connotations of 'rivalry' and 'the desire to attain a goal ahead of someone else', which are integral to the notion of competition, are completely absent from 'perfect competition'. Yet the latter is used – inappropriately – as some sort of benchmark in assessing the former. As a consequence, economic theory often does not make sense to businessmen (see Boettinger 1967), and policies on 'competition' do not promote competition.

5 Karl Mittermaier suggested to me that the epistemology of the third-person perspective is an attempt to convey the idea that 'knowledge' can exist without a knower. In this regard a positivist methodology, prefaced on the desire to describe

241

all aspects of the world, and all the forces at work in it, requires that the whole scheme of things fulfils the epistemological and ontological requirements of Karl Popper's 'World Three' – the world of 'objective knowledge', or 'knowledge without a knower'. To the hermeneuticist, World Three, like the third-person perspective, is an anathema.

6 Parsons' views are echoed in the contributions of economists who have tackled the issue of the relationship between theorist and his subject matter. These economists include Robert Clower, Alan Coddington, F.A. Hayek, F.H. Knight, and G.B. Richardson who typically hold that the theorist, as external observer, has a more extended knowledge than that of the actor, but the nature of the knowledge – what it 'consists of' – is the same as that of the individual. Coddington (1972) uses the terms 'first-person' and 'third-person' viewpoints, for the perspectives of the actor and observer, respectively. Although I have appropriated his terms because I think that they are particularly apposite once they are properly defined and understood, the meaning I ascribe to them is completely different. The third-person perspective, a creation of positive science, is a peculiar artificial epistemology and ontology and is not the viewpoint of an observer in the everyday meaning of the word. On the other hand, the first-person perspective applies to both an actor and an observer, in the ordinary sense of someone who 'sees and notices', or 'carefully watches', or 'pays attention to', particular phenomena. There is no difference between the epistemologies of the actor and the observer who are both understanders or interpreters.

7 It does not matter whether the object is to maximise (e.g. profits or utility), to minimise (e.g. costs), to find an optimal strategy (as in game theory), or to 'satisfice'. The epistemological implications in all cases are the same because each conception of optimising is a third-person perspective.

8 These considerations help to explain why mathematics has proved to be such a useful tool in developing equilibrium theories. Given an epistemology and ontology of things that exist in the world, the theorist can view every mathematical variable as having a real counterpart in the determinate scheme of things out there. In terms of this ontology, knowledge, tastes, expectations, prices, and even time ('weeks' or distinct 'periods'), are conceived as undergoing an actual physical transformation, and emerging with new 'values', just as the values of variables change when equations are manipulated. Furthermore, the changing values of variables in the equations are seen to correspond with transformed knowledge, prices, and so on, so mathematics is able to explain how the world works.

2 NEOCLASSICAL METHODOLOGY

1 Useful overviews of the history and main precepts of the logical positivist and empiricist, hypothetico-deductive conceptions of science are contained in the following works. On the tenets see Benton (1977: chs 3, 4), Caldwell (1982: chs 2, 3), Hollis and Nell (1975: ch. 1), and McCloskey (1983: 484–5). On the history see Losee (1972).

2 In referring to this paradigm as an epistemology, the implication is that there are others. One of these is transcendental phenomenology, as conceived by Husserl, who saw in the method of phenomenological reduction a route to apodeictic knowledge.

3 Various aspects of the problems that confront theorists in pursuing an inductively based science, and of asserting proof on the basis of induction, are examined by Losee (1972: ch. 10) and also by Boland (1982a: ch. 1), Caldwell (1982: ch. 4), and

Hollis and Nell (1975: Introduction and ch. 1), who all place considerable emphasis on the particular form of these problems in economics and the social sciences.

4 McCloskey's precept (5) states that 'subjective "observation" (introspection) is not scientific knowledge'. This is different to the claim that knowledge cannot be acquired *a priori*, since the Kantian view is that *a priori* knowledge is not subjective.

5 From the vantage point of modern methodological analysis, the classical and neoclassical schemes have little in common except the notion of equilibrium, and even that term assumes completely different connotations in neoclassical theory (see Milgate 1979; Petri 1978). Both are based on the idea of the economy as system and share a third-person epistemology, but apart from this, their lack of affinity casts doubt on whether the term '*neoclassical*' was ever apposite.

6 Something of the flavour of the debate is contained in, for example, Schumpeter (1967: 911–8), Tarascio (1968: ch. 2), Jaffé (1976), various papers in Black *et al.* (1973), especially that of Blaug, and Hicks (1976a). See also Gram and Walsh (1978).

7 I examine Menger's eclectic methodology more fully in Chapter 6.

8 In fact, as Kregel (1988: 131–2) points out, although Walras was the founder of general equilibrium, much of the contemporary theory, including the Arrow–Debreu version which was preceded by the contributions of Wald and von Neumann, can be traced to Cassel's *Theory of Social Economy*, first published in 1918. It was the work of Hicks, especially *Value and Capital* (2nd edn. 1946), that introduced Walras to an audience of English-speakers.

9 Surely Shackle is incorrect? We can have knowledge of the past, but the individual's experience is personal. Complete knowledge, arising from experience, is inconceivable. Rather, complete knowledge is a defining characteristic of a third-person perspective, an epistemology which does not accommodate experience.

10 My reservations about the methodology of the orthodox theory of choice are not weakened by the more recent models of choice with 'limited information' or with search and information costs (see Lippman and McCall 1976; Rothschild 1973). The views of Nelson and Winter (1982: 65–71) on the bankruptcy of this theory, including the limited information models, are quite as blunt and uncompromising as those expressed here.

11 Arrow (1968: 377) cites Cournot and Jenkin as earlier proponents of partial equilibrium.

12 As opposed to what is sometimes called the 'logical' time of comparative static and dynamic formulations of equilibrium models. I contrast this latter concept of time, the mathematician's notion of time as a continuum, with Bergson's notion of the *durée*, the 'time' that is experienced.

13 There is now an extensive literature analysing, comparing, and evaluating the contributions of these authors, particularly the work of Kuhn and Feyerabend, which has provoked the greatest reaction. Initially, a general response seemed to be that, in criticising the positivist view of rational science, they were either advocating an approach to science, or documenting a scientific community, which had abandoned objectivity for relativism. Philosophical discourse today holds that there are other directions beyond objectivism and relativism. These are only treated as 'natural' opposites from the standpoint of a philosophy that seek certainty about the world (i.e. an epistemology in Rorty's sense). Accepting the 'subjectivism' of a hermeneutical position does not preclude intersubjective consensus or agreement, based on a variety of criteria including aesthetic ones, on what constitutes an acceptable theory. In this view consensus is not contingent upon discovering 'the world out there as it really is', as permanent and immutable, but upon institutional structures and social approbation which will change over time. A useful and fairly up-to-date examination of these issues in the philosophy

of science, which includes an analysis of the contributions of Kuhn and Feyerabend and explores the origins and assesses the implications of the hermeneutical turn in philosophy, is Bernstein (1983).

3 THE PRACTICES OF NEOCLASSICISTS

1 See also Katouzian (1980: 55–71) and O'Sullivan (1987: ch. 11, especially 165– 8), on the methodology of positive economics in practice.

2 These points assert that the questions that scholars seek to answer are relative to our 'state of knowledge'; influenced by what individuals, perhaps with the support of a scientific community, deem to be important at some time, and also by what that community (which may be a very small one) considers to be legitimate techniques for analysis and problem-solving. The social 'consensus' can and does change for various reasons, not least because of new fashions, or 'tastes', within the community. Aumann (1985, in the section 'Science and Truth', pp. 31–5) has some anecdotes that illustrate the historical relativism of knowledge.

3 Without these devices economists would have to abandon neoclassical partial and general equilibrium and revert to a classical notion of equilibrium that does not involve, or require, a balance of choices and decisions but relies on the operation of impersonal 'long-run forces' to bring the system to equilibrium.

4 The main thrust of Kornai's (1971) critique of general equilibrium theory is that the theory substitutes a 'black box' for the important processes by which information is transmitted in the economy. But, in fact, the mechanisms by which information is provided and transmitted *are* built into equilibrium theory, no matter how inadequate they may be as a description of what actually happens in the economy. The problem is not that of a black box, but of a set of arrangements which is devised purely to obtain a determinate outcome, irrespective of what implications this may have for the purposes to which the theory may be put.

5 Schumpeter states (1967: 911) that all three of the protagonists in the catallactist revolution were concerned with barter activities. They deal with markets for goods that are already in existence – a pure exchange economy. Neoclassical theorists tend to continue in this vein and to overlook the considerations – especially the implications of uncertainty – that arise when an investment and subsequent production activities precede the demand for the item, sometimes by many years. See Joan Robinson (1977: 1321).

6 This was actually a form of recontracting which Walras introduced into later editions of the *Eléments*, with a concept of provisional contracts which he called *bons* ('tickets'). (See Jaffé 1977; 1981). The idea behind recontracting is also carried over, in modern formulations of general equilibrium, in the notion of the 'core'. These formulations provide for a process of bargaining amongst economic units which permits a greater number of feasible equilibrium allocations than could be attained under perfect competition. As the number of participants in the bargaining process increases, however, so the number of feasible allocations constituting the core will narrow down until they eventually approximate allocations established in competitive equilibrium. See Arrow and Hahn (1971: 183–206) and Chipman (1965: 54–9).

7 This statement begs the obvious question of how Hahn knows that the end of the road is near. Is it merely because he feels that Arrow–Debreu GE has little more to say about the questions that Smith posed? In addition, linking Smith, the 'invisible hand', and GE, as Hahn is prone to do (see Hahn 1982), surely indicates a belief that GE *is* able to cast light on 'real', capitalist economies. This inference, however, is confounded a few pages on when Hahn states that while one can

describe an economy with certain properties, 'this of course does not mean that any actual economy has been described. An interesting and important theoretical question has been answered and in the first instance that is all that has been done' (ibid.: 126).

8 Although this paper (Fisher 1979) was published in *Econometrica* (see Fisher 1981), the contrast between the two versions is marked, in respect of the matters that have the closest bearing on my arguments. The later version (Fisher 1981) has been 'sanitised' in that many of the arguments that refer to controversial methodological (especially epistemological) issues, such as dealing with agents' uncertainty and their 'disequilibrium consciousness' (1981: 3–5) have been removed. In short, the analysis is more safely back within a modernist epistemology and the hermeneutical problems have been circumvented or at least have been partly concealed.

9 To be fair to Fisher, in an earlier paper (1976), he demurs at the idea that a household requiring toothpaste in the future should immediately enter the futures market.

4 ON SUBJECTIVISM

1 See Boehm (1982); Littlechild (1983); Wiseman (1983b). Coats (1983) says that he had difficulty in finding a definition of subjectivism. That is not surprising, but the definition that he cites – 'any theory which takes private experience to be the sole foundation of factual knowledge' (ibid.: 89) – is rather narrow and idiosyncratic. Coats does not provide an alternative definition and, after digesting his review of the revival of Austrian economics, the reader is not much wiser about the meaning of the term.

2 As an example of non-Austrian subjectivism, one would look to the work of Keynes, particularly his emphasis on individuals' expectations. The subjectivism is embodied in a concept such as 'user cost' (a notion which today is largely neglected). User cost also brings to mind the tradition of 'LSE cost theory', on which the work of Lionel Robbins had a considerable influence. Some of the important contributions to this tradition are collected in Buchanan and Thirlby (1973) and, in his introduction to the volume, Buchanan (1973) notes its subjectivist flavour and also identifies ties to Austrian economics.

3 The confusion that surrounds the use of the term 'subjectivism' is well illustrated by comparing my use with that of O'Sullivan (1987). Although we are both interested in the methodological tradition of neoclassical theory on the one hand and phenomenology on the other, O'Sullivan refers to the latter as subjectivist-relativist even though Husserl regarded phenomenology as capable of providing knowledge which is apodeictically certain and therefore objective. At the same time O'Sullivan rejects the relativist position on interpretation that modern hermeneutics adopts, although I regard this as truly subjectivist-relativist. The distinction between the third-person and first-person perspectives is useful in clarifying the differences between our positions and in explaining why I believe that O'Sullivan's use of the term subjectivism is inappropriate. The issues are set out briefly in the Appendix to this chapter.

4 This argument applies to individuals who are regarded as 'normal' and I am ignoring pathological cases, such as sociopaths, and severe psychological ones, such as autism.

5 In Austrian economics, subjectivism has come to be associated with recognising the existence of a human mind. The term is used not merely to refer to the fact that people think, and converse with one another, but 'mind' has acquired the

connotation of something that has a real, physical existence, like the notion which Schrag (1985: 26–7) attributes to Descartes: one which 'still called upon the classical doctrine of substance to provide consciousness with a stable support, an abiding and ever-present ego, an Archimedian [sic] point of certainty.' Boehm (1993) reminds us that discussion of the nature of the human mind crops up fairly regularly in Hayek's work and is integral to his theory of knowledge. O'Driscoll and Rizzo's (1985: 20 ff.) 'mind construct', which they postulate as the basis of a subjectivist scheme, is confusing. Such a notion is not found in the subjectivist tradition which is under examination here. It may, however, be appropriate in the context in which these authors use it, for their approach involves a third-person perspective.

6 On the constitution of interpretive schemes embracing ideal types see Schütz (1972: especially 176–201).

7 It is worth remembering, as Benton (1977: 120, 121) points out, that Weber did not regard *Verstehen* as a *method* of social science, 'but an "objective", an "achievement" – . . . a distinctive type of knowledge which may be achieved by a variety of methods, or no "method" at all'.

5 INTERPRETATIVE UNDERSTANDING

1 See Truzzi (1974: 8–9) for a brief statement of Dilthey's approach to the social sciences. Warnke (1987: see especially ch. 1) offers a useful overview, initially from Gadamer's perspective, of the evolution of hermeneutical thinking through 'Romantic hermeneutics' – from Schleiermacher and Dilthey – to Heidegger. Different views emerged concerning the purpose of hermeneutics in respect of textual interpretation: for example, from the idea that the role of hermeneutics was to establish the truth of the text, to that of establishing the author's intention, to shedding light on where (and how) the meaning of the text is established, including the idea that the reader does not simply interpret what is already there but actually co-creates the work.

2 A particularly useful examination of Weber's ideas on the certainty of understanding and on the objectivity of a science of interpretative understanding is that of Freund (1968: 96–101).

3 The interpretation is supported by Freund's (1968: 54–5) reading of Weber.

4 Benton's critique of a lack of objectivity in Weber's approach is apparently of a different nature. Benton (1977: 126) argues that Weber's conceptual position (methodological individualism combined with the idea that historical concepts are constructed according to the criterion of value-relevance) prevents one from determining, along scientific lines, whether the techniques and criteria for understanding cultural objects are objective. Benton's suggestion (ibid.: 127), to overcome this difficulty, is to have a scientific theory of objective techniques and criteria of evaluation, which would produce 'criteria for the construction of concepts and interpretations not dependent upon any relevance to values, or upon any particular ideological standpoint, but upon logical techniques for analysing the structure of conceptual systems'. From a hermeneutical point of view, the weakness of this suggestion, which Weber might possibly have identified, is precisely the problem of providing a value- and ideology-free framework. Once the hermeneutical nature of any conceptual framework is recognised, Benton's suggestion leads to an infinite regress. A framework is needed to evaluate a framework, which is needed to evaluate another framework, and so on.

5 Evidently, it is just such a conception that underpins Kirzner's (1978) concept of error.

6 Husserl was definitely not a relativist but an objectivist because he claimed that it is (transcendental) subjective structures, gained through the philosophical act of pure reflection, the transcendental *epoché*, that form the basis of knowledge of the life-world and of science (see also Bernstein 1976: 128–31).

7 For an overview of Schütz's contribution, see Bernstein (1976: 135–69) and also O'Sullivan (1987: ch. 14).

8 Husserl's ideas sometimes foreshadow Schütz's emphasis on the social nature of understanding. See, for example, Husserl (1970: 327–8).

9 As a supreme irony, Apel (1977) charges the proponents of positive science of the sort of solipsism which they hold to be the problem of subjectivism. The sentiments that lie behind the charge are similar to the point made in the text about subjectivism's failure to recognise that understanding is intersubjective. Apel states that 'modern analytical logic of science, based on semantical reconstruction of the language of science . . . [has] *methodological solipsism* as its tacit presupposition' (Apel 1977: 297). The problem, in his view, is that positive science assumes that '*objective* knowledge should be possible without *intersubjective* understanding by communication being presupposed' (ibid.: 298).

10 I explain below that action also involves retrospection. We cast our minds back over events before taking the next step. The social, intersubjective nature of the life-world means that our activities are inevitably bound up with our relationships with other people, and as we do things we are frequently conscious of our obligations or responsibilities to them.

11 Bernstein (1983) and Taylor (1977) refer to a hermeneutical circle, Warnke (1987) to a hermeneutic circle. The latter seems to be the correct usage.

12 The idea that all knowledge is understanding (from a particular perspective) and that, in this sense, nothing exists beyond understanding, is conveyed in Winch's 'relativist' standpoint, which Benton regards as extreme. See Benton (1977: 121ff.). See also Bernstein (1983: 25ff.).

13 Gadamer sees prejudice and tradition as playing not only necessary, but also positive, roles in interpretation. For a very readable analysis of Gadamer's standpoint, which includes a discussion of how he treats the question of assessing, or evaluating, the 'adequacy of prejudice', see Warnke (1987: ch. 3).

14 Sometimes this statement is literally true. In dealings in financial asset markets, such as a stock market, individuals' changing perspectives, in the light of developments in or outside the market, may involve sudden changes in sentiment, almost from one moment to the next.

6 AUSTRIAN ECONOMICS AND SUBJECTIVISM

1 K. Menger (1973: especially 52–5) considers differences between Austrian and mathematical economists, examining arguments regarding the limitations of a mathematical approach to economics.

2 This book represents a substantial modification of my earlier position. There the distinction between first-person and third-person perspectives, and the significance of the distinction for Austrian economics, is ill defined and is not associated with different epistemologies and ontologies.

3 The Austrian revival, the start of which coincided with the centenary of the publication of Menger's *Grundsätze der Volkwirtschaftslehre* [1871] (1950), provides ample material on which to gain an understanding of Austrian themes. An early English commentary identifying a distinctive Austrian contribution is Bonar (1888). More modern surveys and appraisals, which also provide insight into Austrian methodology, include: contributions to *Atlantic Economic Journal*,

Sept. 1978; the contributions to Boettke (1994); essays in Caldwell (1990); the contributions to Dolan (1976); essays in Grassl and Smith (1986); Hayek (1948a, 1955a); contributions to Hicks and Weber (1973); Kirzner (1973, 1976a); contributions to Kirzner (1982a, 1986); Lachmann (1973a, 1976, 1977b, 1982, 1986); Littlechild (1978, 1990a, 1990b); Mises (1949, 1960, 1969, 1978); Nozick (1977); O'Sullivan (1987); essays in Spadaro (1978); White (1977).

4 As this chapter shows, classifying economists in terms of the criterion of their espousal of a subjectivist methodology is problematic, and additional problems of definition arise from the fact that in the school's formative years, when its members did indeed live in Austria, there were many economists of Austrian nationality who did not, and would not, claim any affiliation to the Austrian School. (See Schumpeter 1967: 844–9 for a list of members of the 'older' Austrian School, including biographical details. Some of the points made below are also discussed by Littlechild 1978: 14–17.) Friedrich von Weiser, both on account of nationality and academic affiliation, is categorised as Austrian, but his contribution does not fit the mould of Austrian subjectivism. Then there are economists who are commonly associated with the Austrian School, but incorrectly so when their methodological positions are considered. Schumpeter is sometimes referred to as a 'second generation' Austrian, as are Fritz Machlup and Gottfried Harberler. Individuals like G.L.S. Shackle have influenced Austrian thinking, but would not consider themselves Austrians. Lachmann views Shackle as a kindred spirit and has done much to incorporate Shackle's ideas into Austrian economics. In a similar category, but a more extreme example, is Keynes, whose writings on expectations ally him with Austrian subjectivism (see Lachmann 1991).

5 A common source for many writers crediting Menger with being an Aristotelian is Kauder (1957). More recently, however, scholars have begun to re-assess this claim. See the contributions in Caldwell (1990), especially Mäki (1990) who classifies Menger as a realist sowing the seeds of realist Austrian theory; Milford (1990); and Silverman (1990), who is particularly critical of the Kauder interpretation, and identifies the cameralist roots of Menger's ideas.

6 Mäki (1990: 289) identifies realism as a 'family' of philosophical doctrines opposed to doctrines such as instrumentalism, phenomenalism, idealism, conventionalism, and others. He defines various kinds of realism including ontological realism: 'X exists . . . "X" is a variable that can be given many qualitative values, such as the world . . . physical objects and mental states'. Mäki also refers to semantic realism, common sense realism – the view that everyday experience has access to what is real – and scientific realism. Scientific realism involves the assertion that scientific theories can represent entities in the world, although common sense may not provide access to these (ibid.: 292–3).

7 According to Barry (1979: 12), Hayek makes use of a similar distinction 'between the objective physical world and the phenomenal world, that is the world we perceive through our senses'.

8 Caldwell (1982: see especially 117–24) is critical of Mises' methodology but is sympathetic to Austrian ideas, and he refers to Kirzner's view that Mises was almost forced into giving his Kantian *a priorism* more prominence than he would have wanted (ibid.: 137, n. 45). Nozick (1977) gives Mises' views an impartial hearing from a philosopher's point of view, while Smith (1986, 1990) also brings a philosopher's perspective to bear in examining Austrian *a priorism* and the relationship between the ideas of Menger and Mises. O'Sullivan (1987: 155–8) regards Austrian *a priorism* as 'extreme', 'philosophically challengeable', and 'not even an accurate description of the general practice of economists' (ibid.: 161). See also Boehm (1982); Katouzian (1980: 39–44); Lachmann (1951, 1976, 1982). On Hayek's *a priorism*, see Hayek (1948d: 67–8).

9 Mises' conviction that the 'only method of dealing with the problem of action is to conceive that action ultimately aims at bringing about a state of affairs in which there is no longer any action . . . .' (Mises 1949: 245) appears, at least from a hermeneutical perspective, completely idiosyncratic. It is certainly not consistent with the way in which we understand the activities of others. There is no presumption that our colleagues or friends do things in order to remove felt uneasiness. Mises' adoption of this approach is puzzling but, perhaps, can be explained in terms of an adherence to Benthamite principles. Action is an attempt to overcome feelings of unease or deprivation, possibly caused by hunger and other symptoms of physiological distress (ibid.).

Mises' justification for postulating tendencies towards equilibrium and his interest in the 'final state of rest' derive from the idea that, rather than trying to achieve something, people act to remove something to end up in a position where they no longer have to act. 'What makes it necessary to take recourse to this imaginary construction [the final state of rest] is the fact that the market at every instant is moving toward a final state of rest' (ibid.: 246). The difference in emphasis between the neoclassical concept of general equilibrium and Mises' final state of rest is interesting. In neoclassical theory, what would happen if equilibrium were established and all agents' 'decisions' were compatible? Presumably a stationary state would prevail where people would go on doing the same thing in period after period. For Mises, however, if everyone succeeded in doing what they were trying to do, namely to remove uneasiness, there would be no need for further action. Perhaps individuals would simply languish and then have to act again to overcome the 'felt uneasiness'.

10 It is just this foundation on which Kirzner (1973) builds his theory of entrepreneurship. These unexploited opportunities provide the scope for entrepreneurial activity, which is characterised by attempts to exploit such opportunities for profit as are discovered to exist (out there) by 'alert' individuals. The puzzle which Kirzner's analysis does not resolve is, where do the unexploited opportunities come from? If entrepreneurs are alert, why have they not spotted them before? If they have spotted them, why have all the profitable opportunities not disappeared by now? Or, if new opportunities can be 'thrown up' as a result of changes that occur, how does anyone know that existing opportunities will last? (If they may not last, then conjecture and speculation are important elements in entrepreneurial activity which have been ignored.) Schumpeter's analysis of the entrepreneur as a force of 'creative destruction' makes the entrepreneur a disequilibrating agent, while competition works to restore equilibrium (see Schumpeter 1955: 74–94, 128–56, 217– 36). By contrast, Kirzner's scheme leaves one half of the implied sequence of events unexplained. Of course, this does not deny the importance of an analysis of entrepreneurship. The question is whether anything is gained by placing that analysis in the context of tendencies towards (or away from) equilibrium.

11 I am using the term in the Kantian sense of what is beyond the limits of experience.

12 I recall Ludwig Lachmann recounting a saying of Terrence Hutchison that 'there are at least five Hayeks'. Hayek-the-economist almost disappeared from view in later years in favour of Hayek-the-social-philosopher and, when he is there, Hayek-the-economist is not always an equilibrium theorist. Sometimes Hayek makes much of interpretative understanding, and sometimes when advocating an evolutionary theory of social change he is hard to distinguish from a modernist. My contention, however, is that tendencies towards equilibrium are an important component of his economic thinking and also characterise his political philosophy, where the evolutionary nature of the social order is a strong element (see Hayek 1973a). Lachmann (1976: 58, n. 5) notes Hayek's early attachment to general

equilibrium. See also Barry's remarks (1979: 42–3) on Hayek's position in respect of the notion of equilibrium. Boehm (1993) identifies various inconsistencies and unresolved issues in Hayek's views on the role of markets and the acquisition of knowledge. The problems are a result of trying to deal with epistemological matters in the context of a third-person, equilibrium framework.

13 I believe that assessment, which is based on an analysis of Lachmann's writings, is correct. On the other hand I also believe that Lachmann's later work, in which he refers to the economics of an 'active mind', is consistent with a conception of a hermeneutic economics, involving individuals who constitute problems (in terms of their plans and expectations).

14 Austrian economists generally try to avoid what Mittermaier (1986) appropriately terms 'mechanomorphisms', though not always successfully. In the nature of the Austrian conceptual framework, mechanical analogies are probably unavoidable, since explanation – the linking of particular economic phenomena to individuals' plans and decisions – is really about showing correlations between things. See Mittermaier on the use of metaphors as means of explanation, and on the questions of whether, and why, the use of mechanomorphisms is problematical.

7 IMPLICATIONS OF INTERPRETATIVE UNDERSTANDING

1 It is precisely the recognition of a mutual interest amongst individuals who regard themselves as competitors that may lead to attempts to try to 'eliminate the competition' in one of two ways: either by forcing the competition out (to which end numerous strategies may be adopted), or by co-operating instead of competing, say by forming a cartel, or by way of a 'gentlemen's agreement'.

2 See Hayek (1955c: 53–9) for his discussion of 'methodological collectivism'. Hayek argues that the collectivist approach 'mistakes for facts what are no more than provisional theories ... to explain the connection between some of the individual phenomena which we observe' (Ibid.: 54). He states that 'wholes as such are never given to our observation but are without exception constructions of our mind. They are not "given facts" ... we spontaneously recognise as similar by their common physical attributes' (ibid.). The difficulty with this type of critique, from the standpoint of hermeneutics, is that it presumes that there is a world 'out there' of individual facts, which can be grasped spontaneously and, unlike the 'wholes', is independent of 'constructions of the mind'.

3 In some respects the evolution of the modern market economy has resulted in certain types of transactions becoming increasingly anonymous and impersonal. Compared with a hundred years ago, manufacturing firms, banks, and even certain retailers, do not now have the same relationships with their customers, and perhaps there is no one in the firm who actually knows a particular customer. Yet this is not true of all transactions and at different levels within a company individuals' relationships with others – both inside and outside the organisation – are important to 'doing business'.

4 The idea of aggregating individuals' preferences would, at any rate, only manifest itself in a scheme where preferences were treated as things that exist in the world, that have a structure (like a shopping list) and, presumably, are durable, so that they can all be scrutinised for compatibility and consistency and then combined. As I argued in Chapter 2, the social welfare function is a creation of a third-person perspective.

5 Compare Hayek's (1967c) explanation of individuals' purchasing decisions, in his response to Galbraith's argument that wants are dependent upon the process of

NOTES

production. This article highlights a phenomenon common amongst economists. They understand perfectly well how the economy 'works' but will not reflect this understanding in their modernist theories. In the article cited, Hayek offers useful insights into the social nature of market activity. Yet none of these insights, which are certainly useful for making a case for advertising, 'spills over' into the theory of advertising or of competitive conduct. As far as economic theory is concerned, it seems to be essential to keep separate one's understanding of market activity and the theory of market activity. Yet by doing so, one is rejecting the very insights that Hayek himself deems important for the social theorist – his understanding of human conduct which forms the basis for the compositive method of 'building up' an explanation of economic phenomena. In fact this apparent paradox is easily explained. When the Austrians, following Mises, say that the nature of human conduct is known to the theorist and therefore forms the starting point of social scientific theory, they do not mean the practical aspects of human conduct, as in going shopping. Instead, what is referred to is the category of action itself. Individuals consciously choose ends and the means to achieve them: people are rational: and economic phenomena can be 'explained' in terms of these '*a priori*' categories.

6 This is not to deny that, on occasion, a manager or employee may make a difference to the way in which, say, the customer perceives his bank. Customers may change branches when the manager is transferred because, from their point of view, the personal relationship that exists with the manager is the most important aspect of their relationship with the bank. The point, though, is that individuals do develop business or other relationships with institutions which can outlast their relationships with particular individuals in those institutions.

7 In recent years, there has been an increased interest in an 'institutional economics'. One attempt to draw together Austrian theory and a theory of institutions is that of Langlois (1982a), which contains a number of additional interwoven threads.

8 Perhaps it should be noted that even the notion of explanation is given different interpretations. Hayek (1948d: 67–8), for example, though at times a proponent of *Verstehen* (see Hayek 1973b: 8), argues that explaining conscious action is 'a task for psychology but not for economics or linguistics, jurisprudence or any other social science. What we do is to merely to classify types of individual behaviour which we can understand ... provid[ing] an orderly arrangement of the material' (Hayek 1973:67).

9 Taylor's position is that 'it is much easier to understand after the fact than it is to predict. Human science is largely *ex post* understanding' (Taylor 1977: 129). This view has much in common with the standpoint of Lachmann (see, for example, Lachmann 1978b: 15–17).

8 MODELS OF INDUSTRIAL LOCATION

1 Until the end of the war, when American writers took up the problems of location, interest in, and contributions to, the theory of location was much stronger in Germany than elsewhere. Isard (1956: 27) attributes this strength to the confluence of the interest of members of the German historical school in the spatial implications of economic development and the impact of Walrasian economics upon German economists.

2 Webber (1972: see especially ch. 2) compares many of the contributions and highlights the assumptions of the various models. Useful overviews of the neoclassical theory of location are also provided by Carrier and Schriver (1966: see ch. 2) and Isard (1956: ch. 2), whose outline of the literature pays particular

attention to the work published in German. Besides sketching a comparison of the models of different theorists, Isard also deals with the concurrent evolution of neoclassical methodology, highlighting the shift from a partial to a general equilibrium approach to location that occurred in the 1920s (Isard 1956: 31–4). See also Hamilton (1974b), Massey (1979), D.M. Smith (1979), and Stafford (1972).

The variety of contributions can be classified in ways that help to indicate where the emphases of the different writers fall. In the models of A. Weber (1929), Palander (1935), and Hoover (1937) the main determinant of location is the desire to minimise costs (the 'least cost approach'), while Isard (1956) also utilises a Weberian approach. In these models the firm's costs are a function of its position in space, determined by its distance from raw materials, as determined by transport costs, and so on. In the 1920s and 1930s, a number of writers, including Fetter (1924), Hotelling (1929), Chamberlin [1933] (1962), and Smithies (1941), produced models that involve locational interdependence. They were influenced by the newer theories of imperfect competition and monopolistic competition that emerged in the 1930s which attempt to model interfirm 'rivalry' (i.e. inter-dependencies), a factor that is missing from the perfectly competitive model (see Schumpeter 1967: 1150–2 on the scholars who contributed, either directly or indirectly, to the formulation of the newer theories based on quasi-monopolistic market structures).

Lösch's [1939] (1954) 'market area approach' takes account of both production costs and market area (Weber's approach omits the latter), but does not deal with locational inter-dependencies among firms. Lösch, who is responsible for formal-ising the analysis of market areas – showing how general location patterns emerge – also provides a basis for the development of central place theory in the hands of Christaller [1933] (1966) and others (see Beavon 1977). Central place models, built on a scheme that defines a spatially organised system, have served to explain settlement hierarchies (see Isard 1956: ch. 3).

3   While I agree with Massey's diagnosis that the problems of orthodox location theory are found at the level of epistemology, I do not agree with her suggestions for the reformulation of location theory (see Massey 1984) with their Marxist-institutionalist foundations. Massey's critique of location theory overlooks the ontological issues, and one of the reasons for rejecting the path that she recommends is that it is deterministic and involves an ontology of things-in-the-world. It is not an approach that allows the theorist to understand how individuals formulate location decisions.

4   A more up-to-date contribution to conceptions of space by Sack (1980) also makes no reference to interpretative understanding of space and spatial relationships (i.e. a hermeneutical approach to spatial considerations). His analysis of 'subjective meanings of space' in the social sciences (ch. 4), much like that of Gould and White (1974), deals with different perceptions from an objectivist standpoint, and the discussion of chorology (ch. 4) indicates that an objectivist psychology of perception provides the root of these 'subjective' meanings.

5   Forer's interest is in spatial concepts that are not independent of time and in the problems of representing these concepts. As he casts it, this is a different set of problems from my hermeneutical one of understanding what 'spatial issues' mean to the individual and, therefore, whether perceptions of spatial relationships have any bearing on location decisions.

6   The notion that a map embraces the whole scheme of things is reinforced by the concept of 'projection', a mechanistic metaphor which suggests that the geo-grapher has succeeded in taking the world out there and converting it in its entirety, without any act of interpretation, into a two-dimensional image which captures all the elements including all the spatial relationships.

7 In an editorial footnote, Friedrich (1928: 102) explains the meaning of Alfred Weber's term, 'isodapanes'. Bearing in mind that the concept refers to things that are influenced by what people do, and that costs themselves have to be identified, classified, and allocated (i.e. interpreted), the idea that 'equal cost' (or 'expense') is inspired by the geographical term 'isotherm' is revealing. It shows how Weber deemed mechanical analogies appropriate when it came to developing models of human activities.

8 These themes are identified and examined in Watts (1987), and the literature is critically reviewed by Krumme (1969), Hamilton (1974b), Keeble (1978), Massey (1979), Wood (1981), Carr (1983), Hayter and Watts (1983), and Taylor and Thrift (1983b).

9 Models of the decision-making process in large organisations, highlighting the factors that play a role in decisions about location, are also presented by Dicken (1971), Lloyd and Dicken (1972: 146–51), Rees (1972a, 1972b, 1974), Stafford (1969), M. J. Taylor (1975), Townroe (1971: ch. 2), and Watts (1987: 168–77) and are outlined by Downs (1970: 69–70). Because the firm's size is a determinant of its structure and its decisions, industrial geographers tend to concentrate on large, generally multiplant, and often multinational enterprises. The activities of the large enterprise, with a number of plants, are more interesting to the geographer, but also contributing to this emphasis is the view (Hamilton 1974b: 14) that '[t]here appears rarely to be a conscious *location policy* except among very large or market-dominant corporations'.

10 On the nature of the individual's 'perception' that forms the basis of decision-making in the theory of the geography of enterprise, see Dicken (1971) and Lloyd and Dicken (1972: 138–46). The latter show, in diagrammatic form, how the behavioural environment is perceived. In brief, the individual is a mechanism, obliged by his characteristics to respond and behave in particular ways. His 'mind', a part of what (to the theorist) exists out there, is treated as a 'filter' which has to 'decode' the information which (to the individual) exists out there, beyond and separate from him. Once decoded, the filtered information is placed into its context in the firm's decision structure, with the object of producing an efficient response (for the firm). A 'considerable amount' of the information transmitted to the individual is apparently received visually (Lloyd and Dicken 1972: 139). The decision-maker is depicted much like a camera that records, through different types of filters, visual images of what happens out there, and stores these images.

11 The reformist neoclassical theorists who seek answers to hermeneutical questions (e.g. Hahn 1970, 1973a) adopt a similar approach to decision-making. In order to deal with 'learning', where the agent interacts with the environment within an equilibrium framework, it appears to be necessary to advance an epistemological dualism. To ensure that plans dovetail, 'the world' must be the same for everyone. Every individual, though perhaps initially somewhat ignorant of the 'true' facts, must eventually come to learn the same things as everyone else. This will only happen if we postulate a complete and unchanging 'reality' behind the perceptions and knowledge of each individual.

12 A related and fundamental question, of how the boundaries of the firm's environment are identified, is unanswerable. The third-person perspective leads to the view that the environment is something out there, beyond the firm. One of the most cogent critiques of this notion of environment, which is widely used in organisational theory, is that of Morgan (1986: see especially ch. 8).

13 Wood (1981: 175) observes that while various writers 'have tried to represent the decision sequence in diagrammatic form ... such is the variety of experience uncovered in investigations of individual firms that it is very difficult to generalise [about decision structures].'

9 LOCATION THEORY AS A NARRATIVE

1 At the end of the previous chapter I drew attention to the contrast between the models that industrial geographers employ and their descriptions of how locations are chosen. This emphasises that scientists use more than one language to discuss problems. In this case it is the language of behavioural theory and the 'natural language' of everyday discourse. As illustrated by the location problem, the various languages may yield not just different, but entirely incongruent interpretations of the problem and its implications. It is puzzling that scientists who profess to be concerned with the quest for 'truth', or who at least hope to achieve a 'correct explanation', do not seem to be troubled by the incongruities and tend to ignore them.

2 Both of these are extremely charitable interpretations of what the theories are about. Like any positivist theory, and at the risk of over-emphasising the point, they do not deal with the conscious activities of people going about their daily social lives, but with things that are assumed to exist in the world, and relationships between these things.

3 As I argued in Chapter 3, the role of devices like the Walrasian auctioneer, recontracting, and futures markets in general equilibrium theory, is precisely to attempt to overcome this problem and to preserve the illusion that agents can possess complete knowledge.

4 In G.L.S. Shackle's important contribution to economics, the issue of uncertainty and also the relationship between time and uncertainty are central considerations. No study of investment decision-making is complete without an examination of his work. The problem of finding a 'language for expectation' is one with which he has grappled (see, *inter alia*, Shackle 1965, 1969, 1970, 1972a), and he makes a serious attempt to develop a formal framework for analysing investments, recognising that while 'expensive tools need much time in which to repay their cost, [t]hat time must needs lie in the future which is out of reach of direct observation, which in strictness is *unknowable*' (Shackle 1970: 97). Of particular interest is Shackle's attempt to reconcile 'unknowledge' with a desire to be able to 'quantify' the prospects of returns from different investments so that the investments can be compared *ex ante*. (See Shackle 1970: 97–105; 1972a: chs 18, 33, 34.)

The account of the hermeneutic circle, however, also highlights a formalism in Shackle's description of decision-making that is at odds with the spirit of his thinking on epistemological issues. The reason may be that for much of his career Shackle has striven to develop a language of subjective probability. There is a sense in Shackle's work that expectations are more than conjecture and that in forming expectations the individual is engaged in trying to construct a complete 'picture' – I use the term deliberately – of different possible states of the world. In contrast, I would argue that, as far as investment decisions are concerned, the people planning the investment have no expectation of a particular outcome, but are either optimistic or pessimistic about the investment being successful.

The difficulty that economists appear to have had both in classifying and appreciating Shackle's *oeuvre* may be tied to the need to understand the distinction between the epistemologies and ontologies of the first-person and third-person perspectives. For much of his contribution revolves around this distinction, with Shackle in effect arguing that the third-person perspective of equilibrium theory does not serve economists' purposes and they need to adopt a first-person perspective. The meaning of his contention (1972: 246) that '[e]conomics, concerned with thoughts and only secondarily with things, the objects of those thoughts, must be as protean as thought itself' is much clearer when the ontology of the first-person perspective – understanding, constituted in the *durée* – is contrasted with that of the third-person – a world of things that exists out there.

5 Many studies do recognise that 'personal factors' may determine the location of a business, but it is usually implied that this is irrational behaviour and that firms should only be paying attention to the objective circumstances out there. Glossing over the question of whether 'personal factors' are not in fact the basis of any decision, Greenhut (1956) holds that, from the appropriate theoretical standpoint, even when decisions cannot be explained in terms of traditional microeconomic determinants of location – when personal factors are important – there is no evidence that industrialists behave irrationally and make inappropriate choices.

6 See, for example, Aangeenbrug 1968; Barr *et al.* 1980; Barr and Fairbairn 1978; Downs 1970; Forer 1978; Huff 1960; McDermott and Taylor 1976; M.J. Taylor 1975, 1978.

7 Various authors have none the less found it useful to conceptualise this image as an areal one. Taylor (1975) formulated the concepts of 'operational' space (as the area defined by the imaginary boundary drawn around the points representing the firm's linkages), 'action' space, and 'information' space. These concepts have found fairly widespread acceptance in industrial geography, despite the fact that they involve the transformation of punctiform 'space' into areal space. Harrison *et. al.* (1979: 334) offer various criticisms of the analysis of spatial relationships in industrial geography. They argue that

> there is a fundamental confusion between 'space' defined as a continuous areal phenomenon and 'space' defined as a discrete, punctiform phenom- enon. . . . [T]he assumption that . . . points can be taken as boundary points on an imaginary line enclosing a continuous space within which the firm operates . . . is a logical fallacy.

These authors also go on to criticise the tendency of conflating 'geographical (map) space on the one hand, and a series of abstract spaces which may or may not be directly related to it, on the other.'

8 In this area again one finds the dichotomy that is evident between the formal models of structures of decision-making on the one hand, and writers' interpreta- tions of how location decisions are made on the other. North (1974) is an important case in point. His discussion of location decisions, based on analysis of survey data, stands in marked contrast to his model. His analysis not only offers useful insights into the factors influencing location, but indirectly it subverts the basis of the received approach to location which emphasises the search for alternative locations. North argues (1974: 242) that

> as far as the locational search and selection process is concerned, two things are abundantly clear. In the first place, it was very rare for firms to perform a strictly objective analysis of alternative locations. . . . Even where firms did employ objective methods . . . the ultimate decision was often made on the basis of hunch . . . and previous experience of an area.

These arguments are important. See also Luttrell (1962: 74). A subjectivist approach to decision-making provides a context and rationale for such inferences.

9 The issue of uncertainty receives scant attention from industrial geographers. When it does, they are up against the problem that their conceptual scheme excludes uncertainty. Pred (1967) deals with uncertainty as a motivating factor in the choice of location (firms try to minimise uncertainty). While Lloyd and Dicken (1972: 157–8) deal with the problem only briefly at the end of a chapter on 'The Decision-Making Process'. The strategies which they suggest for minimising

uncertainty are important and sensible, but they fail to integrate these insights into the theory of location decision-making. Industrial geographers' questions related to uncertainty, concerning the individual's 'picture' of an area, naturally have to fit the epistemology of the behavioural approach. The type of uncertainty upon which the analysis of location problems is premised is uncertainty about the actual 'real world' circumstances (which are apparent to the theorist) that lie behind the 'perceived environment' (that is known to the decision-maker) (see Dicken 1971: 431), or about different possible 'states of nature'. It is postulated that events may have more than one possible outcome, the list of potential outcomes is complete and known (to the analyst of decision-making), but uncertainty arises because the decision-maker has to find out which outcomes are most likely. See also Stafford (1972: Section IV).

10 For this reason it is not at all irrational for different people to hold completely divergent expectations, which is the basis of any speculative market. Each speculator conjectures about the 'behaviour of the market', therefore about what the other participants are thinking and what they are going to do. It is simply not possible for him or anyone else to say beforehand that the 'bears' are more correct or more rational than the 'bulls', or that they have a better chance. It is not possible to reason, on the basis of probabilities or by any other means, about what will happen until we know how people understand. The 'outcome' – what happens in the market – is entirely a consequence of what people think, and depends on how they understand and what they decide to do.

11 Dealing with those location models that incorporate 'locational interdependence', where the locator has to take cognisance of the activities and proximity of other firms, for they affect his revenue, Webber uses game theory to analyse what he calls (1972: ch. 6) 'uncertainty about rivals'. Similar objections apply to its use, in that game theory is an attempt to substitute knowledge for uncertainty (see also Stafford 1972: Section III). Game theory, in Shackle's words, is an 'extraordinary paradox', because although it is a product of a 'great mathematician's originative genius ... it assumes away the whole of that aspect of business, science ... and contest, which allows originative genius to exist' (Shackle 1972a: 422). Shackle is saying that game theory is an attempt to create a system that meets the requirements of a third-person perspective; a system without an open future. Individuals who inhabit a world consisting of game-theoretic rivalry, would live a life without doubt and surprises (they already know the possible strategies that their rivals may adopt), and without uncertainty. For an interpretation of the objectives of game theory, see Aumann (1985).

12 See Richardson (1973) for an illuminating analysis of how oligopolistic market structures contribute to the businessman's ability to cope with uncertainty.

13 Maps are not keys to 'rational' (in the sense of optimal) decisions, but are means of coping with uncertainty (when the individual does not know), though not of removing it. Their value is not in directing the user to undertake the correct course of action, but in helping him to interpret and to understand.

14 Townroe (1969) and others refer to location in the context of an investment by the firm, although there is seldom more than a mention of the interconnection (see, for example, Krumme 1969: 32; Rees 1972a: 204).

10 DECISIONS ABOUT THINGS IN THE WORLD

1 Hamermesh (1983: 1) quotes a definition of (corporate) strategy as 'the pattern of objectives, purposes, or goals and major policies and plans for achieving those

goals, stated in such a way as to define what business the company is in or is to be in and the kind of company it is or is to be.'

2 Overviews of the theory are provided by Edwards (1967a, 1967b). See also Hogarth and Reder (1987) and Kahneman *et al.* (1982) for the contributions of psychologists to behavioural decision theory.

3 See Katz and Kahn (1966: ch. 2) on the 'system concept' that is the foundation of behavioural theory. Their reference to organisations as 'open systems' does not contradict our argument that the epistemology of a third-person perspective denotes a complete, closed system. Openness, for Katz and Kahn and for other behavioural theorists, signifies that the firm is subject to influences from outside. The important consideration is that what is 'outside' is conceived as being complete. The world out there forms a whole entity and is capable of being comprehended in its entirety. Only in this context does optimisation make sense.

4 The third-person perception of the economy, or the market as a system, is identified explicitly in the following quotation from Coleman (1987: 184). He examines the assumptions of models of rational action and argues that:

> the straightforward model of rational action that satisfies normative theory will, despite all the evidence about its descriptive deficiency, be adequate for most problems in economic theory as a descriptive theory. It is deficiencies in the apparatus for moving from the level of the individual actor to the behaviour of the system that hold the greatest promise of gain. The reasons, I believe, lie in part with evolutionary processes in social and psychological organization. . . . [T]here is wider variability in social organization through which individuals' actions combine to produce system-level behaviour.

5 Here again is the epistemological dualism that characterises the behavioural approach to location.

6 The same arguments apply to the tests used to examine decision-makers' 'judgements' and their responses to uncertainty. See the contributions in Kahneman *et al.* (1982), especially Bar-Hillel (1982), Kahneman and Tversky (1982), and Tversky and Kahneman (1982b).

7 There are circumstances, such as tests of skill or strength, where the parameters on which performance will be judged are so carefully laid down that decisions which have to be made, to all intents and purposes, are made against the background of a 'complete system', although the decisions always involve interpretation. These conditions, which are intersubjectively established, are devised so that it is practical to say whether the individual's performance met or fell short of some standard, either in terms of what he achieved or how he got there. The position of a business manager – the way he understands – is not analogous to someone judging a gymnastics contest.

8 Notice how Hogarth (1987: 57) glosses over these issues. Having argued that 'formal, statistical models should be used for prediction where possible', he notes two objections to this suggestion: quantitative data and 'sufficient numbers of past instances'. The first difficulty can be overcome by using qualitative information, 'scaled and represented in numerical form'. The matter of 'past instances' is almost passed over. Hogarth says that 'to build statistical models . . . one needs adequate data sources. However, even when data sources are not rich, some means of statistical combination of data . . . often leads to better predictions.' Hogarth's positivist methodology has taught him to think of 'past instances' and 'qualitative data' like quantitative data, as just other sets of observable things that exist out there.

9 This conception of planning is not unlike the treatment of decision-making in

behavioural theory. The difference between the approaches is a matter of interpretation. Lachmann's position appears to be that what the individual sees out there is the world out there, while the behavioural approach draws a distinction between the circumscribed or limited 'view' of the individual and the complete world 'known' to the theorist. Neither, however, accommodates the idea that the individual constitutes her world.

11 PLANS AND DECISIONS AS UNDERSTANDING

1 At times, however, there is no conflict at all. See Schütz (1972: 65) on the 'Act of attention'.

2 Because it is central to interpretative sociology, Max Weber begins *Wirtschaft und Gesellschaft* [1922] (1964) with a definition of action, which emphasises that action, as distinct from other forms of behaviour, consists of those activities to which 'the acting individual attaches a subjective meaning' (ibid.: 88). In expanding upon this definition, Weber explains action in terms of the concepts 'ends' and 'means'. With good reason, Schütz (1972: 19) criticises Weber's distinction between action and behaviour, pointing out that '[e]ven ... traditional [habitual] ... behaviour has some kind of meaning'. This is the argument that is relevant to the points made here. Much of the individual's daily activity (routine) is habitual, to the extent that it does not involve the process of 'projection' which Schütz associates with planning, but this does not make it any less 'meaningful' in the Weberian sense. I can go into the kitchen and do all sorts of things associated with preparing a meal, and may even cook the entire meal, without being conscious of planning anything, but my activities are still purposeful.

3 Industrial geographers have pointed to these issues, as illustrated by the model of the structure of location decision-making proposed by D. J. North (1974) and the analysis of Townroe (1971: ch. 5). The sources of information depicted in North's model include estate agents, local newspapers, industrialists, personal contacts (see Figures 8.3 and 8.4). While these authors identify various sources of information on which location decisions may be based, McNee (1974) is one of the few contributors in the field of industrial geography who alludes to the importance of social relationships. His article begins with the statement 'decisions and choices are always in the context of society' (ibid.: 47), but the analysis does not live up to this introduction. In sketching the history of the hypothetical Gismo company, McNee glosses over social relations that might shape the changes taking place.

4 Thus, when speaking of the 'complementarity' of investment plans, Lachmann (1978a: 3) makes no reference to relationships among people that complementarity implies. He states that,

> the heterogeneous capital resources do not lend themselves to combination in any arbitrary fashion. For any given number of them only certain modes of complementarity are technically possible, and only a few of these are economically significant.

Although he views the capital structure as being endlessly variable as people's plans change and capital has to be redeployed, he treats the capital stock as a complete, interlocking, but changing system, a conception that masks the importance of relationships between people.

5 It is important to clear up a possible misconception about the concept of the social world, a misconception which Schütz himself wishes to avoid. Elsewhere, with reference to the third-person perspective, I have used the term 'world' to refer to a conception of the scheme of things as complete and self-contained. The term

'social world' simply conforms with Schütz's usage. He argues that 'world' means only 'that different people are consociates, contemporaries, predecessors, or successors to one another' (1972: 143) and is careful to stress that the term is not to be interpreted to mean 'given and complete' – the meaning that I have ascribed to the third-person perspective. Schütz argues (1972: 142, emphasis added) that

> the world of my actual perception is only a fragment of the whole world of my experience, and this . . . is but a fragment of the world of my possible experience, so likewise the social world (itself a portion of this 'whole world') is only *directly experienced by me in fragments as I live from moment to moment.* This directly experienced social world is again, on its side, segmented according to conceptual perspectives. Beyond this domain of directly experienced social reality to which I am anchored by spatiotemporal community, there are still other realms.

6 The fairly well-developed theory of search, and of optimal search behaviour, began with Stigler (1961). See also Alchian (1977b) and Rothschild (1973).

7 The idea of imperfect information has aroused much debate about whether, and why – since the dispersed prices are equilibrium prices – an equilibrium theory is compatible with the existence of a distribution of prices. Would an initial distribution of prices not collapse into a single price in each market so that the need to search disappears (see Rothschild 1973)? This apparent conundrum illustrates that the difficulty of sustaining 'realistic' assumptions about what people know – the idea that there is a distribution of prices, rather than a single one – is irresolvable in the face of the desire to work within an equilibrium framework. The knowledge that individual prices represent elements in a fixed distribution, which epitomises the third-person perspective, also removes uncertainty (unknowledge); the world out there can be known in its entirety.

8 Discussing an epistemology of personal knowledge, Polanyi (1973: 256) states his position in terms which match and support my arguments about decisions resting on judgement. He says that

> in the last resort my statements affirm my personal beliefs. . . . Nothing that I say should claim the kind of objectivity to which in my belief no reasoning should ever aspire; namely that it proceeds by a strict process . . . [and] include[s] no passionate impulse of . . . [the expositor's] own.

9 Watts (1987 174) cites Townroe as noting that this practice is less common, for example, in the United Kingdom than in the United States. Townroe states that firms in the United Kingdom rarely use location consultants, and that the practice is found only among larger firms in the United States. Two comments on this statement are in order. The arguments set out in Chapter 12 explain why one would expect only large firms to hire consultants and my contention that ideas for locations generally 'emerge' out of other considerations explains why one would not necessarily expect firms to hire location consultants; though they may hire consultants in connection with the investment or consultants in the area of strategy, whose advice settles the matter of location.

10 Naturally rhetoric plays an important role in helping people to make up their minds. Managers need to *feel* that they are doing the right thing. Advice from an 'acknowledged expert' who has a reputation for solving business problems, may go some way to allaying fears. In this context it is appropriate for the adviser to point out how particular strategies have been responsible for the success of other firms, and to highlight how successful they have been. Some general recipes for success are well known: 'adopt the Japanese approach of subcontracting'; 'reduce

inventory and other costs by implementing a "just-in-time" manufacturing system'; 'reduce manufacturing costs by licensing the product to low-cost manufacturers of original equipment, or enter into a joint venture with an OEM company'.

12 INVESTMENT DECISIONS

1 Neoclassical theory recognises that the firm has 'commitments' as a consequence of decisions made in the past: commitments that are manifested in the form of fixed costs or a particular capital combination. Yet these do not have any significance for agents other than that it takes 'time' (defined as so many 'periods') before the commitments are discharged. As Hicks (1976b: 137) says, putting the matter in the context of the theory of consumer choice, whatever constraints exist, 'the consumer is supposed to rethink his whole budget'. As a critique of the orthodox approach to decision-making, this statement has two parts. One is that as prices change each agent goes through a ridiculous exercise in which she effectively reconsiders her entire 'future'. In addition, there are no consequences of past decisions to think about. The income that was spent or the investments that were undertaken then do not have repercussions now, or in the future. Even if it is necessary to 'wait' a while, in order to allow fixed costs to run off, given a set of comprehensive 'plans' that direct the agent's decisions through 'future' time periods, whatever set of prices emerges, there is always a way 'out', a means of transforming the current situation into that of the next period. 'Commitments' do not really mean anything. A corollary of a complete (determinate) scheme is that firms and agents always remain infinitely flexible. Whatever someone else does, they have an optimal response. In practice, a commitment means being obliged to do something even though you might not want to, or would prefer to do something else. Whether it is a legal or moral obligation, the decision-maker knows that, having made the commitment, she will not have a way out; she will not be free to do other things. That is why, if she is unsure of the consequences, she may prefer not to commit herself in the first place.

Sir John Hicks and G.L.S. Shackle come to mind as two commentators who have long argued that Marshall's economics is different from the standard axiomatic neoclassical theory. The distinction between the 'market day', 'short period', and 'long period', in part is an attempt to reflect the commitments that arise as a consequence of people's activities. I am sure that they, and others, are right about a fundamental difference between Marshallian and Walrasian economics. For one thing, a virtue of a partial equilibrium approach is that agents do not have to rethink their entire budgets. On the other hand, Marshall's is a determinate analysis. People do not get 'bogged down' in indecision. Firms do not fail because the managers are incompetent administrators, but because prices are too low to enable them to cover their variable costs in the short run. Some firms – the efficient ones – will survive. The ontology of the Marshallian scheme, where economic phenomena, including 'periods', have an existence in the world, does not allow the theorist to express commitments. A partial equilibrium analysis still specifies an entire system and the short-period equilibrium gives way, quite effortlessly, to the long-period equilibrium. In the circumstances of each period firms have a defined path, a natural way 'out', or transition, to the next period.

2 This is the idea behind Keynes's analysis of the effects of short-term expectations on investment opportunities and the 'marginal efficiency of capital'. Those opportunities, however, are interpreted as surviving in a scaled-down form even when the outlook of the business community becomes more pessimistic. My

position is that under these circumstances investment 'opportunities' actually disappear and may never 'come round' again. Some of the people who might have done so if the outlook were more buoyant, do not even think about undertaking investments. They turn their attention to the short-term problems that have arisen and may not ever consider investments again, because some of the firms will go out of business.

3 It was only when the ideas for this chapter were quite far advanced, and I had already made the distinction between small and large firms, that I 'rediscovered' Penrose's (1959) excellent contribution on the theory of the firm. It is difficult to say how much influence this work had on my thinking, having originally read it more than a decade ago. For different reasons – her interest is in the growth of the firm – Penrose's distinction between small and large enterprises is along similar lines to my own, and the insights that she provides are invaluable. Penrose is well aware that her contribution is not part of the orthodox theory of the firm, although she does not identify quite what differentiates it from 'standard' neoclassical theory. The important consideration is that Penrose's is not an equilibrium analysis. Not being constrained by the epistemology and ontology of a determinate scheme, she is able to ask questions which illuminate the circumstances of managers and the factors that bear upon their decisions. The result is a more satisfying explanation of firm's activities than neoclassical theory is able to provide. I should add that the need to divide firms into large and small companies in part depends on whose activities are of interest and on what these people do. If the focus were on workers on the factory floor or lower-rung administrative staff, whose work activities are fairly routine – including their business dealings with people outside the firm itself – and whose authority is limited, the distinction might be unnecessary.

4 The term 'entrepreneurial' should not be understood to mean that the managers of all small businesses are innovative and are willing to take risks for the prospect of high returns. The profitability of many small businesses is low, and although it is referred to as a 'small business', there is a type of activity, such as sidewalk hawking which is prevalent in developing countries, which is no more than a means of subsistence. The 'owner' has no capital and he has no conception, or intention of 'expanding the business', but is trying to earn enough to survive.

5 Chandler's (1962) seminal contribution on corporate strategy postulates and investigates relationships between the way in which large firms are structured and managed, and the strategies of these firms. Later contributions have pursued the same theme, also examining the structure and 'culture' of organisations in terms of whether particular combinations of structure and culture are conducive to better performance by large enterprises.

6 Freund (1968: 59–70) provides a useful definition and explanation of Weber's concept of the ideal type, including some of the pitfalls involved in its application. Lachmann (1970: 26–30), examines the concept, considers its application as a 'fundamental concept' for explaining economic phenomena, and rejects its use in this context. His argument is that 'Weber's ideal type lacks any specific reference to human action and seems to be as readily applicable to the animal kingdom or to the plant world as to the human sphere' (ibid.: 29). His proposal is to 'start from something at once simpler and more comprehensive. . . . *the plan*' (ibid.: 29). I believe, however, that in attempting to understand plans and decisions from a first-person perspective, the ideal types of small and large firms provide a useful starting point. Framed from the point of view of individual's understanding – the bureaucratic *versus* the entrepreneurial business – these types refer specifically to 'human action'.

7 The reason why the financial standing of the large bureaucratic company is

probably the most important factor contributing to the individual's feeling of job security, is because it is poor financial performance more than anything else that leads to 'restructuring', which may be associated with a loss of jobs. An employee is more likely to lose his job when the company does badly than as a consequence of how he performs.

8 Various arguments related to shareholding support the view that public companies, listed on a stock exchange, will adopt investment policies aimed at opportunities with prospects of good, secure returns, rather than ones where not only the return, but also the risk, may be high. Poor earnings associated with a failed investment, even if they do little to influence the long-term profitability of the company, can lead to a sudden fall in the share price, and may make the company vulnerable to takeover. Similarly, a failed investment, if it impinges on the company's cash flow and affects its ability to service its debt, may either lead to a reassessment, and downgrading, of the firm's credit rating, or it may necessitate a rights issue, diluting the shareholding.

9 Williams and Scott (1965) establish that investment decisions are often not made by the people who undertake feasibility studies and who gather information. This means that the planners and decision-makers may well place different interpretations on the information that has been gathered, and feasibility studies may be a vehicle for the planners to 'sell' their views to decision-makers.

10 By virtue of their financial strength, according to Kay and Thompson (1986), large companies are somewhat isolated from the competitive pressures of the capital market.

11 This means that the economist's characterisation of the ideal firm as one that is small and autonomous and is able to enter markets at will (where there are profit opportunities) in order to compete aggressively with other firms of various sizes, is wholly misleading. Small firms cannot readily 'enter markets'. There are all sorts of institutional barriers to them doing so, including being able to meet the criteria which other organisations impose as preconditions for being willing to 'talk' or to 'do business'. Until economics reflects these conditions, why they come about, and what consequences they have, it cannot claim to have provided an adequate theory of 'how markets work'. Furthermore, although the literature on networks tends to focus on their contribution to very small-scale businesses and to informal businesses such as co-operatives, the concept is a useful one when understood as the *Umwelt* of decision-makers, and the notion is relevant to all businesses. Managers in large industrial undertakings no doubt also make use of networks, though probably to a lesser degree than their counterparts in small firms. At any rate, the existence of networks in both contexts is not only worth investigating but also these relationships evidently form an important adjunct to other institutionalised relationships, such as contractual ones, which have been the main focus of economic theory.

12 Compared with the large manufacturer, the small firm will often suffer a cost and price disadvantage. Instead of competing head on, the latter develops niche markets but these are narrow and market conditions are easily upset.

13 In modernist theory, motives only matter if they are expressed in a neutral reference language and identified as things that exist in the world; hence the attempt to ground decisions in a psychology of behaviour. The result is illustrated by Wright (1964). In examining the motives of decision-makers considering investments, he initially argues that the individual is induced to do things by a set of 'desires' and that 'at any moment of time . . . [he] is only aware of a rather small subset of his own desires' (ibid.: 41). Later, Wright's arguments are more sensible. He refers to the existence of different groups with possibly conflicting motives

and suggests that 'conflicting interests may have to be satisfied by a single policy' (ibid.: 53).

14 The nature of this proof is puzzling to say the least. Since no one, including the theorist, has the sort of knowledge that would allow him to try to optimise, and no one knows what the consequences would be if he did, it is difficult to understand how empirical studies can support a finding that people behave as if they were trying to maximise.

15 In arguing for their 'multiple-constituency approach' to the concept of organisation effectiveness, Connolly *et al.* (1980) still tend to reflect the idea that the individuals who comprise the different constituencies view the organisation as an organic whole. These authors' underlying commitment to what, more appropriately, might be termed multiple 'perspectives' is promising, because it is consistent with the consideration that different decision-makers constitute their worlds differently. They cite various studies (ibid.: 212) which conclude that 'strong goal consensus among senior managers of a single organisation cannot be assumed'. This means that different individuals are likely to have different motives and priorities, which may be manifested in disagreement over what course of action to pursue and how best to do so.

16 These arguments pose problems for the researcher who is interested in studying investment decisions. It may prove difficult for him to unravel the process leading up to the investment decision, and to uncover the 'original' motives for taking it. For by the time he gets to make his enquiries, even those directly involved in the discussions and negotiations are likely to have lost sight of the motives, if they were ever articulated. Over time the issues which were once reasonably fresh in the minds of the individuals concerned are going to become even less distinct. Furthermore, many decisions are at least implicitly the result of various compromises which have to be struck when the interests of certain individuals or groups prevail over those of other people.

13 UNDERSTANDING AND LOCATIONS

1 By this I mean that although the firm has no form, there is also no conception of sectarian interests within an organisation, or of vested interests that a decision-maker may have in certain activities within an organisation, which he treats as the interests of 'the firm'.

2 It is not necessarily the plant itself (i.e. the physical manufacturing capability embodied in buildings and equipment), but factors and circumstances associated with the production facility, that may lead the decision-makers to prefer one type of operation and its associated location over another.

3 Without the insights afforded by a subjectivist approach, Penrose's analysis is limited to examining financial and economic determinants of mergers.

4 I reject those theories of economics that build upon analogies of feedback mechanisms as a basis for individuals' or organisations' 'learning' over time, because they too involve a third-person perspective and require a comprehensive system of things that gradually reveals itself over successive 'tries'. In spite of presenting a useful critique of neoclassical economics, the methodology of Nelson and Winter's (1982) alternative approach to an economic theory suffers from this drawback.

5 The spate of acquisitions by corporations and 'corporate raiders' that occurred in the United States and elsewhere during the 1980s, bears testimony to these arguments, illustrating that the quality of an investment prospect is a matter of interpretation (in the *durée*). When economic conditions were buoyant and credit

was readily available, the news media generally hailed these as bold moves and treated the individuals as a new breed of business hero. Not many years later, unable to meet staggering debts as interest rates rose and economic conditions deteriorated, the empires were dismantled and personal fortunes, and in some cases also the savings of the investing public, were lost.

6 The contrast between the critique of the orthodox theory of the firm presented here and other critiques should be noted. Cohen and Cyert (1965), Coase (1973), Liebenstein (1966), Machlup (1967), Nelson and Winter (1982), Simon (1952, 1959), and Thirlby (1973) amongst others (see also Loasby 1967, 1971), argue that the neoclassical view of the efficiency of businesses, and of the nature of business decisions, is misleading. The difference between most of these critiques and mine is that, in general, these writers do not question the 'motives' that neoclassical theory ascribes to firms. Instead, they argue that while firms look for profit opportunities and seek to minimise costs, there are obstacles which prevent them from doing so. Either they do not have full knowledge of their circumstances, or it is impossible to remove all inefficiencies and 'slack' from an organisation, or people do not have the time to find out all they would need to know in order to be able to optimise. The contributions of Nelson and Winter (1982) as well as Coase, Thirlby, and others among the collection of works in Buchanan and Thirlby (1973), some of which date back to the 1930s, are of a different kind, for they identify non-economic motives as normal.

7 From an international development perspective this meant finding ways of encouraging the growth of 'developing' countries (the 'South'), which would enable them to throw off the economic shackles imposed by the developed, capitalist countries (the 'North'). On growth poles and their application to regional planning see Kuklinski (1972) and Kuklinski and Petrella (1974). See Fair (1982) for an overview of different paradigms of spatial development; also Bell (1987) and Massey (1984: ch. 2) on labour and the spatial structures of industry.

8 Industrial decentralisation policy in South Africa has been extensively evaluated. See, *inter alia*, Bell (1973) and contributions in Tomlinson and Addleson (1987: especially Parts 1 and 3). Though these contributors differ somewhat in their interpretation of the motivation behind the policy, all stress that it is closely linked to the implementation of apartheid policies.

9 Over the history of the policy, the form of the inducements offered changed from tax concessions to cash grants (see Dewar *et al.* 1984; Pretorius *et al.* 1986). By the time the surveys were undertaken, companies were receiving incentives in the form of cash payments, and the switch away from tax concessions resulted in an increase in the number of companies willing to decentralise, though the total doing so in any year remained rather small. Various people have stated that these incentives were among the most generous industrial relocation inducements available in any country.

10 From the mid-1970s onwards, the average growth rate of the South African economy declined considerably, a factor which might be expected to encourage small firms in particular to make use of decentralisation benefits.

11 In examining why firms relocate and the circumstances under which they do so, Townroe (1971: 39) expresses a view that must be common to manufacturers in most countries. 'In many ways it is impossible for a manufacturing concern ... not to have some regard to the instruments of public policy when considering a move'. Townroe then enumerates some of the factors related to public policy in Britain which influenced the location decisions of firms in his sample. These include the refusal of planning permission and the failure to obtain an 'industrial development certificate'. Townroe also notes the 'bitterness' and 'frustration' of companies about delays and indecision on the part of local authorities. While such

delays cannot always be overcome, or the problems they cause circumvented, there are occasions on which access to people with authority can speed things up considerably.

12 This is the gist of information conveyed to Addleson *et al*. (1985) in the course of interviews conducted as part of their research into industrial decentralisation policy in South Africa.

14 RETROSPECT AND PROSPECT

1 In this regard Keirstead (as quoted at the beginning of the chapter) is wrong in asserting that neoclassical economics deals with preference and choice. These models, based on a third-person perspective, purport to deal with choice, but are not about how individuals choose.

2 By convention, when measures of 'concentration' are applied in judging the desirability of mergers and takeovers, the number of firms within a country is measured. The 'industry' is the domestic industry. But there is no justification for the convention if the aim is to establish whether there is sufficient competition, which may well be foreign competition. In many cases it is policies like tariff protection, and not the number of local producers, that limits the opportunities for competition. On the ambivalent role of the state in enforcing anti-monopoly legislation see Shenfield (1983).

REFERENCES

Aangeenbrug, R.T. (1968), 'Regional Perception and its Effect on Industrial Location', *Kansas Business Review*, January, 3–12.

Abel, T. (1977), 'The Operation Called Verstehen', in Dallmayr, F.R. and McCarthy, T.A. (eds) (1978), *Understanding and Social Inquiry*, Notre Dame, Ind., University of Notre Dame Press, 81–92. Reprinted from *American Journal of Sociology*, 1948, 54, 211–18.

Adams, J. (1970), 'Book Review of Pred' [1967; 1969], *Journal of Regional Science*, 10, 2, 259–63.

Addleson, M. (1984a), 'Robbins's *Essay* in Retrospect: On Subjectivism and an "Economics of Choice"', *Revista Internazionale di Scienze Economiche e Commercial*, 31, 6, 506–23.

—— (1984b), 'General Equilibrium and "Competition": On Competition as Strategy', *South African Journal of Economics*, 52, 2, 156–71.

—— (1986), '"Radical Subjectivism" and the Language of Austrian Economics', in Kirzner, I.M. (ed.) (1986), *Subjectivism, Intelligibility and Economic Understanding: Essays in Honor of Ludwig Lachmann on his Eightieth Birthday*, New York, New York University Press, 1–15.

—— (1994), 'Competition', in Boettke, P. (ed.), *The Elgar Companion to Austrian Economics*, Aldershot, Edward Elgar, 96–102.

Addleson, M., Tomlinson, R., and Pretorius, F. (1985), 'The Impact of Industrial Decentralisation Policy: The Businessman's View', *South African Geographic Journal*, 67, 2, 179–200.

Albert, L.D. and Kellow, J.H. (1969), 'Decision-Makers' Reactions to Plant Location Factors: An Appraisal', *Land Economics*, August, 376–81.

Alchian, A.A. (1977a) *Economic Forces at Work*, Indianapolis, Liberty Press, 37–71.

—— (1977b), 'Information Costs, Pricing and Resource Unemployment', in Alchian, A.A. (1977a), *Economic Forces at Work*, Indianapolis, Liberty Press, 37–71.

Aldrich, H.E. (1979), *Organisations and Environments*, Englewood Cliffs, NJ, Prentice-Hall.

Apel, K.-O. (1977), 'The *A Priori* of Communication and the Foundation of the Humanities', in Dallmayr, F.R. and McCarthy, T.A. (eds) (1977), *Understanding and Social Inquiry*, Notre Dame, Ind., University of Notre Dame Press, 292–315.

Arrow, K.J. (1968), 'Economic Equilibrium', in Sills, D.L. (ed.) (1968), *International Encyclopedia of Social Sciences*, [New York], The Macmillan Co. and The Free Press, 4, 376–89.

—— (1974), 'Limited Knowledge and Economic Analysis', *American Economic Review*, 64, 1, March, 1–10.

—— (1978), 'The Future and the Present in Economic Life', *Economic Inquiry*, 16, April, 157–69.

Arrow, K.J. and Hahn, F.H. (1971), *General Competitive Analysis*, Edinburgh, Oliver and Boyd.

Arrow, K.J. and Honkapohja, S. (eds) (1985), *Frontiers of Economics*, Oxford, Basil Blackwell.

Artis, M.J. and Nobay, A.R. (1976), *Essays in Economic Analysis: Proceedings of the Association of University Teachers of Economics Sheffield 1975*, Cambridge, Cambridge University Press.

Aumann, R. (1985), 'What is Game Theory Trying to Accomplish', in Arrow, K.J. and Honkapohja, S. (eds) (1985), *Frontiers of Economics*, Oxford, Basil Blackwell, 28–76.

Bar-Hillel, M. (1982), 'Studies of Representativeness', in Kahneman, D. *et al.* (eds) (1982), *Judgement Under Uncertainty: Heuristics and Biases*, New York, Cambridge University Press, 69–83.

Barr, B.M. and Fairbairn, K.J. (1978), 'Linkage and Manufacturer's Perception of Spatial Economic Opportunity', in Hamilton, F.E.I. (ed.) (1978), *Contemporary Industrialization: Spatial Analysis and Regional Development*, New York, Longman, 122–43.

Barr, B.M., Walters, N.M., and Fairbairn, K.J. (1980), 'The Application of Cluster Analysis to Entrepreneurial Perception of Regional Economic Environments', *Environment and Planning A*, 12, 869–79.

Barry, N.P. (1979), *Hayek's Social and Economic Philosophy*, London, The Macmillan Press Ltd.

Beavon, K.S.O. (1977), *Central Place Theory: A Reinterpretation*, London, Longman.

Beenhakker, H.L. (1974), *Capital Investment Planning for Management and Engineering*, Rotterdam, Rotterdam University Press.

—— (1975), *Replacement and Expansion Investments*, Rotterdam, Rotterdam University Press.

Bell, D. and Kristol, I. (eds) (1980), *The Public Interest, Special Issue*, 'The Crisis in Economic Theory'.

Bell, R.T. (1973), *Industrial Decentralisation in South Africa*, Cape Town, Oxford University Press.

—— (1983), 'The Growth and Structure of Manufacturing Employment in Natal', *Occasional Paper* No.7, Institute for Social and Economic Research, University of Durban-Westville.

—— (1987), 'International Competition and Industrial Decentralization in South Africa', *World Development*, 15, 1 (December), 1291–307.

Benton, T. (1977), *Philosophical Foundations of the Three Sociologies*, London, Routledge and Kegan Paul.

Bernstein, R.J. (1976), *The Restructuring of Social and Political Theory*, Oxford, Basil Blackwell.

—— (1983), *Beyond Objectivism and Relativism: Science, Hermeneutics and Praxis*, Oxford, Basil Blackwell.

Beyers, W.B. and Krumme, G. (1974), 'Multiple Products, Residuals and Location Theory', in Hamilton, F.E.I. (ed.) (1974), *Spatial Perspectives*, 76–104.

Black, R.D.C., Coats, A.W., and Goodwin, C.D.W. (eds) (1973), *The Marginal Revolution in Economics: Interpretation and Evaluation*, Durham, NC, Duke University Press.

Blaug, M. (1973), 'Was There a Marginal Revolution?', *History of Political Economy*, 4, 2, Fall, 269–80. Reprinted in Black, R.D.C. *et al.* (eds) (1973), *The Marginal Revolution in Economics: Interpretation and Evaluation*, Durham, NC, Duke University Press, 1–11.

Bleicher, J. (1982), *The Hermeneutic Imagination: Outline of a Positive Critique of Scientism and Sociology*, London, Routledge and Kegan Paul.

REFERENCES

Bliss, C.J. (1975), *Capital Theory and the Distribution of Income*, Amsterdam and Oxford, North-Holland Publishing Co.

Boehm, S.(1982), 'The Ambiguous Notion of Subjectivism: Comment on Lachmann', in Kirzner, I.M. (ed.) (1982a), *Method, Process, and Austrian Economics: Essays in Honour of Ludwig von Mises*, Lexington, Mass., D.C. Heath and Co., 41–52.

—— (1992), 'Austrian Economics Between the Wars: Some Historiographical Problems', in Caldwell, B. and Boehm, S. (eds) (1992), *Austrian Economics: Tensions and New Directions*, Boston, Kluwer Academic Publishers.

—— (1993), 'Hayek and Knowledge: Some Question Marks', typescript revision of paper presented to a conference on *The Economics of F.A. Hayek*, held under the auspices of the Associazione Sigismondo Malatesta, Rocca Malatestiana, Sant'Arcangelo di Romagna, 2–4 July, 1992.

Boettinger, H.M. (1967), 'Big Gap in Economic Theory', *Harvard Business Review*, July–August, 51–8.

Boettke, P. (ed.) (1994), *The Elgar Companion to Austrian Economics*, Aldershot, Edward Elgar.

Boland, L.A. (1979), 'A Critique of Friedman's Critics', *Journal of Economic Literature*, 17, June, 503–22.

—— (1982a), *The Foundations of Economic Method*, London, George Allen and Unwin.

—— (1982b), 'Difficulties with the Element of Time and the "Principles" of Economics or Some Lies My Teachers Told Me', *Eastern Economic Journal*, 8, 1, Jan., 47–58.

Bonar, J. (1888), 'The Austrian Economists and Their View of Value', *Quarterly Journal of Economics*, 2, Oct., 1–31.

Boskin, M.J. (ed.) (1979), *Economics and Human Welfare: Essays in Honour of Tibor Scitovsky*, New York, Academic Press.

Bostaph, S. (1978), 'The Methodological Debate Between Carl Menger and the German Historicists', *Atlantic Economic Journal*, 6, 3, Sept., 3–16.

Buchanan, J.M. (1973), 'Introduction: L.S.E. Cost Theory in Retrospect', in Buchanan, J.M. and Thirlby, G.F. (eds) (1973), *L.S.E. Essays on Cost*, London, London School of Economics and Political Science/Weidenfeld and Nicolson, 1– 16.

Buchanan, J.M. and Thirlby, G.F. (eds) (1973), *L.S.E. Essays on Cost*, London, London School of Economics and Political Science/Weidenfeld and Nicolson.

Caldwell, B. (1982), *Beyond Positivism: Economic Methodology in the Twentieth Century*, London, George Allen and Unwin.

—— (ed.) (1990), *Carl Menger and his Legacy in Economics*, Annual Supplement to Volume 22, *History of Political Economy*, Durham and London, Duke University Press.

Caldwell, B. and Boehm, S. (eds) (1992), *Austrian Economics: Tensions and New Directions*, Boston, Kluwer Academic Publishers.

Carr, M. (1983), 'A Contribution to the Review and Critique of Behavioural Industrial Location Theory', *Progress in Human Geography*, 386–401.

Carrier, R.E. and Schriver, W.R. (1966), *Plant Location Analysis: An Investigation of Plant Locations in Tennessee*, Bureau of Business and Economic Research, Memphis, Tenn., Memphis State University.

—— (1968), 'Location Theory: An Empirical Model and Selected Findings', *Land Economics*, Nov., 450–60.

Carter, C.F. and Ford, J.L. (eds) (1972), *Uncertainty and Expectations in Economics, Essays in Honour of G.L.S. Shackle*, Oxford, Basil Blackwell.

Chamberlin, E.H. (1962), *The Theory of Monopolistic Competition: A Reorientation of the Theory of Value*, 8th edn [1st edn 1933], Cambridge, Mass., Harvard University Press.

—— (1968), *Enterprise and Environment: The Firm in Time and Place*, New York, McGraw-Hill.

Chamberlain, N.W. (1955), *A General Theory of Economic Process*, New York, Harper and Brothers.

Chandler, A.D. (1962), *Strategy and Structure: Chapters in the History of Industrial Enterprise*, Cambridge, Mass., MIT Press.

Child, J. (1972), 'Organisational Structure, Environment and Performance: The Role of Strategic Choice', *Sociology*, 6, 1, 2–22.

Chipman, J.S. (1965), 'The Nature and Meaning of Equilibrium', in Martindale, D. (ed.) (1965), 'Functionalism in the Social Sciences: The Strengths and Limits of Functionalism in Anthropology, Economics, Political Science and Sociology: A Symposium', *Monograph* No. 5, Philadelphia, The American Academy of Political and Social Science, 35–64.

Christaller, W. (1966), *Central Places in Southern Germany*, Baskin, C.W. (trans.), Englewood Cliffs, NJ, Prentice-Hall. [Original German edition 1933, *Die Zentralen Orte in Suddeutschland*, Fischer, Jena].

Clower, R. (1975), 'Reflections on the Keynesian Perplex', *Zeitschrift für National-ökonomie*, 35, 1–2, 1–24.

Coase, R.H. (1973), 'Business Organisation and the Accountant', in Buchanan, J.M. and Thirlby, G.F. (eds) (1973), *L.S.E. Essays on Cost*, London, London School of Economics and Political Science/Weidenfeld and Nicolson, 95–132.

Coats, A.W. (1983), 'The Revival of Subjectivism', in Wiseman, J. (ed.) (1983a), *Beyond Positive Economics*, Proceedings of Section F (Economics) of the British Assn. for the Advancement of Science (York, 1981), London, Macmillan, 87–103.

Coddington, A. (1972), 'Positive Economics', *Canadian Journal of Economics*, 5, 1, Feb., 1–15.

—— (1975a), 'Creaking Semaphore and Beyond: A Consideration of Shackle's "Epistemics and Economics"', *British Journal for the Philosophy of Science*, 26, 2, June, 151–63.

—— (1975b), 'The Rationale of General Equilibrium Theory', *Economic Inquiry*, 13, Dec., 539–58.

Cohen, K.J. and Cyert, R.M. (1965), *The Theory of the Firm: Resource Allocation in a Market Economy*, Englewood Cliffs, NJ, Prentice Hall.

Coleman, J.S. (1987), 'Psychological Structure and Social Structure in Economic Models', in Hogarth, R.M. and Reder, M.W. (eds) (1987), *Rational Choice: The Contrast between Economics and Psychology*, Chicago, University of Chicago Press, 181–5.

Connolly, T., Conlon, E.J., and Deutsch, S.J. (1980), 'Organizational Effectiveness: A Multiple-Constituency Approach', *Academy of Management Review*, 5, 2, 211–17.

Coulter, J. (1974), 'Decontextualised Meanings: Current Approaches to Verstehende Investigations', in Truzzi, M. (ed.) (1974), *Verstehen: Subjective Understanding in the Social Sciences*, Reading, Mass., Addison-Wesley Publishing Co, 134–64.

Cowen, T. (1991), 'What a Non-Paretian Welfare Economics Would Have to Look Like', in Lavoie, D. (ed.) (1991a), *Economics and Hermeneutics*, London and New York, Routledge, 285–98.

Creedy, J. (1980), 'Some Recent Interpretations of Mathematical Psychics', *History of Political Economy*, 12, 2, 267–76.

Cyert, R.M. and March, J.G. (1963), *A Behavioural Theory of the Firm*, Englewood Cliffs, NJ, Prentice-Hall.

Dallmayr, F.R. and McCarthy, T.A. (eds) (1977), *Understanding and Social Inquiry*, Notre Dame, Ind., University of Notre Dame Press.

Deane, P. and Kuper, J. (eds) (1988), *A Lexicon of Economics*, London and New York, Routledge.

Descombes, V. (1985), 'The Fabric of Subjectivity', in Silverman, H.J. and Ihde, D. (eds) (1985), *Hermeneutics and Deconstruction*, Albany, State University of New York Press, 55–65.

Development Bank of Southern Africa (1989a), *Report of the Panel of Experts on the Evaluation of the Regional Industrial Development Programme as an Element of Regional Development Policy in Southern Africa* [No additional details given].

—— (1989b), *Appendices to the Report of the Panel of Experts on the Evaluation of the Regional Industrial Development Programme as an Element of Regional Development Policy in Southern Africa* [No additional details given].

Dewar, D. (1987), 'An Assessment of Industrial Decentralisation as a Regional Development Tool, with Special Reference to South Africa', in Tomlinson, R. and Addleson, M. (eds) (1987), *Regional Restructuring Under Apartheid: Urban and Regional Policies in Contemporary South Africa*, Johannesburg, Ravan Press, 154–80.

Dewar, D., Todes, A., and Watson, V. (1984), 'Industrial Decentralisation Policy as a Mechanism for Regional Development in South Africa: Its Premises and Record', *Working Paper* 30, Urban Problems Research Unit, University of Cape Town.

Dicken, P. (1971), 'Some Aspects of Decision-Making Behaviour in Business Organisations', *Economic Geography*, 47, 426–37.

—— (1977), 'A Note on Location Theory and the Large Business Enterprise', *Area*, 9, 138–43.

Dolan, E.G. (ed.) (1976), *The Foundations of Modern Austrian Economics*, Kansas City, Sheed and Ward, Inc.

Downs, R.M. (1970), 'Geographic Space Perception: Past Approaches and Future Prospects', *Progress in Geography*, 2, 65–108.

Ebeling, R.M. (1986), 'Towards a Hermeneutical Economics: Expectations, Prices and the Role of Interpretation in a Theory of the Market Process', in Kirzner, I.M. (ed.) (1986), *Subjectivism, Intelligibility and Economic Understanding: Essays in Honor of Ludwig Lachmann on his Eightieth Birthday*, New York, New York University Press, 39–55.

—— (1991), 'What is a Price? Explanation and Understanding (With Apologies to Paul Ricoeur)', in Lavoie, D. (ed.) (1991a), *Economics and Hermeneutics*, London and New York, 177–94.

Edgeworth, F.Y. (1881), *Mathematical Psychics* (reprint of 1881 edn), New York, Augustus M. Kelly.

Edwards, W. (1967a), 'The Theory of Decision Making', in Edwards, W. and Tversky, A. (eds) (1967), *Decision Making: Selected Readings*, Harmondsworth, Penguin Books, 13–64.

—— (1967b), 'Behavioural Decision Theory', in Edwards, W. and Tversky, A. (eds) (1967), *Decision Making: Selected Readings*, Harmondsworth, Penguin Books, 65–95.

Edwards, W. and Tversky, A. (eds) (1967), *Decision Making: Selected Readings*, Harmondsworth, Penguin Books.

Elliston, F. and McCormick, P. (eds) (1977), *Husserl: Expositions and Appraisals*, Notre Dame, Ind. University of Notre Dame Press.

Evans, A.W. (1973), 'The Location of Headquarters of Industrial Companies', *Urban Studies*, 10, 387–95.

Fair, T.J.D. (1982), *South Africa: Spatial Frameworks for Development*, Cape Town, Juta and Co.

Fetter, F. (1924), 'The Economic Law of Market Areas', *Quarterly Journal of Economics*, 39, 520–29.

REFERENCES

Feyerabend, P.K. (1978), *Against Method: Outline of an Anarchistic Theory of Knowledge*, London, Verso.

Fisher, F.M. (1976), 'The Stability of General Equilibrium: Results and Problems', in Artis, M.J. and Nobay, A.R. (eds) (1976), *Essays in Economic Analysis: Proceedings of the Association of University Teachers of Economics Sheffield 1975*, Cambridge, Cambridge University Press, 3–29.

—— (1979), 'Stability, Disequilibrium Awareness, and the Perception of New Opportunities', typescript of paper presented as the Econometric Society Presidential Address.

—— (1981), 'Stability, Disequilibrium Awareness, and the Perception of New Opportunities', *Econometrica*, 49, 2, March, 279–317.

Forer, P. (1978), 'A Place for Plastic Space', *Progress in Human Geography*, 2, 230–67.

Freund, J. (1968), *The Sociology of Max Weber*, Ilford, M. (trans.), Harmondsworth, Penguin Books.

Friedman, M. (1953), *Essays in Positive Economics*, Chicago, Ill., University of Chicago Press.

Friedrich, C.J. (trans.) (1928), *Alfred Weber's Theory of the Location of Industries*, Chicago, Ill. University of Chicago Press.

Fusfeld, D. (1980), 'Is Optimising Rational?', Typescript of paper prepared for the annual meeting of the American Economic Association, Denver, Col. Sept. 5–7.

Georgescu-Roegen, N. (1971), *The Entropy Law and the Economic Process*, Cambridge, Mass., Harvard University Press.

Gewirth, A. (1954), 'Subjectivism and Objectivism in the Social Sciences', *Philosophy of Science*, 21, 157–63.

Giddens, A. (1977), *Studies in Social and Political Theory*, New York, Basic Books.

—— (1979), *Central Problems in Social Theory: Action, Structure and Contradiction in Social Analysis*, London, Macmillan.

Gilmour, J.M. (1974), 'External Economies of Scale, Inter-Industrial Linkages and Decision Making in Manufacturing', in Hamilton, F.E.I. (ed.) (1974a), *Spatial Perspectives on Industrial Organisation and Decision-Making*, London, John Wiley, 335–62.

Goddard, J.B. (1978), 'The Location of Non-Manufacturing Activities within Manufacturing Industries', in Hamilton, F.E.I. (ed.) (1978), *Contemporary Industrialization: Spatial Analysis and Regional Development*, New York, Longman, 62–85.

Godsell, G. (1990), 'The Social Networks of South African Entrepreneurs', Unpublished PhD Dissertation, Boston University Graduate School.

Golledge, R.G. and Rushton, G. (eds) (1976), *Spatial Choice and Spatial Behaviour: Geographic Essays on the Analysis of Preferences and Perceptions*, Columbus, Ohio State University Press.

Gould, P. and White, R. (1974), *Mental Maps*, Harmondsworth, Middlesex, Penguin Books.

Gram, H.N. and Walsh, V.C. (1978), 'Menger and Jevons in the Setting of Post-von Neumann-Sraffa Economics', *Atlantic Economic Journal*, 6, 3, Sept., 46–56.

—— (1983), 'Joan Robinson's Economics in Retrospect', *Journal of Economic Literature*, 21, June, 518–50.

Grassl, W. and Smith, B. (eds) (1986), *Austrian Economics, Historical and Philosophical Background*, New York, New York University Press.

Green, H.D. (1977), 'Industrialists' Information Levels of Regional Incentives', *Regional Studies*, 11, 7–18.

Greenfield, S., Strickon, A., and Aubrey, R.T. (eds) (1979), *Entrepreneurs in Cultural Context*, Albuquerque, University of New Mexico Press.

Greenhut, M.L. (1956), *Plant Location in Theory and Practice*, Chapel Hill, North Carolina, University of North Carolina Press.

—— (1963), *Microeconomics and the Space Economy*, Chicago, Ill. Scott Foresman and Co.

Hague, D.C. (1958), 'Alfred Marshall and the Competitive Firm', *Economic Journal*, 68, Dec., 673–90.

Hahn, F.H. (1970), 'Some Adjustment Problems', *Econometrica*, 38, 1, Jan., 1–17.

—— (1973a), 'On the Notion of Equilibrium in Economics: An Inaugural Lecture', Cambridge, Cambridge University Press.

—— (1973b), 'The Winter of Our Discontent', *Economica (N.S.)*, 50, Aug., 322–30.

—— (1978), 'Exercises in Conjectural Equilibria', in Strøm, S. and Werin, L. (eds) (1978), *Topics in Disequilibrium Economics*, London, Macmillan, 64–80.

—— (1980), 'General Equilibrium Theory', in Bell, D. and Kristol, I. (eds) (1980), *The Public Interest, Special Issue*, 'The Crisis in Economic Theory', 123–38.

—— (1982), 'Reflections on the Invisible Hand', *Lloyds Bank Review*, No. 144, April, 1–21.

Hahn, F.H. and Hollis, M. (eds) (1979), *Philosophy and Economic Theory*, Oxford University Press.

Hamermesh, R.G. (ed.) (1983), *Strategic Management*, New York, John Wiley and Sons.

Hamilton, F.E.I. (ed.) (1974a), *Spatial Perspectives on Industrial Organisation and Decision-Making*, London, John Wiley.

—— (1974b), 'A View of Spatial Behaviour, Industrial Organizations and Decision-Making', in Hamilton, F.E.I. (ed.) (1974a), *Spatial Perspectives on Industrial Organisation and Decision-Making*, London, John Wiley, 3–43.

Hamilton, F.E.I. and Linge, G.J.R. (eds) (1979a), *Spatial Analysis, Industry and the Industrial Environment, 1: Industrial Systems*, Chichester, John Wiley and Sons.

—— (1979b), 'Industrial Systems', in Hamilton, F.E.I. and Linge, G.J.R. (eds) (1979a), *Spatial Analysis, Industry and the Industrial Environment, 1: Industrial Systems*, Chichester, John Wiley and Sons, 1–23.

Hansen, B. (1970), *A Survey of General Equilibrium Systems*, New York, McGraw-Hill.

Harrison, R.T., Bull, P.J., and Hart, M. (1979), 'Space and Time in Industrial Linkage Studies', *Area*, 11, 333–8.

Hausman, D.M. (ed.) (1984a), *The Philosophy of Economics: An Anthology*, Cambridge, Cambridge University Press.

—— (1984b), 'Are General Equilibrium Theories Explanatory?', in Hausman, D.M. (ed.) (1984a), *The Philosophy of Economics: An Anthology*, Cambridge, Cambridge University Press, 344–59.

—— (1992), *The Inexact and Separate Science of Economics*, Cambridge, Cambridge University Press.

Hayek, F.A. (1948a), *Individualism and Economic Order*, Chicago, University of Chicago Press, reprinted by Gateway Editions, Ltd, Indiana.

—— (1948b), 'Individualism: True and False', in Hayek, F.A. (1948a), *Individualism and Economic Order*, Chicago, University of Chicago Press, reprinted by Gateway Editions, Ltd, Indiana, 1–32.

—— (1948c), 'Economics and Knowledge', in Hayek, F.A. (1948a), *Individualism and Economic Order*, Chicago, University of Chicago Press, reprinted by Gateway Editions, Ltd., Indiana, 33–56. Reprinted from *Economica (N.S.)*, 13, Feb., 33–54.

—— (1948d), 'The Facts of the Social Sciences', in Hayek, F.A. (1948a), *Individualism and Economic Order*, Chicago, University of Chicago Press, reprinted by Gateway Editions, Ltd, Indiana, 57–76. Reprinted from *Ethics* (1943), 54, 1, Oct., 1–13.

REFERENCES

—— (1948e), 'The Use of Knowledge in Society', in Hayek, F.A. (1948a), *Individualism and Economic Order*, Chicago, University of Chicago Press, reprinted by Gateway Editions, Ltd, Indiana, 77–91. Reprinted from *American Economic Review* (1945), 34, 4, Sept., 519–30.

—— (1948f), 'The Meaning of Competition', in Hayek, F.A. (1948a), *Individualism and Economic Order*, Chicago, University of Chicago Press, reprinted by Gateway Editions, Ltd, Indiana, 92–106.

—— (1955a), *The Counter-Revolution of Science: Studies on the Abuse of Reason*, New York, The Free Press of Glencoe.

—— (1955b), 'Scientism and the Study of Society', in Hayek, F.A. (1955a), *The Counter-Revolution of Science: Studies on the Abuse of Reason*, New York, The Free Press of Glencoe, 13–102. Reprinted from *Economica (N.S.)*, 9, 10, 11, 267–91, 34–63, 27–39.

—— (1955c), 'The Counter-Revolution of Science', in Hayek, F.A. (1955a), *The Counter-Revolution of Science: Studies on the Abuse of Reason*, New York, The Free Press of Glencoe, 105–88. Reprinted from *Economica (N.S.)* (1941), 8, Feb., May, Aug., 9–36, 119–50, 281–320.

—— (1967a), *Studies in Philosophy, Politics, and Economics*, Chicago, University of Chicago Press.

—— (1967b), 'The Theory of Complex Phenomena', in Hayek, F.A. (1967a), *Studies in Philosophy, Politics, and Economics*, Chicago, University of Chicago Press, 22–42.

—— (1967c), 'The *Non-sequitur* of the Dependence Effect', in Hayek, F.A. (1967a), *Studies in Philosophy, Politics, and Economics*, Chicago, University of Chicago Press, 313–17.

—— (1973a), *Law, Legislation and Liberty*, Vol. 1, *Rules and Order*, Chicago, University of Chicago Press.

—— (1973b), 'The Place of Menger's *Grundsätze* in the History of Economic Thought', in Hicks, J.R. and Weber, W. (eds) (1973), *Carl Menger and the Austrian School of Economics*, Oxford, The Clarendon Press, 1–14.

—— (1975), 'Full Employment at Any Price?', *Occasional Paper* 45, London, Institute of Economic Affairs.

Hayter, R. and Watts, H.D. (1983), 'The Geography of Enterprise: a Reappraisal', *Progress in Geography*, 7, 157–81.

Heiner, R.A. (1983), 'The Origin of Predictable Behaviour', *American Economic Review*, 73, 4, Sept., 560–95.

Hicks, J.R. (1937), 'Mr Keynes and the "Classics": A Suggested Interpretation', *Econometrica*, 5, 147–59.

—— (1946), *Value and Capital: An Inquiry into Some Fundamental Principles of Economic Theory*, 2nd edn, Oxford, Oxford University Press.

—— (1965), *Capital and Growth*, Oxford, Oxford University Press.

—— (1969), *A Theory of Economic History*, London, Oxford University Press.

—— (1976a), '"Revolutions" in Economics', in Latsis, S.J. (ed.) (1976), *Method and Appraisal in Economics*, Cambridge, Cambridge University Press, 207–18.

—— (1976b), 'Some Questions of Time in Economics', in Tang A.M. *et al.* (eds) (1976), *Evolution, Welfare and Time in Economics: Essays in Honour of Nicholas Georgescu-Roegen*, Lexington, Mass., Lexington Books, 135–51.

—— (1977), *Economic Perspectives: Further Essays on Money and Growth*, Oxford, Clarendon Press.

—— (1979), *Causality in Economics*, Oxford, Basil Blackwell.

—— (1980), 'IS-LM: An Explanation', *Journal of Post-Keynesian Economics*, 3, 2, Winter 1980/1, 139–54.

REFERENCES

—— (1983a), *Classics and Moderns: Collected Essays on Economic Theory III*, Oxford, Basil Blackwell

—— (1983b), 'Leon Walras', reprinted in Hicks, J.R. (1983a), *Classics and Moderns: Collected Essays on Economic Theory III*, Oxford, Basil Blackwell.

Hicks, J.R. and Allen, R.D. (1934), 'A Reconsideration of the Theory of Value', *Economica (N.S.)*, 1, 52–76, 196–219.

Hicks, J.R. and Weber, W. (eds) (1973), *Carl Menger and the Austrian School of Economics*, Oxford, The Clarendon Press.

Hodgson, G. (1986), 'Behind Methodological Individualism', *Cambridge Journal of Economics*, 10, 211–24.

Hogarth, R.M. (1987), *Judgement and Choice: The Psychology of Decision*, 2nd. edn, Chichester, John Wiley and Sons.

Hogarth, R.M. and Reder, M.W. (eds) (1987), *Rational Choice: The Contrast between Economics and Psychology*, Chicago, University of Chicago Press.

Hollis, M. and Nell, E.J. (1975), *Rational Economic Man: A Philosophical Critique of Neo-Classical Economics*, New York, Cambridge University Press.

Hoover, E.M. (1937), *Location Theory and the Shoe and Leather Industry*, Cambridge, Mass., Harvard University Press.

—— (1968), *The Location of Economic Activity*, [1st edn 1948] New York, McGraw-Hill.

Hotelling, H. (1929), 'Stability in Competition', *Economic Journal*, 39, 41–57.

Huff, D.L. (1960), 'A Topographical Model of Consumer Space Preferences', *Papers & Proceedings of the Regional Science Association*, 6, 159–73.

Husserl, E. (1970), *The Crisis in European Sciences and Transcendental Phenomenology: An Introduction to Phenomenological Philosophy*, Carr D. (trans. with intro.), Evanston, Northwestern University Press.

Hutchison, T.W. (1938), *The Significance and Basic Postulates of Economic Theory*, London, Macmillan.

—— (1973), 'Some Themes from *Investigations into Method*', in Hicks, J.R. and Weber, W. (eds) (1973), *Carl Menger and the Austrian School of Economics*, Oxford, The Clarendon Press, 15–37.

—— (1977), *Knowledge and Ignorance in Economics*, Oxford, Basil Blackwell.

Isard, W. (1956), *Location and Space Economy: A General Theory Relating to Industrial Location, Market Areas, Land Use, Trade, and Urban Structure*, Cambridge, Mass., The MIT Press.

Jaffé, W. (1976), 'Menger, Jevons and Walras De-Homogenised', *Economic Inquiry*, 14, Dec., 511–24.

—— (1977), 'The Birth of Léon Walras's *Eléments*', *History of Political Economy*, 9, 2, 198–214.

—— (1980), 'Walras's Economics As Others See It', *Journal of Economic Literature*, 18, June, 528–49.

—— (1981), 'Another Look at Léon Walras's Theory of *Tâtonnement*', *History of Political Economy*, 13, 2, 313–36.

Jefferson, M. (1983), 'Economic Uncertainty and Business Decision-Making', in Wiseman, J. (ed.) (1983a), *Beyond Positive Economics*, Proceedings of Section F (Economics) of the British Association for the Advancement of Science (York, 1981), London, Macmillan, 122–59.

Jevons, W.S. (1957), *The Theory of Political Economy*, 5th edn [1st edn 1871], New York, Kelly and Millman.

Johnston, J. (1967), 'The Theory of Economic Decision-Making', in Audley, R.J. *et al.* (1967) *Decision Making*, London, British Broadcasting Corporation, 61–9.

Kahneman, D. and Tversky, A. (1982), 'Variants of Uncertainty', in Kahneman, D.

REFERENCES

et al. (eds) (1982), *Judgement Under Uncertainty: Heuristics and Biases*, New York, Cambridge University Press, 509–20.

Kahneman, D., Slovic, P., and Tversky, A. (eds) (1982), *Judgement Under Uncertainty: Heuristics and Biases*, New York, Cambridge University Press.

Kaldor, N. (1934), 'A Classificatory Note on the Determinateness of Equilibrium', *Review of Economic Studies*, 1, 2, Feb., 122–36.

—— (1972), 'The Irrelevance of Equilibrium Economics', *Economic Journal*, 82, Dec., 1237–255.

—— (1979), 'Equilibrium Theory and Growth Theory', in Boskin, M.J. (ed.) (1979), *Economics and Human Welfare: Essays in Honour of Tibor Scitovsky*, New York, Academic Press, 273–91.

Katouzian, H. (1980), *Ideology and Method in Economics*, London, Macmillan.

Katz, D. and Kahn, R.L. (1966), *The Social Psychology of Organisations*, New York, John Wiley and Sons.

Kauder, E. (1957), 'Intellectual and Political Roots of the Older Austrian School', *Zeitschrift für Nationalökonomie*, 17, 4, 411–25.

Kay, J.A. and Thompson, D.J. (1986), 'Privatisation: A Policy in Search of a Rationale', *Economic Journal*, 96, March, 18–32.

Keeble, D. (1978), 'Industrial Geography', *Progress in Human Geography*, 2, 318–23.

Keirstead, B.S. (1972), 'Decision-making and the Theory of Games', in C.F. Carter and J.L. Ford (eds) (1972), *Uncertainty and Expectations in Economics, Essays in Honour of G.L.S. Shackle*, Oxford, Basil Blackwell, 160–74.

Kennedy, C.R. (1985), 'Thinking of Opening Your Own Business? Be Prepared!', *Business Horizons*, Sept.–Oct., 38–42.

Keynes, J.M. (1937), 'The General Theory of Employment', *Quarterly Journal of Economics*, Feb., reprinted in S.E. Harris (ed.) (1949), *The New Economics: Keynes' Influence on Theory and Public Policy*, London, Dennis Dobson Ltd., 181–93.

Kirzner, I.M. (1966), *An Essay on Capital*, New York, Augustus M. Kelly Publishers.

—— (1973), *Competition and Entrepreneurship*, Chicago and London, University of Chicago Press.

—— (1976a), *The Economic Point of View*, 2nd edn, Moss, L.S. (ed. with intro.), Kansas City, Sheed and Ward Inc.

—— (1976b), 'On the Method of Austrian Economics', in Dolan, E.G. (ed. with intro.) (1976), *The Foundations of Modern Austrian Economics*, Kansas City, Sheed and Ward Inc., 40–51.

—— (1976c), 'Philosophical and Ethical Implications of Austrian Economics', in Dolan, E.G. (ed. with intro.) (1976), *The Foundations of Modern Austrian Economics*, Kansas City, Sheed and Ward Inc. (1976), 75–88.

—— (1978), 'Economics and Error', in Spadaro, L.M. (ed. with intro.) (1978), *New Directions in Austrian Economics*, Kansas City, Sheed Andrews and McMeel Inc., 57–76.

—— (1979), *Perception, Opportunity and Profit*, Chicago, University of Chicago Press.

—— (ed.) (1982a), *Method, Process, and Austrian Economics: Essays in Honour of Ludwig von Mises*, Lexington, Mass., D.C. Heath and Co.

—— (1982b), 'Uncertainty, Discovery, and Human Action: A Study of the Entrepreneurial Profile in the Misesian System', in Kirzner, I.M. (ed.) (1982a), *Method, Process, and Austrian Economics: Essays in Honour of Ludwig von Mises*, Lexington, Mass., D.C. Heath and Co., 139–59.

—— (1985), *Discovery and the Capitalist Process*, Chicago and London, University of Chicago Press.

—— (ed.) (1986), *Subjectivism, Intelligibility and Economic Understanding: Essays in*

Honor of Ludwig Lachmann on his Eightieth Birthday, New York, New York University Press.

Klein, L.R. (1972), 'The Treatment of Expectations in Econometrics', in Carter, C.F. and Ford, J.L. (eds) (1972), *Uncertainty and Expectations in Economics, Essays in Honour of G.L.S. Shackle*, Oxford, Basil Blackwell, 175–90.

Knight, F.H. (1933), *Risk, Uncertainty and Profit*, London, London School of Economics and Political Science.

—— (1940), '"What is Truth" in Economics', *Journal of Political Economy*, 48, 1, 1–32.

Kornai, J. (1971), *Anti-Equilibrium: On Economic Systems Theory and the Tasks of Research*, Amsterdam, North-Holland.

Kotler, P. (1971), *Marketing Decision-Making: A Model Building Approach*, New York, Holt, Rinehart and Winston.

Kregel, J.A. (1977), 'On the Existence of Expectations in English Neoclassical Economics', *Journal of Economic Literature*, 15, 2, June, 495–500.

—— (1988), 'Equilibrium', in Deane, P. and Kuper, J. (eds) (1988), *A Lexicon of Economics*, London and New York, Routledge, 128–33.

Krumme, G. (1969), 'Toward a Geography of Enterprise', *Economic Geography*, 45, 30–40.

Kryzanowski, W (1927), 'Review of the Literature of the Location of Industries', *Journal of Political Economy*, 35, 278–91.

Kuhn, T.S. (1962), *The Structure of Scientific Revolutions*, Chicago and London, University of Chicago Press.

—— (1970), *The Structure of Scientific Revolutions*, 2nd edn, Chicago, University of Chicago Press.

Kuklinski, A. (ed.) (1972), *Growth Poles and Growth Centres in Regional Planning*, The Hague, Mouton and Co.

Kuklinski, A. and Petrella, R. (eds) (1974), *Growth Poles and Regional Policies: A Seminar*, The Hague, Mouton and Co.

Lachmann, L.M. (1950), 'Economics as a Social Science', *South African Journal of Economics*, 18, 3, Sept., 3–14. Reprinted in Lachmann, L.M. (1977a), *Capital, Expectations and the Market Process: Essays in the Theory of the Market Economy*, Grinder, W.E. (ed. with intro.), Kansas City, Sheed Andrews and McMeel, Inc., 166–80.

—— (1951), 'The Science of Human Action', *Economica (N.S.)*, 18, Nov., 412–27. Reprinted in Lachmann, L.M. (1977a), *Capital, Expectations and the Market Process: Essays in the Theory of the Market Economy*, Grinder, W.E. (ed. with intro.), Kansas City, Sheed Andrews and McMeel, Inc., 94–111.

—— (1970), *The Legacy of Max Weber: Three Essays*, London, Heinemann Educational Books.

—— (1973), 'Macro-economic Thinking and the Market Economy: An Essay on the Neglect of the Micro-foundations and its Consequences', *Hobart Paper* No. 56, London, Institute of Economic Affairs.

—— (1976), 'From Mises to Shackle: An Essay on Austrian Economics and the Kaleidic Society', *Journal of Economic Literature*, 14, 1, March, 54–62.

—— (1977a), *Capital, Expectations and the Market Process: Essays in the Theory of the Market Economy*, Grinder, W.E. (ed. with intro.), Kansas City, Sheed Andrews and McMeel, Inc.

—— (1977b), 'Austrian Economics in the Present Crisis of Economic Thought', in Lachmann, L.M. (1977a), *Capital, Expectations and the Market Process: Essays in the Theory of the Market Economy*, Grinder, W.E. (ed. with intro.), Kansas City, Sheed Andrews and McMeel, Inc., 25–41.

—— (1977c), 'Methodological Individualism and the Market Economy', in Lachmann,

L.M. (1977a), *Capital, Expectations and the Market Process: Essays in the Theory of the Market Economy*, Grinder, W.E. (ed. with intro.), Kansas City, Sheed Andrews and McMeel, Inc., 149–65.

—— (1977d), 'Mrs. Robinson on the Accumulation of Capital', in Lachmann, L.M. (1977a), *Capital, Expectations and the Market Process: Essays in the Theory of the Market Economy*, Grinder, W.E. (ed. with intro.), Kansas City, Sheed Andrews and McMeel, Inc., 214–34.

—— (1977e), 'Professor Shackle on the Economic Significance of Time', in Lachmann, L.M. (1977a), *Capital, Expectations and the Market Process: Essays in the Theory of the Market Economy*, Grinder, W.E. (ed. with intro.), Kansas City, Sheed Andrews and McMeel, Inc., 81–93.

—— (1977f), 'Sir John Hicks as a Neo-Austrian: Review Article', in Lachmann, L.M. (1977a), *Capital, Expectations and the Market Process: Essays in the Theory of the Market Economy*, Grinder, W.E. (ed. with intro.), Kansas City, Sheed Andrews and McMeel, Inc., 251–66.

—— (1977g), 'The Significance of the Austrian School of Economics in the History of Ideas', in Lachmann, L.A. (1977a), *Capital, Expectations and the Market Process: Essays in the Theory of the Market Economy*, Grinder, W.E. (ed. with intro.), Kansas City, Sheed Andrews and McMeel, Inc., 45–64.

—— (1977h), 'The Role of Expectations in Economics as a Social Science', in Lachmann, L.A. (1977a), *Capital, Expectations and the Market Process: Essays in the Theory of the Market Economy*, Grinder, W.E. (ed. with intro.), Kansas City, Sheed Andrews and McMeel, Inc., 65–80.

—— (1978a), *Capital and Its Structure*, Kansas City, Sheed Andrews and McMeel, Inc.

—— (1978b), 'An Austrian Stocktaking: Unsettled Questions and Tentative Answers', in L.M. Spadaro (ed. with intro.) (1978), *New Directions in Austrian Economics*, Kansas City, Sheed Andrews and McMeel, Inc., 1–18.

—— (1982), 'Ludwig von Mises and the Extension of Subjectivism', in Kirzner, I.M. (ed.) (1982a), *Method, Process, and Austrian Economics: Essays in Honour of Ludwig von Mises*, Lexington, Mass., D.C. Heath and Co., 31–40.

—— (1986), *The Market as an Economic Process*, Oxford, Basil Blackwell.

—— (1991), 'Austrian Economics: A Hermeneutic Approach', in Lavoie, D. (ed.) (1991a), *Economics and Hermeneutics*, London and New York, Routledge, 134–46.

Lakatos, I. (1970), 'Falsification and the Methodology of Scientific Research Programmes', in Lakatos, I. and Musgrave, A. (eds) (1970), *Criticism and the Growth of Knowledge*, Cambridge, Cambridge University Press, 91–196. Reprinted in Lakatos, I. (1978), *The Methodology of Scientific Research Programmes: Philosophical Papers Vol. I*, Worrall, J. and Currie, G. (eds), Cambridge, Cambridge University Press, 8–101.

—— (1976), *Proofs and Refutations*, Cambridge, Cambridge University Press.

Lakatos, I. and Musgrave, A. (eds) (1970), *Criticism and the Growth of Knowledge*, Cambridge, Cambridge University Press.

Langlois, R.N. (1982), 'Economics as a Process: Notes on the "New Institutional Economics"', *Economic Research Reports*, C.V. Starr Centre for Applied Economics, R.R. No. 82–21, September, New York University.

Larson, C.M. and Clute, R.C. (1979), 'The Failure Syndrome', *American Journal of Small Business*, 4, 2, Oct., 35–43.

Latsis, S.J. (ed.) (1976), *Method and Appraisal in Economics*, Cambridge, Cambridge University Press.

Lavoie, D. (1985), *Rivalry and Central Planning: The Socialist Calculation Debate Reconsidered*, New York, Cambridge University Press.

—— (1986), 'Euclideanism versus Hermeneutics: A Reinterpretation of Misesian Apriorism', in Kirzner, I.M. (ed.) (1986), *Subjectivism, Intelligibility and Economic Understanding: Essays in Honor of Ludwig Lachmann on his Eightieth Birthday*, New York, New York University Press, 192–210.

—— (1990), 'Understanding Differently: Hermeneutics and the Spontaneous Order of Communicative Processes', in Caldwell, B.J. (ed.) (1990), *Carl Menger and his Legacy in Economics*, Annual Supplement to Vol. 22, *History of Political Economy*, Durham and London, Duke University Press, 359–77.

—— (ed.) (1991a), *Economics and Hermeneutics*, London and New York, Routledge.

—— (1991b), 'Introduction', in Lavoie, D. (ed.) (1991a), *Economics and Hermeneutics*, London and New York, Routledge, 1–15.

Lawson, T. (1985), 'Uncertainty and Economic Analysis', *Economic Journal*, 95, Dec., 909–27.

Le Breton, P.P. and Henning, D.A. (1961), *Planning Theory*, Englewood Cliffs; NJ, Prentice-Hall.

Leijonhufvud, A. (1968), *On Keynesian Economics and the Economics of Keynes*, New York, Oxford University Press.

—— (1976), 'Schools, "Revolutions" and Research Programmes in Economic Theory', in Latsis, S.J. (ed.) (1976), *Method and Appraisal in Economics*, Cambridge, Cambridge University Press, 65–108.

Leitch, V.B. (1988), *American Literary Criticism from the Thirties to the Eighties*, New York, Columbia University Press.

Liebenstein, H. (1966), 'Allocative Efficiency vs. "X-efficiency"', *American Economic Review*, 56, 3, June, 392–415.

Lippman, S.A. and McCall, J.J. (1976), 'The Economics of Job Search: A Survey', *Economic Inquiry*, 14, 155–89.

Littlechild, S.C. (1977), 'Change Rules, O.K.?: An Inaugural Lecture', University of Birmingham, UK.

—— (1978), 'The Fallacy of the Mixed Economy: An "Austrian" Critique of Economic Thinking and Policy', *Hobart Paper* No. 80, London, Institute of Economic Affairs.

—— (1982), 'Equilibrium and the Market Process', in Kirzner, I.M. (ed.) (1982a), *Method, Process, and Austrian Economics: Essays in Honour of Ludwig von Mises*, Lexington, Mass., D.C. Heath and Co., 85–102.

—— (1983), 'Subjectivism and Method in Economics', in Wiseman, J. (ed.) (1983a), *Beyond Positive Economics*, Proceedings of Section F (Economics) of the British Association for the Advancement of Science (York, 1981), London, Macmillan, 38–49.

—— (ed.) (1990a), *Austrian Economics*, Vol. I, *History and Methodology*, Aldershot, Edward Elgar Publishing Ltd.

—— (ed.) (1990b), *Austrian Economics*, Vol. III, *Market Process*, Aldershot, Edward Elgar Publishing Ltd.

Lloyd, P.E. and Dicken, P. (1972), *Location in Space: A Theoretical Approach to Economic Geography*, New York, Harper and Row.

Loasby, B.J. (1967), 'Managerial Decision Processes', *Scottish Journal of Political Economy*, 14, 243–55.

—— (1971), 'Hypothesis and Paradigm in the Theory of the Firm', *Economic Journal*, 81, Dec., 863–85.

—— (1976), *Choice, Complexity and Ignorance*, Cambridge, Cambridge University Press.

—— (1978), 'Whatever Happened to Marshall's Theory of Value?', *Scottish Journal of Political Economy*, 25, 1, Feb., 1–12.

Lösch, A. (1954), *The Economics of Location* [German 1st edn 1939], Woglom, W.H. with Stolper, W.F. (trans.), New Haven, Yale University Press.

Losee, J. (1972), *A Historical Introduction to the Philosophy of Science*, Oxford, Oxford University Press.

Luttrell, W.F. (1962), *Factory Location and Industrial Movement: A Study of Recent Experience in Great Britain. Vol. 1*, London, National Institute of Social and Economic Research.

Machlup, F. (1946), 'Marginal Analysis and Empirical Research', *American Economic Review*, 36, 519–54.

—— (1967), 'Theories of the Firm: Marginalist, Behavioural, Managerial', *American Economic Review*, 57, 1, March, 1–33.

—— (1974), 'Friedrich von Hayek's Contribution to Economics', *Swedish Journal of Economics*, 76, 498–531.

McCloskey, D.N. (1983), 'The Rhetoric of Economics', *Journal of Economic Literature*, 21, June, 481–517.

—— (1991), 'Storytelling in Economics', in Lavoie, D. (ed.) (1991a), *Economics and Hermeneutics*, London and New York, Routledge, 61–75.

McDermott, P.J. and Taylor, M.J. (1976), 'Attitude, Images and Location: The Subjective Context of Decision-Making in New Zealand Manufacturing', *Economic Geography*, 52, 325–47.

McMillan, T.E. Jr. (1965), 'Why Manufacturers Choose Plant Locations vs. Determinants of Plant Locations', *Land Economics*, August, 239–46.

McNee, R.B. (1960a), 'Toward a More Humanistic Economic Geography: The Geography of Enterprise', *Tijdschrift voor Economische and Sociale Geografie*, 51, 201–5.

—— (1972), 'An Inquiry into the Goal or Goals of the Enterprise: A Case Study', *The Professional Geographer*, 24, 203–10.

—— (1974), 'A Systems Approach of Understanding the Geographic Behaviour of Organisations, Especially Large Corporations', in Hamilton, F.E.I. (ed.) (1974a), *Spatial Perspectives on Industrial Organisation and Decision-Making*, London, John Wiley, 47–75.

Mäki, U. (1990), 'Mengerian Economics in Realist Perspective', in Caldwell, B.J. (ed.) (1990), *Carl Menger and his Legacy in Economics*, Annual Supplement to Vol. 22, *History of Political Economy*, Durham and London, Duke University Press, 289–310.

Manne, A.S. (ed.) (1985), *Economic Equilibrium: Model Formulation and Solution*, Amsterdam, North-Holland.

March, J.G. and Simon, H.A. (1958), *Organisations*, New York, John Wiley and Sons.

Marshall, A. (1919), *Trade and Industry*, London, Macmillan.

—— (1966), *Principles of Economics: An Introductory Volume*, 8th Edn, London, Macmillan.

Martindale, D. (ed.) (1965), 'Functionalism in the Social Sciences: The Strengths and Limits of Functionalism in Anthropology, Economics, Political Science and Sociology: A Symposium', *Monograph* No. 5, Philadelphia, The American Academy of Political and Social Science.

Massey, D. (1979), 'A Critical Evaluation of Industrial-Location Theory', in Hamilton, F.E.I. and Linge, G.J.R. (eds) (1979a), *Spatial Analysis, Industry and the Industrial Environment, 1: Industrial Systems*, Chichester, John Wiley and Sons, 57–72.

—— (1984), *Spatial Divisions of Labour: Social Structures and the Geography of Production*, Basingstoke, Macmillan.

Menger, C. (1950), *Principles of Economics*, Dingwall, J. and Hoselitz, B.F. (ed. and trans.), with intro. by F.H. Knight, Glencoe, Ill., The Free Press. Translated from the German, *Grundsätze der Volkswirtschaftslehre* [1871].

REFERENCES

—— (1963), *Problems of Economics and Sociology*, Nock, F.J. (trans.), Schneider, L. (ed. with intro.), Urbana, University of Illinois Press. Translated from the German, *Untersuchungen über die Methode der Socialwissenschaften und der Politschen Oekonomie inbesondere* [1883].

Menger, K. (1973), 'Austrian Marginalism and Mathematical Economics', in Hicks, J.R. and Weber, W. (eds) (1973), *Carl Menger and the Austrian School of Economics*, Oxford, The Clarendon Press, 38–60.

Meredith, G.C. (1977), *Small Business Management in Australia*, Sydney, McGraw-Hill.

Milford, K. (1990), 'Menger's Methodology', in Caldwell, B.J. (ed.) (1990), *Carl Menger and his Legacy in Economics*, Annual Supplement to Vol. 22, *History of Political Economy*, Durham and London, Duke University Press, 215–39.

Milgate, M. (1979), 'On the Origin of the Notion of "Intertemporal Equilibrium"', *Economica (N.S.)*, 46, 1–10.

Mises, L. von (1936), *Socialism: An Economic and Sociological Analysis*, Kahane, J. (trans.), London, Jonathan Cape.

—— (1949), *Human Action: A Treatise on Economics*, London, William Hodge and Co., Ltd.

—— (1958), *Theory and History*, London, Jonathan Cape.

—— (1960), *Epistemological Problems of Economics*, Princeton, NJ, D. Van Nostrand Co., Inc.

—— (1969), *The Historical Setting of the Austrian School of Economics*, New Rochelle, NY, Arlington House.

—— (1972), *Planned Chaos*, New York, Foundation for Economic Education Inc.

—— (1978), *The Ultimate Foundation of Economic Science: An Essay on Method*, 2nd edn with Foreword by Kirzner, I.M., Kansas City, Sheed Andrews and McMeel, Inc.

Mittermaier, K. (1986), 'Mechanomorphism', in Kirzner, I.M. (ed.) (1986), *Subjectivism, Intelligibility and Economic Understanding: Essays in Honor of Ludwig Lachmann on his Eightieth Birthday*, New York, New York University Press, 236–51.

Monk, R. (1991), *Ludwig Wittgenstein: The Duty of Genius*, London, Vintage.

Morgan, G. (1986), *Images of Organization*, Newbury Park, CA, Sage Publications, Inc.

Morgenstern, O. (1972), 'Thirteen Critical Points in Contemporary Economic Theory: An Interpretation', *Journal of Economic Literature*, 10, 4, Dec., 1168–89.

Morishima, M. (1980), 'W. Jaffe on Léon Walras: A Comment', *Journal of Economic Literature*, 18, June, 550–58.

Moss, S.J. (1980), 'The Neo-Classical Theory of the Firm from Marshall to Robinson and Chamberlin', Manchester Polytechnic Discussion Papers.

Moss, S.J. (1981), *An Economic Theory of Business Strategy: An Essay in Dynamics Without Equilibrium*, Oxford, Martin Robertson.

Natanson, M. (1962), *Literature, Philosophy and the Social Sciences: Essays in Existentialism and Phenomenology*, The Hague, Martinus Nijhoff.

Nelson, R.R. and Winter, S.G. (1982), *An Evolutionary Theory of Economic Change*, Cambridge, Mass., Harvard University Press.

Nishioka, H. and Krumme, G. (1973), 'Location Conditions, Factors and Decisions: An Evaluation of Selected Location Surveys', *Land Economics*, 49, 195–205.

North, D.J. (1974), 'The Process of Industrial Change in Different Manufacturing Organisations', in Hamilton, F.E.I. (ed.) (1974a), *Spatial Perspectives on Industrial Organisation and Decision-Making*, London, John Wiley, 213–44.

North, R.N. (1977), 'Locational Analysis and the Concept of Horizons', *Area*, 9, 163–66.

REFERENCES

Nozick, R. (1977), 'On Austrian Methodology', *Synthese*, 36, 3, Nov., 353–92.

O'Brien, D.P. and Presley, J.R. (eds) (1981), *Pioneers of Modern Economics in Britain*, London, Macmillan.

O'Driscoll, G.P., Jr. (1977), *Economics as a Co-ordination Problem: The Contributions of Friedrich A. Hayek*, Kansas City, Sheed Andrews and McMeel, Inc.

O'Driscoll, G.P., Jr. and Rizzo, M.J. (1985), *The Economics of Time and Ignorance*, Oxford, Basil Blackwell.

Orkin, M. (1979), 'Ideology and the Interpretative Foundation of Science', *Philosophical Papers*, 8, 2, 1–20.

O'Sullivan, P.J. (1987), *Economic Methodology and Freedom to Choose*, London, Allen and Unwin.

Özga, S.A. (1965), *Expectations in Economic Theory*, London, Weidenfeld and Nicolson.

Palander, T. (1935), *Beitrage zur Standortstheorie*, Uppsala, Almqvist und Vicksell Botrycheri z.-b.

Pareto, V. (1971), *Manual of Political Economy*, Schweir, A.S. (trans.), ed. by Schweir, A.S. and Page, A.N., New York, Augustus M. Kelly.

Penrose, E.T. (1959), *The Theory of the Growth of the Firm*, Oxford, Basil Blackwell.

Perroux, F. (1950), 'Economic Space: Theory and Application', *Quarterly Journal of Economics*, 64, 1, 89–104.

Petri, F. (1978), 'The Difference Between Long-Period and Short-Period General Equilibrium and the Capital Theory Controversy', *Australian Economic Papers*, 17, 246–60.

Polanyi, M. (1973), *Personal Knowledge: Towards a Post-Critical Philosophy*, London, Routledge and Kegan Paul.

Popper, K.R. (1963), *Conjectures and Refutations: The Growth of Scientific Knowledge*, London, Routledge and Kegan Paul.

Pred, A. (1967), *Behaviour and Location: Foundations for a Geographic and Dynamic Location Theory, Part I*, Lund: Gleerup, Lund Studies in Geography, Series B, No. 27.

—— (1969), *Behaviour and Location: Foundations for a Geographic and Dynamic Location Theory, Part II*, Lund, Gleerup, Lund Studies in Geography, Series B, No. 28.

Pretorius, F., Addleson, M., and Tomlinson, R. (1986), 'History of Industrial Decentralisation (Part I): The Regional Concentration of Industry and the Historical Basis of the Policy', *Development Southern Africa*, 3, 1 (Feb.), 37–49.

Redlich, F. (1950/1), 'Innovation in Business: A Systematic Presentation', *American Journal of Economics and Sociology*, 10, 285–91.

Rees, J. (1972a), 'The Industrial Corporation and Location Decision Analysis', *Area*, 4, 199–205.

—— (1972b), 'Organisation Theory and Corporate Decisions: Some Implications for Industrial Location Analysis', *Regional Science Perspectives*, 2, 126–35.

—— (1974), 'Decision-Making, the Growth of the Firm and the Business Environment', in Hamilton, F.E.I. (ed.) (1974a), *Spatial Perspectives on Industrial Organisation and Decision-Making*, London, John Wiley, 189–211.

Richardson, G.B. (1960), *Information and Investment: A Study in the Working of the Competitive Economy*, Oxford, Oxford University Press.

—— (1973), 'Planning versus Competition' in Wagner, L. and Baltazzis, N. (eds) (1973) *Readings in Applied Microeconomics*, Oxford, The Clarendon Press in Association with Open University Press, 10–26. Reprinted from *Soviet Studies*, 8, 3 (Jan.), 433–47.

Rizzo, M.J. (ed.) (1979a), *Time Uncertainty and Disequilibrium: Exploration of Austrian Themes*, Lexington, Mass., Lexington Books.

281

—— (1979b), 'Disequilibrium and All That: An Introductory Essay', in Rizzo, M.J. (ed.) (1979a), *Time Uncertainty and Disequilibrium: Exploration of Austrian Themes*, Lexington, Mass., Lexington Books, 1–18.

—— (1982), 'Mises and Lakatos: A Reformulation of Austrian Methodology', in Kirzner, I.M. (ed.) (1982a) *Method, Process, and Austrian Economics: Essays in Honour of Ludwig von Mises*, Lexington, Mass., D.C. Heath and Co., 53–73.

Robbins, L. (1949), *An Essay on the Nature and Significance of Economic Science*, 2nd edn, London, Macmillan.

Robinson, Joan (1948), *The Economics of Imperfect Competition*, London, Macmillan.

—— (1977), 'What Are the Questions?', *Journal of Economic Literature*, 15, 4, Dec., 1319–39.

Rogerson, C.M. (1987), 'Decentralisation and the Location of Third World Multi-nationals in South Africa', in Tomlinson, R. and Addleson, M. (eds with intro.) (1987), *Regional Restructuring Under Apartheid: Urban and Regional Policies in Contemporary South Africa*, Johannesburg, Ravan Press, 294–308.

Rorty, R. (1980), *Philosophy and the Mirror of Nature*, Oxford, Basil Blackwell.

Rothbard, M.N. (1956), 'Toward a Reconstruction of Utility and Welfare Economics', in Sennholz, M. (ed.) (1956), *On Freedom and Free Enterprise: Essays in Honour of Ludwig von Mises*, Princeton, NJ, D. van Nostrand and Co., Inc., 224–62. Reprinted as *Occasional Paper Series*, No. 3, Centre for Libertarian Studies (1977).

Rothschild, M. (1973), 'Models of Market Organisation with Imperfect Information: A Survey', *Journal of Political Economy*, 81, 1283–308.

Sack, R.D. (1980), *Conceptions of Space in Social Thought: A Geographic Perspective*, London, Macmillan.

Samuelson, P.A. (1948), *Foundations of Economic Analysis*, Cambridge, Mass., Harvard University Press.

Sayer, A. (1979), 'Epistemology and Conceptions of People and Nature in Geography', *Geoforum*, 10, 1, 19–43.

—— (1981), 'Concepts of Space in Social Theory: a Critique', *Research Papers in Geography*, No. 7, Brighton, University of Sussex.

—— (1982), 'Explanation in Economic Geography: Abstraction versus General-isation', *Progress in Human Geography*, 6, 68–88.

—— (1985), 'Industry and Space: A Sympathetic Critique of Radical Research', *Environment and Planning D: Society and Space*, 3, 3–29.

Schrag, C.O. (1985), 'Subjectivity and Praxis at the End of Philosophy', in Silverman, H.J. and Ihde, D. (eds) (1985), *Hermeneutics and Deconstruction*, Albany, State University of New York Press, 24–32.

Schumpeter, J.A. (1955) *The Theory of Economic Development: An Enquiry into Profits, Capital, Credit, Interest and the Business Cycle*, Opie, R. (trans.), Cambridge, Mass., Harvard University Press.

—— (1967), *History of Economic Analysis*, Schumpeter, E.B. (ed. from manuscript), London, George Allen and Unwin.

Schütz, A. (1943), 'The Problem of Rationality in the Social World', *Economica (N.S.)*, 10, 38, May, 130–49.

—— (1945), 'On Multiple Realities', *Philosophy and Phenomenological Research*, 5, 4, 533–76.

—— (1972), *The Phenomenology of the Social World*, Walsh, G. and Lehnert, F. (trans.) with intro. by Walsh, G., London, Heinemann Educational Books. Translated from the German, *Der sinnhafte Aufbau der socialen Welt* [1932].

—— (1977), 'Concept and Theory Formation in the Social Sciences', in Dallmayr, F.R. and McCarthy, T.A. (eds) (1977), *Understanding and Social Inquiry*, Notre Dame, Ind., University of Notre Dame Press, 225–39.

Sennholz, M. (ed.) (1956), *On Freedom and Free Enterprise: Essays in Honour of Ludwig von Mises*, Princeton, NJ, D. van Nostrand and Co., Inc.

Shackle, G.L.S. (1958), *Time in Economics*, Amsterdam, North-Holland Publishing Co.
—— (1959), 'Time and Thought', *British Journal for the Philosophy of Science*, 11, 1 Feb., 285–98.
—— (1964), 'General Thought-Schemes and the Economist: The Second Woolwich Economics Lecture', London, Woolwich Polytechnic.
—— (1965), *A Scheme of Economic Theory*, Cambridge, Cambridge University Press.
—— (1967), *The Years of High Theory*, Cambridge, Cambridge University Press.
—— (1969), *Decision, Order and Time in Human Affairs*, 2nd edn, Cambridge, Cambridge University Press.
—— (1970), *Expectation, Enterprise and Profit: The Theory of the Firm*, London, George Allen and Unwin.
—— (1972a), *Epistemics and Economics: A Critique of Economic Doctrines*, Cambridge, Cambridge University Press.
—— (1972b), 'Marginalism: The Harvest, *History of Political Economy*, 4, 2, Fall, 587–602. Reprinted in Black, R.D.C. *et al.* (1973), *The Marginal Revolution in Economics: Interpretation and Evaluation*, Durham, NC, Duke University Press, 321–36.
—— (1974), *Keynesian Kaleidics*, Edinburgh, Edinburgh University Press.
—— (1976), *Time and Choice: Keynes Lecture in Economics*, from Proceedings of the British Academy, Vol. 62, Oxford, Oxford Univerity Press.
—— (1981), 'F.A. Hayek, 1899–', in O'Brien, D.P. and Presley, J.R. (eds) (1981), *Pioneers of Modern Economics in Britain*, London, Macmillan, 234–61.
—— (1983), 'The Bounds of Unknowledge', in Wiseman, J. (ed.) (1983a), *Beyond Positive Economics*, Proceedings of Section F (Economics) of the British Association for the Advancement of Science (York, 1981), London, Macmillan, 28–37.
Shenfield, A. (1983), 'Myth and Reality in Anti-Trust', *Occasional Paper* 66, London, Institute of Economic Affairs.
Silverman, H.J. and Ihde, D. (eds) (1985), *Hermeneutics and Deconstruction*, Albany, State University of New York Press.
Silverman, P. (1990), 'The Cameralistic Roots of Menger's Achievement', in Caldwell, B.J. (ed.) (1990), *Carl Menger and his Legacy in Economics*, Annual Supplement to Vol. 22, *History of Political Economy*, Durham and London, Duke University Press, 69–91.
Simon, H.A. (1952), 'A Behavioural Model of Rational Choice', *Quarterly Journal of Economics*, 69, 99–118.
—— (1957), *Models of Man, Social and Rational*, New York, John Wiley and Sons.
—— (1959), 'Theories of Decision-Making in Economics and Behavioural Science', *American Economic Review*, 49, June, 253–83.
—— (1960), *The New Science of Management Decision*, New York, Harper and Row, Publishers, Inc.
—— (1979), 'From Substantive to Procedural Rationality', in Hahn, F.H. and Hollis, M. (eds) (1979), *Philosophy and Economic Theory*, Oxford University Press, 65–86.
—— (1987), 'Rationality in Psychology and Economics', in Hogarth, R.M. and Reder, M.W. (eds) (1987), *Rational Choice: The Contrast between Economics and Psychology*, Chicago, University of Chicago Press, 25–39.
Smith, B. (1986), 'Austrian Economics and Austrian Philosophy', in Grassl, W. and Smith, B. (eds) (1986), *Austrian Economics, Historical and Philosophical Background*, New York, New York University Press, 1–36.
—— (1990), 'Aristotle, Menger, Mises: An Essay in the Metaphysics of Economics', in Caldwell, B.J. (ed.) (1990), *Carl Menger and his Legacy in Economics*, Annual Supplement to Vol. 22, *History of Political Economy*, Durham and London, Duke University Press, 263–88.

REFERENCES

Smith, D.M. (1970), 'On Throwing out Weber with the Bathwater: A Note on Industrial Location and Linkage', *Area*, 2, 15–18.
—— (1971), *Industrial Location: An Economic Geographic Analysis*, New York, John Wiley and Sons.
—— (1979), 'Modelling Industrial Location: Towards a Broader View of the Space Economy', in Hamilton, F.E.I. and Linge, G.J.R. (eds) (1979a), *Spatial Analysis, Industry and the Industrial Environment, 1: Industrial Systems*, Chichester, John Wiley, 37–55.
Smithies, A. (1941), 'Optimum Location in Spatial Competition', *Journal of Political Economy*, 49, 423–39.
Spadaro, L.M. (ed. with intro.) (1978), *New Directions in Austrian Economics*, Kansas City, Sheed Andrews and McMeel, Inc.
Stafford, H.A. (1969), 'An Industrial Location Decision Model', *Proceedings, Association of American Geographers*, 1, 141–5.
—— (1972), 'The Geography of Manufacturers', *Progress in Geography*, 4, 181–215.
—— (1974), 'The Anatomy of the Location Decision: Content Analysis of Case Studies', in Hamilton, F.E.I. (ed.) (1974a), *Spatial Perspectives on Industrial Organisation and Decision-Making*, London, John Wiley, 169–87.
Steed, G.P.F. (1971), 'Plant Adaptation, Firm Environments and Location Analysis', *Professional Geographer*, 23, 4 (Oct.), 324–8.
Stevens, B.H. and Brackett, C.A. (1967), 'Industrial Location: A Review and Annotated Bibliography of Theoretical, Empirical and Case Studies', *Bibliography Series* No. 3, Philadelphia, Penn., Regional Science Research Institute.
Stigler, G.J. (1961), 'The Economics of Information', *Journal of Political Economy*, 69, 213–25.
Storey, D., Keasey, K., Watson, R., and Wynarczyk, P. (1987), *The Performance of Small Firms: Profits, Jobs and Failures*, London, Croom Helm.
Streissler, E. (1969), 'Structural Economic Thought: On the Significance of the Austrian School Today', *Zeitschrift für Nationalökonomie*, 29, 3–4, 237–66.
—— (1972), 'To What Extent Was the Austrian School Marginalist?', *History of Political Economy*, 4, 2, Fall, 426–41. Reprinted in Black, R.D.C. *et al.* (1973), *The Marginal Revolution in Economics: Interpretation and Evaluation*, Durham, NC, Duke University Press, 160–75.
Streissler, E., Harbeler, G., Lutz, F.A., and Machlup, F. (eds) (1969), *Roads to Freedom: Essays in Honour of Friedrich A. von Hayek*, London, Routledge and Kegan Paul.
Strøm, S. and Werin, L. (eds) (1978), *Topics in Disequilibrium Economics*, London, Macmillan.
Tang, A.M., Westfield, F.M., and Worley, J.S. (eds) (1976), *Evolution, Welfare and Time in Economics: Essays in Honour of Nicholas Georgescu-Roegen*, Lexington, Mass., Lexington Books.
Tarascio, V.J. (1968), *Pareto's Methodological Approach to Economics: A Study in the History of Some Scientific Aspects of Economic Thought*, Chapel Hill, NC, University of North Carolina Press.
Taylor, C. (1977), 'Interpretation and the Sciences of Man', in Dallmayr, F.R. and McCarthy, T.A. (eds) (1977), *Understanding and Social Inquiry*, Notre Dame, Ind., University of Notre Dame Press, 101–31.
Taylor, M.J. (1970), 'Location Decisions of Small Firms', *Area*, 2, 51–4.
—— (1975), 'Organisational Growth, Spatial Interaction and Location Decision-Making', *Regional Studies*, 9, 313–23.
—— (1978), 'Perceived Distance and Spatial Interaction', *Environment and Planning A*, 10, 1171–7.

REFERENCES

Taylor, M.J. and Thrift, N. (1982a), 'Industrial Linkage and the Segmented Economy: 1 Some Theoretical Proposals', *Environment and Planning A*, 14, 1601–13.

—— (1982b), 'Industrial Linkage and the Segmented Economy: 2 An Empirical Reinterpretation', *Environment and Planning A*, 14, 1615–32.

—— (1983a), 'Business Organisation, Segmentation and Location', *Regional Studies*, 17, 6, 445–65.

—— (1983b), 'Industrial Geography in the 1980s: Entering the Decade of Differences', *Environment and Planning A*, 15, 1287–91.

Terreberry, S. (1968), 'The Evolution of Organisational Environments', *Administrative Science Quarterly*, 12, 4, March, 590–613.

Thirlby, G.F. (1973), 'The Economist's Description of Business Behaviour', in Buchanan, J.M. and Thirlby, G.F. (eds) (1973), *L.S.E. Essays on Cost*, London, London School of Economics and Political Science/Weidenfeld and Nicolson, 203–24.

Tollison, R.D. (1982), 'Rent Seeking: A Survey', *Kyklos*, 35, 575–602.

Tomlinson, R. and Addleson, M. (eds with intro.) (1987), *Regional Restructuring Under Apartheid: Urban and Regional Policies in Contemporary South Africa*, Johannesburg, Ravan Press.

Torrington, D. and Weightman, J. (1985), *The Business of Management*, London, Prentice Hall International, UK, Ltd.

Townroe, P.M. (1968), 'Industrial Location and Regional Economic Policy: A Selected Bibliography', *Occasional Paper* 2, Centre for Urban and Regional Studies, The University of Birmingham.

—— (1969), 'Locational Choice and the Individual Firm', *Regional Studies*, 3, 15–24.

—— (1971), 'Industrial Location Decisions: A Study in Management Behaviour', *Occasional Paper* 15, Centre for Urban and Regional Studies, University of Birmingham.

Triffin, R. (1949), *Monopolistic Competition and General Equilibrium Theory*, Cambridge, Mass., Harvard University Press.

Truzzi, M. (ed.) (1974), *Verstehen: Subjective Understanding in the Social Sciences*, Reading, Mass., Addison-Wesley Publishing Co.

Tversky, A. and Kahneman, D. (1982a), 'Judgement under Uncertainty: Heuristics and Biases', in Kahneman, D. *et al.* (eds) (1982), *Judgement Under Uncertainty: Heuristics and Biases*, New York, Cambridge University Press, 3–20.

—— (1982b), 'Causal Schemas in Judgements Under Uncertainty', in Kahneman, D. *et al.* (eds) (1982), *Judgement Under Uncertainty: Heuristics and Biases*, New York, Cambridge University Press, 117–28.

Van de Ven, A.H. (1979), 'Book Review of Aldrich, H.E. (1979)', *Administrative Science Quarterly*, 24, 2, June, 320–6.

Van Peursen, C.A. (1977), 'The Horizon', in Elliston, F. and Mc Cormick, P. (eds) (1977), *Husserl: Expositions and Appraisals*, Notre Dame, Ind., University of Notre Dame Press, 182–201.

Vaughn, K. (1990), 'The Mengerian Roots of the Austrian Revival', in Caldwell, B.J. (ed.) (1990), *Carl Menger and his Legacy in Economics*, Annual Supplement to Vol. 22, *History of Political Economy*, Durham and London, Duke University Press, 379–407.

von Thünen, J.H. (1875), *Der Isolierte Staat In Beziehund auf Landwirtschaft und Nationalokonomie*, 3rd edn [1st edn 1826] Berlin, Schumacher-Zarchlin.

Vroom, V.H. and Yetton, P.W. (1973), *Leadership and Decision-Making*, Pittsburgh, University of Pittsburgh Press.

Wagner, L. and Baltazzis, N. (eds) (1973), *Readings in Applied Microeconomics*, Oxford, The Clarendon Press in Association with Open University Press.

Walras, L. (1954), *Elements of Pure Economics*, Jaffé, W. (trans.), London, Allen and

REFERENCES

Unwin. Translated from the French, *Eléments d'economie politique pure* [1st edn 1874–77].

Warnke, G. (1987), *Gadamer: Hermeneutics, Tradition and Reason*, Cambridge, Polity Press.

Watts, H.D. (1987), *Industrial Geography*, Harlow; Essex, Longman Scientific and Technical.

Wax, M.L. (1974), 'On Misunderstanding Verstehen: A Reply to Abel', in Truzzi, M. (ed.) (1974), *Verstehen: Subjective Understanding in the Social Sciences*, Reading, Mass., Addison-Wesley Publishing Co., Reprinted from *Sociology and Social Research* (1967), 51, April, 323–33.

Webber, M.J. (1972), *The Impact of Uncertainty on Location*, Cambridge, Mass., MIT Press.

Weber, A. (1929), *Theory of the Location of Industries* [German 1st edn 1909], Friedrich, C.J. (trans. with intro. and notes), Chicago, Ill., University of Chicago Press.

Weber, M. (1964), *The Theory of Social and Economic Organisation*, Henderson, A.M. and Parsons, T. (trans.), Parsons, T. (ed. with intro.), New York, The Free Press. Translated from the German, *Wirtschaft und Gesellschaft* [1922].

—— (1977), '"Objectivity" in Social Science and Social Policy', in Dallmayr, F.R. and McCarthy, T.A. (eds) (1977), *Understanding and Social Inquiry*, Notre Dame, Ind., University of Notre Dame Press, 24–37.

Wellings, P. and Black, A. (1987), 'Industrial Decentralisation under Apartheid', in Tomlinson, R. and Addleson, M. (eds with intro.) (1987), *Regional Restructuring Under Apartheid: Urban and Regional Policies in Contemporary South Africa*, Johannesburg, Ravan Press, 181–206.

Weston, J.F. and Brigham, E.F. (1975), *Managerial Finance* (5th edn), London, The Dryden Press.

White, L.H. (1977), 'Methodology of the Austrian School', *Occasional Paper Series* No. 1, New York, Centre for Libertarian Studies.

—— (1982), 'Mises, Hayek, Hahn, and the Market Process: Comment on Littlechild', in Kirzner, I.M. (ed.) (1982a), *Method, Process, and Austrian Economics: Essays in Honour of Ludwig von Mises*, Lexington, Mass., D.C. Heath and Co., 103–10.

Williams, B.R. and Scott, W.P. (1965), *Investment Proposals and Decisions*, London, George Allen and Unwin.

Winch, P. (1958), *The Idea of a Social Science and Its Relation to Philosophy*, London, Routledge and Kegan Paul.

—— (1977), 'The Idea of a Social Science', in Dallmayr, F.R. and McCarthy, T.A. (eds) (1977), *Understanding and Social Inquiry*, Notre Dame, University of Notre Dame Press, 142–58.

Wiseman, J. (ed.) (1983a), *Beyond Positive Economics*, Proceedings of Section F (Economics) of the British Association for the Advancement of Science (York, 1981), London, Macmillan.

—— (1983b), 'Introduction', in Wiseman, J. (ed.) (1983a), *Beyond Positive Economics*, Proceedings of Section F (Economics) of the British Association for the Advancement of Science (York, 1981), London, Macmillan, 1–12.

Wolpert, J. (1964), 'The Decision Process in Spatial Context', *Annals of the Association of American Geographers*, 54, 537–58.

Wood, P.A. (1969), 'Industrial Location and Linkage', *Area*, 1, 2, 32–9.

—— (1981), 'Industrial Geography', *Progress in Human Geography*, 5, 406–16.

World Bank (1984), 'Industrial Location Policies', *The Urban Edge*, 8, 9 (November), 1–6.

—— (1986a), 'Industrial Location Policies: They're Costly and Inefficient in Korea', *Research News*, 7, 1, Summer.

—— (1986b), 'Industrial Location: Lessons for Spatial Planning', *The Urban Edge*, August/September.

Wright, R. (1964), *Investment Decision in Industry*, London, Chapman and Hall.

Zeckhauser, R. (1987), 'Comments: Behavioural versus Rational Economics: What You See Is What You Conquer', in Hogarth, R.M. and Reder, M.W. (eds) (1987), *Rational Choice: The Contrast between Economics and Psychology*, Chicago, University of Chicago Press, 251–65.

Zeitlin, I.M. (1973), *Rethinking Sociology: A Critique of Contemporary Theory*, New York, Appleton-Century-Crofts.

INDEX